# SYMBOLIC COMPUTING WITH LISP AND PROLOG

D0595098

# SYMBOLIC COMPUTING WITH LISP AND PROLOG

**Robert A. Mueller**

*Colorado State University, Quantitative Technology Corporation*

**Rex L. Page**

*Colorado State University, Amoco Research*

**WILEY**

JOHN WILEY & SONS

New York • Chichester • Brisbane • Toronto • Singapore

To the memories of Walter Orvedahl and Barney
Marschner, mentors extraordinaire. Walter, you
always knew the right place to go, and Barney, you
always knew how to get there.

Cover photograph by Geoffry Gove

Unix is a trademark of AT&T Bell Laboratories

Copyright ©1988, by John Wiley & Sons, Inc.

All rights reserved. Published simultaneously in Canada.

Reproduction or translation of any part of
this work beyond that permitted by Sections
107 and 108 of the 1976 United States Copyright
Act without the permission of the copyright
owner is unlawful. Requests for permission
or further information should be addressed to
the Permissions Department, John Wiley & Sons.

*Library of Congress Cataloging in Publication Data:*

Mueller, Robert A.
Symbolic Computing with Lisp and Prolog / Robert A. Mueller, Rex
L. Page

    p.    cm.
    ISBN 0-471-60771-1
    1. LISP (Computer program language) 2. Prolog (Computer program
language)    I. Page, Rex L.    II. Title.
    QA76.73.L23M84   1988
    005.13'3--dc19                     88-23414
                                           CIP

Printed in the United States of America

10  9  8  7  6  5  4  3  2

# PREFACE

Two main themes emerge in this book: symbolic computing and denotational programming. The first portions of the text covers programming, and the later portion discusses symbolic computing in such areas as game playing, language translation, and theorem proving. We present example problems in each of these areas, propose solutions, and then specify working programs in terms of the programming techniques and languages discussed in the first portion of the text.

Two programs accompany each of the applications in symbolic computing—one written in Lisp, the other in Prolog. These stylized programs conform to a collection of programming techniques that we classify as *denotational* in nature. By this we mean that they specify their results directly in terms of their input data. At each level in the specification, results are described entirely in terms of the constituents of the input data at that level. This contrasts with the *operational* approach, in which a sequence of operations, individually operating on their own small parts of the data in a step-by-step fashion, generates the desired output. To use one of the most overworked phrases of our time, denotational programs concentrate on *what* the result is, whereas operational programs emphasize *how* the result is computed.

To illustrate the difference between the denotational and operational forms, consider the following definition of *bread* (slightly paraphrased from *Webster's New Collegiate Dictionary*[1]):

> A leavened and baked food made of a mixture whose basic constituent is flour or meal.

[1] *Webster's New Collegiate Dictionary*, G. & C. Merriam, Springfield, Mass., 1974.

We would consider this definition to be denotational; the characteristic properties of bread are explicit, and the method of making it is implicit. Contrast this with an operational definition, which explicitly delineates the method of construction but leaves the resulting properties implicit:

1. Prepare the dough by mixing the flour, yeast in warm water, etc.

2. Knead the dough with a folding and tearing motion.

3. Allow the dough to recover by placing it in a warm, draft-free place for the required time.

4. Reknead the dough, shape accordingly, and allow it to rise again.

5. Bake in the oven for the required time at a suitable temperature.

6. Remove from the oven and allow to cool on a wire rack.

Denotational programs written in Lisp are *functional programs*: They describe the result as a function of the input; given a particular input, the Lisp system computes the result satisfying the functional specification. In Prolog they are *relational programs*: They describe constraints among the constituents of the input data and the results; combinations of input data and results satisfying these constraints are uncovered by the Prolog system and delivered as output. (There is a close correspondence between functional and relational programs. A function can be thought of as a constraint between potential input data and potential results that associates valid results with appropriate input. A relation does the same thing, although it has a bit more freedom in this regard than does a function, according to the technical definitions of the terms.) In either case, a computer system can derive computations from these specifications. We do not dwell on how such a system is able to do this, but we explain enough about these mechanisms to estimate the computational resources required by programs and to facilitate coping with bugs when they creep in.

Our approach is practical rather than theoretical. We emphasize useful, common programming techniques and show how they can affect the performance of a program. We value algorithms that avoid excessive computation. (We do not present $O(n^2)$ algorithms when linear or $O(n \log n)$ algorithms are available.) However, we do not attempt to pin down details of performance relative to specific configurations of computing hardware. We value programs that elucidate as well as compute, as this, we suspect, is a way out of the software quagmire, if there is one. (Paradoxically, it may also foster the reduction of hardware deficiencies, via massive parallelism, but that is not a primary motif in this presentation.)

This text can be used in several ways: to study some important applications in the area of symbolic computing, to practice techniques of denotational programming in Lisp or in Prolog, or to learn about any combination of these applications and programming techniques. The Lisp portion and the Prolog portion are independent; neither part assumes a knowledge of the other. We present symbolic-computing algorithms in both notations, so that a familiarity with either Lisp or Prolog will be sufficient background for a study of that material. Readers who are already familiar with one of the languages may wish to skip both the programming sections and read only the symbolic computing portion of the text.

Whatever your route, we hope you will enjoy it and find the information useful.

ROBERT A. MUELLER
REX L. PAGE

# ACKNOWLEDGMENTS

Many students persevered through the errors and organizational mistakes in earlier versions of this text and managed, in spite of these, to respond enthusiastically to the subject. We thank them for that, and for the guidance their reactions provided in revisions. Marian Sexton and Charles Sharpe provided an extraordinary number of detailed tips, for which we owe them a great debt. Margaret Sweeney and Joseph Varghese read the original manuscript with a critical eye when few others had seen it. We have some inkling of how hard that job was, and we very much appreciate their efforts.

Several reviewers saw value in the text and offered suggestions that led to important improvements in both context and presentation. We offer them our thanks for their distinctive contributions: Alan Perlis of Yale University for his inspiring endorsement of the concept of the book; David Touretsky of Carnegie-Mellon University for suggesting ways to connect the material to traditional presentations; Frederick Blackwell of California State University, Sacramento; Charles Dyer of the University of Wisconsin; Dennis Kibler of the University of California, Irvine; and Jordan Pollack of New Mexico State University for improving the organization of the text; and Richard Gabriel of Lucid Corporation and Stanford University for helping us reduce the similarity between our prose and pompous imitations of nineteenth-century novelists. Thank you every one.

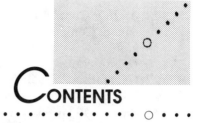

# CONTENTS

1 Lisp, Prolog, and Denotational Programing     1

## SECTION I  Lisp     11

2 Notations for Data in Lisp     13
3 Functions     19
4 Building Lists and Extracting Components     29
5 More List Manipulation Functions     36
6 A Lenient Function: **if**     46
7 Naming Partial Results: **let**     55
8 Recursion     59
9 Debugging     70
10 More Lenient Functions: **and, or**     79
11 Pumping     86
12 Divide and Conquer     97
13 Input and Output     105
14 Higher Order Functions     114
15 Numbers     121

## SECTION II  Prolog     127

16 Notation for Data and Variables in Prolog     129
17 Propositional Facts, Rules, and Queries     137
18 Relations Containing Variables     148
19 Unification: How the Interpreter Instantiates Variables     155
20 Recursion     163
21 Propagation and Accumulation of Results     171
22 Divide and Conquer     182

23 And/Or Control Flow     196
24 Saving Computation with Embedded Or Control     200
25 Not     203
26 Backtracking     207
27 Generating All Solutions Using **bagof** and **setof**     223
28 Inhibiting Backtracking     228
29 Built-in Relations for Program File Access and
   Transformation of Terms     237
30 Program Construction and Debugging     251
31 Numbers     266
32 Input and Output     278
33 Declarative and Procedural Semantics of Logic Programs     291

**SECTION III** Lisp vs. Prolog     301

34 Lisp vs. Prolog: How Do They Relate?     303

**SECTION IV** Applications     311

35 Two-Opponent Games     313
36 Language Parsing     370
37 Automated Theorem Proving     413

Index     465

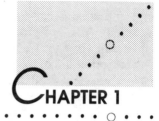

# CHAPTER 1

# LISP, PROLOG, AND DENOTATIONAL PROGRAMMING

Lisp and Prolog are notations for describing relationships between input data and results. They are general-purpose notations in the sense that they can be used to describe any such relationship that is "computable."

What is computable and what is not computable is a philosophical issue that has been debated for about half a century. Although there is no firm answer to the question, most of the discussion falls along these lines: A relationship between input and results is computable if it has a finite description in terms of a finite set of fundamental relationships, each of which can be worked out in a finite amount of time. The set of "fundamental relationships" is a key issue. Philosophers have considered several different fundamental sets (also known as "models of computation") and have found, through careful mathematical analysis, that they all are equivalent. That is, all the proposed models of computation lead to the same set of computable relationships. Lisp and Prolog are complete models in the sense that they are sufficient to describe any computable relationship that can be described via any of the other proposed methods of computation.

There are many other notations for describing computable relationships. You are probably familiar with one or more of them, such as Pascal, Fortran, C, PL/I, Cobol, or Basic. All these notations, or "programming languages" as they are usually called, start from slightly different sets of fundamental operations and from widely different points of view about how these operations should be denoted. They are all highly redundant in the sense that many of their fundamental operations could be eliminated without affecting the set of describable relationships.

Some of the redundancy leads to more concise programs. (A "program" for our purposes is a description in a programming language of a computable relationship.) Other portions of the redundancy are included to make it possible to address certain types of computing hardware in a particularly efficient manner. We will be concerned with both conciseness and efficiency, but we will not be overly concerned with questions of efficient computation that are closely related to underlying hardware.

For this reason, we will not discuss every aspect of Lisp and Prolog. We will cover subsets that are sufficient to describe any computable relationship in such a way that a computer can carry out the computation in a reasonably efficient manner, but not necessarily in the manner that is optimal with respect to a given computer's unique capabilities. The advantage of this approach is that you can spend more time learning general programming techniques and solutions for many computing applications. The disadvantage is that you will not learn all the bells and whistles of either Lisp or Prolog. If that is your goal, you should choose a different book; there are many suitable ones available.

In any programming language, even one that has no built-in redundancy, many different programs describe any given computable relationship. Although it makes us guilty of a vast oversimplification, we classify programs in two categories: *operational* and *denotational*. A program in the operational category describes a computable relationship in terms of a sequence of operations on the input data that eventually leads, in a step-by-step fashion, to the desired results. Thus, an operational program explains a procedure for computing the result. A denotational program, on the other hand, attempts to describe the form of the result in terms of its relationship to the input data. It specifies this relationship directly in terms of the constituents of the input data rather than concentrating on how the result can be derived from the input data in a step-by-step procedure.

To say the same thing one more way, in an operational program a procedure determines a relationship between input and output data; in a denotational program a relationship between input and output data determines a procedure. [1]

---

[1] The terms *iterative* and *procedural* often refer to the operational approach to programming. Names used for the denotational approach include *functional, applicative, declarative,* and *nonprocedural*. People often associate the terms functional and applicative with Lisp and declarative and nonprocedural with Prolog. We chose the term denotational because

For example, suppose we want to write a program that has as its result the word **yes** if its input data is a palindrome, and **no** if it is not. A denotational description might say that the result is **yes** whenever the letters in the input match, exactly, those same letters in reverse order; in all other situations, the result would be **no**. An operational description might go as follows: (1) Compare the first letter in the input data to the last letter; (2) if they are different, then the result is **no**; (3) if they are the same, then compare the second letter to the next-to-last; (4) if they are different, then the result is **no**; (5) continue in this manner until you have examined all the letters and found no differences, in which case the result is **yes**, or until you have determined that the result is **no**. The subsets of Lisp and Prolog that we will discuss favor denotational programs over operational programs.

Lisp was inspired by one of the models of computation that is denotational in nature, specifically, the lambda-calculus model proposed by Alonzo Church in the 1930s and further developed, in various forms, by Schoenfinkel, Curry, and others. In the 1950s, John McCarthy took the lead in developing the original Lisp notation and its supporting computing system, which was a practical implementation of many of the theoretical concepts developed by Church. (We write our programs in Common Lisp, a modern Lisp dialect. If you use a different dialect, you may have to adjust our notation slightly to get your programs to work. We stay within a very small subset of the language; few of the features we discuss will differ in any Lisp dialect.)

Prolog derives from the work of Frege on predicate calculus around the turn of the century, with subsequent refinements by Skolem, Herbrand, Horn, Davis and Putnam, Gilmore, and Robinson (spanning from the 1920s into the 1960s). The computational ramifications of this model were developed by Kowalski, Colmerauer, and others in the 1970s. (We write our Prolog programs in C-Prolog. If your Prolog system plays in a different key, you will have to transpose; we do not think you will find it difficult.)

Because Lisp and Prolog arose from descriptive models of computable relationships, they support the design of denotational programs more directly than do conventional programming languages such as Pascal or C, which are patterned after an operational model of computation developed by Alan Turing, Emil Post, and others. (The Turing model arose at about the same time as the Church model.)

Lisp and Prolog are not the only choices. There are many existing notations that would serve as a basis for illustrating the programming tech-

---

its dictionary meaning matches the idea of programs denoting results rather than operation sequences better than functional (connotes something that is not broken), applicative (useful for a given purpose), or declarative ("well, I declare"). Nonprocedural works, but seems too negative. Semantic specification techniques split naturally into denotational and operational categories, for many of the same reasons as programming, and both terms have gained some popularity in that field.

niques and applications covered in this text. For example, we could have chosen to use the mathematical notation of recursive function theory, or our own variant thereof, or we could have chosen Church's original notation, or Curry's, or Schoenfinkel's, or Skolem's, or Horn's.

The primary disadvantage of choosing one of these notations would be that our programs would stand only as descriptions of computations. They would not support, in a realistic sense, actual computations because we would not have access to a computer system that would automatically carry out the computations described by our programs.

That eliminates notations with no supporting computing system, but there are also many programming languages with excellent support for our chosen computational model that do have computer systems to support them. FP, the variableless programming language introduced by John Backus in the late 1970s would have been a good choice, as would SASL, KRC, or Miranda, the elegant notations developed by David Turner. ML, developed by Robin Milner's group, and Hope, developed by Burstall and associates, ALFL (Paul Hudak), and a host of new arrivals provide still other pleasing alternatives. We did not choose any of these because they are not so widely available as Lisp and Prolog. If you write a program in Lisp or Prolog, there will be many more places that you can use it to perform computations than there will be if you write it in Miranda or Hope.

So the choice of Lisp and Prolog was a pragmatic one: they are adequate, and they are popular — and likely to remain so for a long time.

Lisp can serve as a durable, generic medium for expressing the ideas of modern functional and logic-based (relational) languages. Alan Perlis likes to think of Lisp as the machine language for the programming languages of the future and of Prolog, FP, Miranda, and such as the initial prototypes of these languages. We agree.

Lisp has facilities for dealing effectively with computer architectures as they exist today. In fact, most Lisp programs developed over the past two decades have an operational bent. (Analysis of significant artificial intelligence codes written in Lisp reveals that setq's, rplaca's, and the like account for about 90% of all the function references in such programs. These operations support procedural programming; we do not cover them in this text.) New architectures aimed at supporting the most important parts of Lisp directly have had a commercial presence for half a decade. Prolog machines, SASL machines, and the like build on this experience.

The newer programming languages will facilitate the discovery of the most appropriate language features for effective programming. Lisp may then absorb these features and continue its dominance. Or Prolog may impart such a strong influence on the ideas and products stimulated by Japan's fifth-generation computing effort that programmers will migrate in the Prolog direction. Or later arrivals such as FP or Miranda or Hope may somehow gain a foothold. (Probably none of the above, predictions being what they are.) Regardless of the chosen notation, we believe that the denotational approach will play an increasingly significant role in program design and development.

We cover only a very small part of Lisp in this text. We cover a larger percentage of Prolog (it is smaller than Lisp). The portions of the two languages that we present, and the ways in which we use them, may leave the impression that differences between them are primarily superficial. This is not the case. We simply choose to write all our programs in a denotational form (or nonprocedural, or declarative, or whichever term you prefer), and this minimizes the gulf between Lisp and Prolog.

To illustrate the similarity between Lisp and Prolog, as we use them, consider a pair of specifications of the palindrome relationship. The specification that follows on the left is in the manner of Lisp, and the one on the right is in the manner of Prolog (expressed in a form more akin to informal mathematical notation than to the formal syntax of either Lisp or Prolog).

| **Lisp-like** | **Prolog-like** |
|---|---|
| p(x) is x=rev(x) | p(x) if rev(x,x) |
| rev([]) is [] | rev([],[]) |
| rev(w^x) is append(rev(x),[w]) | rev(w^x,y) if rev(x,z) and append(z,[w],y) |

In the Lisp-like program, p, rev, and append are functions (they deliver transformed versions of their input values). In the Prolog-like programs, p, rev, and append are relations (expressing true or false conditions, depending on their input values). In both programs x, y, and z are phrases, w is a letter from the alphabet, square brackets enclose sequences, and the circumflex represents a sequence formed from an initial component (on the left of the circumflex) and another sequence (on the right).

The Lisp-like program says that the palindrome function is true if its argument is the same as a reversed copy of its argument. It further specifies that the reverse function, when applied to the empty sequence, delivers the empty sequence; when applied to a sequence beginning with the component w and consisting of the components in x following w, the reverse function delivers a sequence constructed by concatenating a reversed copy of x and the sequence with w as its only component.

The Prolog-like program says that a sequence satisfies the palindrome property if it is in a reversed relationship with itself. It further specifies that the empty sequence satisfies the reverse property with itself and that a sequence whose first component is w and whose following components are those of the sequence x satisfies the reverse property with a sequence y if there is a sequence z that satisfies the reverse property with x and if that sequence z together with the sequence with w as its only component satisfies the append property with y.

In case you are curious, the programs that follow describe these same computations in Lisp, Prolog, and C syntax.

```
        Lisp                              Prolog

(defun p(x)                      p(X)  :- rev(X,X).
    (equal x (rev x)))           rev([],[]).
(defun rev(x)                    rev([W|X],Y)  :- rev(X,Z),
    (if (null x)                             append(Z,[W],Y).
        x
      (append (rev (cdr x))
              (list (car x))))))
```

```
                    C

#define False   0
#define True    1
p(x,n)
char x[];
int n;
{int k;
 for (k=0; k<n; k++)
    if (x[k] <> x[n-k-1])
        return(False);
 return(True);
}
```

The C version employs the conventional procedural paradigm. It specifies a sequence of computational steps, leaving the resulting input/output relationship to be deduced from an understanding of the resulting process. The Lisp and Prolog versions, on the other hand, specify the desired input/output relationship, leaving the computational process to be deduced by the processor. For us, Lisp and Prolog serve the same purpose: They provide a practical means of expressing computations in enlightening ways.

## ■ BIBLIOGRAPHY NOTES

In the 1930s and 1940s, logicians explored many of the theoretical foundations of computing. A line of investigation based on lambda-calculus and the related combinatory calculus, pioneered by Church, Curry, Kleene, Rosser, Schoenfinkel, and others inspired practical computing systems for functional programming developed by McCarthy, Landin, and others in the 1950s and 1960s. (Rosser prepared an enlightening history of this work in 1982.) Elegant extensions of these computing systems, have emerged from work by Backus, Burstall, Milner, Turner, and others in the 1970s and 1980s.

Another line of investigation with its roots in predicate calculus and with theoretical contributions from Herbrand, Horn, Skolem, and others in the 1930s, 1940s, and 1950s has led to computing systems that support relational programming grounded in the work of Kowalski, Colmerauer, Robinson, and others in the 1970s. In the 1980s, Clocksin and Mellish provided an implementation of this approach that is practical for computing purposes.

Conventional computing systems, both hardware and software, from the 1950s to the present, have followed a line of investigation pioneered by Turing, Post, and others whose theoretical formulations had more obvious representations in the form of constructable, physical machines than either lambda-calculus or predicate calculus.

John Backus (1978). Can programming be liberated from the von Neumann style? *Comm. ACM* **21**,(8) 613–641.

R. M. Burstall, D. B. MacQueen, and D. T. Sannella (1980). HOPE: An experimental applicative language. *ACM Lisp Conference* (August), 136–143.

Alonzo Church (1932). A set of postulates for the foundation of logic. *Annals Mathematics* **33** (2): 346–366.

Alonzo Church (1936). An unsolvable problem of elementary number theory. *American J. Mathematics* **58**, 345–363.

Alonzo Church and J. Barkley Rosser (1936). Some properties of conversion. *Trans. American Mathematical Society* **39**, 472–482.

Alonzo Church (1941). The calculi of lambda-conversion. *Annals of Mathematical Studies 6*, Princeton University Press, Princeton N.J.

W. F. Clocksin and C. S. Mellish (1981). *Programming in Prolog*, Springer-Verlag, New York.

A. Colmerauer (1973). Les systemes-Q our un formalisme pour analyser et synthetiser des phrases sur ordinateur. *Publication Interne No. 43*, Dept d'Informatique, University of Montreal, 1973.

A. Colmerauer (1978). Metamorphosis grammars. In L. Bolc (ed.), *Natural Language Communication with Computers*, Lecture Notes in Computer Science, Vol. 63. Springer-Verlag, New York.

Haskell B. Curry (1930). Grundlagen der Kombinatorischen Logik. *American J. of Mathematics* **52** 509–536, 789–834.

Haskell B. Curry (1963). *Foundations of Mathematical Logic*, McGraw-Hill, New York.

M. Gordon, R. Milner, and C. Wadsworth (1979). Edinburgh LCF – a mechanized logic of computation. *Lecture Notes in Computer Sciences*, Vol 78. Springer-Verlag, New York.

J. Herbrand (1930). Recherches sur la theorie de la demonstration. *Travaux de la Societe des Sciences et des Letters de Varsovie, Classe III, Science Mathematique et Physique* **33**.

A. Horn (1951). On sentences which are true of direct unions of algebras. *J. Symbolic Logic,* **16** 14–21.

S. C. Kleene (1936). Lambda-definability and recursiveness. *Duke Mathematical J.* **2** 340–353.

Robert Kowalski (1969). Search strategies for theorem-proving. In *Machine Intelligence 5,* Edinburgh University Press, 181–201.

Robert Kowalski (1974). Predicate logic as a programming language. *IFIP 74,* North-Holland, Amsterdam, 569–574.

Robert Kowalski (1979a). Algorithm equals logic plus control. *Comm. ACM* **22**(7), 424–436.

Robert Kowalski (1979b). *Logic for Problem Solving,* North-Holland, New York.

P. J. Landin (1963). The mechanical evaluation of expressions. *Computer J.* **6**(4), 158–165.

P. J. Landin (1965). A correspondence between Algol 60 and Church's lambda-notation. *Comm. ACM* **8** (March), 89–101, 158–165.

P. J. Landin (1966). The next 700 programming langauges. *Comm. ACM* **9**(3), 157–164.

John McCarthy (1960). Recursive functions of symbolic expressions and their computation by machine. *Comm. ACM* **3**(4), 184–195.

Robin Milner (1978). A theory of type polymorphism in programming. *J. Computer and System Sciences* **17**(3), 348–375.

Robin Milner (1984). A proposal for standard ML. *ACM Symposium on Lisp and Functional Programming* (August), 184–197.

Emil Post (1936). Finite combinatory processes. *J. Symbolic Logic* **1**, 103–105.

Emil Post (1944). Recursively enumerable sets and their decision problems. *Bulletin American Mathematical Society* **50**, 284–316.

J. A. Robinson (1965). A machine-oriented logic based on the resolution principle. *J. ACM* **12**(1), 23–41.

J. A. Robinson (1979). Logic: Form and Function. *The Mechanisation of Deductive Reasoning,* North-Holland, New York.

J. Barkley Rosser (1935). A mathematical logic without variables. *Annals Mathematics* **36**, 2nd series, 127–150.

J. Barkley Rosser (1982). Highlights of the history of the lambda-calculus. *Mathematics Research Center Report* 2441, University of Wisconsin (October). Also in *Annals of the History of Computing* **6**(4), 1984, 337–349.

Moses Schoenfinkel (1924). Uber die Bausteine der mathematischen Logik. *Mathematical Annals,* **92**, 305–316. English translation in *From Frege to Goedel: A Source-book in Mathematical Logic, 1879–1931,* Jead Van Heijenoort (ed.), Harvard University Press, Cambridge, Mass., 1967.

Thoralf Skolem (1944). Some remarks on recursive arithmetic. *Det Kongelige Norske Videnskabers Selskabs Forhandlinger* **17**, 103–106.

S. Stenlund (1972). Combinators, lambda-terms and proof theory. Reidel, Dordrecht, Holland.

Simon Thompson (1986). Laws in Miranda. *ACM Conference on Lisp and Functional Programming* (August), 1–12.

Alan Turing (1936). On computable numbers, with an application to the Entscheidungsproblem. *Proc. London Mathematical Society* **42**(2), 230–265. Corrections: **43** (1937), 544–546.

Alan M. Turing (1937). Computability and lambda-definability. *J. Symbolic Logic* **2**, 153–163.

David Turner (1985). Miranda: A non-strict functional language with polymorphic types. Proceedings IFIP International Conference on Functional Programming Languages and Computer Architecture, Nancy, France (September). *Lecture Notes in Computer Science*, Vol 201, Springer-Verlag, New York.

David Turner (1986). An overview of Miranda. *SIGPLAN Notices* **21**(12), 158–166.

M. H. Van Emden and R. A. Kowalski (1976). The semantics of predicate logic as a programming language. *J. ACM* **23**(4), 733–742.

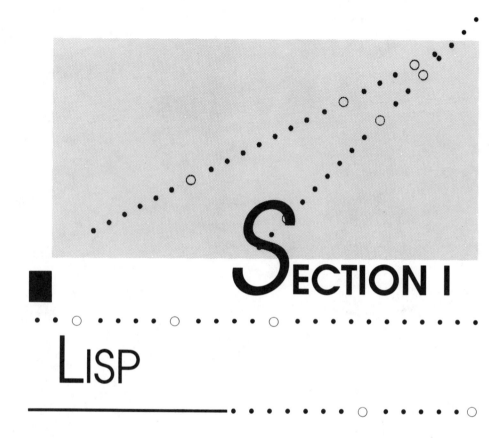

# SECTION I

# LISP

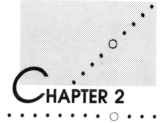

# CHAPTER 2

# NOTATIONS FOR DATA IN LISP

Every programming language has its peculiar way of denoting information. In Lisp, data are represented in terms of sequences with components that are either atoms or other sequences. In Lisp, an atom is denoted by a string of letters and/or digits, and a sequence is denoted by a list of components separated by spaces and enclosed in a matching pair of parentheses. These sequences are called *lists*.[1]

Here are some examples of lists:[2]

---

[1] The notation for lists, and our definition of lists, makes them appear to be symmetric structures that could be viewed as easily from one end as the other. However, Lisp systems represent lists in an asymmetric way that makes the beginning of the list much more easily accessible than the end. In fact, the beginning is directly accessible, and each component contains a link to the next component. Access to the last element requires passing through all these links, and this process involves an amount of work proportional to the number of components in the list.

[2] Actually, **((bean dip) (10 oz) 115)** is not, itself, a list. It denotes a list, but the list itself exists in its own space (and **bean** is not an atom; it merely denotes an atom). By the same token, 194 is not a number; it is a numeral denoting a number (00194, another numeral, denotes the same number). A symbol denoting a thing is not the thing; the thing

---

### Notations Specifying Lists

| | | |
|---|---|---|
| *list* | is | (*component* ... ) |
| *component* | is | *atom* |
| | or | *list* |
| *atom* | is | a contiguous string of letters and/or digits containing no spaces |
| *symbolic-atom* | is | an atom beginning with a letter |
| | Caveat: | Most Lisp systems permit symbolic atoms to have names containing hyphens, underscores, asterisks, slashes, less-than- and greater-than-signs, and other special symbols. Lisp interprets certain atoms as numbers (see Chapter 14). |

---

| | |
|---|---|
| `(Kurt Vonnegut)` | two components: both atomic |
| `( (Deadeye Dick) (Kurt Vonnegut) )` | two components: both lists |
| `(T O O   H O T   T O   H O O T)` | 12 components: all atomic |
| `( (bean dip) (10 oz) 115)` | 3 components: 2 lists, 1 atom |

Components[3] of lists are separated by spaces; the beginning of the list is marked with a left parenthesis; and the end of the list is marked with a matching right parenthesis. Each component is either an atom, that is, a string of letters and/or digits, or another list enclosed in its own set of matching parentheses. The list " `(Kurt Vonnegut)` " has two components: its first component is the atom "`Kurt`" and its second component is the atom "`Vonnegut.`"

By exactly the same logic, " `(Deadeye Dick)` " is a list. Since `(Deadeye Dick)` and `(Kurt Vonnegut)` are both lists, they may, themselves, be components of lists (because the definition of *component* includes *list* as one alternative). Therefore, `((Deadeye Dick) (Kurt Vonnegut))`

---

is something else. This philosophical puzzler arises in different guises in many intellectual pursuits. Forgive us if we occasionally superimpose the two concepts. We will try to be careful in contexts where confusion might ensue from a slip.

[3] Most literature on Lisp refers to components of lists (i.e., lists and atoms) as *symbolic expressions*, or *s-expressions* for short. Lisp systems conventionally represent s-expressions as collections of "cells" containing pointers or other data. Operations to alter these cells are intrinsic in all Lisp systems, but such operations do not interest us because denotational programs never change data - instead, they compute new data from old.

meets the definition of a list. It has two components. (If you thought it had four components, rethink the issue. Remember: The parentheses are important constituents of the list syntax; they group components into sublists.)

## BACKUS-NAUR FORM (BNF)

We will use BNF to describe the forms of expression that Lisp systems can interpret. This notation specifies the syntax of interpretable forms in terms of their constituents. Each constituent is either the name of an interpretable form described elsewhere (a so-called *nonterminal symbol*) or a symbol that stands for itself (a *terminal symbol*).

Names written in lowercase italic letters denote nonterminal symbols. Other names denote terminal symbols. Parentheses occur only in places where the form being described requires them; that is, parentheses are terminal symbols. An ellipsis "..." indicates that the immediately previous item may occur any number of times (including no times at all) in the form being described. Occasionally, we will be less formal and use a phrase in English to describe the form of an interpretable entity (see the definitions of *atom* and *symbolic atom*). In addition to the BNF, we also describe the forms in ordinary English. We include the BNF descriptions for reference and clarification.

## INTERPRETING BNF VIA THE PRINCIPLE OF SUBSTITUTION

It may seem a little mind-boggling, at first, to discover the term *list* used in its own definition. Resolve it like this: A *list* is constructed of *components*, and each *component* is either an *atom* or something that fits the definition of *list* (i.e., something that consists of *components*). Thus, the definition of list illustrates how lists are constructed by the Principle of Substitution.

The Principle of Substitution says that wherever an entity occurs, it may be replaced by an equivalent entity without altering the correctness of the construct containing the entity. Thus, wherever *component* occurs in the definition of *list*, either of the alternative forms for *component* (i.e., *atom* or *list*) may replace it; the result remains a *list*.

The bean dip list exhibits another interesting case. It is heterogeneous: Some of its components are lists, others atoms. But each of its components meets the definition of what a component must be, which makes it a list.

The correspondences between left and right parentheses in the denotation of a list are crucial and must not be taken lightly. Here are some trickier examples.

| | |
|---|---|
| **( (Kurt Vonnegut) )** | one component: a list |
| **()** | no components, the empty-list (remember! the ellipsis in the definition of list indicates that there may be *any number* of components, including none) |
| **( (bean dip) () )** | two components: both lists |
| **( () () )** | two components: both empty lists |
| **( () )** | one component: an empty list |
| **( ( () ) )** | one component: the above list |

It is also important to recognize that any given list will have many different denotations and that Lisp does not distinguish among these. For example, the list

**(bean dip)**

can also be denoted

**(bean                    dip)**

It is the same list as far as Lisp is concerned, even though the second one is written in a slightly different manner from the first.[4] Similarly,

**(T  O  O        H  O  T        T  O        H  O  O  T)**

is the same list as

**(T O O H O T T O H O O T)**

but not the same list as

**(TOO HOT TO HOOT)**

which has only four components rather than twelve.

---

[4]Lisp also ignores letter-case in symbolic atoms (e.g., **Nabokov** and **nabokov** denote the same symbolic atom). Your Lisp system, if it is a very polite one, will use your choice of letter-case when it prints your symbolic atoms (or one of your choices, at least, if you have been inconsistent). More likely, your Lisp system will rudely impose its own letter-case preference on you. When you type **Nabokov**, expect to see your Lisp system type **nabokov**.

Lisp represents all data, both input and results, as lists and atoms. The fundamental operations of Lisp provide ways to extract components from lists, to construct new lists from existing ones, and to denote lists as data to be taken literally. A Lisp program describes a relationship between an input list and a result list. In doing so, it makes certain assumptions about the formation of the input list, and it will construct a result list of a particular form, depending on the input list.

Thus, to write a Lisp program to carry out some "real-world" computation, we will have to decide how to represent input data from the problem we are addressing in terms of lists, and we will have to decide on some way to represent result data so that we can interpret the answer.

## ■ SUMMARY

Lisp represents data in terms of atoms, which are indecomposable symbols, and lists, which are sequences of atoms and/or other lists enclosed in parentheses.

| | | |
|---|---|---|
| *list* | is | (*component* ... ) |
| *component* | is | *atom* |
| | or | *list* |
| *atom* | is | a contiguous string of letters and/or digits containing no spaces |
| *symbolic-atom* | is | an atom beginning with a letter |

## ■ EXERCISES

1. Count the number of components in the following lists.

   ```
   (Granny Smith)
   ((red delicious))
   ()
   ( () () () )
   ( ( () () () ) () )
   ( 27 3 (hut hut hut) )
   ```

2. Which of the lists in Exercise 1 have only atoms as components? Which have only lists as components? Which have both? Neither?

3. Write a list that has four components: The first two are lists of three atoms each, the third a list with two components (the first a list, the second an atom), and the fourth a list of five atoms.

## ANSWERS

1. The lists have 2, 1, 0, 3, 2, and 3 components, respectively.

2. The first list has only atoms as components. The second, fourth, and fifth have only lists (albeit some of these are empty) and the last one has both. The third has neither, since it has no components at all. Technically, Lisp treats the empty list "()" as both a list and an atom (no other list or atom has this dual nature). Therefore, the fourth list in Exercise 1 also contains only atoms and the fifth list contains both lists and atoms, but you were not expected to know this until now.

The empty list has an alternative denotation: "NIL" denotes the same list/atom as "()."

3. ( (x x x) (x x x) ( (x) x ) (x x x x x) )

This is only one of myriad possibilities, of course. Try to match the parenthesis structure in your answer to that of ours. As long as that matches, your answer is ok. Additionally, because of the technicality about the empty list being an atom that you learned about in Exercise 2, any of the x's in our answer could equally well have been "()."

# CHAPTER 3

# FUNCTIONS

The method of describing computable relationships in Lisp is via functions definitions. The fundamental operations of Lisp are, themselves, predefined functions that we can use in combination to compose new functions. Functions are applied to input data (arguments) and deliver results that, in turn, can be fed into other functions as arguments. It is through this mechanism, known as function composition, that we specify all computations in Lisp.

For example, one of the predefined functions in Lisp is the **reverse** function. Its argument is a list, and its result is a new list. The result list has the same components as the argument, but they occur in reverse order. Here are some examples:

**Function: `reverse`**

| **argument** | **result** |
|---|---|
| `(Kurt Vonnegut)` | `(Vonnegut Kurt)` |
| `( (bean dip) (10 oz) 115)` | `(115 (10 oz) (bean dip))` |

---

## FUNCTIONS, ARGUMENTS, AND THE ESSENCE OF COMPUTING

The input data for a function are known as its arguments. A function's result is simply information from its arguments presented in a new form. The function extracts some of the information from its arguments, refashions those data into a new form, and this refashioned form of the input data becomes the function's result.

This is the essence of computing—presenting data in new forms that are more useful for a given purpose. A stereo system is an example of this process. The stereo tuner is a function that has as its input a collection of radio frequency signals. The tuner extracts some of the information from these signals (e.g., it will throw away all the signals outside a certain frequency band) and presents them in a new form to the amplifier. The amplifier, in turn, takes the result from the tuner function and converts it to electrical signals of sufficient strength to drive speakers. The speakers transform the electrical results delivered by the amplifier function into soundwaves.

Thus, a stereo system is a function built from the composition of three subfunctions that, together, transform radio frequency signals into sound waves. As stereo systems become more and more dependent on digital technology, the ways in which designers put together these tuner functions, amplifier functions, and the like become more like the way you write programs for computers—in Lisp or in any other programming language.

---

```
((Deadeye Dick)                    ((Kurt Vonnegut)
        (Kurt Vonnegut))                  (Deadeye Dick))
(T O O H O T T O H O O T)         (T O O H O T T O H O O T)
(TOO HOT TO HOOT)                 (HOOT TO HOT TOO)
```

The components of the result of **reverse** are exactly backward in order from those of its argument, but the internal structure of each component remains the same, as you can see in these examples.

The notation used in Lisp to denote the application of a function to its argument is to form a list in which the first component is the name of the function and the second component is the argument.

To apply **reverse** to the argument **(Kurt Vonnegut)**, we would write

```
(reverse '(Kurt Vonnegut) )
```

## LISP EXPRESSIONS

| | | |
|---|---|---|
| *expression* | is | *function-application* |
| | or | *pure-data* |
| *function-application* | is | *(function-name arg ...)* |
| *function-name* | is | *symbolic-atom* |
| *arg* | is | *expression* |
| *pure-data* | is | *'list* |
| | or | *'atom* |

Meaning:    Result data from function application or the list or atom following the apostrophe is pure data.

Caveat:    The Lisp system must have access to a definition of the function name and the arguments must match, in sequence, with those expected by the function.

The apostrophe preceding **reverse**'s argument is not an incidental speck. Both data and function applications take the form of lists, and there must be a way to specify which is which. The apostrophe in the foregoing expression marks the list or atom as data; that is, it inhibits interpretation of the form following the apostrophe as the application of a function.[1] The apostrophe is a shorthand notation for the application of a special function called **quote** that inhibits interpretation of its argument, thus making it data rather than an expression requiring evaluation. The expressions **'beans**, **'(bean dip)**, and **'((too hot) to (eat))** have precisely the same meaning as the expressions **(quote beans)**, **(quote (bean dip))**, and **(quote ((too hot) to (eat)))**.

In general, atoms in Lisp do not stand for themselves; they represent some function or value. Thus, the atom **reverse**, stands for the function of that name, and not simply for the name itself. If we wanted it to stand for itself, we would mark it with an apostrophe: **'reverse**. On the other hand, the expression

**'(Kurt Vonnegut)**

[1]The apostrophe character has alternative names: single quote and accent acute, for example. Most literature on programming uses the name "single quote." We use "apostrophe" because it seems less clumsy in English sentences.

> **reverse**—reverses the ordering of the components in a list
>
> **(reverse** *lst***)**   is   a list with components that are, in reverse
>                              order, those of *lst*

is pure data; it does not denote an application of a function called **Kurt** to an argument called **Vonnegut**.

Here is how you can get the Lisp system to evaluate functions for you: When the system prompt (perhaps an asterisk) is on the screen, the Lisp system is waiting for you to enter a function application for it to evaluate.

## Examples

```
* (reverse '((bean dip) (10 oz) 115) )
        – you type "(reverse ...)"
(115 (10 oz) (bean dip))
        – system types this
* (reverse '((rapid lube) 12 (5 qt)) )
        – you type this
((5 qt) 12 (rapid lube))
        – system types this
* (reverse '((Van Halen)))
        – watch out ... tricky!
((Van Halen))
        – arg has only 1 component
* (reverse 'rube)
        – don't do this ...
Error:  Wrong kind of argument,
        – arg must be a list!
   you are advised to (reset)
        (typically helpful error message)
```

The **reverse** function is one of a few dozen intrinsic Lisp operations. Another one is the **equal** function, which compares two lists or atoms. The result of the **equal** function is the atom "**T**" if its two arguments are the same; otherwise, its result is the atom "**NIL**" (i.e., the empty list).

## Examples

```
Program:  (equal '(bean dip) '(guacomole) )
Result:   NIL                          2 arguments unequal
```

---

**equal**—checks for equality of two lists or atoms

(**equal** $arg_1$ $arg_2$)　　is　**T**　　if $arg1 = arg2$
　　　　　　　　　　　　or　**NIL**　otherwise

---

Program:　**(equal '(bean dip) '(bean dip) )**
Result:　**T**　　　　　　　　　　　both args denote same list
Program:　**(equal '(Kurt V) '((Kurt V)) )**
Result:　**NIL**　　　1st arg, 2 components; 2nd arg, 1 component

The way to describe more and more complicated computations in Lisp is to apply functions in tandem; that is, to feed the result of one function application into another function as its argument. In this way, we can use a combination of **reverse** and **equal** to describe the palindrome relationship we talked about earlier. You probably recall that a palindrome is a phrase that remains unchanged when its letters are reversed.

We will represent phrases as lists of one-letter atoms. This is not ideal because it leaves out all of the customary punctuation, but we want to concentrate on the computation, not the way the data are presented. Here are some phrases represented in the proposed way:

| Representation in Lisp | Traditional form |
| --- | --- |
| (B O B) | Bob |
| (N A O M I) | Naomi |
| (A B L E W A S I<br>　　E R E I S A W E L B A) | Able was I,<br>　　ere I saw Elba. |
| (T O O H O T T O H O O T) | Too hot to hoot. |
| (H E B A D M A D D O G E H) | He bad mad dog, eh? |

The **equal** function compares two lists, and the **reverse** function reverses the order of the components of a list. These are the two operations needed to specify the palindrome computation. The idea is to compute a reverse copy of a list and compare it to the original.

Program:　**(equal '(B O B) (reverse '(B O B)))**
Result:　**T**　　　　　　　　　　　　Bob is palindrome
Program:　**(equal '(N A O M I) (reverse '(N A O M I)) )**
Result:　**NIL**　　　　　　　　　　Naomi is not palindrome

These expressions describe the palindrome test, but they are tiresome to write (especially retyping the phrase to be tested, once for the first argument to the **equal** function and a second time as the argument to the **reverse** function).

As you must suspect, there is a more convenient way to handle it. We can define a function that puts together the proper composition for an arbitrary argument and use that function to perform the palindrome test. We do this using the **defun** operation. This operation lets us attach a name to an expression. The **defun** operation is a different type of operation than **reverse** or **equal** because it leaves a permanent record of having been performed. The results computed by **reverse** and **equal** are immediately "consumed," either as arguments to other functions within an expresssion or as displayed results. But **defun** attaches a name to an expression for the duration of a computing session in Lisp.

The **defun** function is used to define functions. There are three parts to the definition:

1. The function name          **palindrometest**

2. The dummy argument list   **phrase**

3. The result specification    **(equal phrase ...)**

The function name must be an atom beginning with a letter. The dummy argument list must be a list of atoms, each of which begins with a letter. The result specification designates a result for the function and may invoke other functions by using any combination of the names in the argument list as arguments for these functions, or it may specify a value as pure data (using the apostrophe).

The definition of **palindrometest** that follows specifies that this function is to be a function of one argument (to be referred to as **phrase** in the result specification) and that its value is to be the result of comparing the argument, **phrase**, to its reverse. As you can see, the result specification for **palindrometest** combines the functions **equal** and **reverse** in the same way that we were combining them earlier to perform the **palindrome test**. The only difference is that the dummy argument name, **phrase**, is used in place of the pure data we used earlier. Thus, the dummy argument name does not stand for itself; it is not pure data. Instead it stands in place of data to which the **palindrometest** function will be applied.

Here is a session in which we define **palindrometest** and use it to test a few phrases to see whether or not they are palindromes.

```
Program:   (defun palindrometest (phrase)
                            ; comments ok after ";"
           (equal phrase (reverse phrase) ) )
                            ; exp'n specifying result
```

---

### LISP FUNCTION DEFINITIONS

| | | |
|---|---|---|
| *function-defn* | is | (**defun** *function-name arg-list result-spec*) |
| *function-name* | is | *symbolic-atom* |
| *arg-list* | is | ( *symbolic-atom* ... ) |
| *result-spec* | is | *expression* |

Meaning: Attaches function-name to result-spec; henceforth, the *function-name* may be used to form function applications; the result of such an application will be the value of the *expression* when each occurrence of a symbolic atom from the *arg-list*, other than one within pure data, is replaced by the corresponding argument in the function application.

---

| | | |
|---|---|---|
| Result: | **palindrometest** | defun echoes function-name |
| Program: | **(palindrometest '(B O B) )** | |
| Result: | **T** | "Bob" is a palindrome. |
| Program: | **(palindrometest '(N A O M I I M O A N) )** | |
| Result: | **T** | So is "Naomi, I moan." |
| Program: | **(palindrometest '(T O O H O T T O H O O T) )** | |
| Result: | **T** | "Too hot to hoot," too. |
| Program: | **(palindrometest '(H E B A D M A D D O G E H) )** | |
| Result: | **NIL** | But not "He bad mad dog, eh?" |

There are not too many interesting functions we can describe using only **reverse** and **equal** as our only predefined functions, but to get some practice, we will define a few boring ones. Here is a function that checks to see if its argument is "Naomi," spelled backward.

| | |
|---|---|
| Program: | **(defun bkwdNaomi (phrase)** |
| | **(equal phrase (reverse '(N A O M I) ) ) )** |
| Result: | **bkwdNaomi** |
| Program: | **(bkwdNaomi '(H A T M A N J A C K) )** |
| Result: | **NIL**    "Hat-man Jack" is not Naomi, backwards. |
| Program: | **(bkwdNaomi '(I M O A N) )** |
| Result: | **T**    But "I moan" is. |

## THE PRINCIPLE OF SUBSTITUTION AS THE BASIS OF COMPUTATION

Function composition works like this: The result of a function application inside an expression is substituted in place of that function application (except that substitutions are not performed in pure data, which are marked by apostrophes). By the Principle of Substitution, this does not alter the meaning of the expression.

This is how computation in Lisp proceeds: When an argument needed to compute the result of a function application is, itself, a function application, its result is computed (via the Principle of Substitution, if necessary), and this result is substituted in place of the argument.

This principle seems straightforward, but it leads to some subtle theoretical problems.[2] Consider the expression **(reverse (reverse ' (x reverse)))**. The subexpression **(reverse ' (x reverse))** has the value **(reverse x)**, but we cannot substitute **(reverse x)** for **(reverse ' (x reverse))** in the original expression. This substitution would produce **(reverse (reverse x))**, and Lisp would complain about **x** being "unbound." The problem is that subexpressions that Lisp has evaluated are pure data; further evaluation is inhibited. Thus, the value of the subexpression **(reverse ' (x reverse))** is, in the notation of Lisp programs, **' (reverse x)** rather than **(reverse x)**. If we substitute **' (reverse x)** in place of the subexpression **(reverse ' (x reverse))**, we get **(reverse ' (reverse x))**. This evaluates to the data value **' (x reverse)**, as expected.

Although we cannot overemphasize the importance of the Principle of Substitution as the basis of computation, you should not consider it as a guide to writing programs. In fact, it is a mistake to worry about how the Lisp system is going to compute a function's result when you are designing the function's result specification. Worry instead about whether the result you specify is in concert with the result you want your function to have. In other words, worry about making true statements in your function definitions, not about making computable statements.

---

[2] In theoretical treatments of the lambda-calculus, the substitution principle we are discussing is known as *beta-reduction*. Other forms of substitution (e.g., *alpha-reduction*, used to avoid spurious name conflicts, and *eta-reduction*, used in dealing with functions that ignore some of their arguments) play a role in resolving some of the potential paradoxes that arise in studying computation with the rigor of mathematical logic.

Here is a function with two arguments that check to see if its first argument is the reverse of its second.

Program: **(defun equalreverse (phr1 phr2)**
          **(equal phr1 (reverse phr2) ) )**
Result: **equalreverse**
Program: **(equalreverse '(L O O K) '(K O O L) )**
Result: T
Program: **(equalreverse '(D E E R) '(R E A D) )**
Result: **NIL**

## ■ SUMMARY

| | | |
|---|---|---|
| **(reverse** *lst***)** | is | a list with components that are those of *lst*, but in reverse order |
| **(equal** $arg_1$ $arg_2$**)** | is | **T** if $arg_1 = arg_2$ |
| | or | **NIL** otherwise |

## ■ BIBLIOGRAPHY NOTES

Glaser, Hankin, and Till clearly and concisely explain many of the basic concepts of the lambda-calculus in their text on functional programming, including an excellent discussion of some of the problems that the quote function can lead to.

Hugh Glaser, Chris Hankin, and David Till (1984), *Principles of Functional Programming*, Prentice–Hall, Englewood Cliffs, N.J.

## ■ EXERCISES

1. Define a function **bkwdNaomi** again, but this time use the function **equalreverse** in its *result-specification*.

2. Define the function **bkwdNaomi** without using either the **reverse** function or the **equalreverse** function in the *result-specification*.

# ANSWERS

1. (defun bkwdNaomi (phr) (equalreverse phr '(N A O M I)
 ) )

2. (defun bkwdNaomi (phr) (equal phr '(I M O A N) ) )

# CHAPTER 4

# BUILDING LISTS AND EXTRACTING COMPONENTS

Most Lisp systems have several dozen intrinsic functions (i.e., functions it automatically knows how to perform). We will not use all of them in this text. When we use a new function, we will specify its meaning.

We have omitted some of the functions, many of which are redundant anyway. Over the years, Lisp has acquired alternative forms for equivalent operations. Usually we will stick to one of these forms in the text, primarily to keep the text as brief as possible without omitting central concepts. These omissions will not affect your understanding of Lisp programming in any important way, although they will affect your ability to read programs that use the functions we omit. If you are trying to read such a program, consult your system guide and translate them into familiar terms.

We also omit many functions that are included in Lisp primarily for the sake of addressing certain types of computing hardware in a direct fashion. For example, some Lisp functions make it possible to use programming techniques similar to those commonly used in languages such as Pascal and Fortran. We do not discuss such functions because we emphasize denotational programming techniques. We leave the study of operational programming techniques, whether in Lisp or in any other programming language, to other sources. Therefore, your understanding of Lisp programming techniques, insofar as it is derived from reading this book, will be deficient in the area of operational programming techniques.

The examples in the applications section of this book are described in terms of the functions discussed in the Lisp section. These functions provide enough scope to describe any computable relationship.

The **reverse** function, like all functions, delivers as its result a new presentation of the information in its argument. If its argument is a person's first initial and surname (represented as a list with the first component the initial and the second component the surname), then its result will be the person's name in last-name-first format.

Program:   **(reverse ' (H Williams))**
Result:    **(Williams H)**

Suppose we have a list of names in this initial/surname form, and we would like them all reformatted in the last-name-first form. In other words, we would like to apply the **reverse** function to all the components of the list of names, individually. We do not want to apply the **reverse** function to the list of names as a whole because that will not reformat any of the individual names.

Program:   **(reverse ' ( (H Williams) (R Charles)**
                              **(B King) ) )**
Result:    **((B King) (R Charles) (H Williams))**
           – not what we had in mind

There are many ways to do what we want to do, but all require the use of at least one new function. The one that we are going to use applies the same function repeatedly to a sequence of arguments packaged in a list.

The name of this new function is **mapcar**. Not a very enlightening name is it? Unfortunately, this obscurity is a characteristic of many Lisp function names. Lisp is one of the oldest languages, and when it was being designed, people were far more concerned with figuring out what functions were needed and how they should operate than with how descriptive their names were. This was a natural and completely justified point of view at the time, especially since they had no idea we would still be using the same old names two or three decades later.[1]

---

[1] Names like **mapcar** were partially derived from names of computer components used to express the meanings of the functions on the system that the designers of Lisp were using to experiment with their new notation. In particular the "car" part stands for "contents

---

**mapcar**—constructs a list of transformed components

**(cad...r (mapcar #'** *fn lst***))**     is    **(***fn* **(cad...r** *lst***))**

Note:  **cad...r** extracts a component from its argument, our definition says that each component of **mapcar**'s result is the result of applying **mapcar**'s first argument, which is a function, to the corresponding component of **mapcar**'s second argument, which is a list.

---

So we are stuck with **mapcar**, and a few other weird ones, but it is no real handicap. After a while, it will not even annoy you anymore, except when you try to explain to someone else why a particular function has such an unsuggestive name.

The **mapcar** function does exactly what we want: It applies a function to each of the components of a list, individually, and delivers as its result a list of the results of each of the function applications. The function **mapcar** has two arguments: The first one is the name of the function to be applied, and the second is the list with components that are to be transformed by the function.

```
    → (mapcar #'reverse '( (H Williams) (R Charles)
                                (B King) ) )
((Williams H) (Charles R) (King B))
```

The pound sign/apostrophe mark reminds the Lisp system that **reverse** is the name of a function. Most Lisp systems do not permit the use of a function name as an argument to another function unless the function name used as an argument is marked with the pound sign/apostrophe.[2]

Let us carry this example a little further. Suppose we have a collection of lists, each of which has two components: (1) a name, in initial/surname form, and (2) a list of information pertaining to this individual. We would like to change the format of the name in each list to

---

of address register," which is a computer component the original Lisp implementors used for a pointer to a list element.

[2]Like the apostrophe, the pound sign/apostrophe is a shorthand notation. It stands for an application of the special function called "**function**," which delivers its argument in a form permitting the argument to be interpreted as a function. Thus **#'reverse** is equivalent to **(function reverse)** and permits a function such as **mapcar** to interpret **reverse** as a function.

last-name-first, but leave the other information as is. Our goal will be to write a program to make this transformation.

```
Sample argument:  ( ( (H Williams)
                        ((Jambalaya) (Lost Highway)) )
                  ( (R Charles)   ((I got a woman)) )
                  ( (B King)
                        ((Caldonia)  (Nobody Home))  )  )
          Result:  ( ( (Williams H)
                        ((Jambalya) (Lost Highway)) )
                  ( (Charles R) ((I got a woman)) )
                  ( (King B)
                        ((Caldonia)  (Nobody Home)) ) )
```

If we can put together a function to handle one of the component lists individually, then we can use **mapcar** to apply the function to the whole collection. We simply define a function with an argument that is a list of two components, each of which is a list. The function's result is that same list of two components, except that the first component list is reversed.

Our first thought might be to use **mapcar** to accomplish this:

```
Program:   (mapcar #'reverse '( (H Williams)
                  ((Jambalya) (Lost Highway)) ) )
Result:    ( (Williams H) ((Lost Highway) (Jambalya)) )
```

Unfortunately, this does a little more reformatting than we wanted. It reverses the order of the list of pertinent information as well as converting the name to last-name-first format. We want to apply **reverse** only to one portion of the list, and then to reconstitute the list with the rearranged name taking the place of the original.

To accomplish this we need to use two kinds of functions: one that extracts portions of lists and one that puts lists together from components. First, the extraction functions: **car**, **cadr**, **caddr**, and so forth. The function **car** (another unsuggestive name; same derivation as **mapcar**) extracts the first component of a list. It has only one argument, which must be a list, not an atom, and its result is the first component of that list.

```
Program:   (car '( (H Williams)
                  ((Jambalya) (Lost Highway)) ) )
Result:    (H Williams)
```

The function **cadr** extracts the second component of its argument.

---

**cad**...**r**—extracts a component from a list
| | | |
|---|---|---|
| (**cad**...**r** *lst*) | is | the $n$'th component of *lst* |
| | | where $n - 1$ is the number of **d**'s in **cad**...**r** |
| (**car** '(A B C D)) | is | **A** |
| (**cadr** '(A B C D)) | is | **B** |
| (**caddr** '(A B C D)) | is | **C** |
| (**cadddr** '(A B C D)) | is | **D** |

Caveat: Some Lisp systems limit the number of of **d**'s in **cad**...**r** to three or fewer, allowing only **car**, **cadr**, **caddr**, and **cadddr**

---

Program:   `(cadr '( (H Williams)`
          `((Jambalya) (Lost Highway)) ) )`
Result:    `((Jambalya) (Lost Highway))`

As we suggested earlier, there is a collection of related extraction functions that go by names of the form **cad**...**r**, in which there can be any number of **d**'s (Caveat: Some Lisp systems restrict number of letters between the **c** and the **r** in **cad**...**r**, typically to three or fewer, leaving only four functions of this form: **car**, **cadr**, **caddr**, and **cadddr**. In the next chapter, you will see how to extract deeper components even in the face of this restriction.) The **cad**...**r** function extracts the $n$th element of its argument, where $n$ is one more than the number of **d**'s in the **cad**...**r**. Thus, **caddr** extracts the third element of its argument, **cadddr** extracts the fourth, and so on.

We need only the first two of these functions, **car** and **cadr**, to build the function on which we are working. We are trying to specify a result in which the first component is a reversed version of the first component of the argument. We can get this reversed version of the first component by combining **car** and **reverse**.

Program:   `(reverse (car '( (H Williams)`
          `((Jambalya) (Lost Highway)) ) ))`
Result:    `((Williams H))`

This is part of the result we are trying to build. The other part is the second component of the argument, which we can extract using **cadr**.

Program:   `(cadr '((H Williams)`
          `((Jambalya) (Lost Highway)) ) )`
Result:    `((Jambalya) (Lost Highway))`

---

**list** – constructs a list from components

(**list** $arg_1$ $arg_2$ $\cdots$ $arg_n$)    is    ($arg_1$ $arg_2$ $\cdots$ $arg_n$)

---

Now we have both components of the result we want, but we have no way to put them together. That is the job of the **list** function. It takes any number of arguments and constructs a result list with those arguments as its components.

```
Program:    (list 'H 'Williams)
              - 2 arguments for list
Result:     (H Williams)
              - 2 components in result
Program:    (list '(Jambalya) '(Lost Highway) )
              - 2 args
Result:     ((Jambalya) (Lost Highway))
              - 2 comps
Program:    (list '(H Williams) '((Jambalya)
                                    (Lost Highway)) )
              - 2 args
Result:     ( (H Williams) ((Jambalya) (Lost Highway)) )
              - 2 comps
Program:    (list '(Caldonia) '(Nobody Home)
                                  '(Sweet Sixteen) )
              - 3 args
Result:     ((Caldonia) (Nobody Home) (Sweet Sixteen))
              - 3 comps
```

The function we are looking for can be defined in terms of the functions **reverse, car, cadr,** and **list**.

```
Program:    (list (reverse (car '((H Williams)
                         ((Jambalaya) (Lost Highway))) ))
                  (cadr '((H Williams)
                         ((Jambalaya) (Lost Highway))) ))
Result:     ((Williams H) ((Jambalya) (Lost Highway)))
```

We can use the idea embodied in the foregoing examples to formulate the result specification for a function that carries out the name format conversion for which we have been looking.

```
Program:   (defun lastnamefirst (nameplusinfo)
             (list (reverse (car nameplusinfo)) ; 1st comp
                   (cadr nameplusinfo) )) ; 2nd comp
```
Result:    `lastnamefirst`

```
Program:   (lastnamefirst '((H Williams)
                      ((Jambalya) (Lost Highway))) )
```
Result:    `((Williams H) ((Jambalya) (Lost Highway)))`

```
Program:   (lastnamefirst '((R Charles) ((I got a woman))) )
```
Result:    `((Charles R) ((I got a woman)))`

```
Program:   (lastnamefirst '((B King)
                      ((Caldonia) (Nobody Home))) )
```
Result:    `((King B) ((Caldonia) (Nobody Home)))`

```
Program:   (mapcar #'lastnamefirst
           '(( (H Williams) ((Jambalaya) (Lost Highway)) )
           ( (R Charles) ((I got a woman)) )
           ( (B King) ((Caldonia) (Nobody Home)) )) )
```
Result:

```
           (( (Williams H) ((Jambalya) (Lost Highway)) )
           ( (Charles R) ((I got a woman)) )
           ( (King B) ((Caldonia) (Nobody Home)) ))
```

— mapcar applies lastnamefirst to all components of second arg

## ■ SUMMARY

|  |  |  |
|---|---|---|
| **(car** *lst***)** | is | first component of lst |
| **(cadr** *lst***)** | is | second component of lst |
| **(cad...r** *lst***)** | is | $n$th component of *lst*, where the number d's in **cad...r** is $n - 1$ |
| Caveat: | | Some Lisp systems restrict $n - 1$ to three or fewer |
| **(list** *arg* ···**)** | is | (*arg* ···) |
| **(cad...r (mapcar #'** *fn* *lst***))** | is | (*fn* **(cad...r** *lst***))** |

## ■ EXERCISES

1. What are the results of the following expressions?

```
(car    '((S Dan)
          ((Charlie Freak) (Barrytown))) )
(cadr   '((S Dan)
          ((Charlie Freak) (Barrytown))) )
```

```
(car (cadr      '((S Dan)
                 ((Charlie Freak) (Barrytown))) ))
(cadr (cadr     '((S Dan)
                 ((Charlie Freak) (Barrytown))) ))
(cadr (car      '((S Dan)
                 ((Charlie Freak) (Barrytown))) ))
(cadr (car (cadr  '((S Dan)
                 ((Charlie Freak) (Barrytown))) )))
```

2. What are the results of the following expressions?

```
(list 'H  'Lewis)
(list '(H Lewis)    '(I want a new drug)
                    '(Finally found home)
                    '(Bad is bad) )
(cadr (list 'H 'Lewis '(You crack me up) ))
```

3. What are the results of the following expressions?

```
(mapcar #'car '((H Lewis) (S Dan) (P Floyd)) )

(mapcar #'list '((H Lewis) (S Dan) (P Floyd)) )

(mapcar #'cadr '((H Lewis) (S Dan) (P Floyd)) )
```

4. Define a function, **extr24**, the result of which is a list made up of the second and fourth components of its argument.

5. Define a function, **rev3rd**, the result of which is a reversed version of the third component of its argument.

6. Use **mapcar** and **reverse** to define a function called **interior-reverse** that will reverse each of the components within a list of lists. Example:

```
(interiorreverse '( (A B C) (D E F) (G H I)))
= ((C B A) (F E D) (I H G))
```

7. Assume the argument to a function **deepreverse** is a list, each component of which is a list of lists. Define **deepreverse** in such a way that

```
(cad...r (deepreverse lst)) = (mapcar #'reverse
                                 (cad...r lst))
```

Example: (deepreverse '( ((A B C) (D E F)) ((G H I)) ))

```
= ( ((C B A) (F E D)) ((I H G)) )
```

# ANSWERS

1. `(S Dan)`

   `((Charlie Freak) (Barrytown))`

   `(Charlie Freak)`

   `(Barrytown)`

   `Dan`

   `Freak`

2. `(H Lewis)`

   `((H Lewis) (I want a new drug) (Finally found home) (Bad is bad))`

   `Lewis`

3. `(H S P)`

   `( ((H Lewis)) ((S Dan)) ((P Floyd)) )`

   `(Lewis Dan Floyd)`

4. `(defun extr24 (1st) (list (cadr 1st) (cadddr 1st)) )`

5. `(defun rev3rd (1st) (reverse (caddr 1st)) )`

6. `(defun interiorreverse (1stof1sts)`
   `(mapcar #'reverse 1stof1sts))`

7. `(defun deepreverse (1st) (mapcar #'interiorreverse 1st))`

# MORE LIST MANIPULATION FUNCTIONS

So far we have studied three types of functions: list builders, component extractors, and predicates. **Reverse**, **list**, and **mapcar** build lists in various ways. The components of the list built by **reverse** are the same as those in the argument (but in the opposite order); the **list** function puts together a list with components that are copies of its arguments; and **mapcar** builds a list with components that are transformed versions of the components of its second argument. The **cad...r** functions extract components from lists. And the **equal** function compares its two arguments, delivering the result **T** if they are the same and **NIL** if they are not. The **equal** function is called a predicate because it affirms or denies a property of its arguments.

This is a powerful set of functions but not quite complete. Some list transformations cannot be described without the use of additional functions. For example, suppose we have a list of three components. The first component is a list of two components: the first of these two is the atom "animal," and the second is a list of animals. The second and third components have the same structure, but represent "vegetable" and "mineral," respectively.

Here is an example of such a list:

```
( (animal      (possum sheep armadillo bass anemone
                    bloodhound))
  (vegetable  (persimmon tomato bean kumquat quince
                    hoarhound))
  (mineral    (calcium granite quartz dolomite
                    runciblespoon )) )
```

We might wish to isolate the specific information from this list and discard the categories. We could extract those items using the **cad...r** functions and then package the three extracted lists into one using the **list** function.

```
(defun extractspecifics (allthings)
        (list (cadr (car allthings))
              (cadr (cadr allthings))
              (cadr (caddr allthings)) ))
```

However, if we apply this function to the aforementioned list, the result is not altogether pleasing. It has some distracting extra parentheses in it.

```
-> (extractspecifics
    '((animal      (possum sheep armadillo bass
                    anemone bloodhound))
      (vegetable (persimmon tomato bean kumquat
                    quince hoarhound))
      (mineral    (calcium granite quartz dolomite
                    runciblespoon )) ))

((possum sheep armadillo bass anemone bloodhound)
(persimmon tomato bean kumquat quince hoarhound)
(calcium granite quartz dolomite runciblespoon ))
```

Because our intent is to amalgamate all the specific information, we would prefer a flat result; that is, one with no substructure organizing the specifics into categories. Like this:

```
( possum sheep armadillo bass anemone bloodhound
  persimmon tomato bean kumquat quince hoarhound
  calcium granite quartz dolomite runciblespoon )
```

The former list has exactly three components, each of which is a list of specific items, and the latter has many components, each of which is one of the specific items. With the functions we have studied so far, we cannot construct this flat list from the categorized input data that forms the argument for **extractspecifics**. And this is only one example; many types of reorganizations cannot be described using only the functions **reverse**, **list**, **mapcar**, and **cad...r**. In the remainder of this chapter, we will present several new functions for list manipulation. This completes the set in the sense that no others will be needed to describe any sort of list reorganization.

To solve our problem with the flat list of specifics, we need only one new function: **append**. This function may have any number of arguments, but they must be lists. Append constructs a single list with components that are those of its arguments in their established order, the first argument's components coming first, then the second argument's components, and so forth. This differs from the **list** function. The components of the result of the list function are copies of its arguments. If the **list** function has three arguments, for example, the result list will have three components. On the other hand, the result of the **append** function applied to three arguments will have as many components as the three arguments have in toto.

**Examples:**

```
(append '(A B C) '(D E F))          is  (A B C D E F)
(append '(A B) '(C D E) '(F G H I)) is
                                    ( A B C D E F G H I)
```

but

```
(list '(A B C) '(D E F))            is
                                    ( (A B C) (D E F))
(list '(A B) '(C D E) '(F G H I))   is
                                    ( (A B) (C D E) (F G H I))
```

We can use the **append** function to get the effect we wanted in our **extractspecifics** function:

```
(defun   specifics  (allthings)
        (append  (cadr (car   allthings))
                 (cadr (cadr  allthings))
                 (cadr (caddr allthings))) )
```

The result of this new function, **specifics**, will be the flat list we wanted.

---

**append**—collects components from several lists into one list

$(\textbf{cad}...\textbf{r}\ (\textbf{append}\ lst_1\ lst_2\ \cdots\ lst_n))$   is   $(\textbf{cad---r}\ lst_k)$, where the number of **d**'s in **cad**...**r** is $l_1 + \cdots + l_{k-1} + j$, $l_m$ is the number of components in $lst_m$, and $j$ is the number of **d**'s in **cad---r**

---

```
-> (specifics
    '((animal      (possum  sheep  armadillo  bass
                    anemone  bloodhound))
      (vegetable   (persimmon  tomato  bean  kumquat
                    quince  hoarhound))
      (mineral     (calcium  granite  quartz  dolomite
                    runciblespoon ))) )

(possum sheep  armadillo  bass  anemone  bloodhound
    persimmon  tomato  bean
 kumquat quince  hoarhound  calcium  granite  quartz
    dolomite  runciblespoon)
```

Only one more function and we will have all we need for list manipulation. We can use **cad**...**r** to take lists apart and **append** and **list** to put them together. Using various combinations of these functions, we can rearrange lists in an arbitrary way, as long as we know with how many elements we are dealing. Consider the list of atoms derived by applying the **specifics** function: **(possum sheep ...)**. Suppose, for some reason we want to construct a new list like this one except without its first component: **(sheep ...)**. We could do this by extracting each component needed in the result (using a **cad**...**r** function), making this component into a list (using the **list** function), and then forming the result with **append**.

The expression takes this shape:

```
(append (list (cadr allthings))
        (list (caddr allthings)) ...)
```

Not only is this inconvenient, but it works only because we know in advance with how many components we are dealing. That is, our program is based on a detailed property of the input data—not a very useful

**cdr**—drops the first argument from a list

| | | |
|---|---|---|
| `(cdr (list `$arg_1$` ··· `$arg_n$`))` | is | `(list `$arg_2$` ··· `$arg_n$`)` |
| `(cdr '(a b c))` | is | `(b c)` |
| `(cdr '(a (b c)))` | is | `((b c))` |
| `(cdr '((a b) c))` | is | `(c)` |

**cd...r**—drops the leading component(s) from a list

| | | |
|---|---|---|
| `(cdd...r `$lst$`)` | is | `(cdr (cd...r `$lst$`))` where the number of **d**'s in **cdd...r** is one more than the number of **d**'s in **cd...r** |
| Caveat: | | Some Lisp systems support only the first four of these functions (**cdr**, **cddr**, **cdddr**, and **cddddr**) |
| `(cdr '(a b c))` | is | `(b c)` |
| `(cddr '(a b c))` | is | `(c)` |
| `(cdddr '(a b c))` | is | `()` |

program. (Another, but less fundamental, problem with this approach is the restriction that some Lisp systems place on **cad...r** functions, requiring the number of **d**'s to be three or fewer.)

What we need is a function with a result that is identical to its input list, without its first component. That is the **cdr** function (rhymes with good-er or rudder, depending on whom you talk to—another one of those names related to internal details of the original Lisp system).

As you can see, multiple applications of **cdr** will remove an initial sequence of any length from a list. For example, **(cdr (cdr** *lst*)) is *lst*, sans its first two components, and **(cdr (cdr (cdr** *lst*))) is *lst*, sans its first three components. There is a convenient abbreviation for this type of multiple composition of **cdr**'s: **cddr** is a composition of two **cdr**'s, so that **(cddr** *lst*) is **(cdr (cdr** *lst*)), **cdddr** is a composition of three **cdr**'s, and so on.

The **cad...r** and **cd...r** notations are provided as a matter of convenience, not necessity. They could always be written as compositions of **car** and **cdr**. Some other convenient notations that make the Lisp programmer's life a little easier are **cons** and **last**. For example, the **cons** function inserts a new first element into a list.

**cons**—inserts a component at the beginning of a list

```
(cons c lst )        is  (append (list c) lst)
(cons 'a '(b c))     is  (a b c)
(cons '(a b) '(c))   is  ((a b) c)
(cons '(a) '(b c))   is  ((a) b c)
```

**last**—drops all components of a list except the last

```
(last '())                  is  ()
(last (list arg₁ ··· argₙ)) is  (list argₙ)
(last '(a b c))             is  (c)
(last '((a b) c)            is  (c)
(last '(a (b c))            is  ((b c))
```

## Describing Lisp from Simple Primitives: `car`, `cdr`, `cons`

As you can see from the way we described **cons** and **last** in terms **append** and **list**, we could get by with fewer basic functions. There is no unique basic set, and most Lisp systems include all these functions as independent entities. It turns out, however, that all of them can be encoded in terms of three of the simplest ones: **car**, **cdr**, and **cons**. These functions are, in fact, the traditional starting point when the goal is to describe all of Lisp in terms of the simplest basic concepts. Lisp systems represent lists as chains of "cons-cells." These chains begin at the "car" of the list, which means that accessing the first element of a list or inserting a new first element is much faster than operations on succeeding elements.

```
(cons 'a '(b c))      is   (a b c)
(cons '(a b) '(c))    is   ((a b) c)
(cons '(a) '(b c))    is   ((a) b c)
```

This is equivalent to forming a list with the first argument of **cons** as the only component and appending that list to the second argument of **cons**. That is, the meaning of **cons** can be expressed in terms of **append** and **list**, but **cons** is more convenient to use when the desired result is a list with a newly inserted first component.

The function **last** is a sort of "super-**cdr**": Its result is a copy of its argument with all its components missing except the last.

## ■ SUMMARY

**append**  (**append** $lst_1$ $\cdots$ $lst_n$)
    is   a list made up of all the components from $lst_1$ through $lstn$, in sequence

**cdr**  (**cdr** (**list** $arg_1$ $arg_2$ $\cdots$ $arg_n$))
    is   (**list** $arg_2$ $\cdots$ $arg_n$)

**cdd...r**  (**cdd...r** $lst$)
    is   (**cdr** (**cd...r** $lst$))

**cons**  (**cons** $c$ $lst$)
    is   (**append** (**list** $c$) $lst$)

**last**  (**last** '())
    is   ()
    (**last** (**list** $arg_1$ $\cdots$ $arg_n$))
    is   (**list** $arg_n$)

## ■ EXERCISES

1. What are the results of the following expressions?

   a. **(cons '(a b c) '(x y z))**

   b. **(reverse (cdr '(a b c)))**

   c. **(last (reverse '(a b c)))**

   d. **(reverse (cdr (reverse '(a b c))))**

2. Define a function with a result that is the same as its argument, which is a list, except that the second component is missing.

3. Define a function with an argument that is a list and with a result that is a copy of the list, except that its last component is missing.

4. Define a function with result that is the same as its argument, which is a list, except that it is rotated right one position (i.e., its first component is the last component of its argument, its second component is the first component of its argument, its third component is the second component of its argument, and so on, and its last component is the next-to-last component of its argument).

5. Define a function with input data that is the animal-vegetable-mineral list given at the start of this chapter and with a result that is the same data set except that the first element of each of the specifics lists is missing. (Define a function that does this to one of the categories, then use **mapcar** to apply it to all the categories.)

6. Define a function to transpose the animal-vegetable-mineral list. The list is organized by category, with one component for each category. Rearrange it so that it contains the same information but has two components: first, the list of categories; and second a list with components that are the specifics lists.

## ANSWERS

1. a.   `((a b c) x y z)`
   b.   `(c b)`
   c.   `(a)`
   d.   `(a b)`

2. `(defun delete2nd (lst) (cons (car lst) (cddr lst)) )`

3. `(defun deletelast (lst) (reverse (cdr (reverse lst)))`
   `)`

4. `(defun  rotateright (lst)   (cons (car (last lst))`
   `                        (deletelast lst)))`

5. `(defun  oneclass (class)`
   `     (list (car class) (cdadr class)) )`
   `(defun delete1stspecific (avm)`
   `     (mapcar #'oneclass avm) )`

6. `(defun transpose (avm)`
   `     (list  (mapcar #'car  avm)`
   `            (mapcar #'cadr avm)) )`

# CHAPTER 6

# A LENIENT FUNCTION: IF

Consider the following function.

```
(defun K (x y) (append '(start msg) x '(end msg)) )
```

You might ask yourself why anyone would design a function that completely ignores one of its arguments. Please let us defer this question until later; we cannot give a very good answer right now, except to say that we are trying to illustrate a point in the simplest possible terms.

If we apply **K** to a pair of arguments, we get the expected result.

```
→ (K '(Plz call BillyJoJimBob) 'ignoredanyway)
(start msg Plz call BillyJoJimBob end msg)
→ (K '(Put out the cat) (reverse '(Yak uh t e e yak)) )
(start msg Put out the cat end msg)
```

But we might be tempted to ask ourselves, "How does the computer carry out this computation?" (Please pardon our inconsistency in this

---

**if**—a lenient function to select one of two alternatives
(if $p$ $x$ $y$)    is    $y$ if $p$ is the empty list
                   is    $x$ otherwise
(if NIL 'true-result 'false-result)
            is    false-result
(if 'T 'true-result 'false-result)
            is    true-result
(if (equal '(Downtown Brown) '(Reid)) 'yes 'no)
            is    no

---

matter. We said earlier that we were not going to worry about how the computer computes our results, but only about whether the results we specify are correct. We need to explicate a few details about this computation to explain how to use Lisp in certain circumstances.)

Because **K** never makes use of its second argument, computing it would waste effort. In the second application of **K**, computing a result for the second argument involves reversing the order of a list—not a lot of computation, but enough to illustrate the idea. Since this result is not needed, why compute it? The answer has to do with internal system details, underlying hardware support, and the like. It turns out that under the conditions supporting most Lisp systems, it is faster to evaluate all arguments regardless of whether they will be needed, except in a few special cases.

Some programming systems, however, take a different point of view: They avoid computation whenever possible (Miranda is such a system). The difference can be important, even in the simple case just presented.

Consider the following application of **K**.

```
(K '(Dont talk back) (reverse 'unfortunatelynotignored))
```

If Lisp insists on evaluating the second argument in this case, it will have problems because the **reverse** function blows up on atomic arguments. Therefore, the question of whether unnecessary results are computed affects the meaning of some types of expressions. In this case the meaning is "**Error !*!@%!**" if the system insists on computing the second argument of **K** and "**(start msg Dont talk back end msg)**" if it does not.

For most functions it is not important which choice the system makes. (No one designs function like **K** anyway.) Except in one very special case: the **if** function. This is a function that evaluates exactly two of its three arguments.

This function facilitates describing function results that take one shape or another, depending on some property of the input data. Furthermore, it frequently happens that the unselected result involves a function application that is not computable. Therefore, a Lisp system that forced evaluation of all three arguments of the **if** function would be nearly useless.

For this reason, the **if** function is evaluated under a *lenient* strategy: It computes only those arguments that it needs (namely, its first argument, and then either its second or its third argument, depending on what its first argument turned out to be). We will call functions that avoid evaluating unnecessary arguments *lenient functions* (it is, of course, the evaluation strategy that is lenient, not the function itself).[1] This is in contrast to *strict functions*, which force the evaluation of all of their arguments whether they need them or not.

All the functions introduced in previous chapters, except the function **defun**, are strict functions in Lisp (though none of them need to be completely strict, and they are not in programming systems based on the lenient computation strategy—also called *demand-driven* or *lazy evaluation*). Furthermore, the functions you, yourself, define are strict. (Lisp systems do provide a way to define lenient functions, but now is not the time to go into that subject.)

To get an understanding of how to use the **if** function, let us look at a few examples. Suppose we expect to be supplied with some encoded messages. The code is a variant of pig latin in which certain portions of the message are written in reverse order with a special sound at the end, so we will know which ones are reversed.

```
((ake t ay) (out the) (apers p ay) (and the)
 (ash tr ay))
((ing br ay) (in the) (ogg d ay) (and) (oot p ay)
 (out the) (at c ay))
```

Our goal is to specify the translation that decodes these messages.

```
((t ake) (out the) (p apers) (and the) (tr ash))
((br ing) (in the) (d ogg) (and) (p oot) (out the)
 (c at))
```

Each component of the list that represents the coded message is translated by examining its last component. If its last component is "ay," it

---

[1] The **if** function falls into a special class of lenient functions called *conditionals*. (We will introduce two other conditionals (**and** and **or**) in Chapter 10.) Operational programmers prefer to think of conditionals as "control structures" (i.e., statements that control the sequence of operations that the computation carries out). We prefer to think of them as functions that, like other functions, accept arguments and deliver results, but neglect to evaluate certain arguments in some cases. "Nonstrict" is another term sometimes applied to such functions.

is translated by reversing its order and removing the first element of the reversed list. If not, it is already decoded and should stay as is. Here is this idea expressed in Lisp:

```
(defun  xlatcmp (msgcmp)
   (if (equal (last msgcmp) '(ay))
       (cdr (reverse msgcmp))
       msgcmp
   ))
```

```
(xlatcmp '(ake t ay))   is   (t ake)
(xlatcmp '(out the))    is   (out the)
```

The translator for individual components can be applied to the whole message with **mapcar**, and the result will be the translated message.

```
(defun  xlatmsg  (msg)    (mapcar #'xlatcmp msg) )
```

program:  (xlatmsg '((ake t ay) (out the) (apers p ay)
          (and the) (ash tr ay)) )

result:   ((t ake) (out the) (p apers) (and the) (tr
          ash))

program:  (xlatmsg '((ing br ay) (in the) (ogg d ay)
          (and) (oot p ay) (out the) (at c ay)) )

result:   ((br ing) (in the) (d ogg) (and) (p oot)
          (out the) (c at))

Now let us complicate the matter a little further. Suppose we decide to let the encodings be more flexible by permitting decoded words to appear as atomic components rather than requiring them to be in lists.

**New messages**

```
((ake t ay) out the (apers p ay) and the (ash tr ay))
((ing br ay) in the (ogg d ay) (and) (oot p ay) out the
(ash tr ay))
```

**Decoded messages**

```
((t ake) out the (p apers) and the (tr ash))
((br ing) in the (d ogg) (and) (p oot) out the (c at))
```

This will foul up our **xlatcmp** function because it expects its argument to be a list. The function **last** will not work on atoms, but

---

**atom**—a predicate to test for atoms

| | | | |
|---|---|---|---|
| (atom *arg*) | is | **T** | if *arg* is an atom |
| | is | **NIL** | if *arg* is not an atom |
| (atom '(x y z)) | is | **NIL** | |
| (atom 'x) | is | **T** | |
| (atom '()) | is | **T** | — a strange case: the atom NIL represents '() |

---

**xlatcmp** applies it indiscriminately. To avoid this, **xlatcmp** needs to detect atoms and leave them as is, since they represent already decoded words. To detect atoms, we will need a new predicate function, **atom**. This function's result is **T** if its argument is an atom [including (), the empty list, a.k.a. **NIL**]; if it's argument is not an atom, it delivers the empty list as its result. Like the function **equal**, **atom** is called a predicate because it affirms or denies a property of its argument.

The new version of the component translation function appears next. The **xlatmsg** function does not change, but relies on **xlatcmp** in the same way as before.

```
(defun  xlatcmp (msgcmp)
   (if (atom msgcmp)
       msgcmp
       (if (equal (last msgcmp) '(ay))
           (cdr (reverse msgcmp))
           msgcmp
   )))
```

```
(xlatcmp '(ake t ay))   is   (t ake)
(xlatcmp '(out the))    is   (out the)
(xlatcmp 'the)          is   the
```

The new function **xlatcmp** addresses three cases: (1) an atomic argument; (2) an argument with "ay" as its last component; and (3) an argument of any other form. In the function definition, the expressions specifying the first two potential results are guarded by predicates in applications of the **if** function. The first **if**'s predicate is (atom msgcmp). If this predicate affirms that **msgcmp** is atomic, then the result guarded by that predicate, namely **msgcmp**, is delivered. In this case, the third argument to the first **if**, which is another application of the **if** function, is not needed, and therefore not computed because of the lenient nature of the **if** function. This is fortunate because if the second application of the **if** function were computed, it would require the result of (last msgcmp), which would be unavailable because **last** cannot handle atomic arguments.

---

A WORD ABOUT FORMATTING DEFINITIONS OF FUNCTIONS

---

Many of the functions we design will involve multiple cases. Each case will describe its own potential result for the function, and a sequence of tests, expressed through invocations of **if** will determine the selection of one of the potential results.

We present each invocation of **if** with its three arguments aligned vertically. Often the third argument will be another invocation of **if**, and, again, the three arguments of this nested **if** will be aligned vertically.

At the end of the function definition, we count the number of **if**'s (they are easy to see because of the formatting), add one for the **defun**, and put that many right parentheses on the bottom line. This habit helps us avoid some pesky parenthesis errors.

---

## ■ SUMMARY

| | | | | |
|---|---|---|---|---|
| **if** | **(if** $p$ $x$ $y$**)** | **is** $y$ | if $p$ is **NIL** |
| | | **is** $x$ | otherwise |
| **atom** | **(atom** $arg$**)** | **is T** | if $arg$ is an atom |
| | | **is NIL** | if $arg$ is not an atom |
| **null** | **(null** $arg$**)** | **is** | **(equal** $arg$ **' ())** |

## ■ BIBLIOGRAPHY NOTES

---

Functions that require the values all their arguments are called strict functions. Functions that can compute some of their results without values for some of their arguments are called nonstrict or lenient. We prefer the term "lenient" (coined by Keller, we believe) because it is an antonym for strict without being a made-up term (nonstrict does not appear in our dictionary). Friedman and Wise, Henderson and Morris, and Vuillemin discovered some important implications of lenient functions for practical computing systems. They investigated several computation rules to support such functions—in particular, argument binding mechanisms known variously as lazy evaluation, delayed evaluation, and call-by-need. Manna's text on the theory of computation elucidates such computation rules and explains some of their theoretical implications. Clinger has explored some of the effects of lazy evaluation in the presence of nondeterministic computation.

C. Clinger (1982). Nondeterministic call by need is neither lazy nor call by name. *ACM Symposium on Lisp and Functional Programming* (August) 225–234.

52 ■ LISP

**null**—a predicate to test for the empty list

| | | |
|---|---|---|
| `(null arg)` | is | `(equal arg '())` |
| `(null '())` | is | `T` |
| `(null 'nonNILatom)` | is | `NIL` |
| `(null '(x y z))` | is | `NIL` |

Daniel P. Friedman and David S. Wise (1976). CONS should not evaluate its arguments. In S. Michaelson and R. Milner (eds.), *Automata, Languages, and Programming* . Edinburgh University Press, 257–284.

Peter Henderson and J. H. Morris, Jr (1976). A lazy evaluator. *Third ACM Symposium on Principles of Programming Languages*, 95–103.

Robert Keller, Gary Lindstrom, and Suhas Patil (1979). A loosely-coupled applicative multi-processing system. *National Computer Conference, AFIPS* 613–622.

Robert Keller and Frank Lin (1984). Simulated performance of a reduction-based multiprocessor. *IEEE Computer* (July), 70–82.

Zohar Manna (1974). *Mathematical Theory of Computation*, McGraw–Hill, New York.

Jean Vuillemin (1974). Correct and optimal implementations of recursion in a simple programming language. *J. Computer and System Sciences* 9, 332–354.

## ■ EXERCISES

1. Design a function with "**XXXX**" as its result if its argument is "**damnation**" or "**hellfire**"; otherwise, its result should be the same as its argument.

2. Design a function similar to Exercise 1, except that it should also replace the two curses with **XXXX**'s in case they occur as components in its argument.

3. Design a predicate function with **T** as its result if its argument has three or more components; otherwise, its result should be **NIL**.

4. Design a function with a result that is the first three components of its argument, if its argument has three or more components; if its argument has three or fewer components (or is atomic), its result should be the same as its argument.

5. Design a function with a first argument that is a pattern of three components and with a second argument that is a list. The function should be a predicate that will determine whether the pattern matches any three contiguous components within the first five components of the second argument.

# ANSWERS

1. 
```
(defun censor (wrd)
   (if (equal wrd 'damnation)
       'xxxx
       (if (equal wrd 'hellfire)
           'xxxx
           wrd
       )))
```

2. 
```
(defun deepercensor (phrase)
   (if (atom phrase)
       (censor phrase)
       (mapcar #'censor phrase)
   ))
```

3. 
```
(defun greater3  (arg)
   (if (atom arg)
       NIL                        ; no components
       (if (null (cdr arg))
           NIL                    ; 1 component
           (if (null (cddr arg))
               NIL                ; 2 components
               T                  ; 3 or more
           ))))
```

4. 
```
(defun first3  (arg)
  (if (greater3 arg)
    (list (car arg) (cadr arg) (caddr arg))
                              ; more than 3 cmps
            arg               ; 3 or fewer cmps
  ))
```

5.  ```
    (defun match (pattern lst)
        (if (under3 lst)
            NIL
            (if (equal pattern (first3 lst))
                T
                (if (equal pattern (first3 (cdr lst)))
                    T
                    (if (equal pattern (first3 (cddr lst)))
                        T
                        NIL
        )))))

    (defun under3 (lst)
        (not (greater3 lst)))
    ```
    ```

# NAMING PARTIAL RESULTS: LET

Consider constructing a function to remove all but the last two components of a list. You could extract the first two components of the reversed list and paste them together with the list function.

Program:
```
(defun last2 (lst)
    (if (null lst)                  ; return original list
        lst                         ; if it has no components
        (if (null (cdr lst))                  ; or only one
            lst
            (list (cadr (reverse lst))
                  (car (reverse lst))
        )))
    (last2 '(Granny apple green))
```
Result:    `(apple green)`

This approach may dismay you because it calls for the computation of the reversed list twice.[1] The revised function that follows fixes the problem by supplying the reversed list to a "helping function," which then uses the reversed list twice in specifying its result.

```
(defun last2 (lst)
  (helplast2 (reverse lst)) )
(defun helplast2 (rev)
  (if (null rev)               ; return original list
      rev                      ; if it has no components
      (if (null (cdr rev))     ; or only one
          rev
          (list (cadr rev)
                (car rev))
  )))
```

However, the annoyance of having to dream up names for helping functions annoys most programmers. Fortunately, Lisp provides another way to eliminate common subexpressions. The **let** construct permits attaching names to intermediate values needed at several points in a computation. We use **let** in the following example to avoid the need for the helping function in the definition of **last2**.

```
(defun last2 (lst)
  (let ( (rev (reverse lst)) )
    (if (null rev)                ; return original list
        rev                       ; if it has no components
        (if (null (cdr rev))      ; or only one
            rev
            (list (cadr rev))     ; return first two
                  (car rev)))     ; components if possible
    ))))
```

The **let** construct has two parts: a binding section attaching names to values, and a section specifying the result delivered by the let construct. In our **last2** function, the binding section, **((rev (reverse lst)))** attaches the name **rev** to the reversed list, and the result specification, which follows the binding section, uses **rev** in several places.

---

[1] A clever Lisp system might avoid recomputation of the reversed list by noticing that two of the expressions in the specified result are identical. Elimination of common subexpressions helps a Lisp system get the most out of the computer. Even if programmers eliminate obvious ones, as we will do with **(reverse lst)**, efficient Lisp systems need the ability to avoid recomputation of identical subexpressions because a straightforward translation of a program to a form that a computer can carry out directly will almost always contain some common subexpressions in behind-the-scenes computations, outside the control of the programmer.

**let construct**—binds names to values
**let-construct**   is   **(let (** (*name val*)... **)** *result-spec*)
*name*           is   *symbolic-atom*
*val*              is   *expression*
*result-spec*   is   *expression*

> Meaning:   Bind values to names; the names may be used to designate their values in the result specification. The **let** construct delivers the value computed in its result specification, then discards the name-value bindings.

> Caveat:   If there is more than one name-value pair in the binding section, the values are all computed before being attached to any of the names. Thus, none of the names may be used within the binding section in place of their specified values. To define the value of one name in terms of another, use nested **let** constructs; that is, use another **let** construct as the result specification of the first **let** construct.

## ■ EXERCISES

1. Exercise 4 of Chapter 5 involved defining a function to rotate a list right one position. The answer given in the chapter used the intrinsic function **last** and the function **deletelast** from Exercise 3. Revise **rotateright** using only the intrinsic functions **cons**, **car**, **cdr**, and **reverse** and the **let** construct.

2. Make a similar revision in the definition of **xlatcmp** from Chapter 6.

3. Write a function that will put three extra copies of its own first element at the beginning and three copies of its own last element at the end.

   Program:   **(repeat '(row your boat))**

   Result:   **(row row row your boat boat boat)**

ANSWERS

1. ```
(defun rotateright (lst)
     (let ( (rev (reverse lst) )
       (cons (car rev) (reverse (cdr rev)))
     ))
```

(Note: This definition has efficiency advantages over the function given in the answer to Exercise 4, Chapter 5, where both last and reverse had to traverse the list to get to the last element. The new version should be approximately twice as fast as the old one.)

2. ```
(defun  xlatcmp (msgcmp)
   (if (atom msgcmp)
       msgcmp
       (let ( (revmsg (reverse msgcmp)) )
          (if (equal (car revmsg) 'ay)
              (cdr revmsg)
              msgcmp
          ))))
```

3. ```
(defun repeat (msg)
   (let ( (rev (reverse msg))
          (firstword (car msg)) )
     (let ( (lastword (car rev)) )
       (cons firstword
             (cons firstword
                   (reverse (cons lastword
                                  (cons lastword
                                        rev      )))))
   )))
```
```

# CHAPTER 8

# RECURSION

Suppose we ask, "What is yogurt?", and the answer is "a food made from milk and yogurt-starter." And then we ask, "What is yogurt-starter?", and the answer is "an ingredient used in making yogurt." We have learned only a little about yogurt. The given definition was circular in a not-very-helpful way. But suppose yogurt had been defined as "a food made by placing a small amount of yogurt-starter in warm milk and keeping the mixture warm for several hours," and yogurt-starter had been defined as "a small amount of yogurt."

The definitions remain circular, but they are more helpful. If we can only find a bit of yogurt, we can make more of it (if we can find some milk).

Circular definitions may be useless, but not necessarily so. It depends on how they are constructed. The definition of *list* (from Chapter 2) is circular: a *list* has the form **(component ...)** and a *component* is either an atom or a list. Yet this definition enables us to determine that **(parenthesis (bugaboo)** does not denote a list (because one part that should designate a component, namely " **(bugaboo**" can denote neither

---

INITIAL/SURNAME PAIRS: AN INPUTDATA SPECIFICATION

---

*namedata* is (*name* ...)
*name*      is *initial surname*
*initial*    is *letter*
*surname*  is *symbolic-atom*

**Example:**   `(I Asimov A Christie V Nabokov K Vonnegut)`

---

an atom nor a list). The definition also confirms that **(parenthesis (bugaboo))** does denote a list.

Therefore the definition of *list* is circular in a useful way. Circular definitions, useful or not, are known as *recursions*, and they form the basis for constructing programs in the denotational style. Recursion makes it possible for definitions with only a finite number of terms to describe objects of unbounded size. This is the usual problem in programming: Each program must be a finite collection of symbols, but the programmer rarely has advance knowledge of a bound on the size of either the input data or the result.

Programs containing a finite number of symbols must describe the relationship between input data and results of unbounded size. Many predefined Lisp functions have this capability. For example, the function **append** delivers a result whose size depends on the size of the input data, which is not bounded by any of the rules defining the meaning of **append**. Therefore a function using **append** can describe an unbounded result. Other list construction functions, such as **reverse**, **cons**, and **cdr** also have this property.

None of the foregoing functions transforms the input data on a component-by-component basis, but we have studied a function that does: **mapcar**, which applies a given transformation to each component of one of its arguments and delivers a result with the same number of components as that argument. If we need a result with more or fewer components, we can form it from **mapcar**'s result by using other list manipulation functions, such as **car**, **cdr**, **append**, or **list**.

However, **mapcar** is not the most convenient tool for describing all types of list transformations. Suppose, for example, there is a collection of input data packaged as a list whose components are atoms representing names in the initial/surname format. That is, the atoms come in pairs, the first half of each pair being an initial and the last half being the corresponding surname.

Suppose further, that we need a transformed version of this list in which the initial/surname pairs are grouped as single components. That is, each component of the result list will be a list of two components, the first being an initial and the second being a surname.

---

INITIAL/SURNAME COMPONENTS: A RESULT DATA
SPECIFICATION

---

*nameresult*       is (*name-component* ... )
*name-component* is (*initial surname*)

**Example:** ( **(I Asimov) (A Christie) (V Nabokov) (K Vonnegut) )**

---

Defining this transformation in terms of **mapcar** and the other list manipulators is a little on the clumsy side, at best. But by visualizing the result in a circular fashion, you can construct a very simple definition of the result.

The idea is to perceive the pairing function's result in two cases: (1) When the input data is an empty list (which is not precluded by our specification, because the ellipsis "..." indicates that a *namedata* list may contain zero or more names), then the result should also be the empty list. (2) On the other hand, if the input data are nonempty, then the result is a list whose first component contains the first pair of items in the input data, and the rest of whose items are constructed by applying the pairing function to the input data without its first pair of components.

This definition is circular (i.e., recursive) because at a certain point it requires knowledge of its own meaning. However, at the point where this knowledge is required, this knowledge is applied to simpler input data than what was involved at the beginning. Useful recursive definitions in Lisp normally will have this characteristic: At the point of circularity, the input data will have been simplified in some way.

The function **pairup** expresses our recursive definition in Lisp notation.

```
(defun pairup (namedata)
   (if (null namedata)
        '()                              ; no names
        (cons (list (car namedata)       ; do first
                    (cadr namedata))     ; component
               (pairup (cddr namedata))) ; others via
   ))                                    ;   recursion
```

Program:   **(pairup '(I Asimov A Christie V Nabokov**
                        **K Vonnegut) )**

Result:   **( (I Asimov) (A Christie) (V Nabokov)**
              **(K Vonnegut) )**

The definition of pairup says that its result will have one of two forms: (1) an empty list or (2) a list whose first component is a two-component list constructed from the first two components of the input data, and the rest of whose components are the result of applying the definition to a simpler list, which is like the original argument except that its first two components have been removed. The result is certainly the one we want in case (1). In case (2), the first component of the result is what we want, and the rest of them will be correct as long as the definition can be assumed to be correct for shorter lists. To believe that the definition is correct requires the same sort of leap of faith that one encounters in proofs by mathematical induction.

In fact, the definition of functions through recursion is directly analogous to the construction of proofs by mathematical induction. If you understand one, you will understand the other. If you were able to accommodate the circular definition of lists in Chapter 2, you have already made the required leap of faith. If not, please persevere anyway. Your faith will probably come to you in a flash.

What you need most is experience, and there will be ample opportunity for that. Try out these functions. Watch them deliver results. Try the exercises at the end of this section. If you do not succeed on the first one, look at the answer and test it on the computer. Then try the second one. Keep going until you succeed. Go through the exercises a second or third time if necessary.

Perhaps you would like to have a few more examples under your belt before proceeding. If so, read on. If not, skip to the exercises.

This example involves extracting the first block of components from a list. The function will have two arguments: The first argument tells us how many components to extract from the second argument. We want to extract a block that has the same number of components as the first argument. If the second argument fails to have that many components (i.e., the block is longer than the list), then the result should be identical to the second argument. You can think of this as a sort of "generalized **car**" that extracts the first several components of a list rather than simply the first component.

The desired result is simple to construct when the block is the empty list. In that case, the result should have no components at all; that is, the result is the empty list. The result is equally easy to construct if the second argument is the empty list. In this case, also, the result is the empty list. If both the block and the component list are nonempty, then the first component of the result will be the first component of the second argument, and the rest of the components of the result should be taken from the second argument, sans its first component, according to a block that is one component shorter than the original block.

Again, our description of the result is circular and can be translated into Lisp notation as follows.

---

### IMPORTANCE OF LENIENT IF

The **if**-function does not bother to evaluate one of its arguments. This is especially important in recursive definitions because one of the arguments to the **if** function in such a definition frequently involves another result of the function being defined. If this result had to be completely determined before the **if** function could select its result, the circularity would continue forever. The definition would still be correct, but a computer following a strict evaluation strategy for the **if** function would not find the definition useful. Programming systems that, unlike Lisp, evaluate all functions on a lenient basis are more liberal about recursive definitions. They can make use of recursive definitions in which the argument for the recursive part is not simpler than the original argument (but that is a whole other story in itself).

---

```
(defun prefix (block lst)
  (if (null block)
      '()                          ; empty block
      (if (null lst)
          '()                      ; empty lst
          (cons (car lst)          ; know first component
             (prefix (cdr block)   ; others defined
                (cdr lst)))        ; via recursion
  )))
```

Program: **(prefix '(x x x) '(a b c d e))**
Result: **(a b c)**
Program: **(prefix '(x x x) '(a b))**
Result: **(a b)**
Program: **(prefix '() '(a b c))**
Result: **NIL**
Program: **(prefix '(x z a y) '(a b c d e))**
Result: **(a b c d)**

Harken now back to the Exercises in Chapter 6. There we developed a function to censor certain curse words from phrases, replacing them with **xxxx**'s. The strategy we used was to first design a function that would censor individual words, then we applied that function to whole phrases via **mapcar**.

```
(defun phrasecensor (phrase) (mapcar #'wordcensor
                                 phrase))
```

```
(defun   wordcensor (word)
         (if (equal word 'hellfire)
             'XXXX
             (if (equal word 'damnation)
                 'XXXX
                 word
             )))
```

Program:    **(phrasecensor '(One seldom hears
                                    hellfire today) )**

Result:    **(One seldom hears XXXX today)**

But suppose that instead of replacing the curse words with **XXXX**'s, we had wanted to remove them without a trace. Then our former strategy will not work because **mapcar** produces a list with the same number of components as its (second) argument, so we would have to put something in place of each curse word, thus leaving that trace we are trying to avoid.

However, we can design the function we want with a recursive definition. The idea, as usual, is to separate the problem into simple and more difficult cases and use recursion to help out on the difficult ones. If the phrase is empty, nothing need be removed; if its first word is a curse word, the result should be what you would get if you applied the function to the phrase, sans its first word; and if the first word is not a curse word, the result begins with the first word of the phrase and continues with whatever result would be appropriate if the function were applied to the phrase, sans its first word.

In Lisp that means:

```
(defun   removecursewords (phrase)
    (if (null phrase)
        '()
        (let ( (firstwrd  (car phrase))
               (otherwrds (cdr phrase)) )
          (if (equal firstwrd 'hellfire)
              (removecursewords otherwrds)
              (if (equal firstword 'damnation)
                  (removecursewords otherwrds)
                  (cons firstwrd
                        (removecursewords otherwrds))
          )))))
```

Program:    **(removecursewords '(One seldom hears
                                    hellfire today) )**

Result:    **(One seldom hears today)**

---

**remove**—produces a copy of a list with all components equal to a specified value removed

**(remove** *cmp* *lst*)  is  *lst*
                         if  *lst* is empty
                              **(remove** *cmp* **(cdr** *lst*))
                         if  **(car** *lst*) is *cmp*
                              **(cons (car** *lst*) **(remove** *cmp*
                                                **(cdr** *lst*)))
                              otherwise

Program:  **(remove ' (ogg d ay) ' ((ing br ay) in the (ogg d ay) sheaf))**

Result:   **((ing br ay) in the sheaf)**

Program:  **(remove 'ogg ' ((ing br ay) in the (ogg d ay) sheaf))**

Result:   **((ing br ay) in the (ogg d ay) sheaf)**

---

The intrinsic function **remove** generalizes our **removecursewords** function. One of the exercises suggests expressing our specialized function in terms of the more general function.

## ■ Summary

Recursive definitions use the term being defined as part of the definition. This device makes it possible to describe all manner of computational relationships in a finite amount of space without constraining the amount of input data or results.

The secret to constructing recursive definitions in Lisp is to discover some arguments for which results can be specified directly, and to find a way to describe results for all other arguments as combinations of directly specifiable partial results and/or recursively defined partial results with simpler arguments.

## ■ Bibliography Notes

Several books on functional programming contain material on general principles of recursive programming, including the following.

H. Abelson and G. Sussman (with J. Sussman) (1985) *Structure and Interpretation of Computer Programs*, MIT Press, Cambridge, Mass.

W. H. Burge (1975) *Recursive Programming Techniques*, Addison–Wesley New York.

H. Glaser, C. Hankin, and D. Till (1984) *Principles of Functional Programming*, Prentice–Hall, Englewood Cliffs, N.J.

P. Henderson (1980) *Functional Programming: Application and Implementation*, Prentice–Hall, Englowood Cliffs, N.J.

▪ ## EXERCISES

---

1. Define a function that will remove every other component of a list.

2. Define a function that will insert **xxxx** between every pair of components in a list.

   **(a b c d e)** produces **(a xxxx b xxxx c xxxx d xxxx e)**

3. Define a function that will deliver the "marked suffix" of a list. The marked suffix is everything beyond the atom **xxxx**. (If the list has no mark, the result should be the empty list.)

   **(a b c xxxx d e f g)** produces **(d e f g)**

4. Define a function that will deliver the "marked prefix" of a list. The marked prefix is everything before the atom **xxxx**. (If the list has no mark, the result should be the entire list.)

   **(a b c xxxx d e f g)** produces **(a b c)**

5. Redefine the **removecursewords** function using the predefined function **remove**.

6. Define a generalized **cdr** function called **suffix** with a result that is a list like its second argument but with a number of components missing from the beginning of the list. The number of missing components should be the same as the number of components in **suffix**'s first argument.

7. Define a function that removes every other block of contiguous components from a list. The function will have two arguments. The first argument is a list that determines the block size; specifically, the size of a block is the number of components in the first argument. The second argument is the list from which every other block is to be removed. Picture this list as a sequence of blocks with implicit marks between the blocks. The result should be this list with every other block removed. (Use **suffix** from Exercise 6 and **prefix** from one of the examples in this chapter.)

`((x x)` `(a b` `c d` `e f` `g h` `i))` produces `(a b e f i)`

8. Define a function called **revblks** that reverses the order of the components within every block of a list, where *block* means the same thing it meant in Exercise 7. Again, the function has two arguments: the first determines the block size, and the second is the list whose blocks are to be reversed.

Program: **(revblks** `'(x x x)` `'(a b c` `d e f` `g h i))`
Result: **(c b a** `f e d` `i h g)`

9. Define a function called **tr** that transposes a matrix. The argument will be a list representing a matrix of *m* rows and *n* columns. Specifically, it will be a list with *m* components, each of these representing one row of the matrix (therefore, each component of this list will have *n* components). The result is to be a matrix of *n* rows and *m* columms such that the *j*th component of the *i*th row of the result is the *i*th component of the *j*th row of the argument.

```
(tr  '( (a b c)        is      ( (a d)
         (d e f) )                (b e)
                                  (c f) )
```

## ANSWERS

```
1. (defun oddcmps  (lst)
     (if  (null lst)
         '()
         (if  (null (cdr lst))
             lst
             (cons (car lst) (oddcmps (cddr lst)))
     )))
```

```
2. (defun  speckle (lst)
     (if  (null lst)
         '()                                    ; no components
         (if  (null (cdr lst))
             lst                         ; 1 component
             (append (list (car lst) 'XXXX) ; 2 or more
                     (speckle (cdr lst))    )
     )))
```

```
3. (defun  markedsuffix (lst)
       (if (null lst)
           '()                                    ; no mark
           (if (equal (car lst) 'XXXX)
               (cdr lst)                          ; mark first
               (markedsuffix (cdr lst)))          ; mark beyond
           )))                                    ;  (if any)


4. (defun  markedprefix (lst)
       (if (null lst)
           '()                                    ; no mark
           (if (equal (car lst) 'XXXX)
               '()                                ; mark first
               (cons (car lst)                    ; mark beyond
                   (markedprefix (cdr lst)))
           )))


5. (defun  removecursewords  (phrase)
       (remove 'hellfire  (remove 'damnation  phrase)) )


6. (defun  suffix (block  lst)
       (if (null block)
           lst                          ; empty block
           (if (null lst)
               '()                      ; empty lst
               (suffix (cdr block)
                       (cdr lst))       ; reduced block
           )))


7. (defun oddblks  (block lst)
       (if (null (suffix block lst))
           lst
           (append (prefix block lst)
                   (oddblks block (suffix block
                                     (suffix block lst))))
       ))


8. (defun revblks  (block lst)
       (if  (null lst)
            '()
            (append (reverse (prefix block lst))
                    (revblks block (suffix block lst)))
       ))
```

9. 
```
(defun tr   (mtx)
    (if   (null (car mtx))
        '()                         ; empty matrix
        (cons (mapcar #'car  mtx)   ; first row result
            (tr (mapcar #'cdr mtx))) ; tr matrix sans
    ))                              ;    first column
```

# CHAPTER 9

# DEBUGGING

You now know enough Lisp to describe any computable function. That is not to say it will be easy—programming is a difficult discipline—but only to indicate that it is possible in the theoretical sense.

With all that expressive power, a commensurate potential for trouble is not surprising. Bugs in Lisp programs that have been constructed from a denotational point of view have a different character from bugs in conventional, operational programs. In operational programs, most bugs (other than typos and syntactic errors) occur because of some unexpected interaction among variables. That is, what you told the computer to do was not what you meant to tell it. Denotational programs, on the other hand, rarely contain mistakes of this type. Usually, the expressions you write mean what you thought they meant when you wrote them. It is just that what you meant is the wrong computation.

Therefore, we recommend that you take a new perspective on debugging. Rather than rushing in to see what the program is doing (i.e., debugging by example), spend some time rethinking the functions you meant to express, the assumptions you made about relationships among the input values, output forms, and so on. Probably you will find that some of your assumptions were wrong, and you can fix the functions accordingly.

In other words, debug the program by rethinking what you meant to compute rather than by checking what happens on example data. Only as a last resort should you rely on observing program behavior. When you need this last resort, you can use the procedures discussed in this chapter.

There are three types of trouble in Lisp programming: (Easy Cases 1 and 2) the program blows up—its result is something like **Error !@#$%*!**; (Hard Case 1) the program successfully delivers a result, but not the one you wanted; (Hard Case 2) the program never delivers a result.

When the program blows up, it does so for one of three reasons: (Easy Case 1) it has tried to compute the value of a function for which the given arguments are unsuitable; (Easy Case 2) it has tried to access the definition of a name and has found no definition available; (Hard Case 2') the program has consumed more computer resources than are available (this is usually a symptom of Hard Case 2, which is why we have called it "Hard Case 2'").

Most Lisp systems provide a tool that helps determine what went wrong in Easy Cases 1 and 2. The particular tools we will describe are part of the GCLISP system, a Common Lisp implementation from Gold Hill Computers, Inc. Most other systems will provide similar facilities, but certain details will be different. These tools make it possible to inquire about what sequence of computations lead to the error and to find out what environment the program found itself in at any point during that computational sequence.

*Bug avoidance* is usually preferable to *bug dissection*, and avoidance is not as difficult as it might seem. The strategy here calls for testing each function as you write it. If its definition involves untested functions, these untested functions should be provided as *stubs* that deliver rigged up, but correctly formed, results. Exhaustive testing will not be possible, but even a small amount of testing is worthwhile. When you replace a stub with a tested definition, retest the functions that depend on it.

Bug avoidance will sometimes fail. Suppose it has failed in the manner of Easy Case 1 or 2. The system has printed some sort of error message, and it is not a message that indicates a lack of sufficient resources, which would put you in Hard Case 2' (the term *overflow* will often occur in resource-related error messages). This is the time to use the debug facility.

When the GCLISP interpreter meets an error in a function evaluation, it prints the form of the function invocation, including the values of the arguments, and it moves to a new level of interpretation. At the new level, you can ask the interpreter to compute any functions you wish, using such computations to help you figure out what has been happening. Probably the most useful computation you can request is a *backtrace*. The **backtrace** function directs the interpreter to print the sequence of incomplete function invocations that led to the present erroneous state of affairs. This will help you determine where you have made an improper reference to a function, as illustrated here.

```
level 0 prompt    * (defun revblks (blk lst)
                      (if (null lst)
                          '()
                          (append (reverse (prefix lst))
                                  (revblks block (suffix lst)))
                      ))
reply             REVBLKS

level 0 prompt    * (defun prefix (block lst)
                      (if (null block)
                          '()
                          (if (null lst)
                              '()
                              (cons (car lst)
                                    (prefix (cdr block)
                                            (cdr lst)))
                      )))
reply             PREFIX

level 0 prompt    * (revblks '(x x x) '(a b c d e f))
reply             ERROR:
                  Not enough arguments for: PREFIX
                  While evaluating: (PREFIX (QUOTE (A B C D E F)))

level 1 prompt    1> (backtrace)      ; invoking backtrace from
                                      ; new level of interpreter
reply             (BACKTRACE)         ; most recently invoked function
                  (PREFIX             ; function invoking backtrace
                    (QUOTE (A B C D E F))
                  (REVBLKS            ; function invoking prefix
                    (QUOTE (X X X))
                    (QUOTE (A B C D E F)))
                  NIL                 ; value of backtrace

level 1 prompt    1> _
```

Backtracing points out that **revblks** is the function from which an improper invocation of **prefix** was made. Looking at the definition of **revblks**, we see that **prefix** occurs in only one place, and at that point it is called with only one argument. The first argument, which determines the block size, has been inadvertently omitted. We change this invocation, inserting the missing argument: **(prefix block lst)**, and try again.

```
1> (revblks '(x x x) '(a b c d e f))
ERROR:
Unbound variable: suffix
While evaluating: (SUFFIX (QUOTE (x x x))
                          (QUOTE (A B C D E F)))

2> (backtrace) ; note: level 2 prompt
(BACKTRACE)
(SUFFIX (QUOTE (X X X))
        (QUOTE (A B C D E F)))
(REVBLKS (QUOTE (X X X))
         (QUOTE (A B C D E F)))
```

Looking back at our program, we see that **revblks** calls **suffix**, but **suffix** has never been defined.

```
2> (defun suffix (block lst)
     (if (null block)
         '()
         (if (null lst)
             '()
             (suffix (cdr block)
                     (cdr lst))
     )))
SUFFIX

2> _
```

At this point, if we try again, **revblks** will work properly.

```
2> (revblks '(x x x) '(a b c  d e f))
(C B A  F E D)
2> _
```

Throughout this process of discovering and repairing errors, we have been getting into deeper and deeper levels of interpretation. We started at level 0, where GCLISP uses an asterisk for a prompt. Then level 1 ("**1>**"), and finally level 2 ("**2>**"). At each level, we have access to the full power of the interpreter, and at any time, we can return to the previous level and take up where we left off upon entering the deeper level. This can be useful in debugging complex, deeply nested programs, but our examples will be simple and we will normally want to return to the previous level at once. To do this, simply invoke the function **clean-up-error**.

```
2> (clean-up-error)
Back to: level 1
1> (clean-up-error)
Back to: Top-level
* _
```

So much for the easy cases.

Now suppose the program has delivered a result, but not the correct one (Hard Case 1). This is where moving through the computation one step at a time comes in handy. You can ask the system to move step by step, under your control, by invoking the **step** function with the offending expression as its argument.

To illustrate how the GCLISP facility for stepping through a computation can help, recall the program from Chapter 5 that extracted certain components of its argument and appended these components to form a list. The function, called "**specifics**," had an argument consisting of three components. Each component was a two-element list: a category and a list of specific items in the category. The **specifics** function formed a single list made up of all the items in the two-element lists.

```
* (specifics '((animal     (possum sheep))
               (vegetable  (persimmon tomato))
               (mineral    (calcium granite))))

(POSSUM SHEEP PERSIMMON TOMATO CALCIUM GRANITE)
```

Suppose, instead of the correct definition given in Chapter 5 we had defined the function in the following way.

```
(defun specifics (allthings)
   (append (cadr (car  allthings))
           (cadr (cdr  allthings))
           (cadr (cddr allthings))))
```

We can use a debugging function from GCLISP, called **step**, to follow through a computation. This will help pinpoint the problem.[1] At each state in an evaluation using **step**, the interpreter is ready to evaluate one particular subexpression (known as the current expression) in the full expression to which step has been applied. You can control which subexpression this is by pressing the arrow keys on your keyboard (the ones you normally use for cursor movements). In addition, you can suspend the computation and enter the next level of the interpreter by

---

[1] "Typing is easier than thinking," someone once said. This may account for the popularity of jumping into debuggers before analyzing code. Nevertheless, we believe thinking is much more effective and recommend using debuggers only as a last resort—or when you are too tired to think.

pressing Ctrl-Break, you can ask for a list of your options by pressing question mark, or you can complete the full computation without further stepping by pressing the END key.

down-arrow    move to the subexpression that would be evaluated next

right-arrow    evaluate the current expression

up-arrow    move to the expression that has the current expression as its argument

left-arrow    pretty-print the current expression

ctrl-Break    enter the next level of interpretation

END    complete the computation without further stepping

Below is a session in which we limp through a computation of the foregoing function using **step** and the arrow keys to move along.

```
* (step (specifics '((animal (possum sheep))
                     (vegetable (persimmon tomato))
                     (mineral (calcium granite)))))
(SPECIFICS (QUOTE ((ANIMAL (POSSUM SHEEP))
                   (VEGETABLE (PERSIMMON TOMATO))
                   (MINERAL (CALCIUM GRANITE))))) _ down-arrow
(QUOTE ((ANIMAL (POSSUM SHEEP))
        (VEGETABLE (PERSIMMON TOMATO))
        (MINERAL (CALCIUM GRANITE))))  _          down-arrow
(APPEND (CADR (CAR (ALLTHINGS))
        (CADR (CDR (ALLTHINGS))
        (CADR (CDDR (ALLTHINGS))) _               down-arrow
(CADR (CAR ALLTHINGS)) _                          right-arrow
                -> (POSSUM SHEEP)
(CADR (CDR ALLTHINGS)) _                          down-arrow
(CDR ALLTHINGS) _                                 right-arrow
        -> ((VEGETABLE (PERSIMMON TOMATO))
            (MINERAL (CALCIUM GRANITE)))
(CADR (CDR ALLTHINGS)) = ((MINERAL (CALCIUM GRANITE))
(CADR (CDDR ALLTHINGS)) _
```

At this point, we can see that something is wrong. We expected the formula **(cadr (cdr allthings))** in the definition of specifics to deliver the components **persimmon** and **tomato** from the "vegetables" element of the input structure. Instead, it delivers the entire minerals portion of the structure. Rethinking the formula, we see that **(cdr allthings)** is the culprit. Instead of delivering the vegetables component of the structure, it delivers a list containing both the vegetables and minerals components. What we should have written is **(cadr allthings)**. Similarly, the application of **cddr** to generate the last argument for **append** will deliver the wrong value. We should have written **caddr** instead of **cddr**. Replacing **cdr** by **cadr** and **cddr** by **caddr** in the definition of **specifics** makes the function work as expected.

Perhaps the system appears to be running on forever (Hard Case 2). Pressing the Ctrl-Break will interrupt the program. At this point, the interpreter will be at a new level and will be able to use the debugging facilities to find out where the program is floundering.

The **trace** operation helps track down problems in cases like this. By notifying the interpreter to trace certain functions, you can follow the computation as it unfolds. Applying the **trace** function to the name of a function you want to follow causes the interpreter to report the argument supplied to the function at each invocation. (Later, you can tell the interpreter to stop making these reports by applying the **untrace** function to the name of the function being traced.)

To illustrate the tracing process, consider the following erroneous definition of the **transpose** function from the exercises of Chapter 20.

```
(defun tr (mtx)
   (if (null mtx)
       '()
       (cons (mapcar #'car mtx)
             (tr (mapcar #'cdr mtx)))
   ))
```

The function **tr** is supposed to swap rows with columns in a matrix represented as a list of rows. For example,

```
(tr '((a b c)
      (d e f))
```

should be

((a d)
 (b e)
 (c f)).

But when we try the function as defined here, the system runs and runs, without reporting a result. To interrupt the computation, we press Ctrl-Break, moving the interpreter to a new level. At this point we turn on the trace and try again.

```
1> (trace tr)
T                              ; note: trace returns the value T
```

```
1> (tr '((a b c)
        (d e f))
```

| | |
|---|---|
| Entering: TR, Argument List: (((A B C) (D E F))) | ; so far so good |
| Entering: TR, Argument List: (((B C) (E F))) | ; still ok |
| Entering: TR, Argument List: (((C) (F))) | ; still ok |
| Entering: TR, Argument List: ((NIL NIL)) | ; ok |
| Entering: TR, Argument List: ((NIL NIL)) | ; looks bad |
| Entering: TR, Argument List: ((NIL NIL)) | ; looks worse |
| Entering: TR, Argument List: ((NIL NIL)) | |

.
.
.

... continues forever ...

          ctrl-Break
2> _

From the sequence of invocations of **tr**, we see that it gets hung up on trying to compute the transpose of an empty matrix. We examine the termination condition of the function and realize that **tr** will never be invoked with an empty argument. Instead, the argument representing an empty matrix will be a list of empty lists.

We modify the definition to make **tr** look for a list with a first component that is empty (as in Chapter 20) and then the function works properly.

Hard Case 2' (insufficient resources) is the same, except that the system interrupts itself. Proceed as in Hard Case 2. In fact, the foregoing example, the erroneous **tr**, would eventually report itself out of memory references, and we would proceed to debug it in the same way.

## ■ SUMMARY

**Bug avoidance**

Test as you go; stub functions

**Bug dissection**

| | | |
|---|---|---|
| Easy Case 1 | Error "…anything but insufficient resources…" | (backtrace) |
| Ease Case 2 | Error "…unbound variable…" | (step) |
| | Error "…undefined function…" | (defun …) |
| | | or (step …) |

| Hard Case 1 | result incorrect | (trace fn ...) or (step ...) |
|---|---|---|
| Hard Case 2 | infinite loop | Ctrl-Break, (trace...) |
| Hard Case 2' | Error "...insufficient resources..." | (debug) (trace ...) or (step ...) |

# MORE LENIENT FUNCTIONS: **AND, OR**

Predicates are functions that affirm or deny some property of their arguments. In Lisp, denial is conventionally represented as **NIL**; any other list or atom signifies affirmation. This representation is a basic element of the **if** function; it interprets its first argument as a predicate value. When this value signifies affirmation (i.e., is not **NIL**), the **if** function selects its second argument as its result; when its first argument signifies denial, the **if** function selects its third argument as its result.

Predicates frequently depend on several relationships among portions of their arguments. For example, a list with two components is an atomic

<table>
<tr><td colspan="2">PREDICATE-VALUE CONVENTIONS IN LISP</td></tr>
<tr><td>Denial (falsity):</td><td>**NIL** represents this condition</td></tr>
<tr><td>Affirmation (verity):</td><td>any datum other than **NIL**</td></tr>
</table>

---

**not**—a synonym for null

(**not** *arg*)   is   (**null** *arg*)

Depending on the context, we sometimes prefer one of the synonyms **not** or **null**. We usually prefer **null** when we are thinking of its argument as a list and **not** when we are thinking of its argument as a predicate value.

---

---

(**not** (**null** *arg*))  **and** *arg* **are equivalent Lisp predicates**

As predicates, (**not** (**null** *arg*)) and the value of *arg*, itself, are equivalent. That is, because of the conventional Lisp representation of denial as **NIL** and affirmation as anything but **NIL**, (**not** (**null** *arg*)) signifies affirmation (or denial) exactly when *arg* does.

---

pair if both components are atoms. To test for this property in Lisp, we could check the first component and deliver a denial if it is not an atom. If the first component checks out as an atom, then the result will depend entirely on whether the second component is an atom. We would express this as:

```
(defun atomicpair (pair)
   (if (not (atom (car pair)))
       NIL
       (atom (cadr pair))
   ))
```

Another way to describe our **atomicpair** predicate is that we want its result to indicate affirmation only if both the first component of its argument is an atom and the second component is an atom. This type of "and" combination comes up so frequently in describing predicates that Lisp systems include "**and**" as a predefined function.

Using the **and** function we can simplify the specification of our atomic pair tester.

```
(defun atomicpair (pair)
       (and (atom (car  pair))
            ; first component non-atomic: denial
            (atom (cadr pair))
            ; first comp atomic: result depends on 2nd
       ))
```

Now suppose we want to write a function to test for lists with two or fewer components. A list will satisfy this condition if it is the empty list.

> **and**— selects its last argument if none are **NIL**;
> otherwise, delivers **NIL**
>
> (**and** $arg$)                          is   $arg$
> (**and** $arg_1$ $arg_2$ $\cdots$ $arg_n$)   is   (**if** (**not** $arg_1$)        **NIL**
>                                                (**and** $arg_2$ $\cdots$ $arg_n$))
>
> **Leniency:** Like the **if** function, the **and** function is lenient. It
> does not force the computation of all its arguments.
> Instead, the **and** function computes each argument in
> sequence, from the first toward the last. If the **and**
> function encounters an argument with a value of **NIL**,
> then **NIL** becomes the result of the **and** function; the
> remaining arguments are ignored. If none of the ar-
> guments are **NIL**, then the last argument becomes the
> result.

If it is not the empty list, but is a list with one component, then it also
satisfies the condition. Similarly, if it fails to be a one-component list,
then it will satisfy the condition only if it has exactly two components.
In Lisp, as we know it, we could describe this function as follows.

```
(defun  uptotwo  (lst)
   (if  (null lst)
        'T                          ; has no components
        (if  (null (cdr lst))
             'T                     ; has exactly 1
             (null (cddr lst))      ; exactly 2 or bust
        )))
```

Again, there is another way to describe what we mean. A list has two
or fewer components if it is the empty list, or if it is a one-component list,
or if it has exactly two components. If **and** is ubiquitous as a connective
in constructing predicates, then so is **or**, and Lisp recognizes this by
including **or** as a predefined function.

Using the **or** function, we can define the **uptotwo** predicate in a simpler way.

```
(defun  uptotwo  (lst)
        (or  (null lst)          ; has no components
             (null (cdr lst))    ; has exactly 1
             (null (cddr lst))   ; exactly 2 or bust
        ))
```

**or**— selects its first non-**NIL** argument;
delivers **NIL** if all arguments are **NIL**

(**or** $arg$)            is    $arg$

(**or** $arg_1$ $arg_2$ $\cdots$ $arg_n$)    is    (**if** $arg_1$    $arg_1$

                                        (**or**   $arg_2$ $\cdots$ $arg_n$))

**Leniency:** Like the **if**-function and the **and**-function, the **or**-function is lenient. and does not necessarily compute all its arguments. Instead, the **or** function it computes each argument in sequence, from the first towards the last. If it finds one that is not **NIL**, then that argument becomes the result of the **or** function. If it runs out of arguments before encountering a non-**NIL** value among them, its result is **NIL**.

The leniency of the **and** and **or** functions comes into play especially in recursive functions. The next example illustrates this point. We want to design a predicate that checks to see if a given pattern matches the initial section of a list. That is, the function will be a predicate with a result that affirms the property (i.e., delivers a non-**NIL** result) if the pattern matches and denies the property (i.e., delivers **NIL** as its result) if the pattern fails to match.

Our specification will be recursive. The pattern matches if it is empty (an empty pattern matches anything) or if the list is nonempty and the first components match and the components following the first component match. Here is the Lisp translation of this definition.

```
(defun  matchprefix  (prfx lst)
        (or (null prfx)
                                ; empty prfx matches all
            (and (not (null lst))
                                ; empty lst, no match
                 (equal (car prfx) (car lst))
                                ; unequal start, no match
                 (matchprefix (cdr prfx)
                                ; unmatched suffixes, no match
                              (cdr lst ))
        )))
```

Program:   (**matchprefix** ' (V Nabokov)
                           ' (I Asimov A Christie V Nabokov))

Result:    **NIL**

Program:   **(matchprefix '(V Nabokov)**
                            **'(V Nabokov I Asimov A Christie))**

Result:    **T**

Program:   **(matchprefix '(V Nabokov)**
                   **'((V Nabokov) (I Asimov) (A Christie)))**

Result:    **NIL**

Program:   **(matchprefix '((V Nabokov))**
                   **'((V Nabokov) (I Asimov) (A Christie)))**

Result:    **T**

This example illustrates the importance of paying attention to the ordering of predicates when designing functions in Lisp. Our definition of **matchprefix** is correct, in a logical sense, regardless of the order in which we write the arguments to the **and** and **or** functions. But the ability of a Lisp system to be able to carry out our intended computation critically depends on its computation strategy.

Consider what would happen if a Lisp system chose to compute the arguments to the **and** and **or** functions starting from the last argument and going toward the first. Such a system would compute the result of our application of the **or** function by first computing the result of the **and** application. It would, in turn, compute this result by first computing the result of the (recursive) application of our **matchprefix** function. Looks bad, eh? It would be, too.

Therefore, although the logical correctness of our specifications is of the utmost importance, we will sometimes need to take into account the way in which the Lisp system chooses to compute the results to its lenient functions. Do not get too hung up on this, however. We think you will find that your taste concerning a "proper" ordering of the arguments for the **if**, **and**, and **or** functions will be in concert with that of Lisp—most of the time, anyway.

## ■ SUMMARY

**and**—a lenient function

    **(and** $arg$**)**                 is   $arg$
    **(and** $arg_1$ $arg_2$ $\cdots$ $arg_n$**)**   is   **(if (not** $arg_1$**) NIL**
                                     **(and** $arg_2$ $\cdots$ $arg_n$**))**

**or**—a lenient function

    **(or** $arg$**)**                 is   $arg$
    **(or** $arg_1$ $arg_2$ $\cdots$ $arg_n$**)**   is   **(if** $arg_1$ $arg_1$ **(or** $arg_2$ $\cdots$ $arg_n$**))**

**not**—a synonym of null

    **(not** *arg***)**  is  **(null** *arg***)**

## ■ EXERCISES

1. Design a predicate called **matchpattern** that tests to see if a given
   pattern matches any consecutive sequence of components within
   a list. (Use our **matchprefix** predicate in your definition.) Your
   **matchpattern** function should answer affirmative with these arguments:

   ```
   (matchpattern  '(V Nabokov)
                  '(V Nabokov  I Asimov  A Christie))
   (matchpattern  '((V Nabokov))
                  '((V Nabokov) (I Asimov) (A Christie)))
   (matchpattern  '(I Asimov)
                  '(V Nabokov I Asimov A Christie))
   (matchpattern  '(Asimov A)
                  '(V Nabokov I Asimov A Christie))
   ```

   It should deny the condition in these cases:

   ```
   (matchpattern  '(Asimov Nabokov)
                  '(I Asimov  A Christie  V Nabokov))
   (matchpattern  '(V Nabokov)
                  '((V Nabokov) (I Asimov) (A Christie)))
   ```

## ANSWERS

1. ```
   (defun  matchpattern  (ptrn lst)
           (or (null ptrn)     ; empty ptrn matches all
               (matchnonempty ptrn lst)
                      ; helping function for other case
           ))

   (defun matchnonempty  (ptrn lst)
                      ; ptrn guaranteed non-empty
       (and  (not (null lst))   ; empty lst can't match
             (or (matchprefix ptrn lst)
   ```
   ```

```
                    ; match prefix: affirm
        (matchpattern ptrn (cdr lst))
                  ; match remainder: affirm
    )))
```

**Note:** We have used a *helping function* in this specification. This is to isolate the empty pattern case. We could, of course, include the expression that defines the helping function directly in the definition of matchpattern (at the point where the application of the helping function, **matchnonempty**, occurs). The advantage of not defining it that way concerns the amount of computation involved when a Lisp system applies the **matchpattern** function: without the helping function, it retests for the empty pattern on every level of the recursion. This saves only a little computation in this case, but you can imagine the helping-function technique saving a great deal of computation in other examples.

# PUMPING

The motif for our next few examples will be a data set representing the contents of a (very small) library, organized by subject. The data set will be a list with components that collect all the books in a given category. That is, a component of this list will be a list whose first component names a category (novel, biography, science, etc.) and the rest of whose components are books in that category. Books will be designated by a list whose first component names the author and whose other components are titles written by that author.

All our examples are going to extract and arrange information from this data set. To have a convenient way to refer to the data, without having to display it in several places, we are going to use a trick that you may frequently find useful when you are dealing with fixed collections of data: We are going to define a function whose value is the data set. A function whose value is always the same is known as a constant function. Such a function needs no arguments—it would only ignore them anyway. Therefore the argument-list portion of its definition is an empty list, and an application of the function involves only the function name, no

LIBRARY-CATALOG: A SPECIFICATION OF FORM

| *library catalog* | is | (subject ...) |
|---|---|---|
| *subject* | is | (category books ...) |
| *category* | is | atom |
| *books* | is | (author title ...) |
| *author* | is | (initial surname) |
| *initial* | is | letter |
| *surname* | is | symbolic-atom |
| *title* | is | (atom atom ...) |

**Note:** This definition guarantees that each title is nonempty

arguments. The function's name is going to be **catalog**, and whenever we wish to access this information, we will use the function application, **(catalog)**.

```
(defun  catalog  ()
 '((novel ((A Christy)  (Ten Little Indians)
                        (Murder on the Orient Express))
          ((V Nabokov) (Lolita)
                       (Ada or Ardor))
          ((K Vonnegut)(Breakfast of Champions)
                       (Jailbird)
                       (Deadeye Dick))
          ((A Asimov)  (I Robot))
          ((J LeCarre) (Smileys People)
                       (Tinker Tailor Soldier Spy))
                                                      )
    (biography  ((A Hodges)   (Turing the Enigma))
                ((V Nabokov)  (Nikolai Gogol)
                              (Speak Memory) )
                ((A Asimov)   (In Joy Still Felt)
                              (In Memory Yet Green))
                ((H Troyat)   (Tolstoy))
                                                      )
    (science  ((G Thomas)    (Calculus and Analytic
                                          Geometry))
              ((D Halliday)  (Physics))
              ((A Asimov)    (On Numbers))
                                                      ))
```

One of our goals is to design a function that, given a catalog of this form and an author's name, will construct a list of all the works of the author that are contained in the catalog. In case these works fall into several categories, as they may, we will have to piece together the full list from several sublists (one sublist for each category). That is, we will first extract from the catalog a list in which each component is a list of titles by the author from a certain category.

```
((titleA1 titleA2 titleA3) (titleB1 titleB2)
 (titleC1 titleC2 titleC3))
```

But the result we want is a list in which the titles are the direct components, not one in which the titles are packaged in sublists according to categories.

```
( titleA1 titleA2 titleA3   titleB1 titleB2
  titleC1 titleC2 titleC3 )
```

Put another way, we will want to append several lists together, and the lists to be appended will be the components of a list that we will put together by scanning the catalog. Because the "appendees" are packaged in this way, we cannot use the **append** function directly, but will have to use it as part of another function definition. We will call this operation **unwrap**.

One way to define unwrap is as follows.

```
(defun   unwrap   (ll)
   (if (null ll)
       '()                        ; result=(), if ll=()
       (append (car ll) (unwrap (cdr ll)))
                                  ; result=append, otherwise
   ))
```

This definition specifies the correct result, but a Lisp system making use of it will not be as economical in its use of space in the computer as it could be with other definitions. The problem is that the Lisp system computes the arguments to the **append** function before carrying out the append. That is, it suspends computation of **append** and works on its arguments, **(car ll)** and **(unwrap (cdr ll))**. To do this, it makes a note of where it is in the computation, then proceeds with the computation of the arguments. One of these arguments, **(car ll)**, presents no difficulties, but the other, **(unwrap (cdr ll))**, involves reusing the definition of **unwrap**. This new use of **unwrap** will, in turn, make a note of the state of the computation, suspend another application of **append**, and reapply **unwrap**. This will continue until the successive applications of **cdr** to the original argument have peeled off all its components.

All the "notes" that keep track of the computation take up space in the computer, and none of them can be deleted until the corresponding computation of **unwrap** is completed. If the original argument, **ll**, has

$n$ components, the total space required for these notes before they can begin to be discarded will be proportional to $n$.

The use of this space for notes can be avoided by expressing the function in a different style. The new strategy uses the eventual result list to keep track of the state of the computation. That is, one of the arguments of the function will also be its result, in the simple case, and in the recursive case, the function will append another segment of the result to that argument.

Functions following this strategy accumulate more and more complete partial results by updating an argument, as if they were "pumping up" the argument. This technique is known as *pumping*. Such a function has one more argument than it should have, and this argument is used to build the result. To avoid mentioning the extra argument in every application of the function, the pumping function is normally expressed as a helper for a function that has the proper number of arguments.

The **unwrap** function operates on only one argument. To express it in a pumping style, we will write a helping function, **uwh** (for *unwrap-helper*), that we will use in the definition of **unwrap**. In this way, the **unwrap** function will have only one argument, just as it did before, but, **uwh**, the pumping function that actually carries out the computation, will have two arguments. At the point where **uwh** is applied in the definition of **unwrap**, one of its arguments will simply be a copy of the argument of **unwrap**, and the other will be an empty list, onto which the result will be appended, one segment at a time.

```
(defun  unwrap (ll)    (uwh ll '() )        )

(defun uwh (ll rslt)
   (if (null ll)
       rslt
       (uwh (cdr ll) (append rslt (car ll)))
   ))
```

In this new definition of **unwrap**, the helping function, **uwh**, specifies the construction of the result. The new specification allows the system to economize on notekeeping. Whereas the previous specification had a recursive application of the function as an argument to **append** (which required that the computation of **append** be suspended pending construction of the complete trailing segment of the result), this new function places the recursive application at the top level. Since the arguments for this recursive application of **uwh** can be computed directly, without further recursive applications of **uwh**, a Lisp system following this program will not need to keep an ever-lengthening list of notes on the state of suspended applications of **uwh** that are awaiting computation of their arguments. Instead, it can simply replace the original application of **uwh** with this new application. The new application will be the same as the original one, except that its first argument will be shorter, and its second argument longer (the first component of the original first argument having been appended at the end of the original second argument).

Not all Lisp systems take advantage of this obvious economy, but many do, and that makes pumping an important programming technique.[1] The space savings derived from pumping in the **unwrap** example were not an overwhelming percentage of the total space required for the computation because the amount of space required to represent the result is on the same order as the amount needed to keep track of suspended applications of **unwrap** in the nonpumping definition. When the result is substantially smaller than the input, the savings can be more dramatic (an example of this phenomenon will come later in this chapter).

Although the pumping version of **unwrap** may consume less space than our first version, it consumes more time because the **(append rslt (car ll))** application consumes an amount of computation time proportional to the number of components in the first argument, **rslt**. Unfortunately, this argument accumulates more and more components as the recursion unfolds—that is the pumping trick, building the result up in an argument.

In the first application of **append**, the first argument, **rslt** will be the empty list, and **append** will consume only a small amount of computation time and will deliver a result equal to the first sublist in the argument of **unwrap**. Suppose that **sublist** has $c_1$ components in it. The second application of **append**, which occurs in the recursive application of **uwh**, will have this sublist as its first argument and the second sublist in the original argument of **unwrap** as its second argument. Therefore, after an amount of time proportional to $c_1$ it will deliver a result with $c_1 + c_2$ components, where $c_2$ is the number of components in the second sublist in the original argument of **unwrap**.

This result with $c_1 + c_2$ components becomes the first argument of **append** in the next recursive application of **uwh**, and the second argument will be the third sublist in the original argument of **unwrap**. This application of **append** will consume $c_1 + c_2$ units of time. So far our computation has used up about $c_1 + (c_1 + c_2)$ units of computation time, and this pattern will continue. That is, the total amount of time consumed by **unwrap** will be

$$c_1 + (c_1 + c_2) + (c_1 + c_2 + c_3) + \cdots + (c_1 + c_2 + \cdots + c_n)$$

where $n$ is the number of sublists in the original argument of **unwrap**, and $c_i$ is the number of components in the $i$th sublist.

---

[1]A function like **uwh** in which a recursive invocation occurs at the outermost level is known as *tail recursive*. Lisp systems that take advantage of tail recursion to save space essentially transform such recursions into iteration (i.e., ordinary, conventional looping), which yields performance advantages as well as space savings.

This seems unreasonable, since a similar analysis of the nonpumping version of **unwrap** reveals a computation time of $(c_1 + c_2 + \cdots + c_n)$. The problem occurs because of the first argument of **append** in the definition of **uwh** gets longer and longer as the computation proceeds. To avoid this, we could reverse the order of **append**'s arguments, making the application look like this: **(append (car 11) rslt)**. However, this causes an even more serious problem than high computation times: the result is incorrect. (Remember! If you will be satisfied with incorrect results, you can always compute them very fast.) Whereas our correct versions of **unwrap** would convert

```
((titleA1 titleA2 titleA3) (titleB1 titleB2)
 (titleC1 titleC2 titleC3))
```

to

```
( titleA1 titleA2 titleA3   titleB1 titleB2
  titleC1 titleC2 titleC3 )
```

this faster version would deliver the result

```
( titleC1 titleC2 titleC3  titleB1 titleB2
  titleA1 titleA2 titleA3 )
```

This would be wrong, but, fortunately, it is not too hard to see how to fix it. The problem is that the new version appends the sublists together in the reverse order, compared to the way they were arranged in the argument. To fix this, all we need to do is to reverse the original argument before passing it along to **uwh**.

```
(defun  unwrap (11)  (uwh (reverse 11) '() )          )

(defun  uwh (11 rslt)
   (if (null 11)
       rslt
       (uwh (cdr 11) (append (car 11) rslt))
))
```

This last version will consume about $c_1 + c_2 + \cdots + c_n$ units of time, plus about $n$ units of time to complete the **reverse** before applying **uwh**, and, since it pumps up the result in the same way as the first pumping implementation, the Lisp system may economize on space.

The **unwrap** function is exactly what we need to accomplish our goal of designing a function to extract all the works by a given author in a library catalog of the form we specified earlier. The idea is to apply **unwrap** to a list whose components collect by category the works by the given author; that is, we will apply **unwrap** to a list with components that are, themselves, lists of works by the given author. The result will be a flat list of works, without the by-category substructure.

We can form the list organized by category by selecting from each category in the catalog the entry, if any, for the given author.

```
(defun groupedincategories  (author  libcat)
   (if (null libcat)
       '()
       (cons (select author (cadar libcat))
             (groupedincategories author (cdr libcat)))
   ))
```

```
(defun select  (author  libentries)
   (if (null libentries)
       '()
       (if (equal author (caar libentries))
           (cdar libentries)
           (select author (cdr libentries))
       )))
```

Then the definition of the function we have been looking for is a simple composition of **groupedincategories** and **unwrap**.

```
(defun worksbyauthor (author libcat)
        (unwrap (groupedincategories  author libcat)) )
```

```
Program: (worksbyauthor ' (V Nabokov) (catalog))
Result:  ( (Lolita) (Ada or Ardor)
          (Nikolai Gogol) (Speak Memory) )
```

In the **unwrap** example of the pumping technique, the function's result was about the same size as its argument. Because of this, the pumping computation required about half as much space as the original version. However, when the result is much smaller than the argument, the space savings can be much more dramatic.

Consider the problem of finding the first name (alphabetically) in a list of names. That is, given a list of names, each of which is a symbolic atom, we want a function that will deliver the name from the list that would come first in alphabetical order. For example, if the function were called **first**, then **(first ' (Christy Nabokov Vonnegut Asimov LeCarre))** would be **Asimov**.

Lisp provides functions to compare pairs of symbolic atoms to determine which comes first according to the alphabetical order of their names.

What we need to do is to use **string-lessp** recursively to determine which list component comes first, alphabetically. A simple way to define this function is as follows.

```
(string-lessp (string x) (string y))   is   T
```

is **T** if the name of the symbolic atom **x** precedes that of **y**, alphabetically

or **NIL** if the name of **x** follows that of **y**

Caveat: **x** and **y** must be symbolic atoms; they cannot be lists; letter-case is ignored

```
(string-lessp (string 'Nabokov)
              (string 'Vonnegut))    is   T
(string-lessp (string 'Vonnegut)
              (string 'Asimov))      is   NIL
```

```
(defun first (nonemptylist)
   (if (null (cdr nonemptylist))
       (car nonemptylist)
       (smaller (car nonemptylist)
                (first (cdr nonemptylist))))
   ))

(defun  smaller (x y)
   (if (string-lessp (string x) (string y))
       x
       y
   ))
```

This definition of **first** has the same flaw that the original definition of **unwrap** had. It has a recursive application as an argument for an application of another function, which forces the Lisp system to keep notes about the state of a temporarily suspended application of **first** to carry out a recursive application. In general, this recursion will occur at more and more deeply nested levels until an argument with only one component is supplied to an application of **first**. Thus, at the greatest depth, the Lisp system will have notes about as many suspended computations of **first** as there are components in the original argument.

By designing a helping function with a pumping argument that will represent the best estimate of the smallest component of the list encountered in earlier portions of the computation, we can permit the Lisp system to economize on space. In fact, the system may use only a small, fixed amount of space for the entire computation. The new version of **first** is shown here.

```
(defun  first  (nonemptylist)
   (firsth (cdr nonemptylist) (car nonemptylist)) )

(defun firsth  (lst smallestsofar)
   (if (null lst)
       smallestsofar
       (if (string-lessp (string (car lst))
                          (string smallestsofar))
           (firsth (cdr lst) (car lst))
           (firsth (cdr lst) smallestsofar)
   )))
```

## ■ SUMMARY

*Pumping* is a programming technique in which an extra argument, introduced in a helping function, is used to accumulate the final result, piece by piece. In effect, the pumping argument keeps a record of the state of the computation. Sometimes this programming trick saves space, sometimes it saves time, and sometimes, both.

## ■ BIBLIOGRAPHY NOTES

The idea of accumulating partial results in one of the parameters of a function has been used since the dawn of programming in various guises and under various names. We first heard the technique referred to as *pumping* by Daniel Friedman, but do not know whether or not he was the first to apply that terminology (which comes from the *pumping lemma* in the theory of formal languages).

Henderson discusses the technique in depth in his text on functional programming. Bird discovered some ways to translate programs mechanically from more easily constructed and understood formulations to equivalent programs that use pumping to improve efficiency.

R. S. Bird (1984). The promotion and accumulation strategies in transformational programming. *ACM Trans. Programming Languages and Systems* 6(4) (October), 487–504.

Peter Henderson (1980). *Functional Programming: Application and Implementation*, Prentice–Hall, Englewood Cliffs, N.J.

## ■ EXERCISES

1. The definition of the function **groupedincategories** in this chapter had a recursive application buried in the argument list of an application of **cons**. This is a signal that pumping may provide a way to design a more economical function. Try writing a pumping version of this function.

2. Rewrite the **worksbyauthor** function using pumping directly on the result of **groupsincategory** function rather than by applying **unwrap**.

3. The **reverse** function, which is one of the standard Lisp operations, is a popular example of a case in which much time can be saved by using the pumping technique. Following is a definition of reverse that does not use pumping, but requires a computation time proportional to the square of the number of components of the list that is being reversed. Redesign **reverse**, using pumping, so that it requires an amount of computation time proportional to the number of components in its argument.

```
(defun reverse (lst)
   (if (null lst)
       '()
       (append (reverse (cdr lst)) (list (car lst)))
   ))
```

## ANSWERS

1. ```
   (defun groupedincategories  (author libcat)
      (gch author libcat '()) )

   (defun gch (author libcat rslt)
      (if (null libcat)  rslt
          (gch author libcat
               (cons (select author (car libcat)) rslt))
      ))
   ```

   **Note:** This pumping version of **groupedincategories** builds the result in the reverse order compared to the original version of **groupedincategories**. This could be fixed by applying reverse to the list delivered by **gch** in the new definition of groupedincategories, but, as you will see in the next exercise, this reverse order plays nicely into the hands of the **worksbyauthor** function.
   ```

2. ```
   (defun worksbyauthor (author libcat)
        (wah (groupedincategories  author libcat)   '()
   ) )
   ```

   ```
   (defun wah  (grpd rslt)
      (if (null grpd)
          rslt
          (wah (cdr grpd) (append (car grpd) rslt))
      ))
   ```

3. `(defun reverse (lst)  (revh lst '()) )`

   ```
   (defun revh (lst rslt)
      (if (null lst)
          rslt
          (revh (cdr lst) (cons (car lst) rslt))
      ))
   ```
   ```

# CHAPTER 12

# DIVIDE AND CONQUER

In your experience as a designer of denotational programs, you probably have discovered that an effective way to solve problems is to find one or more subproblems that are in some way simpler or smaller than the original problem, to solve those problems (often by applying the same idea in a circular fashion), and finally to paste the partial solutions together to form the full solution. All the recursive functions that we have designed in our examples and in the solutions to exercises have been constructed in this mode. However, all these solutions have had in common a curious property. Namely, they divided the problem into two parts: one part was trivial to solve, and the other was solved by a recursive application of the function.

For some problems, the most effective division into subproblems has the property that one part has a trivial solution and the other is solved via recursion. But for many problems it is possible to find a better subdivision in which all the subproblems have about the same complexity. When this is the case, the *balance* in complexity among the partial solutions leads to an enormous improvement in the overall computation

---

### GLOSSARY DATA SPECIFICATION

| *glossary-data* | is | (glossary-entry ...) |
|---|---|---|
| *glossary-entry* | is | (term definition) |
| *term* | is | symbolic-atom |
| *definition* | is | (symbolic-atom ...) |

Example

```
((limerick (five line anapestic verse rhyming aabba))
(rhyming (corresponding terminal sounds))
(anapestic (dadaDAH dadaDAH dadaDAH))
(verse (metrical writing))
(versus (against))
(dactylic (DAHdada DAHdada DAHdada)) )
```

---

time required for solving the full problem, compared to what could be had by dividing it into an unbalanced collection of subproblems.

The technique of dividing problems into subproblems of approximately the same complexity, and solving each of those via a recursive application of this same idea, is known as the *divide and conquer* strategy. It is ubiquitous in algorithm design. In this chapter, we will see how to apply this technique to the important problem of arranging a sequence of items in alphabetical order, the so-called *sorting problem*.

Suppose our data are a collection of definitions of terms for a glossary that has been compiled by going through the pages of a book, selecting terms for the glossary, and writing them down along with their definitions. These definitions will be arranged by page number, more or less (depending on how much skipping around we have done while selecting them). We want to write a function that will deliver a new arrangement of these data so that the entries appear in alphabetical order, as they normally would in a glossary.

Following the line of reasoning that we have grown accustomed to in designing functions, we might come up with the following idea: The sorted form of the glossary data consists of the sorted form of all the entries except the first, with the first entry inserted into the appropriate place among them.

Because we are arranging items in alphabetical order, we will again be using the predicate **string-lessp** (from Chapter 11), which confirms or denies an alphabetical relationship between the names of the two symbolic atoms that are its arguments.

```
(defun  insertionsort  (entries)
   (if (null entries)
```

> **insertion sort** — arranging a collection of items by first properly arranging all the items but one, then inserting that item in its appropriate place
>
> When playing trick-oriented card games such as hearts, spades, bridge, and euchre, most people arrange their cards by a technique along the lines of the insertion sort.

```
       ' ()
       (insert (car entries)
               (insertionsort (cdr entries)))
  ))

(defun  insert  (x sorted)
   (if (null sorted)
       (list x)
       (if (orderp x (car sorted))
           (cons x sorted)
           (cons (car sorted) (insert x (cdr sorted)))
   )))

(defun  orderp  (xglossaryentry yglossaryentry)
    (string-lessp (string (car xglossaryentry))
                  (string (car yglossaryentry))  ))
```

Program:  
```
       (insertionsort
          '( (limerick (five line anapestic verse
                         rhyming aabba))
            (rhyming (corresponding terminal sounds))
            (anapestic (dadaDAH dadaDAH dadaDAH))
            (verse (metrical writing))
            (versus (against))
            (dactylic (DAHdada DAHdada DAHdada))
          ))
```

Result:  
```
      ' ( (anapestic (dadaDAH dadaDAH dadaDAH))
          (dactylic (DAHdada DAHdada DAHdada))
          (limerick (five line anapestic verse
                      rhyming aabba))
          (rhyming (corresponding terminal sounds))
          (verse (metrical writing))
          (versus (against))
        )
```

The insertion sort works well when there are only a few items to be arranged, as in a hand of cards. But when there are many items, dozens or hundreds, as in a glossary, the method is hopelessly slow. To get a feeling for how much work is involved, consider the problem of inserting an item into a presorted sequence (this is the result specified by the function called **insert** in our program). Assuming that the item is about as likely to fit near the end as near the beginning, it seems reasonable to estimate that finding the proper spot for the item will require examining about half the items in the presorted sequence.

Because the insertion sort specifies the arrangement via such an insertion at each level, you would have to make the same estimate for the insertion at the next level. The only difference is that the sequence is one item shorter at that point. This line of reasoning continues, and the insertions required will involve shorter and shorter sequences. At the final level, an insertion is made into an empty list, which will require only a small, unit amount, of effort. Thus, the insertion sort requires one insertion into a presorted sequence for each item in the original sequence, which would be $n$ insertions if the original sequence contained $n$ items.

As the average number of items in these presorted sequences will be about $n/2$, we can expect that insertion to require about half as many computational steps as there are components in the sequence into which the new item is being inserted; that is, about $(n/2)/2$ or $n/4$ computational steps. Thus, the computation will require $n$ insertions, each of which requires about $n/4$ computational steps, which would be about $n^2$ over four computational steps altogether. For a 100-item sequence, this would be 2500 steps.

We can get much better performance with only a slight change in the specification of our program. The change involves balancing the size of the subproblems, the essence of the divide-and-conquer strategy.

The specification of the insertion sort follows our habit of splitting the problem into two subproblems, one of which is small (the insertion of the first item into a sorted version of the rest of the sequence) and the other of which is large (the **insertionsort** applied to the remainder of the input). If instead of splitting off only one item for later insertion, we split the sequence in half, sort each half separately, and then merge these two presorted halves together, we will end up with an algorithm that will require about $n*\log_2(n)$ computational steps to complete a sorted arrangement. For a 100-item sequence, this is 700 steps—still a bunch, but almost four times faster than the insertion sort. The comparison between insertion sort and this new algorithm, which we call the *merge sort* because of the process involved in bringing two presorted halves together into a single sorted sequence, gets more and more dramatic as the size of the sequence to be sorted increases. For example, merge sort is about 25 times faster than insertion sort for a 1000-item sequence.

> **merge sort** — arranging a collection of items by first dividing the items into two collections of approximately equal size, then (merge) sorting the two collections independently, and finally, merging the two sorted collections into a complete sorted sequence

To specify the merge sort, we need to consider two problems. One is the problem of splitting the original sequence into two parts (which is the role of the function **split** in the definitions that follow), and the other is the problem of merging two presorted sequences together (the role of the function **merge** that follows). Ironically, we do not need to consider the main subproblem of the algorithm (i.e., the problem of sorting a half-length sequence) because that subproblem is handled "automatically" via a recursive application of the **mergesort** function itself.

The sorting function can be defined as follows (assuming the existence of a subfunction, **split**, defined later.

```
(defun mergesort (seq)
   (if (or (null seq) (null (cdr seq)))
          seq
       (let ( (pair (split seq)) )
         (merge (mergesort (car  pair))
                (mergesort (cadr pair)))
   )))
```

One way to define this splitting function is as follows.

```
(defun split (seq)
   (if (null seq)
       '( () () )                             ; empty arg
       (if (null (cdr seq))
           (list seq '() )                    ; 1-item arg
           (let( (pair (split (cddr seq))) )  ; 2 or more
                (list (cons (car seq) (car pair))
                      (cons (cadr seq) (cadr pair)))
   ))))
```

Finally, there is the **merge** function to consider. Merge constructs a single, sorted list from a pair of lists, each of which is already sorted. The specification of this result again falls back to our usual strategy, that of handling simple arguments directly and more complex arguments recursively. A simple argument for merge is one in which one list in the pair is empty; then the result must be simply the other list from the pair. When both lists in the pair are nonempty, then the first component of the result will be the smaller of the first item in the first list of the pair and the first item in the second list of the pair. The remaining components in the result will result from applying the **merge** function to a new pair in which one item has been omitted from one of the lists in the pair (namely the item that was discovered to be the first component of the result). The following function definition follows this plan.

```
(defun merge (pair)
   (let ( (a (car pair))
          (b (cadr pair)) )
     (if (null a)
         b
         (if (null b)
             a
             (if (orderp (car a) (car b))
                 (cons (car a) (merge (list (cdr a) b)))
                 (cons (car b) (merge (list a (cdr b))))
             )))))
```

The **orderp** predicate is the same as before, of course, and the result of applying **mergesort** to the example glossary data is the same result we got when we applied **insertionsort** to those data.

```
Program:   (mergesort
            '( (limerick (five line anapestic verse
                          rhyming aabba))
               (rhyming (corresponding terminal sounds))
               (anapestic (dadaDAH dadaDAH dadaDAH))
               (verse (metrical writing))
               (versus (against))
               (dactylic (DAHdada DAHdada DAHdada))
            ))
```

```
Result:    ( (anapestic (dadaDAH dadaDAH dadaDAH))
             (dactylic (DAHdada DAHdada DAHdada))
             (limerick (five line anapestic verse
                        rhyming aabba))
             (rhyming (corresponding terminal sounds))
             (verse (metrical writing))
             (versus (against))
           )
```

Thus, the functions **mergesort** and **insertionsort** are equivalent in the sense that they denote the same results for each potential argument, but they differ in the sense that a computer making use of the **mergesort** definition to carry out a computation will be able to perform the sorting process much faster than it could if it had to use, instead, the **insertionsort** definition.

## ▪ BIBLIOGRAPHY NOTES

*The Design and Analysis of Computer Algorithms*, a classic book by Aho, Hopcroft, and Ullman, applies the divide-and-conquer idea in the design of algorithms to solve a great many important problems. These algorithms frequently are faster than their naive competitors by something like a factor of $n/\log(n)$, where $n$ measures the size of the input. For large sets of input data, this will be a very large savings, as in **mergesort** versus **insertionsort**.

The article on the taxonomy of sorting algorithms by Susan M. Merritt presents an enlightening view of different ways to apply the divide-and-conquer strategy to the sorting problem.

A. V. Aho, J. E. Hopcroft, and J. D. Ullman (1974). *The Design and Analysis of Computer Algorithms*, Addison-Wesley, Reading, Mass.

S. M. Merritt (1985). *An Inverted Taxonomy of Sorting Algorithms*, Communications of the ACM 28 (January).

## ▪ EXERCISES

1. Define a new version of the splitting function making use of the pumping technique.

## ▪ ANSWERS

```
1. (defun split (seq)  (sph seq '()  '()) )

   (defun sph (seq  rsltA rsltB)
      (if (null seq)
          (list rsltA rsltB)
          (if (null (cdr seq))
              (list (cons (car seq) rsltA)  rsltB)
              (sph  (cddr seq)
                    (cons (car seq)  rsltA)
```

```
                    (cons (cadr seq) rsltB))
    )))
```

**Note:** The lists in the pair delivered by this version of **split** will both be in reverse order, compared to the original version of **split**. This could be repaired by specifying **(list (reverse rsltA) (reverse rsltB))** as **split**'s result when its first argument is the empty list, and similarly reversing the components of the result in the case of a one-component sequence. However, it does not make much difference since the purpose of **split** is simply to partition the input sequence into two pieces, the order being unimportant because **mergesort** will rearrange it anyway.

# CHAPTER 13

# INPUT AND OUTPUT

It seems always that the orderliness of a programming language breaks down when it comes to input and output of data. Lisp is no exception. The breakdown occurs because most of the features of a programming language are designed to deal with data that are represented in a form that is consistent with the basic notations of the language, whereas input and output must deal with more or less arbitrary notations that are outside the scope of the language. The purpose of input is to convert these arbitrary notations into a form that the language can deal with conveniently, and the purpose of ouput is to reverse this process, that is, to convert the language's internal data representations into whatever form is required for presentation outside the language.

The differences between i/o and the rest of the programming techniques we will be using is even more pronounced than usual because we have chosen to use denotational rather than operational methods. Lisp provides no simple way to take a denotational view of i/o. That is not to say it cannot be done. It can, but the apparatus needed to support it is beyond the scope of this text.

The *input* process converts external representations of data (i.e., representations that are outside the universe of notations that are part of the programming language) to internal representations that the programming language can deal with directly. In Lisp a convenient cop-out solves this problem, a path that we will take forthwith. We are not going to describe any means of writing Lisp programs to transform arbitrary input data into results. Instead, we will assume that any data we wish to provide for one of our Lisp programs are written in the form of a Lisp list (or atom). This will not in any way constrain the types of programs we can develop because we can encode any kind of information into the form of a Lisp list. The only constraint is on the form in which data can be presented to our programs, and since our main interested is on transforming data via functions, we can afford to let the notational conversion problems take a back seat. (To process data presented in a greater variety of forms, one could write programs in any programming language to convert the native form of the data into a Lisp list representation, and then apply a Lisp function to produce the desired results.)

Although we will process only data represented in the form of Lisp constructs, we can make data preparation more convenient by permitting the data to reside on files outside the Lisp program itself. (Up to now, we have been entering the data directly as part of the program.)

The mechanics of processing data from files proceeds as follows. Assume that the data written in a file on your computer system's mass storage facility are denoted in the form of a Lisp list (or atom, in trivial cases). The program, on the other hand, exists in another file. To apply one of the functions from the program file to the list in the data file, use the text-editing facility of your computer system to modify the data file. Define a function in the data file that takes no arguments, but delivers the data as its result. (See the example of the function called catalog in Chapter 9.) Once this is done, you can use the Lisp system to load the function definitions from the program file along with the data-function definition from the modified data file in such a way that any of the functions can be invoked just as if you had typed them into the system directly. To transform the data in the desired way, all you have to do is apply the appropriate function to the value delivered by the data function.

To illustrate the idea, consider the pig latin translation program from one of the early chapters. In this case, the program file would contain the definitions of **xlatmsg** and **xlatcmp** (functions designed to translate pig latin messages into English).

```
program file                    filename: pigxlat

   (defun  xlatmsg  (msg)  (mapcar #'xlatcmp msg) )
   (defun  xlatcmp  (msgcmp)
      (if (equal (last msgcmp) '(ay))
```

```
       (cdr (reverse msgcmp))
       msgcmp
))
```

The data file would consist of a message written in pig latin, in the list form expected by the **xlatmsg** function.

**data file**                       **filename: pigmsg**

```
( (ake t ay) (out the) (apers p ay) (and the)
  (ash tr ay) )
```

Modify the data file to contain a function whose value would be the data.

**data function file**             **filename: pigmsgfn**

```
(defun pigmsg ()
  '((ake t ay) (out the) (apers p ay) (and the)
    (ash tr ay)) )
```

Now use the Lisp system to load the functions defined in the program file and the data function file. The **load** function performs this service. The argument of the **load** function is the name, enclosed in double-quote marks, of the file that you want brought into the system. (Some systems provide this facility under other guises—consult your Lisp user's manual or a local expert.)

Once the contents of the program file and the data function file have been consumed by the Lisp system, it will be ready to accept an application of any of your functions. At this point, you simply apply the function that makes the desired transformation to the value delivered by the data function.

```
Program:  (load "pigxlat")
Result:   t
Program:  (load "pigmsgfn")
Result:   t
Program:  (xlatmsg (pigmsg))
Result:   ((t ake) (out the) (p apers) (and the) (tr ash))
```

No doubt you discovered the program-file trick long ago to avoid re-typing all your functions every time you begin a Lisp session with the computer. The data file differs only slightly from this, and together they provide a means of handling input for Lisp programs that is adequate for the purposes of this text. To deal with more arbitrary forms of input, especially "interactive" input, requires techniques that would detract from our primary thrust, so we leave them to other treatises. We note in our defense that all computer systems will have some limitation on the forms of input and output they accept. For example, some systems can handle data in the form of files of characters, but not in the form of pictorial images. Some systems can deliver output in the form of pictorial images, but not in the form of audio signals. And so on.

Output cannot be dismissed quite so easily as input. If it could, there would be almost nothing to say about it, since all the functions we have written have been capable of delivering their results in a form we could understand (namely, as a Lisp list). They have done this automatically whenever we constructed a direct function application (i.e., a function application not imbedded inside a function definition and not invoked to compute an argument for another function application). For example, the Lisp system responds to the application

```
(xlatmsg '((ont d ay) (awk t ay) (ack b ay)))
```

by displaying the result

```
((d ont) (t awk) (b ack))
```

just as it would respond to any "top level" invocation.

For this reason, there is no obvious need for any special sort of trick to handle output. But there is a problem of scale. Some of the programs that we will discuss in the applications chapter deliver very large result lists, even when their input lists are of reasonable size. The size of these results would strain the memory capacity of many computers. In some cases there will be no solution to this, and we will simply have to admit that the problem is too large to solve in a practical way on the system we have available. However, in most cases it will be possible to construct portions of the result that, once computed, can be delivered as partial results and then discarded. Lisp, as we know it so far, has no mechanism for doing this; it either delivers the complete result, all at once when the computation is complete, or it fails in some way and delivers no result at all.

For example, suppose we want to apply our pig latin translator to a bunch of phrases, rather than just a single phrase. One way to do this would be to write a function that would accept a list of phrases as its argument and apply **xlatmsg** to these phrases individually, constructing a list of translated phrases as its result.

```
(defun  xlatbunch (phrases)
   (if (null phrases)
       '()
       (cons (xlatmsg (car phrases))
             (xlatbunch (cdr phrases)))
  ))
```

Program:    **(xlatbunch**
            **'( ((ake t ay) (out the) (apers p ay)**
            **   (and the) (ash tr ay))**
            **  ((or you) (ont d ay) (et g ay) (no)**
            **   (endin sp ay) (ash c ay))**
            **  ((if you) (ont d ay) (ub scr ay) (that)**
            **   (itchen k ay) (or fl ay))**
            **  ((you aint) (onna g ay) (ock r ay) (and)**
            **   (oll r ay) (no more))**
            **  ((ack y ay) (uh) (ee t ay) (ack y ay))**
            **  ((ont d ay) (awk t ay) (ack b ay))**
            **))**

Result:     **( ((t ake) (out the) (p apers) (and the)**
            **  (tr ash))**
            **  ((or you) (d ont) (g et) (no) (sp endin)**
            **  (c ash))**
            **  ((if you) (d ont) (scr ub) (that) (k itchen)**
            **  (fl or))**
            **  (you aint) (g onna) (r ock) (and) (r oll)**
            **  (no more))**
            **  ((y ack) (uh) (t ee) (y ack))**
            **  ((d ont) (t awk) (b ack))**
            **)**

The size problem is not at all severe in this case, but you can imagine that the list of phrases might be very long. It could be a whole book in pig latin. And in that case, we might need to avoid constructing the complete list of translations before delivering any part of the result. It is important to notice that the reason the function **xlatbunch** is susceptible to delivering partial results is because it requires no knowledge of the translation of the first message after it inserts that message as the first translated phrase in its result. Thus, as far as the remainder of the result is concerned, the first part may as well have been discarded. It is in situations of this kind, and only in situations of this kind, that we will be able to use the output trick to save space in the computer system's memory.

To keep the idea of delivering partial results as consistent as possible with our denotational theme, we are going to think of the output stream as a sequence of lines, just as a list is a sequence of components. One way to construct new lists from old ones is to use the **cons** function, as we have in the definition of **xlatbunch**. The **cons** function requires two arguments, a component (which may be either a list or an atom) and a list. It delivers a new list that is like the original list argument except that it has one additional component at the beginning, namely the one specified in the component argument.

By way of our analogy between lists and output streams, we will describe an output constructor, **print**, that has two arguments. One of these arguments is analogous to the component argument of **cons**. This argument will be explicit in every application of **print**. The other argument will be implicit (i.e., it will not be present explicitly in applications of **print**). This implicit argument, which is analogous to the list argument of **cons**, will be the output stream constructed by the expression following the application of **print**.

The **print** function will be applied only in the definition of a function, and then it will precede the expression that defines the value of the function. Thus, the explicit argument of **print** becomes the first component of the output stream and the remainder of the output stream, which is constructed in the expression following the application of **print**, is the implicit second argument of **print**.[1]

To illustrate how this works, we will recast our **xlatbunch** function in terms of **print** rather than **cons**. In this old form, the value of the function was an application of **cons** in which the first argument (the component argument) was the translation of the first phrase and the second argument (the list argument) was the list of translations of the remaining phrases (obtained via a recursive application of **xlatbunch**). In the new form, **xlatbunch** will be an application of **print** to the translation of the first phrase (corresponding to the first argument in the **cons**), and this will be followed by an expression that recursively applies **xlatbunch** (corresponding to the second argument of **cons**).

```
(defun  xlatbunch (phrases)
   (print (xlatmsg (if phrases (car phrases) nil))
   (if (null phrases)
       '()
       (xlatbunch (cdr phrases)) )
   ))
```

Program:   (xlatbunch
           '( ((ake t ay) (out the) (apers p ay) (and the)
             (ash tr ay))
             ((or you) (ont d ay) (et g ay) (no)
             (endin sp ay) (ash c ay))
             ((if you) (ont d ay) (ub scr ay) (that)
             (itchen k ay) (or fl ay))
             ((you aint) (onna g ay) (ock r ay) (and)
             (oll r ay) (no more))
             ((ack y ay) (uh) (ee t ay) (ack y ay))

---

[1] Your Lisp system may not have a **print** function that behaves like the one we have described. In that case, you can design it yourself, with the help of your Lisp manual or a local expert. The fundamental requirements are two functions: one to print the value of a Lisp expression and another to terminate the printing of a line. Using these two functions, you can put together a **print** function.

```
                      ((ont d ay)  (awk t ay)  (ack b ay))))
Result:      ((t ake)  (out the)  (p apers)  (and the)  (tr ash))
             ((or you)  (d ont)  (g et)  (no)  (sp endin)  (c ash))
             ((if you)  (d ont)  (scr ub)  (that)
              (k itchen)  (fl or))
             ((you aint)  (g onna)  (r ock)  (and)  (r oll)
              (no more))
             ((y ack)  (uh)  (t ee)  (y ack))
             ((d ont)  (t awk)  (b ack))
             nil
             nil
```

The printing version of **xlatbunch** has a curious property: Its value is the empty list, regardless of its argument. We have no interest in the official result delivered by **xlatbunch**. Instead, we use the function to construct the output stream as a sequence of lines, and this output stream does interest us. Despite our lack of interest, the Lisp system insists on printing the value of the function, and that is the source of the extra "**nil**" following the sequence of lines (translated phrases) generated by invocations of **print**.

Observe again the analogy between **cons** and **print** by comparing the two versions of **xlatbunch**. In the second version, **print** is invoked at the beginning of **xlatbunch**, and the argument of **print** is the same as the first argument of **cons** in the original version of **xlatbunch**. The implicit second argument of **print** is the output stream produced by the recursive application of **xlatbunch** in the expression following the application of **print**. This output stream will, of course, be the translated phrases, in sequence, printed in subsequent recursive invocations of **xlatbunch**. This sequence of translated phrases was the second argument of **cons** in the original version of **xlatbunch**.

Sometimes it may be desirable to print groups of lines of information rather than just one. Suppose, for example, that we had wanted our pig latin translator to print the pig latin version of the phrase as well as the English version. We would probably want to label the pig latin and English versions to avoid confusion, and perhaps to leave a blank line between different phrases. We could do this by placing several applications of **print** in front of the recursive application of **xlatbunch**.

```
(defun  xlatbunch (phrases)
   (print (list "pig latin:" (car phrases)))
   (print (list "English:  " (xlatmsg (car phrases))))
   (print (list "          "))
   (if (null phrases)
       '()
       (xlatbunch (cdr phrases)) )
))
```

```
Program: (xlatbunch
         '( ((ake t ay) (out the) (apers p ay) (and the)
            (ash tr ay))
           ((or you) (ont d ay) (et g ay) (no)
            (endin sp ay) (ash c ay))
           ((if you) (ont d ay) (ub scr ay) (that)
            (itchen k ay) (or fl ay))
           ((you aint) (onna g ay) (ock r ay) (and)
            (oll r ay) (no more))
           ((ack y ay) (uh) (ee t ay) (ack y ay))
           ((ont d ay) (awk t ay) (ack b ay))
         ))
Result:  ("pig latin:" ((ake t ay) (out the)
          (apers p ay) (and the) (ash tr ay)))
         ("English:  " ((t ake) (out the) (p apers)
          (and the) (tr ash)))
         ("          ")
         ("pig latin:" ((or you) (ont d ay) (et g ay)
          (no) (endin sp ay) (ash c ay)))
         ("English:  " ((or you) (d ont) (g et) (no)
          (sp endin) (c ash)))
         ("          ")
         ("pig latin:" ((if you) (ont d ay)
          (ub scr ay) (that) (itchen k ay) (or fl ay)))
         ("English:  " ((if you) (d ont) (scr ub)
          (that) (k itchen) (fl or)))
         ("          ")
         ("pig latin:" ((you aint) (onna g ay)
          (ock r ay) (and) (oll r ay) (no more)))
         ("English:  " ((you aint) (g onna) (r ock)
          (and) (r oll) (no more)))
         ("          ")
         ("pig latin:" ((ack y ay) (uh) (ee t ay)
          (ack y ay)))
         ("English:  " ((y ack) (uh) (t ee) (y ack)))
         ("          ")
         ("pig latin:" ((ont d ay) (awk t ay)
          (ack b ay)))
         ("English:  " ((d ont) (t awk) (b ack)))
         ("          ")
         nil
```

In this version of the function we have used a new trick to insert
commentary in the form of arbitrary strings of characters, including special characters such as blanks and colons that would not ordinarily be

contained in the names of atoms. To do this, we simply enclose the commentary in quote marks, and the print function copies it literally, as is, into the output stream. These quoted constructions, known as *strings*, can be used as components in lists whenever you find it desirable.

It could be made a lot fancier, perhaps formatting the lines in some nice way, and you may want to jazz your version up a bit, but we will leave that entirely up to you. In any case, you should place your print function in a file for easy access. Whenever you begin a Lisp session, load this file, which may contain other "utility functions" that you use frequently, so that you can invoke them whenever you need to.

Sometimes you may want to direct your results to a file rather than having them printed on the screen. To do this, simply surround the function invocation whose result you want sent to the file with a let construct binding the symbolic atom **\*standard-output\*** to the file name denoted as a string.

```
(let ((*standard-output* "filename"))
   (your-function your-data...)        )
```

## ■ SUMMARY

| | |
|---|---|
| (**load** "*filename*") | causes the Lisp system to make the function definitions from the designated file available for use in your Lisp session |
| (**print** *expr*) | prints a line (or lines) containing the value of *expr* |
| "*arbitrary characters*" | is a *string;* it may be used as a list component |
| **\*standard-output\*** | is the name of the output stream; you can bind it to a file name, denoted as a string, with a **let** construct |

# HIGHER ORDER FUNCTIONS

An ordinary function transforms data from one form to another. The function describes the transformation in general terms based on the overall form of the data but ignores the exact values that the data will have. For example, the function **reverse** assumes that its argument is a list, not an atom, but it does not care what components the list has; **reverse** works just as well on ' **(A B C)** as it does on ' **(D E F)**.

Higher order functions may accept other functions as part of their data and may deliver functions as their results. The **mapcar** function, for example, expects one of its arguments to be a function, which means that **mapcar** is a higher order function. Programmers use higher order functions to describe common patterns of function usage. This technique simplifies programs by reusing the common patterns with different base functions. Thus, higher order functions and ordinary functions lead to similar sorts of simplifications: They express concepts in general terms, then apply the concepts in varying contexts by specifying different combinations of arguments.

The function **mapcar** requires two arguments: a function and a list. **Mapcar** delivers a result list that contains a new version of the list argument in which each element has been transformed by the function argument.

Program:    **(mapcar #'reverse '((A Christie) (V Nabokov)**
                                     **(K Vonnegut)))**
Result:      **((Christie A) (Nabokov V) (Vonnegut K))**

The function supplied as **mapcar**'s first argument must, itself, require exactly one argument.

Suppose, now, that we need a function similar to **mapcar** except that it accepts functions of two arguments and applies them to list components in pairs.

Program:    **(map2 #'cons '(a (b c) (x y) (z) m ((n) o)))**
Result:      **((a b c) ((x y) z) (m (n) o))**

We write this higher order function, **map2**, without using any special techniques. The only new twist is that we use one of the arguments as a function in the definition of **map2**. All the functions we have written before use their formal arguments as arguments of other functions in the defining expression, not as functions in the defining expression.

This new twist, that of using one of the arguments of a function as a function, rather than as data, means that we will not have the literal name of the function to use in its invocation. Instead, we will have a name that designates, via its value, a function. The Lisp system cannot tolerate this indirect connection to a function name in a function invocation of the usual form, such as **(f x)**, where **f** designates a function.

To invoke a function indirectly via the value associated with a name, we must use the **funcall** facility. The form of the invocation using **funcall** is **(funcall f x)**. This causes the Lisp system to evaluate **f** (e.g., look up its value) before applying it to its argument.

Later we will see situations in which functions deliver other functions as their values. These situations also require the use of **funcall**. For example, if the invocation **(f x)** delivers a function as its value, then we would invoke the resulting function via **funcall**:

**(funcall (f x) y)**

Thus, the first argument of **funcall** is an expression whose value is a function, and the remaining arguments of **funcall** are arguments for an invocation of that function. For example, suppose the name **f** has the value **#'append**. Then **(funcall f '(a b) '(c d))** delivers the value **(a b c d)**. Equivalently, **(funcall #'append '(a b) '(c d))** has the value **(a b c d)**.

We will use the **funcall** facility to invoke functions whenever we need to get around this problem of literal names versus computed values representing functions. In our first example, we need **funcall** to invoke the function passed as an argument to **map2**, as illustrated in the following definition.

```
Program:   (defun map2 (binaryfunction lst)
             (if (null lst)
                 '()
                 (cons (funcall binaryfunction (car lst)
                                               (cadr lst))
                       (map2 binaryfunction (cddr lst))
                 )
             ))
```

We can use **map2** to generalize on the **pairup** function in Chapter 8. The **pairup** function made two-element lists out of each pair of elements in its argument.

```
Program:   (pairup 'A Christie V Nabokov K Vonnegut))
Result:    ((A Christie) (V Nabokov) (K Vonnegut))
```

**Map2**, with the function "**list**" as its function argument, duplicates the effect of **pairup**.

```
Program:   (map2 #'list '(A Christie V Nabokov
                          K Vonnegut))
Result:    ((A Christie) (V Nabokov) (K Vonnegut))
```

This leads to a very simple definition of **pairup**.

```
Program:   (defun pairup (lst)
             (map2 #'list lst) )
```

However, **map2** gives us a more general capability than **pairup** because its first argument might operate on the pairs in other ways. For example, we might want a function that would form the pairs with each pair reversed.

```
Input:    (A Christie V Nabokov K Vonnegut)
Result:   ((Christie A) (Nabokov V) (Vonnegut K))
```

We could, of course, use **mapcar** to apply reverse to all the elements of the result of **pairup**.

```
Program:   (defun reversepairup (lst)
             (mapcar #'reverse (pairup lst)) )
```

Alternatively, we could define a function that takes two arguments and forms a list from the two arguments taken in reverse order. Applying such a function via **map2** would produce an equivalent **reversepairup** function.

program:
```
(defun reversepair (x y) (list y x) )
(defun reversepairup (lst)
         (map2 #'reversepair lst) )
```

This new **reversepairup** program operates more directly than the original. It moves across the list only once, whereas the original traveled across the list twice, once to form the **pairup** version, then to reverse the paired components. However, the necessity for naming the obscure **reversepair** function to use it in the definition of **reversepairup** tries our patience. Fortunately, we can avoid having to come up with the name by using a very important higher order function, **lambda**, that delivers a function as its result.

A lambda expression is a Lisp form invoking the higher order function **lambda** to produce a function as the value of the expression. The form specifies the operations of the function in terms of formal arguments named within the form. Programmers use **lambda** to formulate functions without having to name them.[1]

The syntax of lambda expressions contains a defect similar to the one in the **defun** form. It is this: The form contains a list of formal argument names in parentheses. Normally, the first entity after any left parenthesis in a Lisp expression designates a function (except in quoted expressions). However, in a lambda expression, as in **defun**, the parentheses surrounding the formal arguments only provide grouping, not function invocation. Fortunately, this syntactic defect does not detract from **lambda**'s usefulness.

Lambda expressions and function names are equivalent entities in Lisp. Either may be used in place of the other. When a lambda expression appears in place of a function name following a left parenthesis, the remaining expressions up to the matching right parenthesis become the arguments of the lambda expression. The computation proceeds by substituting these arguments into the result specification of the lambda expression in places where the corresponding formal arguments of the lambda expression appear. This familiar substitution process is identical to the one that takes place when functions are applied by name, rather than by lambda expression.

Using a lambda expression instead of a named function, we construct an equivalent version of **reversepairup**.

---

[1]Lambda expressions form the basis for all function descriptions in Lisp. **Defun** and **let**, for example, can be viewed as shorthand for equivalent lambda expressions. Theoretical treatments of Lisp usually formulate the primitive functions, **car**, **cdr**, and **cons**, as lambda expressions. In fact, Lisp derives from Church's lambda calculus, where **lambda** plays the central role.

---

**lambda**—delivers a function as its value

| *lambda-expn* | is | **(lambda** (*arg-name...*) *result-spec*) |
|---|---|---|
| *arg-name* | is | *symbolic-atom* |
| *result-spec* | is | *expression* |

Note: the *result-spec* expression may contain references to *arg-names*.

The result delivered by **lambda** is a function that, when applied to a list of arguments, evaluates to the same value that the *result-spec* would deliver if all occurrences of the *arg-names* were replaced by the corresponding values in the list of arguments.

**Examples:**

```
((lambda (x y) (append x (reverse y))) '(a b) '(c d))
          is  (a b d c)
(mapcar #'(lambda (x) (list x 'dot)) '(a b))
          is  ((a dot) (b dot))
```

---

Program:  
```
(defun reversepairup (lst)
  (map2 #'(lambda (x y) (list y x)) lst) )
```

The functions **pairup** and **reversepairup** follow the same pattern: They apply **map2**, with an appropriate function as a first argument, to a list. We could simplify the definitions still further by developing a function accepting a function as its argument and delivering as its value a function applying **map2** in the manner illustrated in both **pairup** and **reversepairup**.

Program:  
```
(defun applymap2 (binaryfunction)
  #'(lambda (lst)
       (map2 binaryfunction lst) ))
(defun pairup (lst)
  (funcall (applymap2 #'list) lst) )
(defun reversepairup (lst)
  (funcall (applymap2 #'(lambda (x y)
              (list y x))) lst) )
```

The function **applymap2** accepts a function as its argument and delivers a function as its value. This is a second type of higher order function. The first type accepted a function as its argument and delivered an ordinary data value (e.g., **mapcar** and **map2**). A third possible combination would accept ordinary data as an argument and deliver a function as its value.

Reconsider the **suffix** function from the exercises of Chapter 8. It removed the first few components from a list by successively applying the **cdr** function. The first argument of **suffix** determined the number of components scheduled for removal (i.e., the required number of **cdr** applications): **suffix** applied **cdr** to its second argument as many times as there were components in its first argument.

We can produce a simpler description of **suffix** by constructing a function that delivers as its value another function that consists of repeated applications of **cdr**. The argument of this function will determine the number of repeated applications; in particular, the number of repetitions will match the number of components in the argument. Thus, **(repcdr ' (x x x))** will deliver a function equivalent to three successive applications of **cdr** to a list, making **(funcall (repcdr ' (x x x)) ' (a b c d e))** will be equivalent to **(cdr (cdr (cdr ' (a b c d e))))**.

The new function **repcdr** will facilitate an extremely simple definition of **suffix**.

```
Program:    (defun repcdr (n)
              (if (null n)
                  #'(lambda (lst) lst) ; no cdr's
                  #'(lambda (lst) ; n-1 + 1 cdr's
                       (funcall (repcdr (cdr n)) (cdr lst))
              ))
            (defun suffix (block lst)
              (funcall (repcdr block) lst) )
            (suffix ' (x x x) ' (a b c d e ))
Result:     (d e)
```

# ▪ SUMMARY

---

> **(lambda** (*arg-names...*) *expr***)**   delivers function that evaluates like *expr* when actual arguments are substituted for *arg-names* in *expr*

# ▪ EXERCISES

---

1. Write a function **map3** similar to **map2**, but operating on functions of three arguments instead of two.

2. Write a function, **compose**, that accepts two arguments, both of which are, themselves, functions, and delivers a result that is a function equivalent to applying the two argument functions in succession (*function composition*).

3. Write a function, **dbl**, that delivers as its result a function that makes a list of two elements out of its argument, each element being a copy of the argument: **(funcall (dbl) 'x) is (x x)**.

## ANSWERS

1. ```
(defun  map3 (ternaryfunction lst)
   (if (null lst)
       '()
       (cons (funcall ternaryfunction (car lst)
                             (cadr lst) (caddr lst))
             (map3 ternaryfunction (cdddr lst)))
   ))
```

2. ```
(defun  compose (f g)
   #'(lambda (arg) (funcall f (funcall g arg))) )
```

3. ```
(defun  dbl ()
   #'(lambda (arg) (list arg arg)) )
```
```

# CHAPTER 15

# NUMBERS

Numbers normally do not play a central role in symbolic computing applications. Nevertheless, requirements for counting and measuring frequently emerge as part of a symbolic computation, and this presents a need for numbers. Lisp, like other programming languages, accommodates this need by providing numbers and numeric operations as built-in features.[1]

Numbers are denoted in Lisp by customary decimal numerals: 194, 0, -27, 49.5, 1096.482, and so on. Very large or very small numbers that

---

[1]We have tried to concentrate on nonnumeric symbol manipulation in the preceding chapters, but have not succeeded entirely in that goal. The functions **prefix** and **suffix** (Chapter 8) had what amounted to a numeric argument. We represented this numeric value by a list with components that we ignored entirely, except in using the length of the list (the number of components) to denote a numeric value. This simple representation of numbers satisfied our purposes at the time because our uses for numbers made minimal computational demands. However, an application calling for large numbers or for complicated numeric computations such as addition or multiplication would find this representation much too cumbersome. For such applications we would have to conjure up a more efficient representation if Lisp had not already done this for us.

would have bulky representations in this form can incorporate a scale factor denoting a shift in the decimal point to the right or left: 6.02E23 (Avogadro's number), -1.602E-19 (electron charge, coulombs).

Lisp provides the usual numeric operations (addition, subtraction, etc.), comparison (equal to, less than, etc.), square root, absolute value, trigonometric functions, exponentials and logarithms, and a few others. In general, they operate generically, considering their arguments as numbers rather than as special kinds of numbers (such as integers or fractions). When you use them, you let the Lisp system decide on a representation. That is, you deal with them only through the provided functions. When the Lisp system displays a number to you in printed form, it uses the familiar decimal notation, just as you do when you write a number in your program.

The use of numeric functions is not sufficiently different from that of other functions to warrant many examples, especially since you have probably been dealing with numeric functions on a daily basis for a dozen years or more. Just to solidify the syntax, we will express two of our favorite numerical algorithms as Lisp functions.

Euclid's algorithm determines the greatest common divisor of two integers. Expressed as a Lisp function, it looks like this:

```
(defun  gcd (m n)
   (if (= n 0)
       m
       (gcd n (mod m n)) ))
```

To verify that this algorithm delivers the greatest common divisor, notice that it certainly does in case **n** is zero, for then **m** (the delivered result in case **n** is zero) divides both **n** and **m**, and no number with a larger magnitude than **m** can divide **m**.  Now suppose (hypothetically) that **gcd** functions properly for all magnitudes of its second argument up to, but not necessarily including the absolute value of **n**, where **n** is some nonzero integer. Then the algorithm will deliver **(gcd n (mod m n))** as its result.

Since the magnitude of **(mod m n)** is strictly smaller than that of **n**, our hypothesis indicates that **(gcd n (mod m n))** is the greatest common divisor of **n** and **(mod m n)**. Let $r$ denote **(mod m n)**, which means that $n=qm+r$ for some integer $q$; and let $g$ denote **(gcd n (mod m n))**. Then $g$ divides both **n** and $r$, and no larger number than $g$ divides both **n** and $r$. Furthermore, $g$ divides **m**, for if dividing **m** by $g$ left a remainder, then dividing $n=qm+r$ by $g$ would have to leave a remainder.

Even more important, no larger number than $g$ could divide both **m** and **n** because, if it did, it would also have to divide $r$ (any number that divides two of the three terms **n**, $q$**m**, and $r$ in the equation must also divide the third; otherwise an extraneous remainder would pop up

## Numeric Functions: Arithmetic

| | |
|---|---|
| (+ *number number...* ) | sum of *number*'s |
| (- *number*) | negation of *number* |
| (- *number subtrahend*) | (+ *number* (- *subtrahend*)) |
| (* *number number...* ) | product of *number*'s |
| (/ *number*) | reciprocal of *number* |
| (/ *number divisor*) | (* *number* (/ *divisor*)) |

## Numeric Functions: Comparison

| | |
|---|---|
| (= *number compar*) | **T iff** *number* **and** *compar* **have same value** |
| (/= *number compar*) | (**not** (= *number compar*)) |
| (< *number compar*) | **T iff** *number* **is less than** *compar* |
| (<= *number compar*) | (**not** (> *number number*)) |
| (> *number compar*) | (**and** (/= *number compar*) (**not** (< *number compar*))) |
| (>= *number compar*) | (**not** (< *number compar*)) |

## Numeric Functions: Miscellaneous

| | |
|---|---|
| (**sqrt** *number*) | $\sqrt{number}$ |
| (**abs** *number*) | (**if** (< *number* 0) (- *number*) *number*) |
| (**max** *number number*...) | largest of the *number*'s |
| (**min** *number number*...) | smallest of the *number*'s |
| (**exp** *number*) | $e^{number}$, e=2.71828... |
| (**expt** *number power*) | (**exp** (* *power* (**log** *number*))) |
| (**log** *number*) | Napierian logarithm of *number* |

## Numeric Functions: Trigonometric

| | |
|---|---|
| (**sin** *number*) | sin *number* (radians) |
| (**cos** *number*) | (**sin** (+ *number* (* 2 (**atan** 1)))) |
| (**tan** *number*) | (/ (**sin** *number*) (**cos** *number*)) |
| (**atan** *number*) | arctan *number* (radians) |

NUMERIC FUNCTIONS: INTEGER ARITHMETIC

| | |
|---|---|
| **(signum** *number*) | **(if (>** *number* **0) 1** |
| | **(if (=** *number* **0) 0    -1))** |
| **(floor** *number*) | greatest integer not exceeding *number* |
| **(ceiling** *number*) | **(- (floor (-** *number*)**))** |
| **(truncate** *number*) | **(\* (signum** *number*) **(floor** |
| | **(abs** *number*)**))** |
| **(round** *number*) | **(floor (+** *number* **0.5))** |
| **(mod** *integer clock*) | **(-** *integer* **(\*** *clock* **(floor** |
| | **(/** *integer clock*)**))))** |
| **(oddp** *integer*) | **(= (mod** *integer* **2) 1)** |
| **(evenp** *integer*) | **((oddp** *integer*)**)** |

somewhere, as we argued before). Thus, g must be the greatest common divisor of **m** and **n**.[2]

Another favorite algorithm approximates the area under a curve determined by a function of a single numeric variable (i.e., the definite integral of the function). Such a function determines a curve consisting of the points *{(x,f(x)): x is a number}* in the Cartesian plane. The area our algorithm approximates is that which is bounded by this curve, the vertical lines at *x=a {(a,y): y is a number}* , and at *x=b {(b,y): y is a number}*, and the x-axis *{(x,0): x is a number}*.

The rectangle bounded by these three lines, plus the horizontal line at *y=f(b) {(x,f(b)): x is a number}* provides a crude approximation, *(b-a)f(b)*, to the desired area. The algorithm observes that two rectangles would probably produce a better approximation. One of them would be half the above rectangle (the half bounded by the vertical line at *x=(a+b)/2 {((a+b)/2,y): y is a number}* and the vertical line at *x=b*). The other would be the rectangle bounded by the vertical lines at *x=a* and *x=(a+b)/2*, the x-axis, and the horizontal line at *y=f((a+b)/2) {(x,f((a+b)/2)): x is a number}*. This better approximation would be the sum *(f((a+b)/2)+f(b)) \*(b-a)/2*.

If the difference between the crude approximation and the better one is small enough, we take the better one as the result. If not, we apply the same idea to two curves, the part of the original curve between *x=a* and

---

[2]The insight required in this mathematical induction is essentially the same sort of insight you have been using to construct Lisp programs. Any recursive program is an induction of sorts, and discovering relationships between arguments and results of such programs involves no more than finding an ordering relationship in the sequences of arguments passed along in recursive invocations, then exploiting that ordering to verify the relationships. In our **gcd** induction, we observed that the magnitude of the second argument always decreased in subsequent invocations in the recursion, and we based our argument on that observation.

the midpoint and the part between the midpoint and $x=b$. Eventually, the rectangles will be so small that they will automatically match the desired area very closely.

```
(defun adaptivequadrature (f a b epsilon)
  (let (  (mid (/ (+ a b) 2))
          (crude (* (- b a) (f b))) )
    (let ( (better (/ (* (- b a) (+ (funcall f mid)
                                    (funcall f b))) 2)) )
      (if (< (abs (- better crude)) epsilon)
          better                              ; good enough
          (+ (adaptivequadrature f a mid epsilon)
                                              ; add two
             (adaptivequadrature f mid b epsilon))
                                              ; smaller areas
  ))))
```

■ EXERCISES

1. The **adaptivequadrature** function does a lot of extra computation. In particular, it computes the area of two rectangles to decide whether the approximation is good enough. Then, if it was not good enough, it recomputes those same areas in the next level of recursion. Use the old helping-function-with-an-extra-argument trick to avoid the extra computation.

ANSWERS

```
1. (defun adaptivequadrature (f a b epsilon)
     (defun aqh (a b crude)
       (let (  (mid (/ (+ a b) 2)) )
         (let ( (leftrectangle (* (/ (- b a) 2)
                                  (funcall f mid)))
                (rgtrectangle (/ crude 2))        )
           (if (< (abs (- leftrectangle rgtrectangle))
                  epsilon)
               (+ leftrectangle rgtrectangle); good enough
               (+ (aqh a mid leftrectangle)   ; add two
                  (aqh mid b rgtrectangle) ) ; smaller areas
     ))))
     (aqh a b (* (- b a) (funcall f b))) )
```

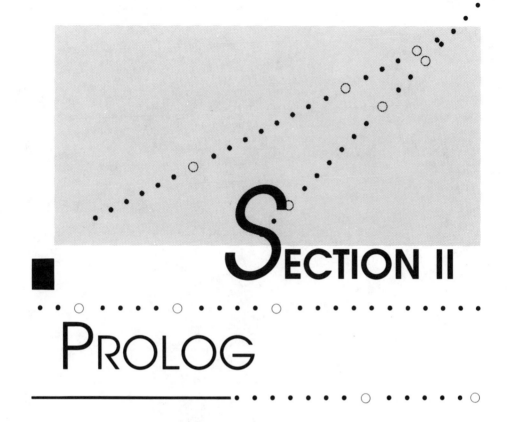

# SECTION II

# PROLOG

# CHAPTER 16

# NOTATION FOR DATA AND VARIABLES IN PROLOG

Prolog contains three principal elements: The *terms* that represent data objects (data structures), the *facts and rules* that specify relationships between terms, and the *queries* that ask questions about how terms are related with respect to a collection of facts and rules.

Terms include such simple objects as *atoms*, *numbers*, and *variables*, and more complex objects called *structures*. The terms of Prolog are similar to the expressions of Lisp in theme, although based on a somewhat different syntax. The BNF notation used to describe data in Lisp will also be used to supply a syntactic definition of Prolog terms. If you skipped the material on Lisp, we suggest you read the short note on BNF contained at the beginning of Chapter 2 (*Notation for Data in Lisp*).

Two types of *atoms* are distinguished in Prolog: *symbolic atoms* and *numbers*[1]. Symbolic atoms refer to specific objects (in the sense of data objects), and to specific relations (in the sense of fact or rule names, which we will elaborate on in the next chapter).

---

[1] Our discussion of numbers is deferred to Chapter 31.

*term*  is  *atom*
  or  *variable*
  or  *structure*

---

**symbolic atom**—identifier for a fixed data object

*symbolic_atom*  is  any sequence of lower- and uppercase letters, digits, and the special symbol *underscore* (_) that begins with a *lowercase* letter. The underscore is useful for constructing mnemonic identifiers by joining multiple words into a single identifier. The resulting identifier tends to be easier to read. (see, e.g., **escape_sequence** in the Examples).

**Examples**

    grandfather
    bill
    r2d2
    escape_sequence

---

Prolog *variables* stand in place of data values. Terms are substituted for variables during computations through a process called *unification*, which is discussed in detail in Chapter 19.

A more complex example of a Prolog term is a *structure*. A structure is a *compound object* built up from component terms. For example, consider the representation of a *graph*. A graph is composed of a set of *nodes* and a set of *edges* that connect nodes. Graph edges are nicely modeled by structures; for example,

**edge (3, 7)**

is a structure that might denote an edge of a graph that connects nodes 3 and 7. The name **edge** is called the *functor* of the structure, and **3** and **7** are called the *components* of the structure. Structures are nicely depicted through the use of *trees*.
For example,

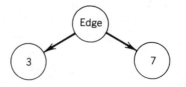

**variable**—identifier used to stand in place of data values

*variable* is any sequence of lower- and uppercase letters, digits, and the special symbol *underscore* (_) that begins with an *uppercase* letter or the underscore.

**Examples**

    X
    L1
    R2D2
    Set_of_Subsets

---

**Tree**—A hierarchical data structure.

*tree* is a finite set one or more of nodes consisting of a *root node* and zero or more disjoint subtrees, $S_1, \ldots, S_m$, each of which is, in turn, a tree.

---

is a tree representation of the structure **edge(3,7)** with root node **edge**, node **3** the root of **edge**'s first subtree, and node **7** the root of **edge**'s second subtree. Note that both the trees rooted by **3** and **7** have zero subtrees.

A more complex structure would be the high-level organization of a university,

    president(  provost,
                vp_for_administration(controller,personnel,
                                        police_department),
                vp_for_research)

with tree representation

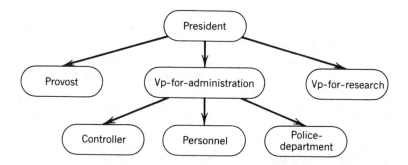

Structures are useful in the representation of objects with a fixed number of components. For example, the foregoing structure with functor

**president** has exactly three components (as does the structure with functor **vp_for_administration**), whereas the structure of the preceding example with functor **edge** has two components. A special type of structure that accommodates a varying number of components is a *list*.

In general, a list either contains no elements (termed the *empty list* and represented by [ ]) or is a structure of two components, the *head* and the *tail*. The head of a list is the first element of the list, and the tail is the list of remaining elements. The elements of a list are *ordered*, so it is meaningful to speak of the *i*th element of a list containing at least $i$ elements, $i \geq 1$. The end of a list is customarily represented as a tail that is the empty list.

Prefix notation is rather cumbersome for describing lists, being a hierarchical representation of an inherently flat structure. For this reason, and the fact that lists are the most important and frequently used structures of symbolic computing, Prolog provides a special syntax for lists. In particular, a nonempty list can be represented by either enumerating the components within the "[" and "]" symbols, $[c_1, \ldots, c_n]$, or separating the list into its first $m$ elements, $m \geq 1$, followed by the remaining tail list with the symbol "|", $[c_1, \ldots, c_n | t]$.

**Examples**

    [ ant,bat,cat ]

is a list containing the elements **ant**, **bat**, and **cat**,

    [ ant | [ bat,cat ] ]

is an equally valid way of expressing this same list, and

    composers(nationality(german),[bach,mozart,brahms],
    [ad1685,ad1756,ad1833])

is a structure containing structure **nationality(german)** as the first component, and lists **[bach,mozart,brahms]** and **[ad1685,ad1756, ad1833]** as the second and third components, respectively.

For notational convenience, we will simply stick with the special list syntax for the remainder of the book.

You most likely noticed that proper names in the foregoing examples were not capitalized, as would be correct in grammatical usage. Doing so would change these terms from atoms to variables, which would take the structure outside the class of fixed data. As such, the structure

    composer(name(berlioz),nationality(french))

**Structure**—A named object composed of component terms

| | | |
|---|---|---|
| *structure* | is | *functor* **(** *component* **[, component ]** … **)** |
| | or | *list* |
| *functor* | is | *symbolic_atom* |
| *component* | is | *term* |
| *list* | is | **[]** |
| | or | **[** *component* **[,** *component* **]** … **]** |
| **[** $c_1, …, c_m$ **|** *t***]** | is | a list whose first $m \geq 1$ components are $c_1, …, c_m$, and whose remaining components are those of the list *t*. |
| | Caveat: | Beware of the different usages of the braces. The braces "**[**" and "**]**" are BNF meta-symbols, whereas the braces "**[**" and "**]**" are the Prolog list delimiter symbols. |

**Examples**

```
composer(bach)
composer(name(berlioz),nationality(french))
composer(name(george,gershwin),
        nationality(american),
        composition(rhapsody_in_blue))
```

contains two terms, **name(berlioz)** and **nationality(french)**, both structures. The structure **name(berlioz)** has a single component, **berlioz**, which is an atom.

In contrast, the structure **name(Berlioz)** as the first component of the structure

```
composer(name(Berlioz),nationality(French))
```

has a single component, the variable **Berlioz**.

The interpretation of a structure is, of course, independent of the form of the structure. However, the example

```
composer(name(berlioz),nationality(french))
```

could be used to convey that someone named "**berlioz**" of nationality "**french**" is a "**composer**".

# ■ SUMMARY

1. Terms can be categorized into *constants*, *variables*, and *structures*.

2. An example of a Prolog constant is a *symbolic_atom*, which serves as the name of a fixed data object, the name of a fact, or the name of a rule. A symbolic_atom begins with a lowercase letter, and may contain any letters, digits, or the underscore.

3. A Prolog variable begins with an uppercase letter or the underscore and may contain any letters, digits, or the underscore. A variable is used to stand in place of data values.

4. A Prolog structure is a *compound object*. It consists of a name, called the *functor*, and a collection of objects, called the *components* of the structure.

5. A Prolog list is a special structure, in which zero or more elements may be enumerated within square braces, " [ " and " ] ", or the list may be decomposed into its first *n* elements followed by the list containing the remaining elements of the list, by separating the enumeration of those *n* elements from the list containing the remaining elements of the list by the vertical bar " | ".

# ■ BIBLIOGRAPHY NOTES

The classic treatment of basic data structures such as trees and graphs is given by

D. E. Knuth (1975) *The Art of Computer Programming. Volume 1: Fundamental Algorithms, (second edition)*, Addison–Wesley, Reading, Mass.

# ■ EXERCISES

1. How many components do each of the following terms have?

   (a) `[ginny, mae]`
   (b) `[ginny, mae|[]]`
   (c) `[ginny, mae|[fha_245]]`
   (d) `composers(nationality(german),[bach,mozart,brahms], [ad1685,ad1756,ad1833])`

---

**binary tree**—A hierarchical data structure

*binary tree*   is   *nil*, representing an empty tree

   or   a root node and two disjoint binary trees that are the left and right subtrees of the root.

---

(e) `[composers([bach,mozart,brahms],[ad1685,ad1756, ad1833],german)]`

(f) `[]`

(g) `[[]]`

(h) `[[]|[]]`

2. Which structures in Exercise 1 are lists?

3. What functors are named in Exercise 1?

4. What structures in Exercise 1 have components that are, themselves, structures?

5. Give an example of a list that has four components. The first two are lists of two structures each, the third a list with two components (the first a list, the second an atom), and the fourth a list of four atoms.

6. An important data structure in computing is the *binary tree.* Although binary trees are *not* special cases of the trees we defined earlier in the chapter, they are certainly similar.

   For example,

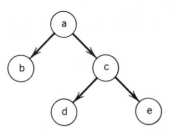

   is a binary tree with root node **a**, node **b** the root of **a**'s left subtree, and node **c** the root of **a**'s right subtree. Give a Prolog representation of this binary tree.

ANSWERS

1. (a) 2

   (b) 2

   (c) 3

   (d) 3

   (e) 1

   (f) 0

   (g) 1

   (h) 1

2. (a), (b), (c), (e), (f), (g), and (h).

3. `composers` and `nationality`.

4. (d), (e), (g), and (h).

5. ```
   [   [german(bach),american(copeland)],
       [birthdate(mozart,1756),birthdate(brahms,1833)],
       [[],four_seasons],
       [callisto,ganymede,europa,io]  ]
   ```

6. A Prolog representation of the given binary tree structure would be

   ```
   tree(a,tree(b,nil,nil),tree(c,tree(d,nil,nil),
   tree(e,nil,nil)))
   ```

   where **tree** is a functor for a 3-ary structure, with the first component representing a node name, the second and third components representing the left and right subtrees of that node (respectively), and **nil** a name representing the empty tree.
   ```

# CHAPTER 17

# PROPOSITIONAL FACTS, RULES, AND QUERIES

The terms discussed in the previous chapter were one of the three principal elements of Prolog. The other two, *facts and rules*, and *queries*, represent components of definitions of relations between terms, and questions about how terms are related by a collection of facts and rules. In this chapter, we begin to discuss how relations are defined, and how it is determined whether a sequence of terms is related with respect to a collection of relation definitions.

The basic entity in this scheme of things is the *relation*.

The syntax of Prolog facts, rules, and queries pertains to relations, be they of the propositional or more general variety. We will present the fundamental syntax and semantics of Prolog in this chapter through examples that use only propositional relations. In the next chapter we will talk about more general relations.

A Prolog *fact* expresses an unconditional relation between terms.

A Prolog *rule* resembles a fact, except that it asserts the truth of a relation that is guaranteed only under certain conditions.

**Relation**—relates a collection of terms

| *relation* | is | *identifier* |
| | or | *identifier* (*component* [, *component* ] ... ) |
| *component* | is | *term* |
| *identifier* | is | *symbolic_atom* |

Notes: A relation with *n* components is called an *n-ary* relation. *n* is said to be the *arity* of the relation.

A *0-ary* relation is called a *propositional relation*, or simply a *proposition*.

In both forms of relations, the *identifier* is called the *name* of the relation.

Syntactically, a *structure* formed by a functor and a collection of *n* components can only be distinguished from an *n-ary* relation within the context of a Prolog program or computation.

**Examples**

`solar_system(sun,planets(mercury,venus,earth))`

is a 2-ary relation with name **solar_system**, and terms **sun** (which is a *symbolic_atom*) and **planets(mercury,venus,earth)** (which is a *structure* with *functor* **planets** and *components* **mercury**, **venus**, and **earth**.

`round`

is a propositional relation.

---

**Fact**—asserts the truth of a relation

*fact*   is   *relation*.

Caveat: Note the period that follows the relation in the syntactic definition of a *fact*.

**Examples**

```
round.
ball_is_blue.
```

---

**rule**—asserts the conditional truth of a relation

| | | |
|---|---|---|
| *rule* | is | *conclusion* : - *condition* [, *condition* ]... . |
| *conclusion* | is | *relation* |
| *condition* | is | *relation* |

Notes: Each rule must contain at least one condition.

Like facts, rules are terminated with a period.

The use of the terms *conclusion* and *condition* is intended to convey the meaning of these syntactic components of a rule in its Prolog interpretation.

The use of the term *head* in place of *conclusion* and the term *goal* in place of *condition* prevails in the Prolog literature. We based our choice of this alternative terminology on our belief that these terms more clearly indicate their meaning.

The meaning of a rule will be coming forthwith.

**Example**

```
x_grandfather_z :- x_grandfather_y,
                   y_grandfather_z.
```

---

A rule logically connects a collection of relations in a conditional form. In particular, the rule

$$conclusion \quad :- \quad condition_1,$$
$$..., $$
$$condition_m.$$

is read,

the relation *conclusion* is true
**if**
$condition_1$ is true **and**
··· **and**
$condition_m$ is true.

We might use the relation **x_grandfather_z** to mean "**x** *is the* **grandfather** *of* **z**", the relation **x_father_y** to mean "**x** *is the* **father** *of* **y**", and the relation **y_father_z** to mean "**y** *is the* **father** *of* **z**". As such, the rule would be read:

**x** *is the* **grandfather** *of* z if    **x** *is the* **father** *of* **y** and
                                          **y** *is the* **father** *of* **z**.

The comma (",") separating the relations **x_father_y** and **y_father_z** is interpreted as a *logical and*. The *logical and* of two relations is interpreted to be *true* whenever both relations are *true*, and *false* otherwise.

The ":-" symbol separates the single relation to its left (e.g., the relation "**x_grandfather_y**" in the preceding example) from the list of relations separated by commas to its right (e.g., the list "**x_father_y**, **y_father_z**" in the preceding example). The relation to the left of the connective :- is called the *conclusion* of the rule, whereas the relations to the right of :- individually comprise the *conditions* of the rule and are compositely referred to as the *conditional-part* of the rule.

The :- is interpreted as *logical implication*. A relation x *logically implies* a relation y if y is *true* whenever x is *true*.

We use the term *statement* to refer to either facts or rules. A collection of statements with a common conclusion name $P$ is called a *definition of relation* $P$[1]. For example,

```
x_grandfather_z :- x_father_y,
                   y_father_z.
x_grandfather_z :- x_father_y,
                   y_mother_z.
```

is a Prolog definition of the relation **x_grandfather_z**. When multiple statements comprise the definition of a relation, the statements serve as *alternate* specifications that imply the truth of the relation being defined. Thus, continuing with our interpretation of the example relations, this relation definition would be read:

**x** is the **grandfather** of **z** if **x** is the **father** of **y** and **y** is the **father** of **z**; or, **x** is the **grandfather** of **z** if **x** is the **father** of **y** and **y** is the **mother** of **z**.

It should be noted that the Prolog interpreter attempts to infer the truth of a rule by evaluating the relations in the condition part from *left* to *right*. Also, when several statements define relation $R$, the Prolog interpreter attempts to infer query or condition references to $R$ by evaluating the statements of $R$ in a *top* to *bottom* order.

The ability to express relations using the logical connectives *and, or,* and *implication* gives Prolog considerable descriptive power. One important additional connective, *logical negation*, is interpreted as *true* if its single argument is *false*,and *false* otherwise. Prolog does provide negation directly. Its role somewhat differs from the other connectives presented, and we will discuss it after we have described the more fundamental facilities of Prolog.

---

[1]In the Prolog literature, the term *procedure* is used to describe what we call a *definition*. We choose this terminology to emphasize the denotational theme of our presentation of Prolog.

**Query**—a question asking whether a sequence of terms are related

*query* is ?- *relation* [ , *relation* ].... .

Notes: Each query must contain at least one relation.

Like facts and rules, queries terminate with a period.

Both the theory of logic programming and Prolog interpreters treat condition and query relations as a common entity. Our use of distinct terms for the two aims at making their contextual use more clear.

**Example**

```
?- x_grandfather_z,
   y_father_x.
```

The other major component of Prolog is the *query*. A query is essentially a condition relation, asking some question with respect to a collection of facts and rules. However, whereas conditions appear in the rules of a relation definition, queries are posed directly to the Prolog interpreter.

For example, from the definition of the relation **x_grandfather_z**, and the additional facts

```
x_father_y.
y_mother_z.
```

it can be inferred that **x_grandfather_z**. How? We begin with the query

```
?- x_grandfather_z.
```

The relation definition

```
x_grandfather_z :- x_father_y,
                   y_father_z.
x_grandfather_z :- x_father_y,
                   y_mother_z.
```

specifies that **x_grandfather_z** if **x_father_y** and **y_father_z**. Our data base of relation definitions contains the fact **x_father_y**, but there is no way to infer the truth of **y_father_z**, so this rule does not help. However, that relation definition also specifies that **x_grandfather_z** if **x_father_y** and **y_mother_z**. Our data base contains both the facts **x_father_y** and **y_mother_z**, so we conclude that **x_grandfather_z** is true.

When a query you enter is determined by the Prolog interpreter to be *true*, it responds with "**yes**".

```
?- x_grandfather_z.
```

**yes**

As this simple example illustrates, a Prolog computation is an attempt to *infer* the truth of a query.

Our first example contained only one relation definition comprised of two facts, but Prolog programs typically contain many relation definitions, each possibly containing several facts and/or rules. To begin to see how this works, we will consider the construction of a propositional relation for determining whether a corporation is legally exempt from federal tax.[2]

The basic statute dealing with organizations that are exempt from Federal income tax is section 501(c)(3) of the code. Under that section a wide variety of organizations can be recognized as exempt, including labor unions, social clubs, some cemeteries, and credit unions.

This is both a little too complex and a lot too vague to consider accurately characterizing in Prolog at this stage of the discussion, so a description of a simplified view of the code will be developed.

---

### SECTION 501(C)(3) OF THE FEDERAL TAX CODE

Section 501(c)(3) of the Code provides for the exemption from taxation of:
Corporations, and any community chest, fund, or foundation, organized and operated exclusively for religious, charitable, scientific, testing for public safety, literary, or educational purposes, or to foster national or international amateur sports competition (but only if no part of its activities involve the provision of athletic facilities or equipment), or for the prevention of cruelty to children or animals, no part of the net earnings of which inures to the benefit of any private shareholder or individual, no substantial part of the activities of which is carrying on propaganda, or otherwise attempting to influence legislation, (except as otherwise provided in subsection (h)), and which does not participate in, or intervene in (including the publishing or distributing of statements), any political campaign on behalf of any candidate for public office.

---

[2]Although this example is based on the 1985 tax code, it presents a grossly oversimplified view of the actual process of determining exempt status of organizations.

First, we note that the definition given by the code can be broken up into several parts in order to determine whether an organization meets the exemption requirements.

The first requirement is that an organization must be a corporation, community chest, fund, or foundation. We will call this requirement the *organizational test*, and describe it in Prolog by the following relation definition:

```
organizational_test :- corporation.
organizational_test :- community_chest.
organizational_test :- fund.
organizational_test :- foundation.
```

The second condition imposes the requirement that an organization be operated exclusively for the purposes enumerated under section 501(c)(3) of the tax code. This requirement will be referred to as the *operational test*. Basically, the operational test is satisfied if the organization must be operated for religious, charitable, scientific, or other listed purposes. In a similar fashion, we get the following Prolog relation definition that describes the operational test:

```
operational_test :- religious.
operational_test :- scientific.
operational_test :- charitable.
operational_test :- public_safety.
operational_test :- literary.
operational_test :- educational.
operational_test :- amateur_athletic.
operational_test :- prevention_of_cruelty.
```

Questions often arise in this area because of the difficulty involved in defining distinctly what is meant by concepts such as *charitable* or *religious*. These are extremely subjective concepts that can cause much debate. For our purposes, we will simply assume that an organization is charitable if it provides both disaster aid and shelter for the homeless.

```
charitable :- disaster_aid,
              shelter_for_homeless.
```

As for the religious test, we will require that it have either a "church", "temple", or "mosque" to hold services in, and that it holds weekly services.

```
religious :- structure_test,
             weekly_services.
```

```
structure_test :- church.
structure_test :- temple.
structure_test :- mosque.
```

The next question to resolve is whether the the organization's net earnings are used to benefit private parties. What this question really relates to is the possibility that private individuals, and particularly insiders with respect to the organization, might make use of the organization's exempt status to generate personal gain. Lawyers refer to this condition as the *inurement test*.

Such gain can be generated in a variety of ways, such as having the organization pay excessive salaries or having the organization buy property from an insider at an excessive price.

```
inurement_test :- no_excessive_salaries,
                  no_bogus_property_transactions.
```

The final two questions are related to legislative and political activities. Section 501(c)(3) of the tax code indicates that no substantial part of an organization's activities can consist of attempts to influence legislation. As for political activities, section 501(c)(3) organizations are not allowed to participate in political campaigns at all. We will combine these into a *political test*.

```
political_test :- no_lobbying,
                  no_campaigning.
```

The exempt status test can then be completed by the following entry-level relation definition:

```
exempt :- organizational_test,
          operational_test,
          inurement_test,
          political_test.
```

The Prolog system can use this representation of the tax code to infer the exempt status of an organization if we enter a few basic facts about the organization in question.

```
corporation.
```

```
shelter_for_homeless.
```

```
leukemia_fund.
```

```
march_of_dimes.
```

```
amateur_athletic.
```

```
cultural_patron.
```

```
literary.
```

```
disaster_aid.
```

```
no_lobbying.
```

```
no_excessive_salaries.
```

The query

```
?- exempt.
```

is posed, and the interpretation begins.

The definition of the relation **exempt** states that **exempt** is *true* if all of **organizational_test**, **operational_test**, **inurement_test**, and **political_test**, is true. Consider first **organizational_test**, which is true if any of **corporation**, **community_chest**, **fund**, or **foundation** is true. As we asserted **corporation** as a fact, we conclude that **organizational_test** is true.

Next, consider **operational_test**, which is true if any of **religious**, **scientific**, or **charitable** is true. There is a relation definition for determining whether **religious** is true that requires that **structure_test** and **weekly_services** be true. Now, **structure_test** is true if any of **church**, **temple**, or **mosque** is true. However, there are neither facts nor rules for any of these relations, so we conclude that **structure_test** is false, and, in turn, that **religious** is false.

The next relation to evaluate is **scientific**. There are neither facts nor rules for **scientific** so we conclude that it is false.

Another possibility is for **charitable** to be true. The relation definition for **charitable** requires that **disaster_aid** and **shelter_for_homeless** both be true. There are asserted facts for each of these relations, so **charitable** is true.

This implies that **operational_test** is true. This brings us to the **inurement_test** relation, which requires that both **no_excessive_salaries** and **no_bogus_property_transactions** be true. There is an asserted fact for **no_excessive_salaries**, but neither facts nor rules for **no_bogus_property_transactions**. Therefore, **inurement_test** is false, and likewise, **exempt** is false.

The result of the query is then the following:

```
?- exempt.
no
```

## ■ SUMMARY

1. A *relation* has the form $r$ or $r(t_1,...,t_m)$, $m \geq 1$, where $r$ is a *symbolic_atom* and each of $t_1,...,t_m$ are *terms*.

2. In the former case, $r$ is a *0-ary*, or *propositional*, relation. A relation $r(t_1,...,t_m)$, $m \geq 1$, is called an *m-ary* relation.

3. Relations can assume the value true or false.

4. A Prolog *fact* asserts the truth of a relation unconditionally.

5. A Prolog *rule* asserts the truth of a relation $(r)$ conditional on the truth of all of one or more relations $(c_1,...,c_m, m \geq 1)$. The relation $r$ is called the *conclusion* of the rule, and the relations $c_1,...,c_m$ are called the *conditions* of the rule. Each $c_i$, $1 \leq i \leq m$, is called a *condition*.

6. Facts and rules are the *statements* used to form definitions of relations in Prolog.

7. A *relation definition* defines a relation $p$ as a collection of facts with relation name $p$ and rules with conclusion relation name $p$.

8. A *query* is an interrogation of the Prolog interpreter in reference to one or more relations.

## ■ BIBLIOGRAPHY NOTES

The application of automated reasoning and artificial intelligence in law has been a growing area of study. A notable example in the area of tax law is the TAXMAN system of McCarty. A critical survey of contemporary issues in artificial intelligence and exempt tax law is given by Hair and Mueller.

L. T. McCarty (1977) Reflections on TAXMAN: An experiment in artificial intelligence and legal reasoning. *Harvard Law Review* **90**, 837–893.

L. T. McCarty (1980) The TAXMAN project: Towards a cognitive theory of legal argument, in B. Niblett (ed), *Computer Science and Law: An Advanced Course*, Cambridge University Press, New York, pp. 23–43.

D. C. Hair and R. A. Mueller (1985) *Knowledge-based Expert System Methods in Exempt Organization Tax Law*, Technical Report CS-85-03, Department of Computer Science, Colorado State University, Fort Collins, Col.

# ■ EXERCISES

1. Write a propositional fact or rule that describes each of the following (in each case, there are many good answers):

   (a) "music is loud"

   (b) "mary is the aunt of billy"

   (c) "bill is the grandfather of chris if tom is the father of chris and bill is the father of tom"

   (d) "if tom and warren are brothers, and linda is the daughter of warren, then linda is the niece of tom"

2. What additional statements could be added to the given statements in the tax code example to permit **exempt** to be inferred?

## ANSWERS

1. (a) `music_is_loud`.

   (b) `mary_aunt_billy`.

   (c) bill_grand_father_chris :- tom_father_chris,
                        bill_father_tom.

   (d) linda_niece_tom :- tom_brother_warren,
                        linda_daughter_warren.

2. It would be sufficient to assert the following relations as facts: **no_bogus_property_transactions** and **no_campaigning**.

# RELATIONS CONTAINING VARIABLES

With the basics of defining and querying relations established in terms of propositional relations, we can now look at the more general forms of relations. In general, a relation is of the form $r(t_1,...,t_m)$, $m \geq 1$, where $t_1,...,t_m$ are terms.

Recall the proposition **x_grandfather_y** that was used to express that **x** was the **grandfather** of y. If we wanted similarly to express the relation "**y** is the **grandfather** of **z**," a new and different proposition would be needed, for example, **y_grandfather_z**. In general, if propositions were used to express this type of relation, a *distinct* proposition would be needed for each distinct pair of objects that were related by **grandfather**.

By using a *2-ary* relation, say *grandfather*$(t_1,t_2)$, the single relation name *grandfather* can be used to relate as many pairs of distinct terms as you desire. Thus, we could use the facts

```
grandfather(bill,mary).
```

```
grandfather(bill,bob).
```

to assert that **bill** is the **grandfather** of **mary**, and **bill** is the **grandfather** of **bob**. This helps somewhat, but being limited to relating only fixed terms still forces us to enumerate all the possibilities. What we need is some way to denote generic terms; that is, terms that stand for whole classes of possibilities. For this, Prolog provides the notion of *variable*.

Recall from Chapter 16 that a Prolog variable is written as an atom that begins with either an uppercase letter or the underscore symbol ("_"). For example, the names

**_cup_of_coffee      X      Y      MI5agent      R2D2**

are all valid variable names, whereas among

**cup_of_coffee      x      y      3CPO**

none are valid variable names.

In general, a Prolog variable can have any term as its value. A variable assumes a value through a process called *instantiation*. Armed with variables, a general definition can be written for the *grandfather* relation:

```
grandfather(X,Z)  :- father(X,Y),
                     father(Y,Z).
grandfather(X,Z)  :- father(X,Y),
                     mother(Y,Z).
```

The relation definition can be read:

For all terms **X** and **Z**, **X** is the **grandfather** of **Z** if there exists a term **Y** such that **X** is the **father** of **Y** and **Y** is the **father** of **Z**, **or**, for all terms **X** and **Z**, there exists a term **Y** such that **X** is the **father** of **Y** and **Y** is the **mother** of **Z**.

In other words, it states that **grandfather(X,Z)** is true if at least one of the following is true:

1. If **X** and **Z** are instantiated to *any* terms (say $t_X$ and $t_Z$), there is a term $t_Y$ that can be substituted for each occurrence of **Y** in the conditional part of the rule such that both the conditions **father**$(t_X, t_Y)$ and **father**$(t_Y, t_Z)$ are true.

2. If **X** and **Z** are instantiated to *any* terms (say $t_X$ and $t_Z$), there is a term $t_Y$ that can be substituted for each occurrence of **Y** in the conditional part of the rule such that both the conditions **father**$(t_X, t_Y)$ and **mother**$(t_Y, t_Z)$ are true.

We can make two important observations about the interpretation of variables in a Prolog program:

1. All occurrences of the same variable name *within a single statement* denote the same variable. Variables occurring in distinct statements denote distinct and unrelated variables.

   Thus, in the foregoing example, the variable **X** in the first statement of the relation definition of **grandfather** is unrelated to the variable **X** in the second statement of that definition.

2. Variables permit single statements to assert many different facts or conclusions. A fact containing variables asserts that all instances of that fact that result from consistently instantiating its variables are true.[1]

   A rule containing variables asserts that each instance of its conclusion that results from a consistent instantiation of all the variables in the rule is true, provided that all the conditions resulting from that instantiation are true.

For example, the rule

```
grandfather(bill,X)  :- father(bill,Y),
                        father(Y,X).
```

can be read:

For all terms **X**, **bill** is the **grandfather** of **X** if there exists a term **Y** such that **bill** is the **father** of **Y** and **Y** is the **father** of **X**.

Using the following specification of *grandfather*:

```
grandfather(X,Z)  :- father(X,Y),
                     father(Y,Z).

grandfather(X,Z)  :- father(X,Y),
                     mother(Y,Z).
```

and asserting the following collection of facts:

---

[1] By *consistent instantiation*, we mean that the same term is substituted for all occurrences of the same variable in a statement. There is one exception: the variable denoted by the underscore symbol (_) need not stand for the same term throughout the statement. It may be instantiated with one term at one point in the statement and with a different term at another point in the statement. The underscore variable is used as a wild card in rule specifications to avoid having to create different variable names for all places where the underscore appears.

```
father(john,bill).
father(bill,mary).
father(bill,tom).
father(tom,chris).
father(tom,bob).
mother(mary,june).
mother(mary,katie).
```

the Prolog interpreter can infer certain facts about the *grandfather* relation in response to queries.

Suppose we posed the query

```
?-   father(X,bill).
```

which would be read: "Is there an instantiation of **X** that makes **father(X,bill)** true?"

In other words,

Does there exist a term $t_X$ that can be substituted for **X** such that **father($t_X$,bill)** is true?

Prolog would respond with

```
yes.  X = john
```

Note that when there are variables in the terms of a query, the interpreter delivers the values used to instantiate those variables to establish the truth of the query. When a query containing variables is determined to be false, the implication is that there are *no* terms that can be substituted for the variables that make the query true. The response in this case is simply **no**.

What would you expect to result from the following query?

```
?-   father(bill,X).
```

Clearly, both **X=mary** and **X=tom** are valid answers. The Prolog interpreter will return the first answer it can infer, which in this case is **X=mary**. It then asks whether we wish it to search for other solutions. If we respond in the affirmative, **X=tom** would be the response. As there are no additional solutions, a further request for another solution would be answered with **no**.

Requests for alternative instantiations of variables that make a query true are achieved by typing "**;**" followed by a carriage return when the interpreter returns with one set of variable/term substitutions that make the query true.

Prolog is capable of inferring the truth of a query using both facts and rules. For example, if we put forth the query

```
?-  grandfather(bill,Grandchild).
```

the response would be

```
yes.  Grandchild=chris.
```

Would you like to see how the interpreter arrives at this conclusion? Well, the query can be expressed prosaically as:

Does there exist a term $t_{Grandchild}$ that can be substituted for **Grandchild** such that **grandfather(bill, $t_{Grandchild}$)** is true?

To discover this result, the Prolog interpreter begins by using the two rules that define the **grandfather** relation.

```
grandfather(X,Z)  :- father(X,Y),
                     father(Y,Z).

grandfather(X,Z)  :- father(X,Y),
                     mother(Y,Z).
```

It substitutes **bill** for each occurrence of **X** in the first statement of the definition and substitutes **Grandchild** for each occurrence of **Z** in the first statement of the definition.

The result is the following "instantiated" version of the relation definition:

```
grandfather(bill,Grandchild)  :- father(bill,Y),
                                  father(Y,Grandchild).

grandfather(X,Z)  :- father(X,Y),
                     mother(Y,Z).
```

Thus, the answer is true if the interpreter can first find an object **Y** such that **father(bill,Y)** is true, and then verify that **father(Y,Grandchild)** is also true. If not, then the second statement with the variables **X** and **Z** instantiated to **bill** and **Grandchild**, respectively, must be true or else the query is false.

The first shot would be to use the fact

```
father(bill,mary)
```

thus instantiating **Y** with **mary**. But this leads to a dead end, since there is no term $t_{Grandchild}$ such that **father(mary, $t_{Grandchild}$)**.

Do things now come to a screeching halt with failure and rejection? Fortunately not. The Prolog interpreter continues its search; it goes back to **father(bill,X)** and discovers that it is also true for **father(bill,tom)**. One further step reveals that **father(tom,chris)** is a fact, so the Prolog interpreter responds in the affirmative with

**yes. Grandchild = chris**

Note that after it was determined that **father(mary,Grandchild)** was false for all terms $t_{Grandchild}$, the interpreter *uninstantiated* **Y** before attempting to instantiate it with another term (e.g., in this case **tom**).

For now, do not worry about how the Prolog interpreter is able to infer queries when there are many possible variable instantiations that need to be considered before one that satisfies a query is found. We will discuss the *and/or* control flow and built-in *backtracking* mechanism of Prolog in Chapters 23 and 26.

# ▪ SUMMARY

1. Variables permit a single relation to assert many facts, conditions, or conclusions.

2. A variable is instantiated when a term is substituted in its place.

3. Consistent instantiation requires all occurrences of the same variable within a single statement to be instantiated to the same value.

4. Variables occurring in separate statements are unrelated, even if they have the same name.

# ▪ EXERCISES

1. Give a relational definition of "aunt" (assuming "sister" and "father") and "cousin" (assuming "father", "brother", "sister", and "mother") in Prolog.

ANSWERS

1. ```
   aunt(A,X)  :- sister(A,B),
                 parent(B,X).

   cousin(C,S)  :- parent(F,C),
                   sibling(F,B),
                   parent(B,S).
   parent(P,C)  :- father(P,C).
   parent(P,C)  :- mother(P,C).
   sibling(C,S)  :- brother(C,S),
   sibling(C,S)  :- sister(C,S).
   ```
   ```

# CHAPTER 19

# UNIFICATION: HOW THE INTERPRETER INSTANTIATES VARIABLES

A principle called *unification* governs the process of instantiating variables with terms. Unification is basically an attempt to *match* two terms, by instantiating the variables contained in the terms. Thus, substitution plays a central role in the process.

A *substitution* is a set of mappings from variables to terms, written

$$\{(X_1, t_1), \ldots, (X_m, t_m)\}$$

where $X_1, \ldots, X_m$ are distinct variables and $t_1, \ldots, t_m$ are terms.

A substitution $\alpha = \{(X_1, t_1), \ldots, (X_m, t_m)\}$ is *applied* to a term $t$, written $t\alpha$, by simultaneously replacing each occurrence of $X_i$ in $t$ by $t_i$ ($1 \leq i \leq m$).

For example, let $\alpha = \{(X, [a, b]), (Y, tree(L, R))\}$. Then

$$
\begin{aligned}
[X, x]\alpha &= [[a, b], x] \\
[X, Y]\alpha &= [[a, b], tree(L, R)] \\
tree(X, Y)\alpha &= tree([a, b], tree(L, R))
\end{aligned}
$$

---

## MOST GENERAL UNIFIERS

A most general unifier $\beta$ of two terms $t_1$ and $t_2$ has the following properties:

1. It is a unifier of $t_1$ and $t_2$, and

2. For every other unifier $\alpha$ of $t_1$ and $t_2$, $t_1\alpha$ is an instance of $t_1\beta$ and $t_2\alpha$ is an instance of $t_2\beta$. That is, if $\alpha$ is a unifier of $t_1$ and $t_2$, then there exists a substitution $\gamma$ such that

$$t_1\alpha = (t_1\beta)\gamma = (t_2\beta)\gamma = t_2\alpha$$

Note: The unification of two terms is denoted by their most general unifier if they unify, and is undefined otherwise.

---

For any substitution $\alpha$ and term $t$, we call $t\alpha$ an *instance* of $t$. Thus, $[[a,b],x]$ is an instance of $[X,x]$ since $[X,x]\alpha = [[a,b],x]$, with $\alpha = \{(X, [a,b])\}$.

A substitution $\alpha$ is said to *unify* two terms $t_1$ and $t_2$ whenever $t_1\alpha = t_2\alpha$. Similarly, two terms *unify* if there is a substitution that unifies them.

The substitution $\{(X,cat),(Y,dog),(Z,animal(dog))\}$ is a *unifier* of the terms [dog,animal(Y)] and [Y,Z].

There is no unifier for the terms [dog,animal(X)] and [X,animal(cat)].

In general, if two terms can be unified, then there are many substitutions that unify them. In such cases, we can talk about a *most general unifier*.

For example, the substitution $\alpha = \{(X,cat),(Y,dog),(Z,animal(dog))\}$ is a *unifier* of the terms [dog,animal(Y)] and [Y,Z], but not the most general unifier. A most general unifier of [dog,animal(Y)] and [Y,Z] would be $\beta = \{(Y,dog),(Z,animal(dog))\}$. Note that for $\gamma = \{(X,cat)\}$, $t_1\alpha = (t_1\beta)\gamma$.

Unification is a basic computational mechanism in the interpretation of Prolog programs. The unification of terms is attempted each time the Prolog interpreter attempts to infer a query or a condition in a rule. It determines not only how variables are instantiated to terms, but also, in part, how a computation proceeds. It combines *pattern matching*, *conditional selection*, and *substitution* into a single high-level control mechanism.

To aid in the debugging of Prolog programs, we give an operational accounting of the unification algorithm and its role in Prolog computations.

Suppose we wish to define a relation that assumes that the first argument $L_1$ is instantiated and that the second argument $L_2$ is uninstan-

tiated. The second argument is instantiated by the execution of the
relation definition as follows:

$$L_2 = \begin{cases} \text{atom}, & \text{if } L_1 = \text{bx2} \\ [\,], & \text{if } L_1 = [\,] \\ X, & \text{if } L_1 = [X] \\ Y, & \text{if } L_1 = [X|Y] \end{cases}$$

The following program satisfies this specification; It contains four
facts:

```
decomp(bx2,atom).
decomp([ ],[ ]).
decomp([X],X).
decomp([X|Y],Y).
```

The relation definition **decomp** realizes its conditional behavior through
the unification mechanism. Assuming the variable **z** to be initially uninstantiated, the query

```
?-  decomp([ ],Z).
```

would be answered with **yes**, with **z** instantiated to the value **[ ]**. This
results from the successful unification of the terms in the respective
positions of the query relation **decomp([ ],Z)** with the fact relation
**decomp([ ],[ ])**.

In general, Prolog seeks to *resolve* the inference of a relation emanating
from either a query or a condition of a rule by searching the data base
of facts and rules from top to bottom for either a fact relation or the
conclusion relation of a rule that has the same relation name, the same
relation arity, and with terms that unify with those in the respective
positions of the relation. We say that a query (or condition) relation
and a conclusion relation *resolve* if they have the same relation name,
the same relation arity, and their terms in each respective component
position unify.

Thus, in the case of the query **decomp([ ],Z)**, the first statement in
the data base (i.e., the four-fact program) would be **decomp(bx2,atom)**.
The interpreter first checks to see if the two relations have the same
name and arity. If not, the relations do not resolve and the computation
cannot continue with that fact. In the case of this example, both relations have the relation name **decomp** that is of *arity 2*, so unification is
attempted on each component of the relation.

The first component of the query relation is the empty list, **[ ]**,
whereas the first argument of the fact relation is the constant **bx2**. This
will bring things to a temporary halt, as a constant can never unify with
a list.

In fact, *a constant will only unify with another identical constant, with a variable that is instantiated to the identical constant, or with an uninstantiated variable.*

In the case of a list, *a list will only unify with another list containing the same number of elements, where the elements in the corresponding positions of the two lists unify, with a variable instantiated to the same, or with an uninstantiated variable.*

Thus, our query relation does not resolve with the first data base fact. The Prolog interpreter will then proceed to the next fact, **decomp([ ],[ ])**, which again, has a common name and *arity*. This time, however, the first arguments are both empty lists. So the conditions for list unification are trivially satisfied.

What about the second arguments? Well, the second argument of the condition relation is **z**, whereas the second argument of the fact relation is **[ ]**. Recall that we assumed that **z** was initially uninstantiated.

Then these arguments will unify, since *an uninstantiated variable will unify with any other term, including another uninstantiated variable.* When an uninstantiated variable is unified with a term, it is instantiated to the value of that term. In the special case of the unification of two uninstantiated variables, if one of the variables becomes instantiated while they are unified, the other assumes the same value.

The situation in our example is then clear: **decomp([ ],Z)** resolves with **decomp([ ],[ ])**, allowing the query to be successful and the uninstantiated variable **z** to assume the value **[ ]**.

What form must a query or condition relation take to resolve with the third fact, **decomp([ X ],X)**? Besides the obvious necessity of being a relation of the same functor and *arity*, its first argument must be a list containing a single element, whereas its second argument must be the single element of the first argument.

Thus, the query

```
?-  decomp([hello],Z).
```

will fail to resolve with the first two data-base statements, but will resolve with the relation **decomp([X],X)**. Why? Because **[hello]** is a list containing the single element **hello** and **z** is uninstantiated. Thus, the term unification is successful and **z** is instantiated to **hello**.

What if, instead, we assumed that **z** was initially instantiated to the value **goodbye**, and we posed the same query? The first arguments will again unify, with variable **X** assuming the value **hello**. But as the second argument is **X**, and **X** is now instantiated to the constant **hello**, the interpreter cannot unify the distinct constants **hello** and **goodbye**. Thus, the relations will fail to resolve.

Should a query or condition relation fail to resolve with any of the first three data-base facts, the fourth fact, **decomp([X|Y],[Y])**, represents the last chance. In this case, we must have a nonempty list as the first argument and the list obtained by removing the first element of the first argument list as the second argument.

In fact, given the *context* of this fact, the query or condition relation must be a list that contains at least *two* elements or else it would have resolved with the third fact. This is a consequence of the Prolog interpreter's searching strategy, namely from top to bottom.

Consider the query

```
?-  decomp([ant,bat,cat],Z).
```

where **Z** is assumed to be initially uninstantiated.

This query will not resolve with any of the first three facts, so the fourth fact is considered. This will be successful, since the fact variable **X** can assume the value **ant**, and the fact variable **Y** the value **[bat,cat]**. The result would be to instantiate **Z** to the value **[bat,cat]**.

How about something more interesting? Suppose we pose the query

```
?-  decomp([ant,bat,cat],[Z1|Z2]).
```

where **Z1** and **Z2** are assumed to be initially uninstantiated.

Again, this query will not unify with any of the first three facts. In considering how things match up with the fourth fact, we again observe that the fact variable **X** will assume the value **ant**, and the fact variable **Y** will assume the value **[bat,cat]**.

The unification procedure will then attempt to unify the term **[Z1|Z2]** with **[bat,cat]**. The result would be to instantiate **Z1** to the first element of **[bat,cat]**, that is, **bat**, and to set **Z2** to the rest of the list, that is, **[cat]**.

You may have wondered about situations where you wish to unify all terms with a particular component of a relation. A simple solution is to introduce a variable not appearing elsewhere in the statement to be that component. However, since this is the only occurrence of the variable, then any value it may assume resulting from unification will never be read. Thus, its usage is somewhat unusual and may be misleading (e.g., someone reading the program might think you are missing references to that variable).

It is precisely for such situations that Prolog offers a special term represented by the underscore symbol, "_".

Since the underscore term is never instantiated, it will never have a specific value associated with it. It loosely represents a "wild term" or "place marker" that matches any other term.

## Resolving Relations via Unification in Prolog

Let $f_1(t_{11}, \ldots, t_{1m})$ and $f_2(t_{21}, \ldots, t_{2n})$ be a query or condition relation and a conclusion relation. Then the following rules determine whether $f_1$ and $f_2$ will unify:

1. $f_1$ and $f_2$ must be identical symbolic atoms.

2. $m = n$.

3. Each of the $m = n$ terms in the corresponding argument positions must unify, that is, $t_{11}$ must unify with $t_{21}$, $t_{12}$ must unify with $t_{22}$, and so on.

The term unification rules are as follows:

3a. If either of the two arguments $t_{1i}$ and $t_{2i}$ are constants (either atoms or numbers), then the other argument must currently have or be able to assume that identical constant value.

3b. If either of $t_{1i}$ and $t_{2i}$ are structures, then their unification rules are identical to those for a query or condition relation and a conclusion relation (simply check for identical *functor* names in step (1), common structure arity in step (2), and continue with term unification in step (3)).

3c. If either of $t_{1i}$ and $t_{2i}$ are lists, then the other argument must currently have or be able to assume a list as its value, where the list contains the same number of elements, each of the pairs of elements in corresponding positions of the two lists must unify as terms.

3d. If either of $t_{1i}$ and $t_{2i}$ are instantiated variables, they are covered by the foregoing rules, depending on the values they represent.

3e. If both $t_{1i}$ and $t_{2i}$ are uninstantiated variables, they unify. Further, if either is instantiated while they are unified, the other assumes the same instantiated value.

## Underscore Symbol (_)

The *underscore symbol* (_) is a term that unifies with any other term (including another underscore) but is never instantiated.

Note: A relational statement $R$ obtained from another statement $S$ by substituting underscore terms for variables that occur exactly once in $S$ is equivalent to $S$.

## ■ SUMMARY

1. A basic computational mechanism in Prolog is *relation resolution*. A query or condition relation and a conclusion relation *resolve* if they have the same relation name, the same relation arity, and their terms in each respective component position unify.

2. Unification is a process of matching terms. It determines, in part, not only how variables are instantiated to values, but also how a computation proceeds. It combines *pattern matching, conditional selection*, and *substitution* into a single, high-level control mechanism.

3. When Prolog seeks to resolve a query or condition of a rule, it searches the data base of facts and rules from top to bottom for either a fact relation or the conclusion relation of a rule that will unify with the query or condition relation.

4. The unification procedure can be described recursively; such a description is given in the text of the chapter.

## ■ BIBLIOGRAPHY NOTES

The resolution of Prolog relations and the unification of Prolog terms is based on the *resolution theorem proving* method of Robinson. For discussions of resolution theorem-proving, see any of Manna, Nilsson, Bundy, or Wos and coworkers.

J. A. Robinson (1965) A machine-oriented logic based on the resolution principle. *J. ACM* **12**(1): 23–41.

Z. Manna (1974) *Mathematical Theory of Computation*, McGraw–Hill, New York.

N. J. Nilsson (1980) *Principles of Artificial Intelligence*, Tioga Publishing, Palo Alto, Calif.

A. Bundy (1983) *The Computer Modelling of Mathematical Reasoning*, Academic Press, New York.

L. Wos, R. Overbeek, E. Lusk, and J. Boyle (1984) *Automated Reasoning: Introduction and Applications*, Prentice-Hall, Englewood Cliffs, N.J.

# ■ EXERCISES

1. For each pair of terms, state whether they unify. If they do unify, give their most general unifiers.

   (a) **X** and **x**.

   (b) **[X]** and **x**.

   (c) **[X|[Y|Z]]** and **[x]**.

   (d) **[X|[Y|Z]]** and **[a,b,c,d,e]**.

   (e) **[X|[X|Z]]** and **[a,b,c,d,e]**.

   (f) **[X|[Y,Z]]** and **[a,b,c,d,e]**.

   (g) **house(bathroom,bedroom,garage([Cars]))** and **house(A,B,C)**.

## ANSWERS

1. (a) Yes. Their most general unifier is given by the substitution {(**X, x**)}.

   (b) No. The term **[X]** is a list containing a single element, whereas the term **x** is a symbolic_atom.

   (c) No. The term **[X|[Y|Z]]** is a list containing two or more elements, whereas the term **[x]** is a list containing exactly one element.

   (d) Yes. Their most general unifier is given by the substitution {(**X, a**),(**Y,b**),(**Z, [c,d,e]**)}.

   (e) No. The term **[X|[X|Z]]** is a list containing two or more elements, in which the first two elements unify. The first two elements of the term **[a,b,c,d,e]** do not unify.

   (f) **[X|[Y,Z]]** and **[a,b,c,d,e]**. No. The term **[X|[Y,Z]]** is a list containing exactly three elements, whereas the term **[a,b,c,d,e]** is a list containing exactly five elements.

   (g) Yes. Their most general unifier is given by the substitution {(**A,bathroom**),(**B,bedroom**) , (**C,garage([Cars])**)}.

# CHAPTER 20

■

# RECURSION

Virtually all useful relation definitions in Prolog employ some form of recursion. Informally, *recursion* is a form of specification in which the meaning of something is defined in terms of itself. This permits specifications containing a finite number of symbols to denote relationships that call for an unbounded amount of computation, just as loops do in conventional programs.

To illustrate the power and convenience of recursion in Prolog, consider the 2-*ary* relation, **member(X, L)**, which is *true* if the term $X$ is a component of the list $L$, and *false* otherwise.

We will develop the relational definition using a methodology in which the result of a simple test indicates that either a relation **member(X, L)** can be inferred or denied immediately, or the relation **member(X, L)** may be inferred or denied by a *simpler* condition, **member(X, L1)**, where $L1$ contains one fewer component than $L$. The computation required to answer a query about the member relation terminates because it asks a sequence of questions about simpler and simpler arguments, finally arriving at one it can verify directly.

## Relational Meaning of List Membership

1. $X$ is in $L$ if $X$ is the first element of $L$.

2. If $X$ is not the first element of $L$, then $X$ is in $L$ if and only if $X$ is in the list containing the remaining elements of $L$.

The test alluded to is *"is X the first element of L?"* Given a query or condition relation $R$, if the result of the test is *true*, then $R$ is *true*. If the result is *false*, then $R$ is *true* if and only if the simpler relation *"X is contained in the list L1"* can be inferred.

Based on this idea, the relation **member** is defined in Prolog as:

```
member(X, [X|Y]).
member(X, [Q|Y]) :- member(X,Y).
```

The first statement is *true* if the second argument of the relation is a list containing one or more elements (i.e., **[X|Y]**) and the first element of that list is the first element of the relation.

The second statement is *true* if the second argument is a list containing one or more elements and the first argument (**X**) satisfies the **member** relation with the list obtained from the second argument by omitting the first element.

If we entered the query

```
?- member(y, [w,x,y,z]).
```

with the **member** program entered into the data base, the query would be determined to be true.

This follows from the second statement of the Prolog definition of **member**, which is *true* if the second argument is a list containing one or more elements and the first argument satisfies the **member** relationship with that list sans its first element. The second argument, **[w,x,y,z]**, is a list containing four elements, and the first argument, **y**, is a member of **[x,y,z]**.

Note that in the definition of **member** some variables need not be instantiated to verify the statements. (The instantiation of **Y** in the first statement is unnecessary, and the instantiation of **Q** in the second statement is unnecessary.) This is a good place to use the underscore variable. Whenever there is a single occurrence of a variable in a Prolog statement, that variable can be replaced with the underscore without altering the meaning of the program. In the case of the fact, **member(X, [X|Y])**, note that **Y** is simply a place marker. We could replace it with the underscore to obtain an equivalent fact that is easier to write (we do not have to conjure up the name **Y**), easier to read (there is no confusion about the use of the values **Y** denotes), and easier for the Prolog interpreter to process (no instantiation is required).

```
member(X, [X|_]).
```

For the rule, **member(X, [Q|Y]) :- member(X,Y)**, the occurrence of **Q** in the second argument of the conclusion relation is again simply a place marker. Replacing it gives the following equivalent rule:

```
member(X, [_|Y]) :- member(X,Y).
```

Like all Prolog definitions of relations, the definition of **member** contains information leading to a *yes/no* decision. The substitution of fixed data for variable arguments in a query is reminiscent of computations in many other languages, including Lisp.

---

### RELATIONAL MEANING OF APPENDED LISTS

$L$ is the list obtained by appending lists $L_1$ and $L_2$ if

1. $L_1 = [\ \ ]$ and $L_2 = L$, or

2. $L_1 = L$ and $L_2 = [\ \ ]$, or

3. $L_1 = [x_1, ..., x_i]$, $L_2 = [x_{i+1}, ..., x_n]$, and $L = [x_1, ..., x_n]$.

---

For our second example, consider a relational definition of *append*. Basically, *append* relates a list $Z$ with the list obtained by appending the elements of a list $Y$ to the elements of a list $X$.

We will define a *3-ary* relation **append(X,Y,Z)**, which is true if **Z** is the list obtained by appending list **X** with list **Y**.

First, a few observations:

1. Appending the empty list with any list **L** yields **L**.

2. For any nonempty list **L**, **L=[A|X]**, appending **L** with any other list **Y** will produce the list **[A|Z]**, where **Z** is the list obtained by appending **X** with **Y**.

These observations can be rewritten as recursive relations, motivating the following Prolog program:

```
append([],L,L).
append([A|X],Y,[A|Z]) :- append(X,Y,Z).
```

The first statement handles the trivial case of appending the empty list to another list without the need for recursion. The second statement denotes that a list $L$ of $m_1 + m_2 \geq 1$ elements is the list obtained by appending list $L1$ of $m_1 \geq 1$ elements, and list $L2$ of $m_2 \geq 0$ elements, if

1. The first elements of $L1$ and $L$ are the same, and

2. The list obtained by appending the elements of $L1$ sans its first element, with the elements of $L2$, is the list $L$ sans its first element.

## Examples

First something conventional.

```
?- append([ant,bat],[cat,dog],L).
```

```
yes. L = [ant,bat,cat,dog]
```

```
?- append([butter,battle],[book],[butter,battle,book]).
```

```
yes.
```

Next, something a little more interesting.

```
?- append([cat,in,the,hat],S,[cat,in,the,hat,by,
                                      dr,seuss]).
```

```
yes. S = [by,dr,seuss]
```

```
?- append([one],L,[one,two,three,four]).
```

```
yes. L = [two,three,four]
```

The response of the Prolog interpreter can be easily explained in terms of a piece of the relation we gave for *append*:

$L = [x_1, \ldots, x_n]$ is the list obtained by appending lists $L_1 = [x_1, \ldots, x_i]$ and $L_2$ if either $L_2 = [\ ]$, where $i = n$, or $L_2 = [x_{i+1}, \ldots, x_n]$, where $1 \leq i < n$.

Given $L =$ [one,two,three,four] and $L_1 =$ [one],

**Definition 2.** [one,two,three,four] is the list obtained by appending lists [one] and $L_2$ if $L_2 =$ [two,three,four], $1 \leq 1 < 4$.

## RELATIONAL MEANING OF A LIST PREFIX

1. [ ] is a prefix of any list.

2. The list $P = [x_1, \ldots, x_i]$ is a prefix of the list $L = [x_1, \ldots, x_n]$, where $1 \le i \le n$.

That is, by letting $i = 1$, we get $x_1$=**one**, $x_2$=**two**, $x_3$=**three**, and $x_4$=**four**.

The relational definition of *append* lends itself to simple denotations of many related list decision problems. Consider the problem of determining whether the elements of one list are a *prefix* of another list.

Note that **append(L1,L2,L)** is *true* if and only if **L1** is a prefix of **L**, according to the relational definitions of *append* and *prefix* (we leave it to you to verify this). Thus, a relational definition of **prefix** in Prolog would simply be

```
prefix(P,L) :- append(P,_,L).

?- prefix([cat,in,the,hat],[cat,in,the,hat,by,dr,seuss]).

yes.

?- prefix([P|[and,ham]],[green,eggs,and,ham])

yes. P = [green,eggs]
```

We want to design a Prolog relation that removes all but one of the contiguous occurrences of the same term from a list of terms.

For example, the list

```
[too,too,much,of,a,very,very,very,good,thing]
```

would be related to

```
[too,much,of,a,very,good,thing]
```

However, the list

```
[mary,hartman,mary,hartman]
```

would be related to

[mary,hartman,mary,hartman]

Let us make some observations about a 2-*ary* relation, "**remove_contiguous**".

1. Nothing can be removed from an empty list of terms.

2. If the first two elements of the list are the same, then the result is that obtained from removing contiguous elements from the given list *sans* its first element.

3. If neither 1 nor 2 is true, then the result is given by inserting the first element at the beginning of the list obtained by removing contiguous elements from the given list *sans* its first element.

Represented in Prolog, these observations translate to:

```
remove_contiguous([],[]).
remove_contiguous([X,X|L],R) :- remove_contiguous
                                          ([X|L],R).
remove_contiguous([X|L],[X|R]) :- remove_contiguous
                                          (L,R).
```

Note that the second statement must appear before the last statement. If the two statements were interchanged, the relation would hold for any two lists with the same elements.

```
?- remove_contiguous([big,jo,jo,white,and,little,arnold,
          arnold,are,members,of,lambda,lambda,lambda],L).

yes. L = [big,jo,white,and,little,arnold,are,members,
          of,lambda].

?- remove_contiguous([rollum,rollum,rollum,keep,them,
          doggies,rollin],[rollum,keep,them,doggies,rollin]).

yes.
```

# ■ SUMMARY

Recursive definitions use the relation being defined as part of the definition. This use of circular definition makes it possible to describe all manner of computational relationships in a finite amount of space without constraining the amount of input data or results.

The secret to constructing recursive definitions in Prolog is to discover some terms for which results can be specified directly and to find a way to describe results for all other terms as combinations of directly specifiable partial results and/or recursively defined partial results with simpler terms.

# ■ Bibliography Notes

Several books on functional programming contain material on general principles of recursive programming, including Burge, Henderson, and Glaser, Hankin, and Till.

W. H. Burge (1975) *Recursive Programming Techniques.* Addison–Wesley, Reading, Mass.

P. Henderson (1980) *Functional Programming: Application and Implementation.* Prentice–Hall, Englewood Cliffs, N.J.

H. Glaser, C. Hankin, and D. Till (1984) *Principles of Functional Programming.* Prentice–Hall, Englewood Cliffs, N.J.

# ■ Exercises

1. Define a 2-*ary* relation, **suffix**, in Prolog, without the use of **append** as defined in this chapter. The relational meaning of **suffix** is

   (a) [ ] is a suffix of any list.

   (b) A list $P = [x_i, \ldots, x_n]$ is a suffix of a list $L = [x_1, \ldots, x_n]$, where $1 \leq i \leq n$.

2. Define another 2-*ary* relation, **suffix**, in Prolog, which uses **append**.

3. Define a 3-*ary* Prolog relation **prefix_before_suffix(P,S,L)**, that is *true* if **S** is a suffix of **L** (as denoted in 1), and **P** is the list of elements that precede **S** in **L**.

4. Define a 2-*ary* Prolog relation, **sublist**, whose relational meaning is as follows:

   (a) [ ] is a sublist of any list.

   (b) A list $S = [x_i, \ldots, x_j]$ is a sublist of a list $L = [x_1, \ldots, x_n]$, if $1 \leq i \leq j \leq n$.

5. Define a 3-*ary* relation **prefix_before_sublist(P,S,L)**, that is *true* if **S** is a sublist of **L** (as denoted in 4), and **P** is the list of elements that precede **S** in **L**.

## ANSWERS

1. ```
   suffix(L,L).
   suffix(S,[_|L]) :- suffix(S,L).
   ```

2. ```
   suffix(S,L) :- append(_,S,L).
   ```

3. ```
   prefix_before_suffix(P,S,L) :- append(P,S,L).
   ```

4. ```
   sublist(S,L) :- prefix(S,L).
   sublist(S,[_|R]) :- sublist(S,R).
   ```

5. ```
   prefix_before_sublist([],S,L) :- prefix(S,L).
   prefix_before_sublist([X|P],R,[X|L]) :-
                           prefix_before_sublist(P,R,L).
   ```
   ```

# PROPAGATION AND ACCUMULATION OF RESULTS

A common problem in computing is finding the smallest and largest elements of a set. We will refer to this as the *min/max problem.*

Let **minmax(Min,Max,L)** be a 3-*ary* relation that is *true* if:

1. **L** is a nonempty list,

2. **Min** is the smallest element in **L**, and

3. **Max** is the largest element in **L**.

We will assume that a 2-*ary* relation **order(X,Y)** exists and carries the value *true* if **X** precedes (or matches) **Y**, and *false* if **X** follows **Y**.

One way to approach a relational definition of **minmax** that can be directly mapped into Prolog is based on the following observations:

1. If **L** contains a single element $x$, then both **Min** and **Max** are $x$.

2. If **L** contains two or more elements $[x_1, \ldots, x_n]$, **Min** is the smaller of $x_1$ and $Min2$ and **Max** is the larger of $x_1$ and $Max2$, where $Min2$ and

$Max2$ are the smallest and largest elements of the list $[x_2, \ldots, x_n]$ (i.e., the list $L$ without its first element).

In Prolog, this translates to

```
minmax(X,X,[X]).
minmax(Min,Max,[X|L])  :- minmax(Min2,Max2,L),
                          min(X,Min2,Min),
                          max(X,Max2,Max).


min(X,Y,X)  :- order(X,Y).
min(X,Y,Y)  :- order(Y,X).


max(X,Y,X)  :- order(Y,X).
max(X,Y,Y)  :- order(X,Y).
```

This definition specifies the correct result, but a Prolog system making use of it will not be as economical in its use of space in the computer as it could be with other relational definitions. The problem is that the conditions `min(X,Min2,Min)` and `max(X,Max2,Max)` cannot be inferred until `minmax(Min2,Max2,L)` has been inferred, as the Prolog interpreter attempts to infer the conditions of the rule from left to right.

Thus, assuming the third term `[X|L]` of the conclusion is a list of $n$ elements, there will be $n-1$ **min** relations and $n-1$ **max** relations waiting to be initiated as conditions after the recursion of the condition `minmax(Min2,Max2,L)` has terminated with the fact `minmax($x_n$,$x_n$,[$x_n$])`, where $x_n$ is the last element of $L$. All the waiting conditions take up space in the computer, and none of them can be deleted until they have been either denied or inferred.

Although this is not necessarily a serious problem, the need for this space can be avoided by expressing the relation definition in a different style. The new style will be to "carry" along the largest and smallest of those list elements already examined. *Propagating* these intermediate results avoids the need to leave conditions waiting to be processed.

This approach will require introducing two additional arguments in which to propagate the results. We now describe the basis for a 5-*ary* relation, `minmax5(Min,Max,L,Cmin,Cmax)`. The argument `Cmin` represents the smallest element thus far scanned, whereas the argument `Cmax` represents the largest element thus far scanned.

Given this meaning of `minmax5`, the following statements are evident:

1. If `L` is empty, then `Min` is `Cmin` and `Max` is `Cmax`.

2. If `L` contains one or more elements $[x_1, \ldots, x_m]$, then

   (a) `minmax5(Min,Max,[$x_1$,...,$x_m$],Cmin,Cmax)` is `minmax5(Min, Max,[$x_2$,...,$x_m$],$x_1$,Cmax)` if $x_1$ is smaller than `Cmin`.

RELATIONAL MEANING OF `MINMAX5 (MIN, MAX, L, CMIN, CMAX)`

For 2-*ary* order relation **order** and list representation $L$ of set $S$,

`minmax5 (Min, Max, L, Cmin, Cmax)` if 1. `order (Min, $x$)` for all elements $x$ in the list $[Cmin|L]$, and

2. `order ($x$, Max)` for all elements $x$ in the list $[Cmax|L]$

where **order** is supplied as a 2-*ary* relation.

(b) `minmax5 (Min, Max, [$x_1, \ldots, x_m$], Cmin, Cmax)` is `minmax5 (Min, Max, [$x_2, \ldots, x_m$], Cmin, $x_1$)` if $x_1$ is larger than **Cmax**.

(c) `minmax5 (Min, Max, [$x_1, \ldots, x_m$], Cmin, Cmax)` is `minmax5 (Min, Max, [$x_2, \ldots, x_m$], Cmin, Cmax)` if $x_1$ falls between **Cmin** and **Cmax** (inclusive).

Furthermore, since $x_1$ will fall into one of the categories (a), (b), or (c), we have all cases covered.

This motivates the following definition of **minmax5** in Prolog:

```
minmax5 (Cmin, Cmax, [], Cmin, Cmax).
minmax5 (Min, Max, [X|L], Cmin, Cmax) :- order (X, Cmin),
                            minmax5 (Min, Max, L, X, Cmax).
minmax5 (Min, Max, [X|L], Cmin, Cmax) :- order (Cmax, X),
                            minmax5 (Min, Max, L, Cmin, X).
minmax5 (Min, Max, [X|L], Cmin, Cmax) :- minmax5 (Min, Max, L,
                            Cmin, Cmax).
```

You might object to the need to deal with two additional arguments. If so, you are justified. It is almost always bad policy to dump the vestiges of implementation considerations on the individuals who use a program.

Fortunately, this is easily dealt with by *hiding* the 5-*ary* behind a 3-*ary* relation. The 3-*ary* relation represents the interface between the 5-*ary* relation and the rest of the world. For this example, we would define the following 3-*ary* relation **minmax (Min, Max, L)** as follows:

```
minmax (X, X, [X]).
minmax (Min, Max, [X|L]) :- minmax5 (Min, Max, L, X, X).
```

As a second example of where recursively propagating results can be useful, we will consider the simulation of the simplest and perhaps most

FINITE STATE AUTOMATA (FSA)—A MODEL OF COMPUTING
MACHINERY

*FSA* is a model of a computing machine consisting of a *finite set of states*, and a *set of transitions between states* that are triggered by the occurrence of *input symbols*.

*Notes:* The operation of an FSA entails scanning a finite sequence of input symbols from left to right and making state transitions on each symbol scanned, as defined by the set of state transitions.

There is one special state called the *initial state* of the FSA. When an FSA begins to scan a sequence of input symbols, it always starts in the initial state.

There is a special subset of the set of states called the *final state set*.

After the entire sequence of input symbols has been scanned, the FSA is left in some state (say *S*). If *S* is a final state, then the FSA *accepts* the sequence of input symbols. If not, it rejects it.

well-known mathematical model of a computing machine: the *finite state automaton*.[1]

FSA's are commonly described using *state transition diagrams*, in which states are given as labeled nodes, the initial state is marked with a dash (–), each final state is marked with a plus (+), and an arc from state *X* to state *Y* labeled with symbol *S* specifies that a transition is made to state *Y* when the FSA is in state *X* and the symbol *S* is scanned.

**Example**

Figure 21.1 is a state transition diagram of an FSA that accepts input sequences of *x*'s and *y*'s that contain an even number of *x*'s and an odd number of *y*'s.

The state labeled "ee" is the state the FSA is in after an even number of *x*'s and an even number of *y*'s have been scanned; this is also the initial state, so it is marked with a dash (—). The FSA is in the "eo" state after an even number of *x*'s and an odd number of *y*'s have been scanned; this

---

[1]The automaton model of computation forms a basis of procedural programming paradigms, whereas the lambda and predicate calculus models lay a foundation for denotational programming paradigms. Either paradigm can simulate the other, although finite automata, by themselves, are not quite enough.

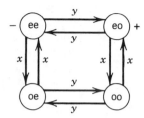

**Figure 21.1** Simple Example of an FSA.

is the only final state, signifying acceptance, so it is marked with a plus (+). The state "oo" occurs after an odd number of $x$'s and an odd number of $y$'s have been scanned, and the state "oe" after an odd number of $x$'s and an even number of $y$'s have been scanned.

To simulate an FSA in Prolog, we will define the FSA as a collection of relations. First, the fact **initial_state(S)** will assert that **S** is the initial state of the FSA. Next, the fact **final_states(F)** will define **F** to be the list of final states of the FSA. Finally, the set of state transitions are given as a collection of facts of the form **next_state(Current_State, Input_Symbol, Next_State)**, with one fact for each state transition.

For the example FSA described herein, a Prolog description of that FSA would be as follows:

```
initial_state(ee).

final_states([eo]).

next_state(ee,x,oe).
next_state(ee,y,eo).

next_state(oe,x,ee).
next_state(oe,y,oo).

next_state(oo,x,eo).
next_state(oo,y,oe).

next_state(eo,x,oo).
next_state(eo,y,ee).
```

Given this form of Prolog definition of an FSA, we now define a 1-*ary* relation **fsa(Input_Sequence)** that is *true* if **Input_Sequence** is

---

RELATIONAL MEANING OF **FSA(INPUT_SEQUENCE)**

---

**fsa(Input_Sequence)**  if  $([Input\_Sequence, S_0] \xrightarrow{*} S_n,$
where **initial_state($S_0$)**,
**final_states(F)**, and
**member($S_n$, F)**.

---

RELATIONAL MEANING OF **SCAN(INPUT_SEQUENCE, S)**

---

**scan(Input_Sequence, S)**  if  $([Input\_Sequence, S] \xrightarrow{*} S_n,$
where **final_states(F)**, and
**member($S_n$, F)**.

*Note:*  **fsa** is a special case of **scan** where the starting state of the computation is the designated initial state.

---

accepted by the FSA. The relation **fsa** will be defined in terms of a relation **scan**, which scans the input sequence from left to right, making state transitions according to the relation **next_state**, and accepting when the entire sequence has been scanned and the FSA is left in a final state.

To denote the **fsa** relation, we begin with some notation. Let *a* be any symbol that can occur in an **Input_Sequence**, and $\alpha$ any **Input_Sequence** of length $\geq 0$. Then for any finite state automaton defined by the **initial_state**, **final_states**, and **next_state** relations, we introduce a relation " $\xrightarrow{*}$ ", defined on *a*, $\alpha$, and states $s_0$, $s_1$, and $s_n$ as follows:

$([], s_0) \xrightarrow{*} s_0$  *the empty Input_Sequence, a special case*
$([a \mid \alpha], s_0) \xrightarrow{*} s_n$  *if* **next_state**$(s_0, a, s_1)$ *and* $(\alpha, s_1) \xrightarrow{*} s_n$

Informally, $(\alpha, s_0) \xrightarrow{*} s_n$ states that $s_n$ is the FSA state reached after scanning $\alpha$ from state $s_0$.

Note that the relation **fsa** is independent of the specific elements of an FSA definition (i.e., the initial state, the set of final states, and the state transitions). In this sense, **fsa** is a universal interpreter for finite state automata. To make it simulate a different automaton, simply change the definitions of the **initial_state**, **final_state**, and **next_state** relations.

The idea is to *propagate* the current state in the recursion of **scan**, so that when the sequence has been scanned, an accept/reject decision can be made immediately. The definition of the relations **fsa** and **scan** in Prolog are

```
fsa(Input_Sequence)  :-  initial_state(S),
                         scan(Input_Sequence, S).

scan([], State)  :-  final_states(F),
                     member(State, F).

scan([Symbol|Seq], State)  :-  next_state(State, Symbol, Next),
                               scan(Seq, Next).
```

where **member** is defined as in Chapter 20 (Recursion).

The condition **initial_state(S)** in the definition of **fsa** causes the interpreter to instantiate **S** with the initial state of the FSA. Similarly, the condition **final_states(F)**, in the definition of **scan**, instantiates **F** with the set of final states of the FSA. Given a current state (**State**) and an input symbol (**Symbol**), the condition **next_state(State, Symbol, Next)**, in the definition of **scan**, instantiates **Next** with the next state of the FSA, as determined by the state transition facts.

```
?- fsa([x,y,x,x,y,y,x]).

yes.

?- fsa([]).

no.

?- fsa([y]).

yes.
```

Another example of propagation is accumulating partial results in the components of relations. This is nicely illustrated through the relational definition of list reversal.

To obtain a computationally useful description of list reversal, we offer the following observations:

1. Reversing the empty list trivially yields the empty list.

2. If we have a nonempty list **L** and we remove its first element **x** to obtain the new list **L1**, then we can obtain the reverse of **L** by simply placing **x** at the end of the reverse of **L1**.

---

RELATIONAL MEANING OF LIST REVERSAL

1. [   ] is the list obtained by reversing [   ].

2. $[x_n, \ldots, x_1]$ is the list obtained by reversing $[x_1, \ldots, x_n]$, $n \geq 1$.

**Example**

`[one,two,three]` is the list obtained by reversing `[three,two, one]`.

---

This motivates a definition of a 2-*ary* relation, **reverse(L,R)**, which is given in Prolog as:

```
reverse([],[]).
reverse([H|L],R)  :-  reverse(L,L1),
                      append(L1,[H],R).
```

This definition of list reversal is correct, but it has an undesirable property: It uses time and space inefficiently. This can be seen by noting that each execution of the rule

```
reverse([H|L],R)  :-  reverse(L,L1),
                      append(L1,[H],R).
```

results in the lists **L1** and **[H]** being appended. Further, assuming our definition of **append** in Chapter 20 (Recursion), there will be $m$ recursive steps in the inference of the relation **append(L1,[H],S)** if **L1** is a list of length $m$.

As there are $n$ recursive steps used in inferring **reverse(L,R)** if **L** is a list of length $n$, the Prolog interpreter will attempt to infer **append** on lists of length $1, 2, \ldots, n - 1$. Noting that

$$\sum_{i=1}^{n-1} i \ \ = (n^2 - n)/2$$

we see that **reverse** uses time and space that is roughly quadratic in the length of the list being reversed, which means we are handling each element several times (about $n/2$ times if there are $n$ elements in the list).

Intuitively, it seems that each element should only have to be manipulated once in reversing the list. The problem is that we are appending each element at the end of the reversed list of elements that followed it

---

### Relational Meaning of REVERSE3 (L, P, S)

reverse3(L,P,S)   if   reverse(L,R) and append(R,P,S).

---

in the given list, and, in doing so, we are forced to rescan elements that have already been placed in their final positions of the result list.

The goal, then, is to eliminate the use of **append** in the rule that produces the recursion. We do this by accumulating the result in a third argument. The new list reversal will require about $n$ steps (roughly linear time in the length of the list).

The new *3-ary* relation, **reverse3(L, P, S)**, is denoted to be *true* if **S** is the list obtained by appending list **L** reversed with list **P**.

To form a basis for a relational definition of **reverse3** in Prolog, we make the following observations:

1. **reverse3([],P,P)** is *true*, since the reverse of **[]** is **[]**, and appending **[]** with **P** yields **P**.

2. **reverse3([X|R],P,S)** is equivalent to **reverse3(R, [X|P],S)**.

Then the Prolog definition of the relation **reverse** using **reverse3** would be:

```
reverse(L,R) :- reverse3(L,[],R).

reverse3([],P,P).
reverse3([X|L],P,S) :- reverse3(L,[X|P],S).


?- reverse([b,o,b],X).

yes. X=[b,o,b]

?- reverse([a,b,c],[c,b,a,a]).

no.

?- reverse(X,[a,b,c]).

yes. X=[c,b,a]
```

## ■ SUMMARY

*Pumping* is a programming technique in which an extra component is introduced to accumulate the final result, piece by piece. The use of the pumping component surplants the need to postpone computation, and often saves space by allowing the internal state of the computation to be dynamically discarded. This programming technique can therefore save both space and time.

## ■ BIBLIOGRAPHY NOTES

The idea of accumulating partial results in logic program relation components is an outgrowth of the same technique used in functional programming. See the bibliographic remarks at the end of Chapter 11 in the Lisp section on *Pumping* for bibliographic references.

## ■ EXERCISES

1. Define a relation, **equal_a_b(L)**, in Prolog, where **equal_a_b(L)** is *true* if **L** contains an equal number of **a** and **b** terms.

2. Define a relation, **swap_prefix_suffix(K, L, S)**, in Prolog, where **swap_prefix_suffix(K, L, S)** is *true* if

   (a) **K** is a sublist of list **L**[2] , and

   (b) **S** is the list obtained by appending the suffix of **L** following an occurrence of **K** in **L**, with **K** and with the prefix that precedes that same occurrence of **K** in **L**.

   **Examples**

   ```
   ?- swap_prefix_suffix([c,d], [a,b,c,d,e],S).

   yes. S=[e,c,d,a,b]

   ?- swap_prefix_suffix([c,e], [a,b,c,d,e],S).

   no.

   ?- swap_prefix_suffix(K, [a,b,c,d,e], [b,c,d,e,a]).

   yes. K=[a]
   ```

---

[2]The term "sublist" is defined by the relation **sublist** described in the exercises of Chapter 20 (*Recursion*).

ANSWERS

1. ```
equal_a_b(L) :- eqab(L,[]).

eqab([],[]).

eqab([a|L],[a|S]) :- eqab(L,[a,a|S]).
eqab([a|L],[b|S]) :- eqab(L,S).

eqab([b|L],[b|S]) :- eqab(L,[b,b|S]).
eqab([b|L],[a|S]) :- eqab(L,S).
eqab([C|L],S)     :- eqab(L,S).
```

2. ```
swap_prefix_suffix(K,L,S) :- swapps(K,L,S,[]).

swapps([],L,S,Acc)     :- append(L,Acc,S).
swapps(K,L,S,Acc)      :- append(K,P,L),
                          append(P,K,S1),
                          append(S1,Acc,S).
swapps(K,[X|L],S,Acc)  :- swapps(K,L,S,[X|Acc]).
```

# CHAPTER 22

# DIVIDE AND CONQUER

Having dealt with data structures and algorithms, you most likely discovered that an effective way to solve problems is to find one or more subproblems that are in some way simpler or smaller than the original problem, to solve those problems (often by applying the same idea in a circular fashion), and finally to glue the partial solutions together to form the full solution.

All the recursive relations that we have designed in our examples and in the solutions to exercises have been constructed in this mode. However, all these solutions have had in common a curious property. Namely, they divided the problem into two parts: One part was trivial to solve and could be represented as either a fact or nonrecursive rule, and the other was solved by a rule that included recursive conditions.

This is an effective solution for some problems. But for many problems it is possible to find a better subdivision in which the subproblems have about the same complexity. When this is the case, the *balance* in complexity among the partial solutions can lead to an enormous improvement in the overall computation time required for solving the full problem, compared to what could be had by dividing it into an unbalanced collection of subproblems.

The technique of dividing problems into subproblems of approximately the same complexity, and solving each of those via a recursive application of this same idea, is known as the *divide and conquer* strategy. Ubiquitous in algorithm design, algorithms designed with this strategy save untold thousands of hours of computer time every year. In this chapter, we will see how to apply this technique to the important problem of arranging a sequence of items in alphabetical order, the *sorting problem*.

Suppose our data are a collection of record albums. Most fastidious record collectors insist on having their albums sorted by recording artist, to allow for fast and easy access. We will assume that each data element is a structure, **album(artist,title)**, and our goal will be to write a Prolog relation definition that will arrange a list of album structures in alphabetical order of artist.

Following the line of reasoning that we have grown accustomed to in designing recursive denotations of relations, we might come up with the following idea: the sorted collection of album structures can be obtained by selecting the alphabetically smallest structure and placing it in front of the sorted list of remaining structures.

We will assume that the alphabetical ordering is determined by the relation **order(X1,X2)**. Our definition of **order** uses a built-in Prolog alphabetical order relation, **compare**.

```
selection_sort([],[]).
selection_sort(X,[A|Y])  :- minimum(X,A),
                            delete_element(A,X,Z),
                            selection_sort(Z,Y).

delete_element(X,[X|Y],Y).
delete_element(X,[Y|Z],[Y|Q])  :- distinct(X,Y),
                            delete_element(X,Z,Q).

minimum([X],X).
minimum([album(ArtistX,TitleX),
                    album(ArtistY,TitleY)|Z],M)  :-
        order(ArtistX,ArtistY),
        minimum([album(ArtistX,TitleX)|Z],M).
minimum([album(ArtistX,TitleX),
                    album(ArtistY,TitleY)|Z],M)  :-
        order(ArtistY,ArtistX),
        minimum([album(ArtistY,TitleY)|Z],M).

order(X,X).
order(X,Y)  :- compare(<,X,Y).
```

selection sort— arranging a collection of items by selecting an item that precedes all other items, sorting the remaining items, and then placing that item in front of the sorted list.

Note: A common playground situation involves two captains picking teams from a group. One team captain will begin by selecting the "best" individual in the group, the other then selects the "best" of the remaining individuals, and the process repeats until each individual is assigned a team. If one simply looks at the order in which individuals are assigned to teams, this corresponds to the order in which items are assigned their positions in the list resulting from a selection sort.

## ALPHABETICAL ORDER RELATIONS ON ATOMS

compare($Op, T_1, T_2$) is *true* if the result of comparing the terms $T_1$ and $T_2$ is $Op$, where $Op$ is one of the following:

= if $T_1$ is identical to $T_2$
< if $T_1$ precedes $T_2$ in alphabetical order
> if $T_1$ follows $T_2$ in alphabetical order

Notes The **compare** relation will, in general, relate terms (rather than simply atoms). In this more general context, it is said to relate a *standard order*, that involves the *arity* (number of components) of a term and the "age" of the value assumed by a variable (rather than variable name). We suggest you consult the user's manual for the Prolog interpreter you are using for the details of its standard order relation.

## RELATIONAL DENOTATION OF SELECTION_SORT(L,S)

selection_sort(L,S) if S is a sorted permutation of list L.

```
distinct(X,Y) :- compare(<,X,Y).
distinct(X,Y) :- compare(>,X,Y).

?- selection_sort([album(rolling_stones,sticky_fingers),
                   album(bb_king,live_at_the_regal),
                   album(pink_floyd,
                         dark_side_of_the_moon),
                   album(who,whos_next),
                   album(von_karajan,
                         tchaikovsky_symphony),
                   album(who,
                         meaty_beaty_big_and_bouncy),
                   album(marsalis,
                         handel_trumpet_concerto),
                   album(delucia_dimeola_mclaughlin,
                         friday_night_in_san_francisco),
                   album(vsop,vsop)],S).

yes. S = [album(bb_king,live_at_the_regal),
          album(delucia_dimeola_mclaughlin,
                friday_night_in_san_francisco),
          album(marsalis,handel_trumpet_concerto),
          album(pink_floyd,dark_side_of_the_moon),
          album(rolling_stones,sticky_fingers),
          album(von_karajan,tchaikovsky_symphony),
          album(vsop,vsop),
          album(who,whos_next),
          album(who,meaty_beaty_big_and_bouncy)]
```

The selection sort works well when there are only a few items to be arranged, as in a small record collection. But when there are many items—dozens or hundreds—as in a typical record collection, the method is hopelessly slow.

To get a feeling for how much work is involved, consider the problem of selecting the smallest item from a list of $n$ elements. Any program that performs this task must make $n-1$ comparisons. Why? Well, if we make less than $n-1$ comparisons, at least two elements were never compared. Therefore, it will not be known which of these elements is smaller, and the program could not be sure whether one of these elements was the smallest.

Similarly, the cost of deleting an arbitrary element in a list of length $n$ will require, on average, that about $n/2$ items be examined. It can be seen that **selection_sort(L, S)** will require that the smallest element be determined $n-1$ times on lists of length $n$, $n-1$, ..., 1, and that an element be deleted from successive lists of length $n$, $n-1$, ..., 1. Thus, the number of steps needed by **selection_sort(L, S)** will be roughly $n^2$, when $L$ is of length $n$.

We can get much better performance from a sorting algorithm that exploits the division of the problem into (hopefully) balanced subproblems, the essence of the divide-and-conquer strategy. The result will be an algorithm, first proposed by C. A. R. Hoare,[1] that tends to require about $n \log_2 n$ computational steps to complete a sorted arrangement. For a 100-item sequence, this is roughly 700 steps—still a bunch, but many times faster than the selection sort. The comparison between selection sort and this new algorithm, *quicksort* gets more and more dramatic as the size of the sequence to be sorted increases.

The quicksort of a list $L$ is based on the following principles:

1. If $L$ is empty, then the sorted result is empty.

2. Given any element of a nonempty list $L$ (say $x$), and two lists, $Lt$ and $Ge$, such that

   (a) $Lt$ and $Ge$ collectively contain, exactly, the elements of $L$ *sans* the element $x$,

   (b) Each element in $Lt$ is smaller than the element $x$, and

   (c) Each element in $Ge$ is larger than or equal to the element $x$,

   the sorted arrangement of $L$ is exactly the list obtained by appending the sorted arrangement of $Lt$ with the list beginning with element $x$ and followed by the sorted arrangement of $Ge$.

Thus, quicksort works by either mapping an empty list to an empty list, or appending the (quick) sorted arrangements of two sublists, each smaller in size than the original list. However, although each sublist is guaranteed to be smaller than the original list, *there is no guarantee that the sublist sizes will be balanced*. Should the element $x$ be the smallest element of a list of size $n$, then $Lt$ will be of length 0 whereas $Ge$ will be of length $n - 1$. Similarly, should the element $x$ be the largest element of a list of size $n$, then $Lt$ will be of length $n - 1$ whereas $Ge$ will be of length 0.

This unfortunate circumstance means that, when at each recursive step the largest or smallest element is chosen to be the "partition element" $x$, a quicksort of an $n$ element list will incur about $n^2$ steps. In other words, without a guarantee of balancing, quicksort may be as slow as a selection sort.

There is, however, another way of looking at the time complexity of quicksort; namely, the *expected time*. If it assumed that $x$ tends to be the median element, then an expected time analysis of quicksort reveals that it requires on the order of $n \log n$ steps, which is as fast as a

[1]C. A. R. Hoare, (1962) Quicksort, *Computer Journal* 5(1), 10–15.

> **quicksort—** arranging a collection of items by dividing them into three groups, an element $x$, all other elements that precede $x$ (say $S$), and the remaining elements that do not precede $x$ (say $G$), and placing $x$ immediately after the (quick) sorted elements of $S$ and immediately before the (quick) sorted elements of $G$.

comparison sort can get. This expected time complexity is significant, as it is generally believed that a "well-tuned" implementation of quicksort is likely to run faster than any other sorting algorithm.

Quicksort has been analyzed extensively, the most detailed study being done by R. Sedgewick.[2] If you are interested in the expected time analysis of quicksort, see either Sedgewick's thesis or Aho, Hopcroft, and Ullman.[3]

It is evident that there are two crucial relations involved in quicksort. One is the quicksort relation, which is relationally defined both recursively and in terms of a relation that determines the sublists $Lt$ and $Ge$. The other is the relation that determines the sublists.

Let us begin with the latter. The relation that determines the sublists $Lt$ and $Ge$ is called a *partition relation*, since it partitions a list into two sublists. The term *partition* comes from elementary set theory. In mathematics, a *partition* of a nonempty set $A$ is a collection of nonempty subsets of $A$ that are pairwise disjoint (i.e., contain no common elements) and that exhaust $A$ (i.e., the union of all the subsets is precisely $A$).[4]

In quicksort, a partition of exactly two sublists is determined by a partition element and the list to be partitioned. As such, we will define a 4-*ary* relation, **partition(P,L,Lt,Ge)**.

For the quicksort itself, we will define a 2-*ary* relation, **quick(L,S)**, that is *true* whenever **S** is a sorted permutation of **L**.

Using the **append** relation previously defined, we offer the following Prolog program for the quicksort:

```
partition([],_,[],[]).
partition([A|L],P,[A|Lt],Ge)  :- order(A,P),
                                 partition(L,P,Lt,Ge).
partition([A|L],P,Lt,[A|Ge])  :- order(P,A),
                                 partition(L,P,Lt,Ge).
```

---

[2] R. Sedgewick (1975) *Quicksort*, Ph.D. thesis, Department of Computer Science, Stanford University, Palo Alto, Calif.

[3] A. V. Aho, J. E. Hopcroft, and J. O. Ullman (1974) *The Design and Analysis of Computer Algorithms*. Addison–Wesley, Reading, Mass.

[4] Note, though, that our use of the term *partition* is not perfectly consistent with its mathematical definition, since it is possible for one of the two sublists to be empty.

---

RELATIONAL DENOTATION OF **PARTITION(P,L,LT,GE)**

---

**partition(L,P,Lt,Ge)** if
1. **L** is a permutation of the list obtained by appending the list **Lt** with the list containing the element **P** followed by the elements of the list **Ge**.
2. $x <$**P**, for each element $x$ in **Lt**.
3. $y \geq$**P**, for each element $x$ in **Ge**.

---

```
quick([],[]).
quick([P|L],S)  :- part(L,P,Lt,Ge),
                   quick(Lt,LtSorted),
                   quick(Ge,GeSorted),
                   append(LtSorted,[P|GeSorted],S).
```

For a second example of divide-and-conquer, we enter the world of tournament competition. A tournament determines the "best," "second best," and so on, from a field of competitors. What constitutes "best" is some form of match, which orders two competitors.

In this sense, a tournament differs little from a sort. The only differences are that a tournament typically finds the first few "best" competitors rather than orders all competitors, and the terms "better" or "best" are commonly used rather than "smaller" or "smallest." The latter is irrelevant if we simply let a relation **order(X1,X2)** determine the "better" of two competitors (data elements).

If we are interested in simulating a tournament that determines the "best" and "second best" of a group of competitors, it can be viewed as the problem of determining the "smallest" and "second smallest" elements of a list. This problem has been studied for some time.

One notable study was conducted by C. L. Dodgson, who is better known by his pseudonym, Lewis Carroll. In a serious albeit humorous essay on lawn tennis tournaments,[5] Dodgson observed that the tournaments were being conducted incorrectly. In particular, the so-called *single-elimination* style of tournament that continues to be pervasive today (consider the NCAA College Basketball Tournament), is unjust[6] in that the team that loses in the final game to the tournament winner is automatically designated runner-up (or second best). That team may be the runner-up, but so may any of the other teams that only lost to the winner. More matches are needed to resolve the situation fairly.

Dodgson attempted to design a fair tournament that minimized the number of competitor matches. Although he did not succeed in coming

---

[5] The essay appeared in the *St. James Gazette*, August 1, 1883, pp. 5–6.
[6] Not as unjust as the college football championship competition, however.

up with a minimal match tournament, he did improve things. Those interested in a more complete account of Dodgson's work on tournament design are encouraged to read an interesting synopsis given by Knuth.[7]

The design of a correct algorithm for computing the smallest and second smallest of a list of elements is, of course, easily solved. By simply extracting the first two elements of a sorted arrangement of the list, we obtain the desired result. This, however, means that $O(n \log n)$ comparisons would be incurred. In the tournament sense, this would be unacceptable to both competitors and spectators.

Another approach would be to use the **minimum** relation given in the selection sort example of this chapter, first on the original list, and then on the elements of that list *sans* the first element. This is an improvement, but is still unacceptable. With this approach, there would be $n - 1$ matches to establish the winner, and $n - 2$ matches to determine the runner-up, given a field of $n$ competitors. The total of $2n - 3$ matches is still substantial.

Since we have already observed that at least $n - 1$ matches are required to establish a winner, the problem clearly lies in the method used to select the runner-up. It will be seen that only an additional $\lceil \log_2 n \rceil - 1$ matches are needed after the winner is selected to determine the runner-up[8]. Knuth discusses this and proves that at least $n - 2 + \lceil \log_2 n \rceil$ matches are needed to correctly determine both a winner and runner-up.[9]

To obtain a minimal comparison first/second tournament, we will apply divide-and-conquer. The idea is based on the following observations:

1. The tournament winner is determined by the winner of the match between the winner of a competitor group $G_1$ and the winner of a competitor group $G_2$, provided $G_1$ and $G_2$ partition the original group. In other words, divide the original group into any two groups, determine the winners of each group, and let the tournament winner be decided by a match between the two group winners.

2. The runner-up is always one of the competitors that lost only to the winner in the first phase of the tournament.

Our approach is then to determine the winner from a field of $n$ competitors in such a way that

1. Exactly $n - 1$ matches are used to determine the winner,

2. The winner always plays at most $m = \lceil \log_2 n \rceil$ matches, and

3. Exactly $m - 1$ matches are used to determine the runner-up.

[7]D. E. Knuth (1975) *The Art of Computer Programming. Volume 3: Sorting and Searching,* second edition. Addison–Wesley, Reading, Mass.

[8]If $x$ is any real number, $\lceil x \rceil$ is the least integer greater than or equal to $x$. It is usually called the *ceiling function.*

[9]Knuth, *op. cit.,* pp. 209–217.

This can be accomplished using the stated observations, provided the partitioning of competitors into groups is always a *balanced* partitioning. That is, we want to always divide the competitors into near-equal size groups. We can define a 3-*ary* relation, `split(L,G1,G2)`, that is *true* if `G1` and `G2` partition `L`, and `G1` either contains the same number of elements as `G2`, or one more element.

This is accomplished if:

1. An empty list is partitioned into two empty lists,

2. A list containing one element is partitioned into a list containing that element and an empty list, and

3. For a list containing two or more elements, $[X_1, X_2, X_3, \ldots, X_n]$, partition $[X_3, \ldots, X_n]$ into two approximately equal size lists $L1$ and $L2$, and return the lists $[X_1|L1]$ and $[X_2|L2]$ as the two sublists.

Based on this strategy, we define the splitting relation as:

```
split([],[],[]).
split([X],[X],[]).
split([C1,C2|L],[C1|L1],[C2|L2]) :- split(L,L1,L2).
```

Next, we will design a relation that determines both the winner and the runner-up candidates using a minimal number of matches. Each competitor will be represented as a 2-*ary* structure, `competitor(Id, Victory_list)`, where `Id` identifies the competitor and `Victory_list` is the list of other competitors that `Id` has defeated in a given round of the tournament. Thus, at the start of each of the two rounds, each competitor's `Victory_list` is empty.

In the first round, a winner is determined together with those competitors the winner defeated in that round (i.e., the runner-up candidates). In the second round, the same is done with the runner-up candidates to find the runner-up. The outcome of a match between two competitors is simulated through the use of the well-used `order(X1,X2)` relation, the specifics of which are left to you.

The 3-*ary* relation, `tournament(Field,Winner,Runner_up)`, is *true* if `Winner` and `Runner_up` are the first and second elements of a sorted arrangement of `Field`, as determined by the relation `order`. It is defined in terms of a 2-*ary* relation, `round(Field,competitor(Winner,Runners))`, which is *true* if `Winner` is the `Id` of the first element of a sorted arrangement of `Field`, as determined by the relation `order`, and `Runners` is the list of competitors determined to follow `Winner` in the said order as a result of direct comparison (i.e., matches).

Adding definitions for these three relations to that given for `split` produces the following Prolog program:

```
tournament(Field,Winner,Runner_up) :-
           round(Field,competitor(Winner,Runners)),
           round(Runners,competitor(Runner_up,_)).

round([X],X).

round([C1,C2],Winner) :- match(C1,C2,Winner).

round(Field,Winner) :- split(Field,Group1,Group2),
                       round(Group1,Winner1),
                       round(Group2,Winner2),
                       match(Winner1,Winner2,Winner).

split([],[],[]).

split([X],[X],[]).

split([C1,C2|L],[C1|L1],[C2|L2]) :- split(L,L1,L2).

match(competitor(C1,L1),competitor(C2,_),
           competitor(C1,[competitor(C2,[])|L1]))
      :- order(C1,C2).

match(competitor(C1,_),competitor(C2,L2),
           competitor(C2,[competitor(C1,[])|L2])).
```

Assuming that alphabetical order on **Id** components was used to resolve matches, the following query would be responded to with the result below:

```
?- tournament([competitor(connors,[]),
              competitor(mac_enroe,[]),
              competitor(lendl,[]),
              competitor(budge,[]),
              competitor(laver,[]),
              competitor(borg,[]),
              competitor(tanner,[]),
              competitor(gerulaitis,[]),
              competitor(trabert,[]),
              competitor(newcombe,[])],First,Second).

yes. First = borg. Second = budge.
```

---

INFIX ALPHABETICAL ORDER RELATIONS ON ATOMS

$T_1 == T_2$    is *true* if atom $T_1$ is identical to atom $T_2$.

$T_1 \setminus == T_2$    is *true* if atom $T_1$ is not identical to atom $T_2$.

$T_1$ @< $T_2$    is *true* if atom $T_1$ precedes atom $T_2$ in alphabetical order.

$T_1$ @> $T_2$    is *true* if atom $T_1$ follows atom $T_2$ in alphabetical order.

$T_1$ @=< $T_2$    is *true* if atom $T_1$ does not follow atom $T_2$ in alphabetical order.

$T_1$ @>= $T_2$    is *true* if atom $T_1$ does not precede atom $T_2$ in alphabetical order.

---

# ▪ SUMMARY

The basic idea behind divide-and-conquer is to partition a problem into parts (which are typically of equal or roughly equal size), solve the newly created problems, and then use the solutions to the smaller problems to obtain a solution to the original problem. Divide-and-conquer algorithms tend be be recursive in nature, since the smaller problems can typically be solved using the same divide-and-conquer procedure as the problem from which they were extracted. They can also be very efficient, particularly when the problem is partitioned into roughly equal-sized subproblems, and the effort required to partition the problem and construct the solution from the solutions to the subproblems is, at most, proportional to the size of the problem.

# ▪ SUPPLEMENTAL: INFIX ALPHABETICAL ORDERING RELATIONS

C-Prolog also allows the use of the more conventional infix form of alphabetical ordering relations. The infix alphabetical ordering relations are given here.

# ▪ BIBLIOGRAPHY NOTES

The divide-and-conquer technique has been well known for many years. Some nice discussions of the design and analysis of divide-and-conquer (and other types of) algorithms are given in Aho, Hopcroft, and Ullman and Horowitz and Sahni.

A. V. Aho, J. E. Hopcroft, and J. D. Ullman, (1974) *The Design and Analysis of Computer Algorithms.* Addison–Wesley, Reading, MA.

E. Horowitz, and S. Sahni (1984) *Fundamentals of Computer Algorithms.* Computer Science Press, Potomac, MD

# ■ EXERCISES

1. Rewrite the selection sort in such a way that the **delete_element** relation can be eliminated.

2. Write a Prolog procedure **quickacc** that implements quicksort without explicitly using **append**.

3. Pretend you are a sports commentator, and describe how the matches would have unfolded in determining the winner and runner-up in the example **tournament** query given in this chapter, assuming the tournament was conducted as defined by the relation **tournament**.

## ANSWERS

1. The relation **delete_element** is eliminated by accumulating the list of elements scanned in the inference of **minimum**, until the minimum element has been determined, and then returning both the minimum element and the remaining elements in the list.

   This requires introducing two additional arguments into the **minimum** relation to obtain a 4-*ary* relation, **minimum(L, E, P, S)**, which is *true* if **E** is the minimum of the elements in lists **L** and **P**, and **S** is the list of remaining elements of **L** and **P**.

```
selection_sort([],[]).
selection_sort(X,[A|Y]) :- minimum(X,A,[],Z),
                           selection_sort(Z,Y).

minimum([X],X,A,A).
minimum([album(ArtistX,TitleX),
        album(ArtistY,TitleY)|Z],M,A1,A2) :-
       order(ArtistX,ArtistY),
       minimum([album(ArtistX,TitleX)|Z],M,
               [album(ArtistY,TitleY)|A1],A2).
minimum([album(ArtistX,TitleX),
        album(ArtistY,TitleY)|Z],M,A1,A2) :-
       order(ArtistY,ArtistX),
```

```
minimum([album(ArtistY,TitleY)|Z],M,
        [album(ArtistX,TitleX)|A1],A2).

order(X,X).
order(X,Y) :- X@<Y.
```

2. To construct a Prolog procedure that implements quicksort without explicitly using **append**, a third argument is introduced to accumulate the elements of the result. In particular, define **quickacc(L,S,I)** to be *true* when $S$ is a list obtained by appending a properly ordered permutation of the list **L** with the list **I**. First, observe that if **L=[]**, then **S=I**. A procedural representation of this relation satisfies the definition and will serve as a termination condition. In general, let **L=[H|T]**. Then **S** is the list obtained by appending a sorted permutation of the list **L** with the list **I** if:

   (a) **A** and **B** are the lists of elements from **T** that are less than and greater than or equal to **H**, respectively,

   (b) **S** is the list obtained by appending a sorted permutation of the list **A** with the list **[H|Y]**,

   (c) **Y** is the list obtained by appending a sorted permutation of the list **B** with the list **I**.

This yields the following Prolog procedure:

```
quickacc([],S,S).

quickacc([H|T],S,I):- part(H,T,A,B),
                      quickacc(A,S,[H|Y]),
                      quickacc(B,Y,I).
```

where **part** is as previously defined, and **quickacc** is used to obtain a sorted list **S** from a list **L** via the goal **quickacc(L,S,[])**.

3.                Round 1. Winner Determination

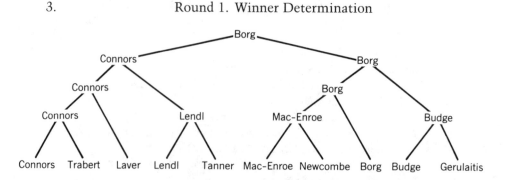

Round 2. Runner-up Determination

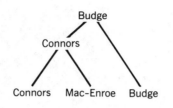

# AND/OR CONTROL FLOW

We will now turn our attention to the flow of control in Prolog program computations. There are two types of control flow: *and* control and *or* control.

*And* control describes the execution of the condition part of a rule. Specifically, the Prolog interpreter tests the conditions of a rule from left to right. The conclusion is verified if there is a consistent instantiation of values for the variables in the conditions that allows all conditions to be inferred.

Thus, if we have a rule

$$conclusion :- \quad condition_1,$$
$$condition_2,$$
$$\ldots$$
$$condition_m.$$

we resolve the rule successfully if we resolve

*condition₁* <u>and</u> *condition₂* <u>and</u> ⋯ <u>and</u> *condition_m*

successfully. This interpretation is directly attributable to the *declarative semantics* of logic programs described in Chapter 33 (*Declarative and Procedural Semantics of Logic Programs*). It does, however, have a procedural component: the order in which the conditions are tested. In mathematical logic, the *and* predicate has the same value regardless of how its clauses are ordered. In Prolog's computational logic, the order of the clauses can affect termination of the computation.

Consider, for example, a 2-*ary* relation **sublist**.

Using the relation **append** defined in Chapter 20 (*Recursion*), we could define **sublist** as

```
sublist(S,L)  :- append(_,L1,L),
                 append(S,_,L1).
```

This definition of **sublist** could be verbalized as: "*S* is a sublist of *L* if *L*1 is any suffix of *L* and *S* is a prefix of *L*1."

It would be logically equivalent to state that: "*S* is a sublist of *L* if *S* is a prefix of some list *L*1 and *L*1 is any suffix of *L*". This statement corresponds to the following definition of **sublist**.

```
sublist(S,L)  :- append(S,_,L1),
                 append(_,L1,L).
```

Now, consider the query

```
?- sublist([c,b],[a,b,c,d]).
```

If this query were made relative to the first definition of **sublist**, the interpreter would determine that **[c,b]** was not the prefix of any of the five suffixes of **[a,b,c,d]**: **[a,b,c,d]**, **[b,c,d]**, **[c,d]**, **[d]**, **[]**. However, if the query were made relative to the second definition of **sublist**, the interpreter would attempt to find one of the *infinite* number of lists that have **[c,b]** as a prefix that also happen to be a suffix of **[a,b,c,d]**. In this case, the query would never terminate. We suggest you try this if you are not convinced.[1]

*Or* control describes the ability of the Prolog interpreter to resolve a condition relation with any of a set of fact and rule statements that constitute a definition of that relation. Consider a relation $c(t_1, \ldots, t_m)$ and a set of statements that define it.

---

[1] If you are interested in the computational processes associated with the computations resulting from the query applied relative to the two definitions of **sublist**, we suggest you first read Chapter 26 (*Backtracking*).

---

## RELATIONAL MEANING OF THE SUBLIST OF A LIST

1. [ ] is a sublist of any list.

2. A list $S = [x_i, \ldots, x_j]$ is a sublist of a list $L = [x_1, \ldots, x_n]$, if $1 \le i \le j \le n$.

---

$c(arg_{11}, \ldots, arg_{1m}) :- \; condition - part_1.$
$c(arg_{21}, \ldots, arg_{2m}) :- \; condition - part_2.$

.
.
.

$c(arg_{n1}, \ldots, arg_{nm}) :- \; condition - part_n.$

The Prolog interpreter resolves $c(t_1, \ldots, t_m)$ successfully if it completes the successful resolution of

$c(arg_{11}, \ldots, arg_{1m}) :- \; condition - part_1.$
     **or**
$c(arg_{21}, \ldots, arg_{2m}) :- \; condition - part_2.$
     **or**

.
.
.

     **or**
$c(arg_{n1}, \ldots, arg_{nm}) :- \; condition - part_n.$

As with *and* control, the semantics of *or* control has a procedural component: The order in which the statements of a relation definition are given will affect the meaning of the relation. A simple example illustrates this point. The definition of the relation **append** is generally given as

```
append([],L,L).
append([A|X],Y,[A|Z]) :- append(X,Y,Z).
```

The query

```
?- append(P,Q,R).
```

relative to this definition would instantiate **P** to **[]** and **Q** and **R** to any identical lists.

However, that same query relative to the following definition of **append** would yield a nonterminating computation.

```
append([A|X],Y,[A|Z]) :- append(X,Y,Z).
append([],L,L).
```

# ■ SUMMARY

Prolog contains two types of control flow: *and* control and *or* control. The *and* control describes the execution of the condition part of a rule. Specifically, we execute the conditions of the rule from left to right, with the rule completing execution successfully if each condition is resolved successfully.

The *or* control describes the ability of the interpreter to resolve a condition relation with any of a set of fact/rule statements that constitute a definition of that relation.

# ■ BIBLIOGRAPHY NOTES

The view that conventional algorithms and programs expressed in Algol-like languages are composed of a *logic component* and a *control component*, whereas a logic program expresses only the logic component of an algorithm, is from Kowalski.

R. A. Kowalski (1979) Algorithms=Logic+Control, *Communications of the ACM* **22**(7) 424–436.

# ■ EXERCISES

1. Using the *and/or* interpretation of control flow in Prolog, give verbal descriptions of the following relation definitions:

    (a) `sublist(S,L) :- append(_,L1,L),`
    `                    append(S,_,L1).`
    (b) `append([],L,L).`
    `    append([A|X],Y,[A|Z]) :- append(X,Y,Z).`

## ANSWERS

1. Some representative interpretations are

    (a) `sublist(S,L)` *if* `append(_,L1,L)` *and* `append(S,_,L1)`.
    (b) `append([],L,L)` *or*
    `    append([A|X],Y,[A|Z])` *if* `append(X,Y,Z)`.

# SAVING COMPUTATION WITH EMBEDDED OR CONTROL

A convenient way to express the concept of *or* control within the condition part of a rule uses the special symbol "$;$".

In interpreting "$c_1 ; c_2$", the Prolog interpreter will attempt to satisfy $c_1$ first, and if not successful, then $c_2$. Note that if $c_1$ fails, all variables instantiated during the attempted resolution of $c_1$ are "undone" before the execution of $c_2$ is initiated.

In general, you may connect an arbitrarily complex pair of expressions containing relations, the "$,$", and the "$;$". Keep in mind, though,

---

OR-CONTROL SYMBOL: "$;$"

Let $c_1$ and $c_2$ be any sequence of condition relations.
$c_1 ; c_2$   is   *true*, if $c_1$ is true or if $c_2$ is true.

---

that the " , " has higher precedence than the " ; ", so parentheses may be needed to express your control flow logic accurately.

Typically, the use of the " ; " is most convenient when there would be two or more rules with a common conclusion and different bodies. To see this, consider the problem of computing the smallest element in a nonempty list, relative to the ordering relation **order**.

We will assume **order(X,Y)** to be true if **X** is less than **Y**, with respect to some ordering relation. We leave the choice of the relation to you. The strategy of our procedure is based on the following observations:

1. If list **L** contains a single element **x**, then **x** is the smallest element in **L**.

   If **L** contains at least two elements, let **x** and **y** be two such elements, and **M** the list containing the remaining elements of **L**.

2. If **order(x,y)** is true, then **min(L)=min(L1)**, where **L1** is **L** with the element **y** removed.

3. If **order(x,y)** is false, then **min(L)=min(L2)**, where **L2** is **L** with the element **x** removed.

This gives way to the following Prolog relation definition:

```
min([X],X).
min([X,Y|Z],M) :- order(X,Y),
                   min([X|Z],M).
min([X,Y|Z],M) :- min([Y|Z],M).
```

Note that the conclusion relations of the two rules are identical. We could therefore replace this procedure with the equivalent one obtained by introducing the " ; " symbol; that is,

```
min([X],X).
min([X,Y|Z],M) :- ( order(X,Y), min([X|Z],M) ) ;
                   min([Y|Z],M).
```

Given the precedence rules for " , " and " ; ", this could be further simplified to

```
min([X],X).
min([X,Y|Z],M) :- order(X,Y),
                  min([X|Z],M) ;
                  min([Y|Z],M).
```

The " ; " symbol may also be used in queries to instruct the interpreter to backtrack on the last condition executed in an attempt to return different instantiations to variables.

# ■ SUMMARY

A convenient way to express the concept of *or* control within a rule uses the special symbol "`;`". In general, the use of the "`;`" is most convenient when there would be two or more rules with a common conclusion and different condition parts. Given two condition statements, $c_1$ and $c_2$,

$$c_1 \; ; \; c_2$$

is *true* if either $c_1$ is true or if $c_2$ is true. Prolog will attempt to satisfy $c_1$ first, and if not successful, then $c_2$. If $c_1$ fails, all variables instantiated during the attempted resolution of $c_1$ are "undone" before the execution of $c_2$ is initiated.

# ■ EXERCISES

1. Rewrite the following relation definition to include only a single rule. What advantage does the new relation definition offer?

```
partition(_[],X,X,Y,Y,Z,Z).
partition(Key,[A|L],X_temp,X2,Y_temp,Y,Z_temp,Z) :-
compare(<,A,Key),
    partition(Key,L,[A|X_temp],X2,Y_temp,Y,Z_temp,Z).
partition(Key,[A|L],X_temp,X2,Y_temp,Y,Z_temp,Z) :-
compare(=,A,Key),
    partition(Key,L,X_temp,X2,[A|Y_temp],Y,Z_temp,Z).
partition(Key,[A|L],X_temp,X2,Y_temp,Y,Z_temp,Z) :-
compare(>,A,Key),
    partition(Key,L,X_temp,X2,Y_temp,Y,[A|Z_temp],Z).
```

ANSWERS

1. 
```
partition(_[],X,X,Y,Y,Z,Z).
partition(Key,[A|L],X_temp,X2,Y_temp,Y,Z_temp,Z) :-
(compare(<,A,Key),
partition(Key,L,[A|X_temp],X2,Y_temp,Y,Z_temp,Z));
(compare(=,A,Key),
partition(Key,L,X_temp,X2,[A|Y_temp],Y,Z_temp,Z));
(compare(>,A,Key),
partition(Key,L,X_temp,X2,Y_temp,Y,[A|Z_temp],Z)).
```

The single rule definition only requires a single unification step, regardless of how **A** relates to **Key**, whereas the original definition may take as many as 3 for each **A**.

C HAPTER 25

# Not

Set manipulation is among the most common problems in computation. A simple way to represent a set in Prolog is to use a list that is assumed to contain at most one instance of any term. That is, should a term be a member of the set, it occurs once in the list; otherwise, it is not a member of the set.

In Chapter 20 (*Recursion*), we gave a definition of a relation, **member**, to determine whether an element was a member of the list representation of a set.

```
member(X, [X|Y]).
member(X, [Q|Y]) :- member(X,Y).
```

Another important set operation is intersection.

Condition 1 can be defined in Prolog as a fact, whereas conditions 2 and 3 can be defined as rules in terms of the relation **member**. However, condition 2 can only be inferred when **member**($P,Y$) is *false*. To implement this rule in Prolog, we can use the meta-relation **not**.

---

## Relational Meaning of Set Intersection

1. $X \cap Y$ is [] if $X$ is [].

2. $X \cap Y$ is $X' \cap Y$ if $X = \{P\} \cap X'$ and $P$ is not a member of $Y$.

3. $X \cap Y$ is $\{P\} \cup (X' \cap Y)$ if $X = \{P\} \cap X'$ and $P$ is a member of $Y$.

---

With the meta-relation **not**, we define the 3-*ary* relation **intersect(S1,S2,**:
which is *true* if **I** is the list of elements common to the lists **S1** and **S2**,
where no duplicate elements occur in either **S1** or **S2**:

```
intersect([],_,[]).
intersect([X|L],Y,[X|I])  :- member(X,Y),
                             intersect(L,Y,I).
intersect([X|L],Y,I)      :- not(member(X,Y)),
                             intersect(L,Y,I).
```

The use of **not** to "guard" a statement (i.e., to prevent the statement
from resolving unless a designated condition is true) must be done with
care. In situations where the condition is costly (in time or space) to
resolve, it is generally not wise to resolve it more than once. The time
and space required to resolve the **member** relation is linear in the length
of the second argument, so it might be reasonable to resolve it twice, as
in the definition of **intersect** above.

Should you wish to only compute a condition once in cases such as
**intersect**, you can resort to the use of the embedded or control. This
is illustrated with the different **intersect** relation given below.

```
intersect([],_,[]).
intersect([X|L],Y,S)  :- ( member(X,Y),
                           intersect(L,Y,I),
                           eq(S,[X|I])  ;
                         /* or */
                           intersect(L,Y,S).
eq(X,X).
```

You should be cautioned that these two definitions of **intersect** do
not define exactly the same relation. Should "backtracking" occur, the
second definition might perform differently than you would expect (i.e.,
not relate two sets to their set intersection). Backtracking is the subject

**not**—a meta-logical operator that effects *"negation as failure"*

**not** ($g$)    is    *true,* if $g$ is not provable as a Prolog condition

Note:    Variables in the arguments of condition $g$ cannot
be instantiated by either the success or the failure
of **not** ($g$). As such, *negation by failure is simply
a test.* In the case of the failure of **not** ($g$),
variables are never instantiated as the result of
**not** ($g$)'s failure. In the case of the success of
**not** ($g$), condition $g$ must have failed, so none of
the variables in its arguments are instantiated.

Caveat:    Because of these instantiation problems, the
negation as failure operation can sometimes
produce questionable results. Consider the
following procedure:

```
animal(cat).
vegetable(turnip).
```

The condition:

```
?- not(animal(X)), vegetable(X).
```

will fail in Prolog systems as we have described
them. The problem is that **not(animal(X))** fails
and causes the entire condition to fail. Note,
though, that the condition

```
?- vegetable(X), not(animal(X)).
```

will succeed, as would be expected. Thus, while
the interpretation of the "**,**" is *and,* which is both
commutative and associative in predicate logic,
the order of evaluation can make the difference
between success and failure in Prolog.

It has been shown that if **not** is applied only to
conditions with no uninstantiated variables, this
problem will not arise. See the Bibliographic Notes
at the end of the chapter for more details.

of the next chapter. After reading this chapter, you will see precisely why the two definitions of **intersect** are not equivalent.

# ■ BIBLIOGRAPHY NOTES

The characterization of the **not** operator of Prolog as *negation as failure* is from Clark. It is also discussed by Kowalski. A theoretical discussion of negation by failure is given by Lloyd.

K. L. Clark (1978) Negation as failure. In H. Gallaire and J. Minker (ed), *Logic and Databases*, Plenum Press, New York, pp. 293–322.

R. A. Kowalski (1979) *Logic for Problem Solving.* North-Holland, Amsterdam.

J. W. Lloyd (1984) *Foundations of Logic Programming.* Springer-Verlag Publishing, New York.

# ■ EXERCISES

1. Indicate the results of the following queries:

   (a) `?- not(member(a, [b,a,b,y]))`.

   (b) `?- not(member(c, [b,a,b,y]))`.

   (c) `?- member(X, [b,a,b,y])`.

   (d) `?- not(member(X, [b,a,b,y]))`.

   (e) `?- not(not(member(X, [b,a,b,y])))`.

## ANSWERS

1. The queries would be resolved as follows:

   (a) **no.**

   (b) **yes.**

   (c) **yes.    X=b**

   (d) **no.**

   (e) **yes. X=_**

   *Note:* **X=_** indicates that **X** is uninstantiated.

# CHAPTER 26

# BACKTRACKING

The computations of Prolog programs generally involve both *success* and *failure* in the sense of condition resolution. When the resolution of a condition succeeds, control flow continues in the conventional forward direction.

When a condition fails to resolve, control will *backtrack* in an attempt to find other ways to ultimately achieve success (i.e., infer the truth of the condition). Consider the condition $c(t_1, \ldots, t_m)$ and the following set of statements in the Prolog definition of $c$,

$$
\begin{aligned}
c(arg_{11}, \ldots, arg_{1m}) \; :- \quad & b_{11}, \\
& b_{12}, \\
& \ldots, \\
& b_{1r_1}. \\
c(arg_{21}, \ldots, arg_{2m}) \; :- \quad & b_{21}, \\
& b_{22}, \\
& \ldots, \\
& b_{2r_2}.
\end{aligned}
$$

$$\vdots$$

$$c(arg_{n1}, \dots, arg_{nm}) \; :- \quad \begin{aligned} & b_{n1}, \\ & b_{n2}, \\ & \dots, \\ & b_{nr_n}. \end{aligned}$$

Assume $c(t_1, \dots, t_m)$ unifies with the conclusion of the first rule of the definition, and that the first $i - 1$ conditions, $b_{11}, \dots, b_{1(i-1)}$, are executed and successfully resolved. Further, assume that the execution of the next condition, $b_{1i}$, fails. This will trigger *backtracking*.

The backtracking invoked by the Prolog interpreter can be described as:

1. Uninstantiate each variable in the condition $b_{1(i-1)}$ that was instantiated as a result of successfully executing $b_{1(i-1)}$. That is, attempt to resatisfy $b_{1(i-1)}$ under the same circumstances as existed when the interpreter originally attempted to satisfy it.

2. Next, return to the relation that was the last control point of the successful computation of $b_{1(i-1)}$. If this was a fact, simply look for the next fact/rule of the definition of this relation whose conclusion relation unifies with $b_{1(i-1)}$. This is simply an application of *or* control flow.

   If this last control point was the last condition relation of a rule, attempt to resatisfy this condition using the same procedure.

3. If $b_{1(i-1)}$ is successfully resatisfied, then continue forward again and attempt to resolve $b_{1i}$ under the new variable instantiations.

   If $b_{1(i-1)}$ fails, then continue backward attempting to resatisfy $b_{1(i-2)}$, and so on.

4. If we backtrack to $b_{11}$, and it fails to resatisfy, then we apply the *or* control flow and go to the next fact/rule in the procedure with a conclusion relation that unifies with the condition $c(t_1, \dots, t_m)$.

5. If we fail to resolve with the last fact/rule of the definition, then the condition relation $c(t_1, \dots, t_m)$ fails and the Prolog interpreter backtracks on it.

Let us give an example of backtracking in action. Suppose we wish to determine whether there are two unifiable elements somewhere in a list. We will pull the cobwebs off the **append** procedure and use it to specify a relation to verify this condition. Then we will analyze the process of backtracking involved in satisfying a **multiple_elements** query for a given list.

Recall the **append** procedure,

```
append([ ],P,P).
append([A|X],Y,[A|Z])  :-  append(X,Y,Z).
```

Now, observe the following principle:

If there are two identical elements in a list **L**, then

```
?- append(_,[E|M],L),  append(_,[E|_],M).
```

is true for some values of **E** and **M**.

This justifies the following procedure:

```
multiple_elements(E,L)  :-  append(_,[E|M],L),
                            append(_,[E|_],M).
```

Basically, the condition statement of **multiple_elements** says that:

There exists a value for **E**, preceded by arbitrary elements, that is followed by a list that contains an occurrence of the same value in the list **L**.

That is, multiple occurrences of the same element exist in the list. To see where backtracking comes in, consider the following query:

```
?- multiple_elements(Element, [a,b,c,b]).
```

The computation for the query contains the following steps:

1. Unify the query with **multiple_elements(E, L)**. This instantiates **L** with the value **[a,b,c,d]** and initiates processing of the conditions in the rule that defines **multiple_elements**.

2. Attempt to unify **append(_,[E|M],[a,b,c,b])** with the first conclusion in the definition of **append**: **append([],P,P)**. This succeeds because **E** instantiated to **a**, and **M** instantiated to **[b,c,b]**.

3. The interpreter then invokes the next condition of **multiple_elements**, attempting to unify **append(_,[a|_],[b,c,b])** with **append([],P,P)**. This fails because the second argument list begins with the element **a**, whereas the third argument list begins with the element **b**.

4. Attempt to unify **append(_,[a|_],[b,c,b])** with the second conclusion in the definition of **append**: **append([A|X],Y,[A|Z])**. This succeeds and instantiates **A_1** to **b**, **Z_1** to **[c,b]**, **Y_1** to a list beginning with **a**, and **X_1** to an arbitrary list.

5. Invoke the condition, attempting to unify **append(_, [a|_], [c,b])** with **append([],P,P)**. This fails because the second argument list begins with the element **a**, whereas the third argument list begins with the element **c**.

6. Attempt to unify **append(_, [a|_], [c,b])** with **append([A|X], Y, [A|Z])**. This succeeds: **A_2** instantiates to **c**, **Z_2** to **[b]**, **Y_2** to a list beginning with **a**, and **X_2** to an arbitrary list.

7. Invoke the condition in the rule whose conclusion was unified in step 6, attempting to unify **append(_, [a|_], [b])** with **append([],P,P)**. This fails because the second argument list begins with the element **a**, whereas the third argument list begins with the element **b**.

8. Attempt to unify **append(_, [a|_], [b])** with **append([A|X], Y, [A|Z])**. This succeeds: **A_3** instantiates to **b**, **Z_3** to **[]**, **Y_3** to a list beginning with **a**, and **X_3** to an arbitrary list.

9. Invoke the condition in the rule whose conclusion was unified in step 8, attempting to unify **append(_, [a|_], [])** with **append([],P,P)**. This fails because the second argument list begins with the element **a**, whereas the third argument list is empty.

10. Attempt to unify **append(_, [a|_], [])** with **append([A|X], Y, [A|Z])**. This also fails because the third argument is an empty list.

    We have exhausted all the facts and rules of the definition of **append** in attempting to satisfy the condition **append(_, [a|_], [])**. None of the conclusions were verified, so we backtrack.

11. Backtracking takes us first to reconsider the *parent* condition of **append(_, [a|_], [])** from step 10, which is **append(_, [a|_], [b])**, from step 8.

    We have tried all ways to satisfy **append(_, [a|_], [b])**, so we move back to its parent condition, **append(_, [a|_], [c,b])**, from step 6.

    The same applies, so we back up to **append(_, [a|_], [b,c,b])**, from step 4, which was initiated as the second condition of the rule for **multiple_elements**.

    This fails as well, so we are now forced to backtrack to the first condition of the rule for **multiple_elements**, namely, **append(_, [E|M], L)**.

12. We are now back where we were at step 2, with the exception that the last attempt to resolve **append(_, [E|M], L)** was accomplished with the fact **append([],P,P)**. Thus, the interpreter attempts to resatisfy the condition using the second statement of the **append** definition.

Attempt to unify **append(_, [E|M], [a,b,c,b])** with **append([A |X], Y, [A|Z])**. This succeeds: **A_1** instantiates to **a**, **Z_1** to **[b,c,b]**, **Y_1** to **[E|M]**, and **X_1** to an arbitrary list.

13. Attempt to unify the condition in the second statement, whose conclusion was unified in step 12; that is, the condition **append(_, [E |M], [b,c,b])**, with the first conclusion in the definition of **append: append([],P,P)**. This succeeds: **[E|M]** instantiates to **[b,c,b]**.

14. Thus, **E** instantiates to **b**, and **M** instantiates to **[c,b]**, and the first condition in the definition of **multiple_elements** is verified.

15. Invoke the second condition of **multiple_elements**, attempting to unify **append(_, [b|_], [c,b])** with **append([],P,P)**. This fails because the second argument list begins with the element **b**, whereas the third argument list begins with the element **c**.

16. Attempt to unify **append(_, [b|_], [c,b])** with **append([A|X], Y, [A|Z])**. This succeeds: **A_2** instantiates to **c**, **Z_2** to **[b]**, **Y_2** to a list beginning with **b**, and **X_2** to an arbitrary list.

17. Invoke the condition in the rule whose conclusion was unified in step 16, attempting to unify **append(_, [b|_], [b])** with **append([],P,P)**. This succeeds, so the recursion begins to unwind.

18. **Y_1** now unifies with and is instantiated to **[b]**.

19. The computation terminates with **Element** unified to **b**.

Figure 26.1 summarizes the computation in schematic form.

The backtracking in this computation was necessary for the given algorithm, because the algorithm basically guesses an element that might have multiple occurrences, and then checks for a second occurrence of that element. If that search fails, then it must reattempt the process with a new guess. If you have as much trouble following the details of computational processes as we do, Figure 26.1, the trace of a relatively simple backtracking process, should help convince you of the futility of understanding (or debugging) large programs by tracing their execution. An important advantage of denotational programming is that it focuses attention on input/output relationships rather than on computational processes. Operational programs, on the other hand, can only be understood as computational processes from which input/output relationships may be derived, at great labor.

Nonetheless, we understand that many people are more comfortable with programming language after they have traced through a few of the processes that an interpreter of the language generates. For this reason, we perservere with a second example of backtracking. The problem we will attack next is the *graph-coloring* problem. Suppose we are given an

```
1    <Goal>    multiple_elements(Element,[a,b,c,b])
|
1    <Unify>   multiple_elements(E,L)
|
1                 Element=E, [a,b,c,b]=L
|
| 2     <Goal>    append(_,[E|M],[a,b,c,b])
|
| 2     <Unify>  append([],P,P)
|
| 2                 E=a, M=[b,c,b]
|
| 2     <Goal>    append(_,[a|_],[b,c,b])
|
| 2     <Unify>  append([A|X],Y,[A|Z])
|
| 2                 A=b, X=_, Y=[a|_], Z=[c,b]
|
|   3     <Goal>    append(_,[a|_],[c,b])
|   |
|   3     <Unify>  append([A|X],Y,[A|Z])
|   |
|   3                 A=c, X=_, Y=[a|_], Z=[b]
|   |
|   | 4    <Goal>    append(_,[a|_],[b])
|   | |
|   | 4    <Unify>  append([A|X],Y,[A|Z])
|   | |
|   | 4                 A=b, X=_, Y=[a|_], Z=[]
|   | |
|   |   5    <Goal>    append(_,[a|_],[])
|   |   |
|   |   5    <FAIL>    append(_,[a|_],[])
|   | |
|   | 4    <Re-Try> append(_,[a|_],[b])
|   | |
|   | 4    <FAIL>    append(_,[a|_],[b])
|   | |
|   3     <Re-Try> append(_,[a|_],[c,b])
|   |
|   3     <FAIL>    append(_,[a|_],[c,b])
|
| 2       <Re-Try> append(_,[a|_],[b,c,b])
|
| 2       <FAIL>    append(_,[a|_],[b,c,b])
```

```
|
| 2      <Re-Try> append(_,[E|M],[a,b,c,b])
|
| 2      <Unify>  append([A|X],Y,[A|Z])
|
| 2               A=a,  X=_,  Y=[E|M],  Z=[b,c,b]
|
| 2      <Goal>   append(_,[E|M],[b,c,b])
|
| 2      <Unify>  append([],P,P)
|
| 2               E=b,  M=[c,b]
|
| 2      <Goal>   append(_,[b|_],[c,b])
|
| 2      <Unify>  append([A|X],Y,[A|Z])
|
| 2               A=c,  X=_,  Y=[b|_],  Z=[b]
|
|  3       <Goal>   append(_,[b|_],[b])
|  |
|  3       <Unify>  append([],P,P)
|
| 2      <EXIT>   append(_,[b|_],[c,b])
|
1   <EXIT>    multiple_elements(b,[a,b,c,b])
```

FIGURE 26.1

undirected graph $G$ with vertex set $V$ and edge set $E$, and a set of colors. The problem is to *assign a single color to each vertex so that no two vertices connected by an edge are assigned the same color.*

Graph coloring is an interesting problem with many practical applications. For example, the 1984 Olympic organizers wanted to assign colored placards to seats in the stadium so as to display the flags of all participating nations. One requirement would be to avoid locating flags so that parts of different flags with common colors were adjacent. This could be (and might have been) solved by framing the problem in terms of graph coloring. Another important application of graph coloring, and one of great importance in computing, has to do with efficient use of computer hardware in compiled programs. Optimizing compilers use graph coloring to compute efficient assignments of the fastest and most precious memory elements of computers (registers) to variables generated by high-level programs.

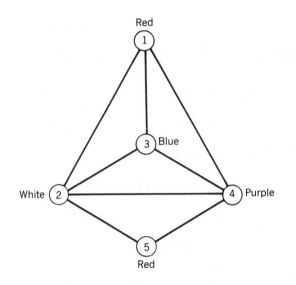

**Figure 26.2**

Figure 26.2 contains a graph and a valid coloring of the graph. There are many algorithms for coloring graphs. We will illustrate one that employs backtracking. First we state the assumptions.

We will assume that each edge in the graph is asserted as a fact of the form **edge(i, j)**, where **i** and **j** are vertices, that each color **c** is asserted as a fact of the form **color(c)**. We define a 3-*ary* relation, **graph_color(V, A, C)**, which is *true* if **C** is a valid coloring of the vertices of **V** that is consistent with the vertex/color assignments of **A**.

In defining the relation, we will assume that the first component is an instantiated list of vertices, the second an initially empty list that will be used to hold the list of vertex/color assignments that have already been computed, each element having the form **vc(v, c)**, where **v** is a vertex and **c** is a color, and the third argument being initially uninstantiated and finally instantiated to a complete assignment list of colors to vertices should there exist a valid coloring.

The asserted edge set for the graph shown in Figure 26.2, plus the asserted facts for the color set {**red, white, blue, purple**}, is given in Figure 26.3. Note that the order in which the facts for either the edges or the colors are given is arbitrary.

To find a coloring of a graph, one can simply enumerate each possible combination of vertex/color assignments until a valid coloring is discovered or all possibilities have been exhausted and failure can only be inferred. It should be noted that while this strategy is correct in principle, it will tend to be very slow as there are generally many combi-

```
color(red).
color(white).
color(blue).
color(purple).

edge(1,2).
edge(1,3).
edge(1,4).
edge(2,3).
edge(2,4).
edge(2,5).
edge(3,4).
edge(4,5).
```

FIGURE 26.3

nations of possible colorings. Nonetheless, the intention is to illustrate backtracking, so we put the efficiency consideration aside for now.

An operational strategy for coloring a graph that uses backtracking to enumerate all possible combinations would then be:

1. For the first vertex $v$, guess a color and assign it to $v$.

2. Check to be sure that no vertex adjacent to $v$ has been assigned that same color.

3. If no conflict exists and all vertices have been assigned colors, then return the computed coloring. If no conflict exists and some vertices remain uncolored, then guess a color for the next vertex in $V$ and repeat step 2.

4. If there is a conflict, then "undo" the assignment, attempt to guess a color not previously assigned to this vertex, and then go back to step 2.

5. If all color assignments to this vertex have been already tried with respect to the previous color assignments, then backtrack to the previous vertex assigned a color, "undo" the previous assignment, and attempt to guess a color not previously assigned to this vertex. Then repeat step 2.

6. If at any point all alternatives have failed, then the procedure fails.

We begin with denotations of three relations.

The Prolog definition of relation **graph_color** in terms of these three relations (and the relation **member**) is given next.

---

RELATIONAL DENOTATION OF **GRAPH_COLOR(V,A,C)**

**graph_color(V,A,C)** if
1. **V** is any subset of the graph vertices.
2. **A** and **C** are each a list of pairs, **vc(V,C)**, where **V** is a vertex and **C** is a color assigned to **V**, that collectively assign exactly one color to each vertex of the graph.
3. There are no pairs **vc(V1,C)** and **vc(V2,C)** from the collective pairs of **A** or **C** whenever **edge(V1,V2)** (or **edge(V2,V1)**) is asserted.

---

RELATIONAL DENOTATION OF **COLORING(V,C,T)**

**coloring(V,C,T)** if
1. **V** is a graph vertex.
2. **C** is a color.
3. **T** is a list of pairs, **vc(V',C')**, where **V'** is a vertex and **C'** is a color assigned to **V'**, containing no pairs **vc(V1,C')** and **vc(V2,C')** whenever **edge(V1,V2)** (or **edge(V2,V1)**) is asserted.
4. There is no pair **vc(V1,C)** from **T** whenever **edge(V,V1)** (or **edge(V1,V)**) is asserted.

---

RELATIONAL DENOTATION OF **ADJ(V,C,T)**

**adj(V,C,T)** if
1. **V** is a graph vertex.
2. **C** is a color.
3. **T** is a list of pairs, **vc(V',C')**, where **V'** is a vertex and **C'** is a color assigned to **V'**, containing at least one pair **vc(V1,C)** such that **edge(V,V1)** (or **edge(V1,V)**) is asserted.

```
graph_color([],L,L).
graph_color([V|L],T,F) :- coloring(V,C,T),
                          graph_color(L, [vc(V,C)|T],F).


coloring(V,C,T) :- color(C),
                   not(adj(V,C,T)).

adj(V,C,T) :- (edge(V,W) ; edge(W,V)),
              member(vc(W,C),T).

member(X,[X|_]).
member(X,[_|L]) :- member(X,L).
```

Consider first the statements in the definition of **graph_color**. The fact,

```
graph_color([],L,L).
```

asserts that when all vertices have been assigned colors (as indicated by the first argument being **[]**), the accumulated color assignments that are instantiated to the second argument variable are unified with and instantiated to the third argument variable.

The rule,

```
graph_color([V|L],T,F) :- coloring(V,C,T),
                          graph_color(L, [vc(V,C)|T],F).
```

asserts that if we have a nonempty list of vertices yet to be assigned, **[V|L]**, and **T** is instantiated to the current list of assignments, then if we validly color **V** with **C**, and **graph_color** the remaining vertices in list **L** with respect to the previous assignments and the assignment of **C** to **V**, we will have successfully colored the graph with the assignments instantiated to variable **F**.

The definition of relation **coloring** attempts to assign vertex **V** a color **C** that does not conflict with the existing assignments of **T**. It consists of the single rule,

```
coloring(V,C,T):- color(C),
                  not(adj(V,C,T)).
```

Basically, it begins by "guessing" a color. This is accomplished by unifying **C** with the first asserted color in the program data base. Next, it calls **adj** to determine whether there is an adjacent vertex already assigned that color. As we only wish to continue if *no* such adjacency exists, we place the meta-command **not** in front of the call to **adj**.

Consider the case where the condition **not(adj(V,C,T))** fails. Then we backtrack to the condition **color(C)** and attempt to unify **C** with a different color. We can use the backtracking control to seesaw back and forth between the two conditions until an acceptable color is found, or we determine that there is no assignable color for **v** that does not introduce an adjacency conflict.

When the latter occurs, we simply backtrack to the assignment of the previous vertex, and either reassign it a color and proceed forward with the computation or continue to backtrack.

The definition of relation **adj**,

```
adj(V,C,T):- (edge(V,W) ; edge(W,V)),
             member(vc(W,C),T).
```

simply determines whether an adjacency conflict exists between the newly colored vertex and the previous assignments. Such a conflict arises if there exists any vertex **W** such that there is either an edge from **V** to **W** or **W** to **V**, and **W** has already been assigned the color **C**.

We can watch **graph_color** in action on the graph shown in Figure 26.2 with respect to the color set {**red,white,blue,purple**}, by initiating a computation with the query

```
?-  graph_color([1,2,3,4,5],[],G).
```

The computation proceeds as follows:

1. Attempt to unify **graph_color([1,2,3,4,5],[],G)** with **graph _color([],L,L)**. The unification fails because **[1,2,3,4,5]** is not empty.

2. Attempt to unify **graph_color([1,2,3,4,5],[],G)** with **graph _color([V|L],T,F)**. This succeeds: **V_1** instantiates to **1**, **L_1** to **[2,3,4,5]**, **T_1** to **[]**, and **F_1** is yet to be determined.

3. Invoke the condition **coloring(V,C,T)** and attempt to unify **coloring(1,C,[])** with **coloring(V,C,T)**, which succeeds.

4. Invoke **color(C)** to instantiate **C** with **red**. (We assume the edge and color assertion orderings given in Figure 26.3.)

5. Invoke the condition **adj(1,red,[])**. This successfully unifies with **adj(V,C,T)**: **V_1** instantiates to **1**, **C_1** to **[red]**, and **T_1** to **[]**.

6. There are no assignments in **T_1**, so **member** will eventually fail. Thus, **not(adj(1,red,[]))** succeeds, and we continue with the condition **graph_color([2,3,4,5],[vc(1,red)],F)**.

7. Attempt to unify **graph_color([2,3,4,5],[vc(1,red)],F)** with **graph_color([],L,L)**. The unification fails because **[2,3,4,5]** is not empty.

8. Attempt to unify `graph_color([2,3,4,5],[vc(1,red)],G)` with `graph_color([V|L],T,F)`. This succeeds: `V_2` instantiates to 2, `L_2` to `[3,4,5]`, `T_2` to `[vc(1,red)]`, and `F_2` is yet to be determined.

9. Invoke the condition `coloring(V,C,T)` and attempt to unify `coloring(2,C,[vc(1,red)])` with `coloring(V,C,T)`, which succeeds.

10. Invoke `color(C)` to instantiate `C` with `red`.

11. Invoke the condition `not(adj(2,red,[vc(1,red)])`. Here, we find edges `edge(2,3)`, `edge(2,4)`, and `edge(2,5)`, but the **member** condition for each fails. We then discover `edge(1,2)`, and find that `vc(1,red)` belongs to `T`. Thus, `adj(2,red,[vc(1,red)])` succeeds, and `not(adj(2,red,[vc(1,red)]))` fails.

12. So we backtrack to `color(C)` and instantiate `C` with the next asserted color, `white`. The condition `not(adj(2,white,[vc(1,red)]))` will then succeed, so we recurse and move forward again.

13. Attempt to unify `graph_color([3,4,5],[vc(2,white),vc(1,red)],F)` with `graph_color([],L,L)`. The unification fails because `[3,4,5]` is not empty.

14. Attempt to unify `graph_color([3,4,5],[vc(2,white),vc(1,red)],G)` with `graph_color([V|L],T,F)`. This succeeds: `V_3` instantiates to 3, `L_3` to `[4,5]`, `T_3` to `[vc(2,white),vc(1,red)]`, and `F_3` is yet to be determined.

15. Invoke the condition `coloring(V,C,T)` and attempt to unify `coloring(3,C,[vc(2,white),vc(1,red)])` with `coloring(V,C,T)`, which succeeds.

16. Invoke `color(C)` to instantiate `C` with `red`.

17. The condition `adj(3,red,[vc(2,white),vc(1,red)])` will fail because there is an edge connecting vertices 1 and 3.

18. We backtrack to `color(C)` and instantiate `C` with the next asserted color, `white`. However, the condition `adj(3,white,[vc(2,white),vc(1,red)])` will also fail because there is an edge connecting vertices 2 and 3.

19. So we backtrack to `color(C)` and instantiate `C` with the next asserted color, `blue`. As there are no other vertices assigned the color `blue`, `adj(3,blue,[vc(2,white),vc(1,red)])` succeeds.

20. Attempt to unify `graph_color([4,5],[vc(3,blue),vc(2,white),vc(1,red)],F)` with `graph_color([],L,L)`. This fails because `[4,5]` is not empty.

21. Attempt to unify **graph_color([4,5],[vc(3,blue),vc(2, white),vc(1,red)],G)** with **graph_color([V|L],T,F)**. This succeeds: **V_4** instantiates to **4**, **L_4** instantiates to **[5]**, **T_4** to **[vc(3,blue),vc(2,white),vc(1,red)]**, and **F_4** is yet to be determined.

22. Invoke the condition **coloring(V,C,T)** and attempt to unify **coloring(4,C,[vc(3,blue),vc(2,white),vc(1,red)])** with **coloring(V,C,T)**, which succeeds.

23. Invoke **color(C)** to instantiate **C** with **red**.

24. The condition **adj(4,red,[vc(3,blue),vc(2,white),vc(1, red)])** will fail because there is an edge connecting vertices 1 and 4.

25. We backtrack to **color(C)** and instantiate **C** with the next asserted color, **white**. However, the condition **adj(4,white,[vc(3, blue),vc(2,white),vc(1,red)])** will also fail because there is an edge connecting vertices 2 and 4.

    Similarly, we backtrack to **color(C)** and instantiate **C** with the next asserted color, **blue**. Unfortunately, there is also an edge from 3 to 4.

    Finally, we instantiate **C** to **purple**, and as there are no other vertices assigned the color **purple**, **adj(4,purple,[vc(3,blue), vc(2,white),vc(1,red)])** succeeds.

26. Attempt to unify **graph_color([5],[vc(4,purple),vc(3, blue),vc(2,white),vc(1,red)],F)** with **graph_color([], L,L)**. This fails because **[5]** is not empty.

27. Attempt to unify **graph_color([5],[vc(4,purple),vc(3, blue),vc(2,white),vc(1,red)],G)** with **graph_color([V| L],T,F)**. This succeeds: **V_5** instantiates to **5**, **L_5** to **[]**, **T_5** to **[vc(4,purple),vc(3,blue),vc(2,white),vc(1,red)]**, and **F_5** is yet to be determined.

28. Invoke the condition **coloring(V,C,T)** and attempt to unify **coloring(5,C,[vc(4,purple),vc(3,blue),vc(2,white), vc(1,red)])** with **coloring(V,C,T)**, which succeeds.

29. Invoke **color(C)** to instantiate **C** with **red**.

30. The condition **adj(5,red,[vc(4,purple),vc(3,blue),vc(2, white),vc(1,red)])** will succeed because no edge connects vertices 1 and 5.

31. Attempt to unify **graph_color([],[vc(5,red),vc(4, purple),vc(3,blue),vc(2,white),vc(1,red)],F)** with **graph_**

`color([],L,L)`. This succeeds, unifying **F** to **[vc(5,red),vc(4, purple),vc(3,blue),vc(2,white),vc(1,red)]**. The recursion unwinds, and the query succeeds with **G** instantiated to **[vc(5,red),vc(4,purple),vc(3,blue),vc(2,white),vc(1, red)]**.

## ▪ SUMMARY

When a condition fails to resolve, control will *backtrack* in an attempt to find other ways to ultimately achieve success. Backtracking is a backward flow of control in which the interpreter attempts to resatisfy conditions, yielding different variable instantiations, with the hope of being able to satisfy the failed condition under the new instantiations.

The " ; " symbol may also be used in the top-level command mode to instruct the interpreter to backtrack on the last condition executed in an attempt to return different instantiations to variables.

## ▪ EXERCISES

1. Suppose that each edge from node *x* to node *y* in a directed graph is asserted as a fact of the form **edge(x,y)**. Define a 1-*ary* Prolog relation, **hamiltonian(Node_List)**, that is true whenever **Node_List** is a list representation of the set of *all* graph nodes and the graph contains a *hamiltonian circuit*, that is, a path that begins and ends at the same node and passes through each other node in **Node_List** exactly once.

    The graph in the following example contains vertices $\{1, 2, 3, 4\}$ and the five edges that are asserted. Close inspection reveals a hamiltonian circuit that goes from 1 to 3 to 2 to 4 and back to 1. Your program should be capable of determining the presence of such a circuit.

    ```
    edge(1,2).
    edge(1,3).
    edge(2,4).
    edge(3,2).
    edge(4,1).

    ?- hamiltonian([1,2,3,4]).

        yes.
    ```

ANSWERS

1. ```
/*
    Select an edge from First to Next and let this
    represent the starting point in the circuit.
    Maintain a list of all graph nodes that have not
    yet been ENTERED in the path being constructed.
    When the list becomes empty, a hamiltonian
    circuit has been discovered provided there is an
    edge from the last node entered to the node
    where the path started (i.e., First).
*/

hamiltonian(Node_List) :-
    edge(First,Next),
    delete(First,Node_List,List1),
    delete(Next,List1,List2),
    ham_circuit(First,Next,List2).

ham_circuit(First_Node,Current_Node,[]) :-
    edge(Current_Node,First_Node).
ham_circuit(First_Node,Current_Node,
                        Current_Node_List) :-
    edge(Current_Node,Next_Node),
    delete(Next_Node,Current_Node_List,L),
    ham_circuit(First_Node,Next_Node,L).

delete(X,[X|L],L).
delete(X,[Y|L],[Y|L1]) :-
    X\==Y,
    delete(X,L,L1).
```
```

# GENERATING ALL SOLUTIONS USING **BAGOF** AND **SETOF**

An important use of backtracking is to accumulate multiple solutions. That is, defining relations that search out a new solution after each solution is computed. We can illustrate this use of backtracking by addressing the problem of computing all elements that appear in a list more than once in adjacent elements.

For example, for the argument list

```
[1,2,2,2,3,1,3,3]
```

we would compute a list containing the elements **2** and **3**.

An element repeats in a list **L** if the query

```
?-  append(_,[X,X|_],L)
```

is true for any value of **X**, where **append** is as previously defined.

Thus, if we executed the query

```
?-  append(_,[X,X|_],[1,2,2,2,3,1,3,3])
```

---

RELATIONAL DENOTATION OF **BAGOF (T,Q,S)**

---

**bagof(T,Q,S)** if

1. **T** is a term.

2. **Q** is a query.

3. **S** is the nonempty list of all instances of **T** for which **Q** is true. That is, the query **Q** is satisfied in all possible ways, and for each instantiation of the variables in the arguments of **Q**, **T** is instantiated and recorded as such in the list **S**.

*Note:*

1. The relation **bagof** is an alternative to iteration in program control. It effectively repeats invoking the query **Q**, searching for *all* values of its variables that make **Q** true.

2. For **bagof** to be useful, the term **T** must contain instances of variables that occur in the query **Q**. Each time **Q** is satisfied, the values assumed by the variables are substituted in places where they occur in **T**, and a copy of the resulting term is placed in **S**.

3. A query of **bagof** will only succeed if the query **Q** succeeds at least once.

4. The query **Q** must be satisfiable in only a finite number of ways. Otherwise, the execution of **bagof** becomes analogous to that of an infinite loop.

---

it would terminate successfully, unifying **X** with the value **2**. (You try it to be sure.)

Now, if we responded to the completed computation with a "**;**", the interpreter would backtrack and search for the next such element in the list. Since there is a sequence of three **2**'s, it would again instantiate **X** to **2**.

Another "**;**" would prompt the interpreter to instantiate **X** to **3**, and one more would result in failure.

There are built-in Prolog relations that automatically invoke backtracking to accumulate a list of all terms related to the successful resolution of a condition statement (**bagof**) or a list of all terms related to the successful resolution of a condition statement containing no duplicates (**setof**).

To illustrate **bagof**, let us go back to the repeated element instances example. First, suppose we wanted to record each element that initiated a repeated sequence of itself in the list **L**. Then we could use the query

```
?-  bagof(X,append(_,[X,X|_],L),S).
```

Thus, the computation of

```
?-  bagof(X,append(_,[X,X|_],[1,2,2,2,3,1,3,3]),S).
```

would instantiate **S** to [2,2,3].

Recall the previous backtracking-based relation for coloring a graph, **graph_color**. Instead of wishing to see a single coloring assignment, we may require all possible colorings. This can be achieved using **bagof**.

For example, consider the graph shown in Figure 27.1, and the color set {**red,white,blue**}. Assume the graph and color set are asserted as required by **graph_color**.

Then the computation for the query

```
?- bagof(L,graph_color([1,2,3,4,5],[],L),S).
```

would instantiate **S** to the list of assignments shown in Figure 27.2.

The relation **setof** is identical to **bagof** with the exception that **S** will contain no duplicate entries.

To illustrate **setof**, we will re-consider the problem of computing the intersection of two sets that are represented as lists. In Chapter 25 (*Not*), we defined **intersect** as:

```
intersect([],_,[]).
intersect([X|L],Y,[X|I])   :- member(X,Y),
                                 intersect(L,Y,I).
intersect([X|L],Y,I)       :- not(member(X,Y)),
                                 intersect(L,Y,I).
```

Using **setof**, we get the following alternate relation definition of set intersection:

```
intersect(X,Y,S):- setof(Z,(member(Z,X),member(Z,Y)),S).
intersect(_,_,[]).
```

Note that the second rule is given for the case where the intersection is empty. Also, note that we could replace **setof** with **bagof** in the **intersect** procedure provided that neither **X** nor **Y** contain duplicate elements.

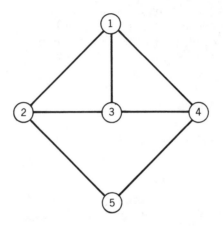

FIGURE 27.1

```
[vc(5,red),vc(4,white),vc(3,blue),vc(2,white),vc(1,red)],
[vc(5,blue),vc(4,white),vc(3,blue),vc(2,white),vc(1,red)],
[vc(5,red),vc(4,blue),vc(3,white),vc(2,blue),vc(1,red)],
[vc(5,white),vc(4,blue),vc(3,white),vc(2,blue),vc(1,red)],
[vc(5,white),vc(4,red),vc(3,blue),vc(2,red),vc(1,white)],
[vc(5,blue),vc(4,red),vc(3,blue),vc(2,red),vc(1,white)],
[vc(5,red),vc(4,blue),vc(3,red),vc(2,blue),vc(1,white)],
[vc(5,white),vc(4,blue),vc(3,red),vc(2,blue),vc(1,white)],
[vc(5,white),vc(4,red),vc(3,white),vc(2,red),vc(1,blue)],
[vc(5,blue),vc(4,red),vc(3,white),vc(2,red),vc(1,blue)],
[vc(5,red),vc(4,white),vc(3,red),vc(2,white),vc(1,blue)],
[vc(5,blue),vc(4,white),vc(3,red),vc(2,white),vc(1,blue)]
```

FIGURE 27.2

## ■ SUMMARY

An important use of backtracking is the accumulation of multiple solutions. That is, defining a relation that searches out new solutions after it computes each solution.

There are built-in Prolog relations that automatically invoke backtracking to accumulate a list of all terms related to the successful resolution of a condition statement (**bagof**), or a list of all terms related to the successful resolution of a condition statement containing no duplicates (**setof**).

## RELATIONAL DENOTATION OF **SETOF (T, Q, S)**

**setof(T, Q, S)**   if   1. **T** is a term.

2. **Q** is a query.

3. **S** is the nonempty list of all *distinct* instances of **T** for which **Q** is true. That is, the query **Q** is satisfied in all possible ways, and for each instantiation of the variables in the arguments of **Q**, **T** is instantiated and, if not already present in this form in list **S**, is entered in **S**.

*Note:*   1. The relation **setof** is similar to **bagof**, except only distinct instances of term **T** are entered into the list *S*. Thus, the notes given in the display box for **bagof** apply to **setof** as well.

2. The relation **bagof** typically operates much faster than **setof**. Therefore, if duplicates do not matter (or are known not to exist), **bagof** would be the preferable relation to use.

## ▪ EXERCISES

1. Assume that each edge from node *x* to node *y* in a directed graph is asserted as a fact of the form **edge(x, y)**. Define a 2-*ary* Prolog relation, **into_node(Node, Node_List)** that is true whenever **Node_List** is a list representation of the set of *all* graph nodes **X** such that **edge(X, Node)**.

### ANSWERS

1. `into_node(Node, Node_List) :-`
   `                 setof(N, edge(N, Node), Node_List).`

# INHIBITING BACKTRACKING

The last major topic on the basics of backtracking is how to constrain it. This is accomplished with a special control operator called *cut* and denoted by an exclamation point (!). Cuts are used as conditions in rules. As a condition, a cut signals success, which means that the interpreter will proceed to the next condition in the rule. This rule will have been used in an attempt to verify a query or a condition in some other rule, and this query or condition is known as the parent condition. Encountering a cut while trying to verify a parent condition affects the interpreter's subsequent backtracking behavior in the course of that verification. If the interpreter is forced to backtrack to verify the parent condition, it will not backtrack to conditions prior to the cut in the rule where the cut was encountered, nor will it attempt to use other rules than the rule containing the cut in the attempt to verify the parent condition.

As a consequence, all variables that are instantiated when the cut is encountered will remain with those instantiated values for the duration of the interpreter's attempt to verify the parent condition, and if the

---

**Cut (!)**—a control operator that inhibits backtracking

!    is    a control operator that always succeeds as a condition, that will never be resatisfied during backtracking, and that prohibits further *or* control in attempting to resolve the condition that invoked the rule it is contained in.

*Note:*    The introduction of a cut operator into a definition of relation $P$ reduces the set of conditions $S$ that satisfy $P$ to a subset of $S$.

---

rule containing the cut fails to support the parent condition, the parent condition fails.

To summarize, if it is not possible to satisfy the rule under the current variable instantiations, the parent condition will fail. The interpreter is locked into the given rule and will not attempt to unify with other facts or rules using the *or* control flow.

The cut is generally used to either improve the efficiency of program execution or to establish a functionality that requires the control of backtracking. For the former, the use of the cut can improve the speed of interpretation by indicating that certain conditions need not be retried. Following dead-end paths can be very time consuming and should be avoided when possible. The use of cut can also reduce space requirements since the interpreter need not store the dynamic state of the computation necessary to support backtracking when it is sure that backtracking cannot occur.

In terms of functionality, three common uses of the cut operator can be identified: to commit the interpreter to a choice of a rule, to eliminate the chance of seeking alternative/multiple solutions, and to directly cause the parent condition to fail. We will discuss each of these usages, illustrating them with examples.

In many instances it is useful to make the successful unification of a condition with a fact or the conclusion of a rule a sufficient condition for committing the interpreter to using only this fact or rule in its attempt to satisfy the condition. Semantically, this use of cut serves to convert the default *inclusive or* control to *exclusive or* control. It is especially useful when it prevents the possibility of an infinite computation if backtracking is attempted.

Consider the problem of finding a path from one vertex $V$ to another $W$ in a graph $G$. Using the representation of graphs discussed in Chapter 25 (*Not*), let $[V_1, \ldots, V_m]$ represent a path from $V_1$ to $V_m$ in terms of the sequence of vertices along the path. We can develop a solution to the problem based on the following observations:

1. $[V, W]$ is a path from $V$ to $W$ in $G$ if there is an edge from $V$ to $W$ in $G$.

2. $[V|P]$ is a path from $V$ to $W$ in $G$ if there exists a vertex $U$ such that there is an edge from $V$ to $U$ and a path $P$ from $U$ to $W$ in $G$.

We define a 3-*ary* relation, **path(V,W,P)**, to be *true* if the sequence of vertices that is the list $P$ constitutes a path from $V$ to $W$ in graph $G$, where $G$ is defined as a collection of facts of the form **edge(x,y)** representing edges of $G$ from **x** to **y** (as in Chapter 25, *Not*).

From the observations, the following Prolog definition of **path** might suggest itself:

```
path(V,W,[V,W])  :- edge(V,W).
path(V,W,[V|P])  :- edge(V,U),
                    path(U,W,P).
```

Given the following definition of a simple graph,

```
edge(1,2).
edge(2,3).
edge(1,4).
edge(3,4).
edge(4,1).
```

the query below would be responded to as follows:

```
?- path(1,4,Path).

yes. Path = [1,4]
```

Now, if the interpreter responses were followed in turn by a semicolon, the following session would result:

```
?- path(1,4,Path).

yes. Path = [1,4] ;

     Path = [1,2,3,4] ;

     Path = [1,2,3,4,1,4] ;

     Path = [1,2,3,4,1,4,1,2,3,4]
```

and so on.

Backtracking on a successful query to this definition of **path** always leads to a new path. If **bagof** were invoked on such a query, the computation would not terminate. To eliminate this problem, we judiciously insert a cut. Since we are only interested in the existence of one path from one vertex to another, we change the rule

```
path(V,W,[V,W])  :- edge(V,W).
```

to

```
path(V,W,[V,W])  :- edge(V,W),
                    !.
```

However, this does not in any way constrain the potential backtracking in the rule

```
path(V,W,[V|P])  :- edge(V,U),
                    path(U,W,P).
```

Therefore, **bagof(P,path(2,4,P),S)** would be obligated to deliver the infinite set **{[2,3,4], [2,3,4,3,2,3,4], [2,3,4,3,2,3,4,3, 2,3,4], ...}**, which means it would never terminate. To prevent this, we need a cut as the last condition of the rule, too. With these two cuts, the **path** relation will never discover more than one path between vertices.

The foregoing use of cuts prevented nonterminating computations in the presence of an infinite number of solutions to a query. A second reason for using cuts is to terminate the search for alternative solutions when it is known that at most one solution exists.

To illustrate this use of the cut, consider the relation **partition(L,P, Lt,Ge)** defined in Chapter 22 (*Divide and Conquer*) to be *true* if **L** is a permutation of the list obtained by appending the list **Lt** with the list containing the element **P** and the list **Ge**, and for each element $x$ in $Lt$, $x < P$, and for each element $y$ in $Ge$, $y \geq P$.

A Prolog definition of this relation is:

```
partition([],_,[],[]).
partition([A|L],P,[A|Lt],Ge)  :- order(A,P),
                                 partition(L,P,Lt,Ge).
partition([A|L],P,Lt,[A|Ge])  :- partition(L,P,Lt,Ge).
```

Consider the query and response

```
?- partition([a,b,c,e,f,g,h],d,Smaller,Larger_or_Equal).

yes.  Smaller = [a,b,c]  Larger_or_Equal = [e,f,g,h]
```

made with respect to the foregoing definition and an alphabetic **order** relation.

If a "**;**" was then typed in, the interpreter would attempt to backtrack in order to find another solution, for example,

```
?- partition([a,b,c,e,f,g,h],d,Smaller,Larger_or_Equal).

yes.   Smaller = [a,b,c]   Larger_or_Equal = [e,f,g,h] ;

       Smaller = [a,b]   Larger_or_Equal = [c,e,f,g,h] ;
```

This is clearly not consistent with the denotation given for **partition**. The problem lies with the statements

```
partition([A|L],P,[A|Lt],Ge)  :- order(A,P),
                                  partition(L,P,Lt,Ge).

partition([A|L],P,Lt,[A|Ge])  :- partition(L,P,Lt,Ge).
```

in the definition of **partition**.

Specifically, the interpreter would backtrack to the last point where the statement

```
partition([A|L],P,[A|Lt],Ge)  :- order(A,P),
                                  partition(L,P,Lt,Ge).
```

was used to infer a condition.

In this case, the condition would be **partition([c,d,e,f,g,h],d, Lt,Ge)**, for some instances of variables **Lt** and **Ge**.

It would then try to satisfy **partition([c,d,e,f,g,h],d,Lt,Ge)** with the next statement,

```
partition([A|L],P,Lt,[A|Ge])  :- partition(L,P,Lt,Ge).
```

Now, since there is no **order** condition "guarding" the rule, the recursion will continue successfully from here. However, the element **c** is inserted into the wrong group.

One way to rectify the problem would be to replace the last statement by the following statement:

```
partition([A|L],P,Lt,[A|Ge])  :- not(order(A,P)),
                                  partition(L,P,Lt,Ge).
```

Certainly correct, this reflects the denotational style of programming. However, some might argue that this solution is inefficient. That is, the last statement is executed each time **order(A,P)** fails in the preceding statement or when backtracking is invoked. For the former case, this additional condition is extraneous.

The problem can also be solved by introducing a cut strategically. In particular, whenever **order(A,P)** succeeds in the second statement of the definition, we do not want the third statement tried. Thus, we simply place a cut after **order(A,P)** to achieve the desired goal. The result is shown here:

```
partition([],_,[],[]).
partition([A|L],P,[A|Lt],Ge)  :- order(A,P),
                                   !,
                                   partition(L,P,Lt,Ge).
partition([A|L],P,Lt,[A|Ge])  :- partition(L,P,Lt,Ge).
```

Whenever **order(A,P)** succeeds, the success or failure of **partition** will depend entirely on the rule containing the cut. The next rule will not be examined, so it does not need a guard.

The third common use of the cut forces a parent condition to fail immediately. Semantically, this use of cut can be interpreted as:

If some collection of conditions $c_1, \ldots, c_m$ are all true, then parent condition $c$ is false.

Thus, it allows us to express the fact that a designated set of logical conditions is sufficient for parent condition failure.

This use of cut can be accomplished by combining the built-in proposition **fail**, which always fails, with the cut. The cut/fail combination,

```
?-  !,
    fail.
```

always causes the parent condition to fail because the cut prevents any backtracking after **fail** has been executed.

We could, for example, use the cut/fail combination to define the built-in relation **not(G)**, which succeeds if condition **G** fails and fails if **G** succeeds. Using cut/fail, we have the following definition of **not**:

```
not(G)  :- call(G),
            !,
            fail.
not(_).
```

where **call** is a built-in relation that simply evaluates the query that is its argument. If **G** succeeds, then the cut/fail combination will execute and cause **not(G)** to fail. Similarly, if **G** fails, then control drops down to the fact **not(_)** that will succeed for any argument.

For a second example, we return to the graph coloring program previously given. Recall the definition of the relation **graph_color**,

```
graph_color([],L,L).
graph_color([V|L],T,F)  :- coloring(V,C,T),
                            graph_color(L,[vc(V,C)|T],F).

coloring(V,C,T):- color(C),
                  not(adj(V,C)).
```

```
adj(V,C,T):- (edge(V,W) ; edge(W,V)),
             member(vc(W,C),T).

member(X,[X|_]).
member(X,[_|L]):- member(X,L).
```

We can rework the definition of the adjacency relation **non_adj** to exploit the cut/fail combination. The relation **adj** will succeed when two vertices connected by an edge are assigned the same color. We will define the relation **non_adj** to be *true* when there exist no such adjacent vertices. The new relation **graph_color** with the **non_adj** relation is defined as:

```
graph_color([],L,L).
graph_color([V|L],T,F) :- coloring(V,C,T),
                          graph_color(L,[vc(V,C)|T],F).

coloring(V,C,T):- color(C),
                  non_adj(V,C,T).

non_adj(V,C,T):- (edge(V,W) ; edge(W,V)),
                 member(vc(W,C),T),
                 !,
                 fail.
non_adj(_,_,_).

member(X,[X|_]).
member(X,[_|L]):- member(X,L).
```

The first rule of **non_adj** searches for the existence of an invalid adjacency. If one is found, then the cut/fail combination is executed, and the parent condition fails. This, in effect, causes it to guess and test a new color assignment.

Should the search for an invalid assignment fail, then the cut/fail combination will not be executed. Instead, control will drop to the next rule and simply succeed.

Careful scrutiny of the nature of the modification to the original procedure will reveal that we simply integrated the logic of the built-in relation **not** directly into **non_adj**. This can generally be done. Whether it is advisable is subject to considerations of programming style and performance.

# ■ SUMMARY

1. Backtracking can be inhibited with a special relation, "!", called the *cut*. Informally, whenever a cut is executed, it always succeeds and, for the purpose of verifying the parent condition, effectively locks the interpreter into the rule being processed and to the instantiations of the variables in effect at the point of the cut.

2. The use of the cut is generally motivated by a need to either improve the efficiency of program execution or to establish a functionality that requires the control of backtracking.

   For the former, the use of the cut can improve the speed of interpretation by indicating that certain conditions need not be retried. The use of cut can also reduce space requirements since the interpreter need not store away the dynamic state of the computation necessary to support backtracking when it is sure that backtracking cannot occur. For the latter, the use of cut can prevent nonterminating computations.

3. In terms of functionality, there are three common uses of the cut operator: to commit the interpreter to a choice of a rule, to eliminate the chance of seeking alternative/multiple solutions, and to directly cause the parent condition to fail.

# ■ BIBLIOGRAPHY NOTES

The various roles of the cut operator are discussed by Clocksin and Mellish. A theoretical discussion of the semantics and completeness properties of the cut is given by Lloyd.

W. F. Clocksin and C. S. Mellish (1980) *Programming in Prolog*. Springer-Verlag, New York.

J. W. Lloyd (1984) *Foundations of Logic Programming*. Springer-Verlag, New York.

# ■ EXERCISES

1. The *3-ary* relation **intersect(S1,S2,I)** is *true* if **I** is the list of elements common to the lists **S1** and **S2**, where no duplicate elements occur in either **S1** or **S2**:

```
intersect([],_,[]).
intersect([X|L],Y,[X|I])  :- member(X,Y),
                                intersect(L,Y,I).
intersect([X|L],Y,I)       :- not(member(X,Y)),
                                intersect(L,Y,I).
```

where **member(X, L)** is *true* if **X** is a member of list **L**. Insert a cut in such a way that it does not alter the meaning of the relation but makes its execution more efficient.

2. Consider the following definition of a relation for performing the union operation on list representations of sets:

```
union([],_,[]).
union([X|L],Y,I)  :-      member(X,Y),
                          union(L,Y,I).
union([X|L],Y,[X|I])  :- union(L,Y,I).
```

Contrast this definition of **union** with the definition that follows, which includes a cut operator in the third statement.

```
union([],_,[]).
union([X|L],Y,I)  :-      member(X,Y),
                          !,
                          union(L,Y,I).
union([X|L],Y,[X|I])  :- union(L,Y,I).
```

## ANSWERS

1.
```
intersect([],_,[]).
intersect([X|L],Y,[X|I])  :- member(X,Y),
                               !,
                               intersect(L,Y,I).
intersect([X|L],Y,I)       :- intersect(L,Y,I).
```

2. The first definition of **union** will create invalid list representations of the set that is component 3 of a query relation in cases where the query succeeds for the first time with the second statement (i.e., when the first element of the first component is a member of the list that is the second component) and the query backtracks and succeeds for the second time with the third statement. This cannot happen with the second definition of **union**, since the cut following the reference to **member** in the second statement inhibits further backtracking.

# CHAPTER 29

# BUILT-IN RELATIONS FOR PROGRAM FILE ACCESS AND TRANSFORMATION OF TERMS

Most Prolog interpreters and compilers provide built-in relations for entering relation definitions into the program data base and for meta-logical tests and transformations dealing with terms. We will discuss these categories of built-in relations as they are provided in EdCAAD C-Prolog.

## ■ RECORDING RELATION DEFINITIONS

The truth of a Prolog query is always dependent on the definition of the queried relation; specifically, the definition currently recorded in the program data base. Some relations are built-in, so their definitions are always present in this data base. Definitions of user-defined relations must, however, be explicitly entered into the data base.

There are two general ways of recording relation definitions: entering definitions recorded in a file, and entering definitions directly through a query. The latter method has the potential disadvantage of entering

> **consult** — a built-in relation that enters into the program data base the relation definitions in a file and executes the directives contained in the file.
>
> **consult** (*filename*) is always *true* and can never be resatisfied . and has the side effect of entering relation definitions and executing directives contained in the file called *filename*
>
> **Note:** If *filename* is not a proper Prolog atom (e.g., it is designated by a UNIX directory path), simply delimit it with single quotes: *'filename'*.
>
> **Example:**
>
> ```
> ?- consult('languages/prolog_routines/testprog').
> ```

the relation definition only for the duration of the current interpreter session. Let us begin with "file consulting."

To "consult" a file during a Prolog session, the built-in relation **consult** (*filename*) is used, where *filename* is a Prolog atom. This relation will always succeed exactly once for a given parent query. It has the "side effect" of entering the relation definitions in the file called *filename* at the end of the program data base and executing the directives[1] contained in the file. Relation definitions and directives may be mixed arbitrarily in the file and are processed in the order in which they are encountered (from beginning to end).

Suppose, for example, that the program data base currently contains only the built-in relations and that the file **appendfile** contains the following statements:

```
append([],L,L).
append([A|X],Y,[A|Z]) :- append(X,Y,Z).
```

Then the following query would enter those statements as definitions of the relation **append** into the program data base to allow for future queries:

```
?- consult(appendfile).

appendfile consulted  164 bytes  0.116668 sec.
yes.
```

---

[1] "Directives" are defined in this chapter.

```
?- append([step],[by,step],X).

X = [step,by,step]
```

After processing a **consult** query, the interpreter always prints the name of the consulted file, the number of bytes of storage used to represent the relation definitions contained in the file in the program data base, and the compute time used to process the query.

The relation definitions are always entered at the end of the program data base in the order in which they are encountered. Thus, if file **test1** contained the single statement

```
reply(1).
```

while the file **test2** contained the single statement

```
reply(2).
```

then consulting **test2** after **test1** would result in the statement **reply(2)** being placed after the statement **reply(1)** in the program data base.

```
?- consult(test1).

test1 consulted   68 bytes   0.050000 sec.

?- consult(test2).

test2 consulted   32 bytes   0.033334 sec.

?- reply(N).

N = 1
```

In addition to relation definition statements, you can also have *directives* in a consulted file. There are two types of directives recognized by the EdCAAD C-Prolog interpreter: *queries* and *commands*.

We have already discussed queries in Chapter 17 (*Propositional Facts, Rules, and Queries*) and used them extensively in examples. Queries are what you typically enter to evaluate relations when interacting with the Prolog interpreter at the user level. The only thing that is new is that queries can also be placed in files to be consulted. The effect is the same: the interpreter evaluates each of the queries in the sequence following the "?-" in the file. If *all* queries evaluate to *true*, then the interpreter prints the values of all variables occurring in the queries that made the query relations *true*. If the interpreter is unable to find values for these variables that simultaneously satisfy all the query relations, then it answers "no."

A very similar directive is the *command*. Commands are identical in syntax to the queries, except they begin with the symbols ":-." Their interpretation is likewise similar, the only difference being that *the values of the variables that occur in the command relations are not printed to the current output*. Thus, commands are interpreted in a way that is identical to the interpretation of a list of condition relations that form the right side of a rule. Commands are often preferred to queries as directives occurring in consulted files, since we usually do not want the values of the variables printed.

For example, suppose you have organized a large program into a collection of three files, say $f1$, $f2$, and $f3$. Rather than typing in three **consult**'s each time you wished to read in the program, you could define another file, say $f$, to contain the following command:

```
:- consult(f1), consult(f2), consult(f3).
```

Then, you simply need to consult $f$ to read in all three files.

```
?- consult(f).

f consulted  ... bytes ... sec.
```

Note that you may also execute commands from the user level when interacting with the Prolog interpreter. In the user level, the interpreter will always prompt you with the query symbols, "**?-**." Simply type in a command, beginning with the symbols "**:-**", and the interpreter will switch from query to command mode. You would only want to do this when you did not wish to have the values of the variables appearing in the directive relations printed.

Sometimes there are situations in which you want to read in relation definitions that supplant definitions already in the program data base. If you consult a file that contains statements defining a relation, and there are already statements defining that relation in the current program data base, then the new statements are simply appended to the bottom of the program data base. The alternative is to use the built-in relation **reconsult**.

Reconsulting is most often used in debugging situations in which a program is modified in a file, and the file is then reconsulted to replace the previous version.

The EdCAAD C-Prolog interpreter provides an alternative syntax for consulting and reconsulting that is somewhat more concise.

A second general way of entering relation definition statements in the program data base is to "assert them" as arguments. For example, suppose you wished to enter the statement **append([A|X],Y,[A|Z])  :-**

**reconsult**—a built-in relation that replaces relation definitions and executes directives contained in a file.

**reconsult** (*filename*)     is     always *true* and can never be resatisfied, and has the side effect of replacing relation definitions and executing directives contained in the file called *filename*. In the case of new relation definitions, any statements defining those relations that currently reside in the program data base are first discarded, and then the new definitions are entered into the program data base.

## ALTERNATIVE SYNTAX FOR CONSULTING AND RECONSULTING

**[fref₁, ..., frefₙ]**     is     always *true* and can never be resatisfied and has the side effect of consulting (reconsulting) the $n \geq 1$ referenced files in the list. Each of **fref₁** through **frefₙ** is either a file name or a file name preceded by the symbol "-."

If **frefᵢ** is a file name, the file name is consulted.

If **frefᵢ** is a file name preceded by -, the file name is reconsulted.

**Examples:**     ?- [file1,-file2,-file3, file4].

would consult **file1**, reconsult **file2**, reconsult **file3**, and then consult **file4**.

**Caveat:**     We are using list syntax in *representing a relation*: this should not be confused with the use of lists for *representing terms*.

append(X,Y,Z) directly into the program data base. Then the relation "assert" could be used as follows:

```
?- assert((append([A|X],Y,[A|Z]) :- append(X,Y,Z))).

yes. A = _0
     X = _1
     Y = _6
     Z = _7
```

The result of this query would be to enter the statement append([A| X],Y,[A|Z]) :- append(X,Y,Z) directly into the program data base. There are several points to note. First, note that the statement was surrounded by what appears to be an additional unnecessary pair of parentheses. In general, the additional parentheses ensure that the statement is not misread by the interpreter. We suggest you always include such an additional set of parentheses to be safe.

A second point to note is the nature of what is printed by the interpreter after the **assert** query succeeded. Each of the variables that occurs in the statement are listed. The funny underscore number they are equated to is just an internal reference that you may ignore.

There are several slight variations on **assert**, which direct the location of the asserted statement in the program data base. These are listed in the display box about **assert**.

Several methods of removing clauses from the program data base are also provided in EdCAAD C-Prolog. One, "retracting", removes the first occurrence of a statement that matches the argument. The other, "abolishing", removes all statements defining a relation with a specified name and a specified *arity*.

If you simply wish to determine whether the program data base contains a statement with a specified conclusion and (in the case of a rule) conditional part, there is a built-in relation called **clause**.

It is sometimes convenient to be able to test the dynamic status of a Prolog term during a computation or to manipulate various forms of terms. EdCAAD Prolog offers a collection of so-called meta-logical relations for this purpose.

**Examples:**

```
- var(X). /* assuming X is currently uninstantiated */
yes.

?- nonvar(f(X)).
yes. X = _0

?- atom(this_is_a_Prolog_atom).
yes.
```

**Assert**—enter a statement directly into the program data base

| | | |
|---|---|---|
| **assert**(*statement*) | is | always *true* and can never be resatisfied and has the side effect of entering *statement* directly into the program database. |
| **Notes:** | | The placement of *statement* in the program data base is implementation dependent. |
| | | The argument *statement* may be either a fact or a rule. |
| **asserta**(*statement*) | is | interpreted identically to **assert**(*statement*), except it is always placed *before* any other statement currently in the program data base for the same relation. |
| **assertz**(*statement*) | is | interpreted identically to **assert**(*statement*), except it is always placed *after* any other statement currently in the program data base for the same relation. |
| **Caveats:** | | The built-in **assert** relations may be used to modify the program while it is running. Self-modifying programs are very difficult to understand and should be avoided whenever possible. |
| | | Note also that any statements entered into the program data base during a session with the Prolog interpreter will disappear after the session is terminated. Thus, when a more permanent recording is preferred, put the statements in a file and use **consult** (or **reconsult**). |

```
?- number(0.29)
yes.

?- integer(481)
yes.

?- atomic(trek620)
yes.
```

---

## REMOVING RELATION DEFINITION STATEMENTS FROM THE PROGRAM DATA BASE

**retract**(*term*) is     always *true* whenever the program data base contains a statement that matches the argument *term*; it has the side effect of removing the first such statement from the program data base.

**Notes:**     The argument *term* must not be a variable.

The interpreter may backtrack on a query to retract, which has the effect of successively removing statements that match the argument *term*.

**abolish**(*name*, *arity*) is     always *true*, and has the side effect of removing all statements defining a relation with name *name* and arity *arity* from the program data base.

**Note:**     The argument *name* must be a Prolog atom.

The argument *arity* must be an integer.

**Caveat:**     The built-in **retract** and **abolish** relations may be used to modify the program while it is running. Self-modifying programs are very difficult to understand and should be avoided.

---

```
?- functor(teams(cardinals,royals),F,2).
yes. F = teams

?- arg(1,teams(cardinals,royals),C).
yes. C = cardinals

?- teams(cardinals,royals) =.. [Func,C1,C2].
yes. Func = teams   C1 = cardinals   C2 = royals

?- name(royals,L).
yes. L = [114,111,121,97,108,115]
```

**Clause**—determines whether the program data base contains a statement with a designated conclusion and conditional part.

| | | |
|---|---|---|
| `clause`(*conclusion, conditional-part*). | is | always *true* whenever the program data base contains a statement with a conclusion that matches the argument *conclusion* and a conditional part that matches the argument *conditional-part*. |
| | **Note:** | Should the statement you wish to enquire about be a *fact*, the argument *conditional-part* must unify with *true*. |

## META-LOGICAL RELATIONS FOR TESTING TERMS

| | | |
|---|---|---|
| `var`(*term*) | is | *true* whenever *term* is an uninstantiated variable. |
| `nonvar`(*term*) | is | *true* whenever *term* is not an uninstantiated variable. |
| `atom`(*term*) | is | *true* whenever *term* is instantiated to a Prolog atom. |
| `number`(*term*) | is | *true* whenever *term* is instantiated to a Prolog number. |
| `integer`(*term*) | is | *true* whenever *term* is instantiated to an integer. |
| `atomic`(*term*) | is | *true* whenever *term* is instantiated to a Prolog atom or number. |

## META-LOGICAL RELATIONS FOR MANIPULATING TERMS

**functor** (*term*, *name*, *arity*)   is   *true* whenever *term* is a structure with functor *name* and arity *arity*.

**Note:**   If *term* is an atom or a number, then *term* and *name* must unify and *arity* must unify with 0.

Before the execution of a query of **functor**, if *term* is an uninstantiated variable, then *name* and *arity* are either instantiated to an atom and a nonnegative integer, or instantiated to an integer and 0, respectively, and the result of the query will be to unify *term* with the most general term having the designated functor *name* and arity *arity*. If *term* is initially an uninstantiated variable and *name* and *arity* do not satisfy these conditions, then the Prolog interpreter will print an error message.

**arg** (*int*, *term*, *component*)   is   *true* whenever *component* is the (*int*)th component of the term *term*.

**Note:**   Before the execution of a query of **arg**, *int* must be instantiated to a positive integer and *term* must be instantiated to a structure. If these initial conditions are not satisfied, the query will simply fail.

*struct* **=..** *list*   is   *true* whenever *struct* is a structure, *list* is a list whose head element is the functor of *struct* and whose tail is the list of components of *struct*.

## META-LOGICAL RELATIONS FOR MANIPULATING TERMS

|  |  |  |
|---|---|---|
| | **Note:** | If *struct* is an uninstantiated variable, then *list* must be instantiated to either a list with fixed length with a Prolog atom as its head element, or to a list whose single element is a number. |
| **name** (*atomic*, *list*) | is | *true* whenever *list* is the list of ASCII codes corresponding to the respective characters of *atomic*, where *atomic* is either a Prolog atom or number. |
| | **Note:** | If *atomic* is an uninstantiated variable, then *list* must be instantiated to a list of ASCII character codes. |

## ▪ SUMMARY

1. **consult** is a built-in relation that *enters* relation definitions and executes directives contained in a file. **reconsult** is a built-in relation that *replaces* relation definitions and executes directives contained in a file. There is an alternative syntax for consulting and reconsulting files that is more concise. Specifically, [**fref**$_1$, ..., **fref**$_n$] is always *true* and can never be resatisfied, and has the side effect of consulting (reconsulting) the $n \geq 1$ referenced files in the list. Each of **fref**$_1$ through **fref**$_n$ is either a file name or a file name preceded by the symbol "-." If **fref**$_i$ is a file name, the file name is consulted. If **fref**$_i$ is a filename preceded by -, the file name is reconsulted.

2. **assert** enters a statement directly into the program data base. **assert** (*statement*) is always *true* and can never be resatisfied and has the side effect of entering *statement* directly into the program data base.

3. **retract** removes a statement from the program data base. **retract** (*term*) is always *true* whenever the program data base contains a statement that matches the argument *term*, and has the side effect of removing the first such statement from the program data base.

**abolish** also removes statements from the program data base.
**abolish**(*name, arity*) is always *true* and has the side effect of
removing all statements defining a relation with name *name* and
arity *arity* from the program data base.

4. **clause** determines whether the program data base contains a statement with a designated conclusion and conditional part.

5. There are a variety of built-in meta-logical relations for testing terms.

   **var**(*term*) is *true* whenever *term* is an uninstantiated variable.

   **nonvar**(*term*) is *true* whenever *term* is not an uninstantiated variable.

   **atom**(*term*) is *true* whenever *term* is instantiated to a Prolog atom.

   **number**(*term*) is *true* whenever *term* is instantiated to a Prolog number.

   **integer**(*term*) is *true* whenever *term* is instantiated to an integer.

   **atomic**(*term*) is *true* whenever *term* is instantiated to a Prolog atom or number.

6. There are also a variety of built-in meta-logical relations for manipulating terms.

   **functor**(*term, name, arity*) is *true* whenever *term* is a structure with functor *name* and arity *arity*.

   **arg**(*int, term, component*) is *true* whenever *component* is the (*int*)th component of the term *term*.

   *struct* =.. *list* is *true* whenever *struct* is a structure, *list* is a list whose head element is the functor of *struct* and whose tail is the list of components of *struct*.

   **name**(*atomic, list*) is *true* whenever *list* is the list of ASCII codes corresponding to the respective characters of *atomic*, where *atomic* is either a Prolog atom or number.

## ■ BIBLIOGRAPHY NOTES

Each implementation of Prolog has a particular set of built-in relations. The relations given in this chapter are those in EdCAAD C-Prolog. Additional material on them can be found in Clocksin and Mellish.

W. F. Clocksin and C. S. Mellish (1981) *Programming in Prolog.* Springer-Verlag, New York.

## ■ EXERCISES

1. Give the response to each of the following queries:

   (a) `?- Term=xxx, var(Term).`

   (b) `?- var(term).`

   (c) `?- nonvar([Term]).`

   (d) `?- atom(_3CPO).`

   (e) `?- atom(r2D2).`

   (f) `?- number(three_CPO)`

   (g) `?- number(2.81)`

   (h) `?- atomic(three_CPO).`

   (i) `?- functor(S,functor,0).`

   (j) `?- functor(star_wars(three_CPO,r2d2,`
   `                       Ronny_Reagan),F,A).`

   (k) `?- arg(2,star_wars(three_CPO,r2d2,Ronny_Reagan),`
   `          X).`

   (l) `?- Struc =..[star_wars,three_CPO,r2d2,`
   `                 Ronny_Reagan].`

   (m) `?- name(r2d2,Name).`

   (n) `?- name(Who,[51,67,80,79]).`

## ANSWERS

1. (a) **no**

   (b) **no**

   (c) **yes**

   (d) **no**

   (e) **yes**

   (f) **no**

   (g) **yes**

   (h) **yes**

(i) **yes**
**S=functor**

(j) **yes**
**F=star_wars    A=3**

(k) **yes**
**X=r2d2**

(l) **yes**
**Struc=star_wars(3CPO,r2d2,Ronny_Reagan).**

(m) **yes**
**Name=[114,50,100,50]**

(n) **yes**
**Who='3CPO'**

# CHAPTER 30

# PROGRAM CONSTRUCTION AND DEBUGGING

The program construction and debugging ideas of this chapter will, we hope, reduce the frustration involved in creating solutions to symbolic computing problems in Prolog. The denotational style of programming helps avoid those dreaded program bugs. You are already familiar with that. Here, we offer other preventive measures to reduce the incidence of common problems. To begin with, laying your program out in a well organized, conventional way will make it easier to read and reduce the overall programming effort.

## ■ PROGRAM LAYOUT

A program of any substance will almost always require many categories of relations. Some popular groups of relations are those for performing basic list manipulation (e.g., **append**, **prefix**, **suffix**), set manipulation (e.g., **member**, **subset**, **union**), searching, sorting, and format-

251

ted input and output. Other logical relation groupings may be evident depending on the program size and application area.

Always partition the program relations into some logical groupings, and place each logical group into a distinct and mnemonically named file.

It is also best to keep the groups small when possible. If you think it might be too much trouble to manage such a group of files, reconsider the material on file consulting in Chapter 29 (*Built-in Relations for Program File Access and Transformation of Terms*). You will find a convenient way to place a command for consulting all relevant files from a single file, so you need only consult a single file.

In laying out the relation definitions in a given file,

Cluster the statements of a relation definition together, and separate the clusters with white space.

This helps to delineate the various relation definitions and will greatly improve readability. In addition, we suggest that when a rule contains several conditions,

Place each condition relation on a separate line.

For example,

```
minmax(X,X,[X]).
minmax(Min,Max,[X|L])  :- minmax(Min2,Max2,L),
                          min(X,Min2,Min),
                          max(X,Max2,Max).

min(X,Y,X)  :- order(X,Y).
min(X,Y,Y)  :- order(Y,X).

max(X,Y,X)  :- order(Y,X).
max(X,Y,Y)  :- order(X,Y).
```

The final and perhaps most important touch is the documentation.

Annotate each definition cluster with comments that describe the variables and components of the statements and the relation computed.

You might select some distinguished symbol pattern to consistently display the relation definition documentation. Adding in such documentation for the foregoing example would produce the following:

```
/* **************************************************

minmax(Min,Max,L) is true if:

(1) L is a nonempty list of values comparable by the
    relation 'order'.

(2) Min is the smallest element in L, if L is nonempty.

(3) Max is the largest element in L, if L is nonempty.

(4) L is initially instantiated to a nonempty list.

*************************************************** */

minmax(X,X,[X]).
minmax(Min,Max,[X|L]) :- minmax(Min2,Max2,L),
                         min(X,Min2,Min),
                         max(X,Max2,Max).

/* **************************************************

min(X,Y,Z) is true if:

(1) All three arguments are initially instantiated to
    values comparable by the relation 'order', and

(2) Z is the smaller of X and Y.

*************************************************** */

min(X,Y,X) :- order(X,Y).
min(X,Y,Y) :- order(Y,X).

/* **************************************************

max(X,Y,Z) is true if:

(1) All three arguments are initially instantiated to
    values comparable by the relation 'order', and

(2) Z is the larger of X and Y.
```

---

## TIPS ON PROGRAM LAYOUT

1. Always partition the program relations into some logical groupings, and place each logical group into a distinct and mnemonically named file.

2. Cluster the statements of a relation definition together, and separate the clusters with white space.

3. Place each condition relation on a separate line.

4. Annotate each definition cluster with comments that describe the variables and components of the statements and the relation computed.

---

```
**************************************************** */

max(X,Y,X)  :- order(Y,X).
max(X,Y,Y)  :- order(X,Y).
```

 # ERRORS TO AVOID

Errors will virtually always be present in early versions of a program even when good program composition practices are adhered to. What follows is a checklist of common types of bugs.

### SPELLING ERRORS

It is real easy to introduce misspelled relation names, variable names, and structure names (unless you are a much better than average typist). A misspelled name usually results in a failed unification at some point in a computation. You can scrutinize your program for spelling errors, but you still may miss some. EdCAAD C-Prolog has several built-in relations that are useful in flushing out misspelled names.

### MISSING COMPONENTS

Another common error is a missing component in a structure or relation. This can be very hard to spot. You can use the built-in relations just given to help locate these problems.

## BUILT-IN RELATIONS THAT LIST CURRENTLY KNOWN NAMES

| | |
|---|---|
| **current_atom**(*Atom*) | generates, through backtracking, all currently known atoms and returns each through the argument *Atom*. When backtracking is attempted after the last known atom has been returned, the query fails. |
| **current_functor**(*Name,Functor*) | generates, through backtracking, all currently structure functors and for each one, returns its name through argument *Name* and its most general term through argument *Functor*. |
| *Note:* | If *Name* is initially instantiated, then only structures with that name are returned. |
| **current_predicate**(*Name,Predicate*) | generates, through backtracking, all current relation names and for each one, returns its name through argument *Name* and its general form through argument *Predicate*. |
| *Note:* | If *Name* is initially instantiated, then only relations with that name are returned. |

## BUILT-IN RELATIONS THAT LIST CURRENTLY KNOWN RELATION DEFINITIONS

`listing` is always *true* and can never be resatisfied and has the side effect of listing all relation definitions that are currently in the program data base.

`listing(R)` is always *true* and can never be resatisfied and has the side effect of doing one of the following:

1. If $R$ is a Prolog atom, then all definitions of relations with name $R$, currently in the program data base, are listed.

2. If $R$ is of the form *Name/Arity*, then all definitions of relations with name *Name* and arity *Arity*, currently in the program data base, are listed.

3. If $R$ is a list of elements of either form 1 or 2, then listing is applied to each list element as described in 1 and 2.

## INCORRECT DELIMITER SYMBOLS

Leaving out a delimiter symbol, particularly a period ("`.`") that should end a statement in a relation definition, can have very unexpected results. When the period is missing, the interpreter will continue to read past the end of the statement and include everything it finds as part of that statement until either a syntax error is evident or, if you are unlucky, until another period is scanned. In the latter case, the statement that is entered into the program data base is likely to be much different from that you intended.

These problems can sometimes be detected through the use of another EdCAAD C-Prolog built-in relation.

## INCORRECT RELATION BOUNDARY CONDITIONS AND GUARDS

Incorrect boundary conditions in traditional program loops or in recursive program definitions are always troublesome. The best medicine here is prevention through careful program construction. Be sure that all boundaries are considered and that each is correctly represented via Prolog statements.

A problem more specific to Prolog programs is the proper "guarding" of relation definition statements. A *guard* is a logical condition that enables the execution of a program statement. Consider the simple case of defining a relation for determining the smaller of two values (as described earlier in this chapter). A common way of defining such a relation is

```
min(X,Y,X) :- order(X,Y).
min(X,Y,Y).
```

The rationale for this definition would most likely be

The smallest of **X** and **Y** is **X** if $X \leq Y$, and **Y** otherwise.

This definition is correct provided *no backtracking occurs.* That is, consider the following query:

```
?- min(1,2,M).
```

**yes**. M=1

Now, suppose you follow that query with a semicolon (";") to request another solution. The response would be

```
?- min(1,2,M).
```

**yes**. M=2

This is not what you would wish to happen! The situation could be easily rectified by adding an appropriate guard to the second statement of the relation definition, to yield the following definition:

```
min(X,Y,X) :- order(X,Y).
min(X,Y,Y) :- order(Y,X).
```

## CARELESS USE OF THE CUT OPERATOR

In practice, cuts are often used to counteract interpreter/compiler inefficiencies. Because this practice requires a full understanding of the process that will occur when the program is interpreted, it's only a matter of time before impulsiveness dominates rational thinking and a bug is introduced!

There is not much to say about this, other than to offer a warning that such bugs can be difficult to recognize and to suggest you heed the advise given in Chapter 8 on cut usage. Tracking down these bugs may remind you more of debugging conventional programs than of your experience with denotational programming. This should be expected because cut concentrates on process rather than on result.

---

COMMON ERRORS TO AVOID

1. Spelling errors.

2. Missing components in relations or structures.

3. Incorrect delimiter symbols.

4. Incorrect relation boundary conditions and guards.

5. Careless usage of the cut operator.

---

## TRACING AND SPYING

When errors occur and the problem is not evident through any of the methods just suggested, there are facilities in EdCAAD C-Prolog that permit you to observe computations in progress. These facilities are not sophisticated, but they do provide the basic mechanisms needed to break up a computation to isolate bugs. There are several ways of observing computations in EdCAAD C-Prolog, particularly *exhaustive tracing* and *selective spying*.

## TRACE

Putting the interpreter in trace mode allows you to observe each step of a computation. This is done by simply executing the query "**trace**." Once the interpreter is placed in trace mode, it will print information about the steps of a computation as directed by the user.

Several options are available during a program trace. When the interpreter prints out a query and waits for a user response, typing a carriage return results in the interpreter executing a single step, printing the result, and waiting for the next response. The result will be an indication either that a condition has been satisfied or that another condition will be evaluated in the next steps of the computation.

Consider the following definition of the relation **append** and the session in which **trace** is set and **append** is queried:

```
append([],L,L).
append([A|X],Y,[A|Z]) :- append(X,Y,Z).


?- trace.

yes.

?- append([a,b],[c,d],L).
```

```
(1) 1 call: append([a,b],[c,d],_10)?

(2) 2 call: append([b],[c,d],_18)?

(3) 3 call: append([],[c,d],_25)?

(3) 3 exit: append([],[c,d],[c,d])?

(2) 2 exit: append([b],[c,d],[b,c,d])?

(1) 1 exit: append([a,b],[c,d],[a,b,c,d])?

yes.  L = [a,b,c,d]
```

A parenthesized number (*n*) indicates that this is the *n*th step of the computation. The next number is *the depth of recursion*. A "**call**" indicates that the following relation will be queried, whereas an "**exit**" indicates that the following relation has been satisfied. The funny numbers (e.g., _**10**) are internal references to variables.

Another option is to ask the interpreter to execute all steps required to satisfy a query, and return at the step after which it has succeeded or failed. This is accomplished by typing an "**s**" followed by a carriage return.

```
?- trace.

yes.

?- append([a,b,c,d],Y,[a,b,c,d,e,f]).

    (1) 1 call: append([a,b,c,d],_7,[a,b,c,d,e,f])?

    (2) 2 call: append([b,c,d],_7,[b,c,d,e,f])? s

  > (2) 2 exit: append([b,c,d],[e,f],[b,c,d,e,f])? s

    (1) 1 exit: append([a,b,c,d],[e,f],[a,b,c,d,e,f])?

yes.  Y = [e,f]
```

Should you wish to abort the computation during a trace, respond with an "**a**" followed by a carriage return. Should you wish to turn off the trace mode after the computation is completed, execute the query "**notrace**."

## SPYPOINTS

More often than not, you will have a good idea of where a bug might be located in your program, and it becomes useful to be able to localize a trace. This can be done in EdCAAD C-Prolog through the use of *spypoints*. A spypoint is associated with all relations with a given name (say **R**) by executing the following query:

    ?- spy R.

The interpreter will respond by printing out each occurrence of **R** for varying arity (e.g., there may be definitions of both a 2-*ary* and a 3-*ary* relation named **R**). The execution of a program will then cause the interpreter to evaluate all steps until a query to a relation currently associated with a spypoint is made, when it prompts you with a "**call**" line. At this point, you may exercise any of the options discussed for **trace**, or type in an "**l**." The latter will tell the interpreter to execute all steps until the next reference to a spypoint is encountered. Spypoints can be removed by executing a query to "**nospy**" with the relation name as the argument (using the same non-standard syntax as is used for **spy**).

## INTERRUPTING PROGRAM EXECUTION

In situations where the interpreter is running and you wish to interrupt it (e.g., you might suspect the program is in an infinite loop), hit the interrupt key on your terminal. When running EdCAAD C-Prolog under Berkeley UNIX, this would be the "break" key. On detecting an interrupt, the interpreter will suspend program execution and prompt you with the following:

    Action (h for help):

Responding with an "**h**" causes the interpreter to print the various options and, again, wait for some action to be specified. Typing an "**a**" will abort the program execution and take you back to the user level again. Typing a "**c**" will allow the program to continue execution at the point it was interrupted. Typing a "**d**" causes the interpreter to switch on trace/debugging mode and prompt you with a trace response, as discussed earlier.

## BREAK LEVELS

When the interpreter is running in trace/debugging mode, we mentioned several possible responses (a carriage return and an "**s**" followed by a carriage return). Should you wish to temporarily re-enter user level to execute further queries while the partial computation remains suspended, you can type a "**b**" followed by a carriage return to enter a *break level*.

## Relations for Interacting with the UNIX vi Editor

**vi** (*Filename*)    makes a system call to **vi** to edit file *Filename*. After exiting from **vi**, the file is automatically reconsulted so that the changes are incorporated into the data base. If *Filename* contains special characters such as "." or some other such character, then it is advisable to delimit *Filename* with single quotes.

```
vi(X) :- name(vi,Z),
         name(X,X1),
         append(Z,[32|X1],Z1),
         system(Z1),
         reconsult(X).
```

**vitx** (*Filename*)  is  similar to the **vi** relation just defined, but it does not reconsult the file after exit from the **vi** editor.

```
vitx(X) :- name(vi,Z),
           name(X,X1),
           append(Z,[32|X1],Z1),
           system(Z1).
```

## Relations for Interacting with the UNIX more File Viewer

**more** (*Filename*)  is  somewhat similar to the **vitx** relation. It calls the **more** command and does not reconsult the file afterward.

```
more(X) :- name(more,Z),
           name(X,X1),
           append(Z,[32|X1],Z1),
           system(Z1).
```

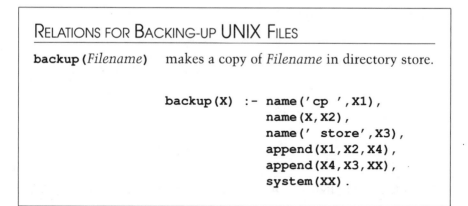

## RELATIONS FOR INTERACTING WITH THE UNIX GREP PATTERN MATCHER

**grep**(*Expression*)     searches through all the files in the current directory for any text string matching *Expression*. Since this uses the Unix command **grep**, there are some limitations. For one thing, the matched strings have to be on a single line. The file names for the files that have occurrences of *Expression* are printed out.

```
grep(X) :- name('grep -l',X1),
           name(X,X2),

append(X1,[32,39|X2],X3),

append(X3,[39,32,42],X4),
        system(X4).
```

## RELATIONS FOR BACKING-UP UNIX FILES

**backup**(*Filename*)     makes a copy of *Filename* in directory store.

```
backup(X) :- name('cp ',X1),
             name(X,X2),
             name(' store',X3),
             append(X1,X2,X4),
             append(X4,X3,XX),
             system(XX).
```

Using the break option is particularly useful for altering the spypoints on your program, or generally being able to alter an aspect of the program so as to complete the suspended computation without beginning again. The system end-of-file character (a "control-D" on Berkeley UNIX systems) will terminate a break and return you to the point at which the break was executed. There may be arbitrarily deep levels of breaks, and the end-of-file character will simply raise you up one break level when executed. Should you wish to terminate a computation from within a break level, simply execute the query "**abort**", and the computation will be halted and control will return to the top user level.

## TRACE/DEBUG MODE

When a traced computation has ended, the interpreter will automatically turn off the "trace/debug" mode. If you have executed a query to **trace**, simply enter a query to "**debug**" to reestablish the trace/debug mode. Similarly, the mode can be suspended by entering a query to "**nodebug**."

## ▪ PROGRAM REPAIRS

We will finish this chapter on debugging by providing a few handy relations that allow you to move between an EdCAAD C-Prolog session and the UNIX (UNIX is a trademark of AT&T Bell Laboratories) system level without having to exit from Prolog. The programs were written by Joseph Varghese, who is gratefully acknowledged. We assume you are familiar with the UNIX commands that are invoked by these relations.

## ▪ SUMMARY

1. A nicely formatted program makes debugging much easier. Some tips for laying out a Prolog are

   (a) Always partition the program relations into some logical groupings and place each logical group into a distinct and mnemonically named file.

   (b) Cluster the statements of a relation definition together, and separate the clusters with ample white space.

   (c) Place each condition relation on a separate line.

   (d) Minimally, place comments along with each relation definition cluster that describe the variables and components of the statements and the relation computed in terms of the variables.

2. The following built-in relations list currently known names:

   (a) **current_atom**(*Atom*) generates, through backtracking, all currently known atoms and returns each through the argument *Atom*. When backtracking is attempted after the last known atom has been returned, the query fails.

   (b) **current_functor**(*Name,Functor*) generates, through backtracking, all currently known structure functors and for each one, returns its name through argument *Name* and its most general term through argument *Functor*.

(c) **current_predicate**(*Name,Predicate*) generates, through back-tracking, all currently relation names and for each one, returns its name through argument *Name* and its general form through argument *Predicate*.

3. The following built-in relations list currently known relation definitions:

   (a) **listing** is always *true* and can never be resatisfied and has the side effect of listing all relation definitions that are currently in the program data base.

   (b) **listing**(*R*) is always *true* and can never be resatisfied and has the side effect of doing one of the following: (1) if *R* is a Prolog atom, then all definitions of relations with name *R*, currently in the program data base, are listed, (2) if *R* is of the form *Name/Arity*, then all definitions of relations with name *Name* and arity *Arity*, currently in the program data base, are listed, or (3) if *R* is a list of elements of either form (1) or (2), then listing is applied to each list element as described in (1) and (2).

4. Some common errors to avoid are: spelling errors, missing components in relations or structures, incorrect delimiter symbols, incorrect relation boundary conditions and guards, and careless use of the cut operator.

5. Several interactive debugging modes are built into EdCAAD C-Prolog. A trace feature permits step-by-step execution of the program with display of all variable values. A less selective but more efficient method of debugging is the use of *spypoints*. With spypoints, the program execution can be broken at very selective locations in the program.

## ■ BIBLIOGRAPHY NOTES

Each implementation of Prolog has a particular set of debugging features. The debugging commands given in this chapter are those in ED-CAAD C-Prolog. Additional material on them can be found in Clocksin and Mellish.

W. F. Clocksin and C. S. Mellish (1981) *Programming in Prolog*, Springer-Verlag, New York.

# ■ EXERCISES

1. Select several of the Prolog relation definitions given in previous chapters and comment them according to the the program layout guidelines. What additional tips would you give on program layout based on your experience in documenting programs of other languages?

2. Consult the programs you selected for debugging in Exercise 1 and trace their execution on selected queries. Try setting spypoints on some of the relations you defined and observe the execution of several queries with the spypoints set.

# CHAPTER 31

# NUMBERS

Traditionally, numbers have been the most important group of symbols in computing. As such, it is not surprising that most introductory texts on programming languages and methodologies have developed their subject matter largely through numeric examples. Our subject matter is symbolic computing in a more general sense, so we have made a concerted effort not to use numeric examples as a crutch. However, since numbers are an important part of symbolic computing, Prolog includes many special facilities for numeric computing. To begin with, there are several ways to denote numbers in Prolog.

Numeric expressions in Prolog are similar to those in the more common programming languages. Prolog does, however, provide a special syntax for unifying a variable or number with a numeric expression. The special syntax is for convenience rather than out of necessity.

Prolog numeric expressions are conventional *infix* expressions using parentheses for grouping and with multiplication and division operators computed before addition and subtraction. The available operators pro-

## NUMBER

| | | |
|---|---|---|
| *number* | is | *unsigned_number* |
| | or | - *unsigned_number* |
| *unsigned_number* | is | *integer* |
| | or | *fixed_point_real* |
| | or | *floating_point_real* |
| *integer* | is | *digit digit* ... |
| | *Caveat:* | No spaces between *digit*'s. |
| *fixed_point_real* | is | *integer* . *integer* |
| | or | - *integer* . *integer* |
| | *Caveat:* | No spaces around the decimal point. |
| *floating_point_real* | is | *fixed_point_real* **e** *integer* |
| | or | *fixed_point_real* **e** - *integer* |
| | *Caveat:* | No spaces around the **e** or the minus sign. |

**Notes:**

1. EdCAAD C-Prolog has trouble with negative fractions. If you want to enter a signed *fixed_point_real* or *floating_point_real*, surround the unsigned number with parentheses.

2. Fractions should always begin with "**0.**", not simply "**.**", or the interpreter will parse it incorrectly.

**Examples:**

**12**, **001**, **229**, and **–33** are unsigned and signed *integer*'s.

**1.1**, **0.01**, and **22.3** are *fixed_point_real*'s.

**1.125e1**, **0.01e-1**, and **7.3e-10** are *floating_point_real*'s.

**-(22.3)** and **-(7.3e-10)** are numeric expressions denoting negative fixed-point and floating-point quantities.

---

**IS**—SPECIAL SYNTAX FOR UNIFYING VARIABLES (NUMBERS) WITH NUMERIC EXPRESSIONS

---

*V* **is** *Expr*   is  true whenever *V* is a variable or a number, *Expr* evaluates to a number, and *V* unifies with *Expr*.

Note:  Each occurrence of a variable in *Expr* must be instantiated to a number before *expr* is evaluated.

**Examples:**    **T is 3\*X+1**
               **1 is 3 mod 2**

---

## EdCAAD C-PROLOG ARITHMETIC OPERATORS

---

Let $X$ and $Y$ be any Prolog numeric expressions.

| | |
|---|---|
| $X + Y$ | Addition |
| $X - Y$ | Subtraction |
| $X * Y$ | Multiplication |
| $X/Y$ | Division |
| $X//Y$ | Integer Division |
| $X$ **mod** $Y$ | $X$ modulo $Y$, where $X$ and $Y$ are integer-valued. |
| $-(X)$ | Unary Negation |
| $X\hat{}Y$ | $X^Y$ |

---

vided by EdCAAD C-Prolog include all the basic arithmetic operators, functions for exponentials and logarithms, sinusoidal functions, and bit-manipulation functions.

The standard arithmetic relational operators are provided for determining the relative magnitude of numeric expressions.

Finally, we give the relative precedence of the numeric functions and relations. Note that parentheses can always be used to dictate the order of expression evaluation.

To illustrate the use of Prolog in solving numeric problems, we will consider several examples. A simple place to begin is with the *factorial* function, $n!$, defined as follows:

$$n! = n * (n - 1) * (n - 2) * \cdots * 2 * 1 \quad (n \geq 1)$$

We will define our 2-*ary* factorial relation **factorial** based on the following assumption and observation:

$$(1)\ 0! \ = \ 1$$
$$(2)\ n! \ = \ n * (n - 1)! \quad (n \geq 1)$$

## EdCAAD C-Prolog Exponential, Logarithmic, and Sinusoidal Functions

Let $X$ and $Y$ be any Prolog numeric expressions.

| | |
|---|---|
| $exp(X)$ | $e^X$ |
| $log(X)$ | $\log_e X$ |
| $log10(X)$ | $\log_1 0X$ |
| $sqrt(X)$ | $\sqrt{X}$ |
| $sin(X)$ | $\sin X$ |
| $cos(X)$ | $\cos X$ |
| $tan(X)$ | $\tan X$ |
| $asin(X)$ | $\arcsin X$ |
| $acos(X)$ | $\arccos X$ |
| $atan(X)$ | $\arctan X$ |
| $floor(X)$ | $\lfloor X \rfloor$ |

## EdCAAD C-Prolog Bit-Manipulation Functions

Let $X$ and $Y$ be any Prolog numeric expressions.

| | |
|---|---|
| $X/\backslash Y$ | integer bitwise conjunction |
| $X\backslash/Y$ | integer bitwise disjunction |
| $X << Y$ | integer bitwise left shift of $X$, $Y$ positions |
| $X >> Y$ | integer bitwise right shift of $X$, $Y$ positions |
| $\backslash X$ | integer bitwise negation |

*Note:* These operators are completely dependent on the particular form in which the system chooses to represent numeric values as bit patterns.

## EdCAAD C-Prolog Numeric Comparison Relations

Let $X$ and $Y$ be any Prolog numeric expressions.

| | |
|---|---|
| $X =:= Y$ | the values of $X$ and $Y$ are equal. |
| $X = \backslash = Y$ | the values of $X$ and $Y$ are not equal. |
| $X < Y$ | the value of $X$ is less than that of $Y$. |
| $X > Y$ | the value of $X$ is greater than that of $Y$. |
| $X =< Y$ | the value of $X$ is less than or equal to that of $Y$. |
| $X >= Y$ | the value of $X$ is greater than or equal to that of $Y$. |

---

### RELATIVE PRECEDENCE OF EDCAAD C-PROLOG NUMERIC FUNCTIONS

Operators of equal precedence are grouped together. The groups are given in *increasing* order of precedence.

$is, =:=, = \backslash =, <, >, =<, >=$

$+, -, /\backslash, \backslash/$

(unary) $-$

$*, /, //, <<, >>$

$X$ **mod** $Y$

$X\char`^Y$

---

Note that although factorial is a 1-*ary* function, we will define it as a 2-*ary* relation. This is consistent with a general principle of mathematics that states that any *n-ary* function can be described as an $(n + 1)$-*ary* relation. In the relational representation, $n$ components correspond to $n$ arguments to the associated *n-ary* function, and the $(n + 1)st$ component corresponds to the result of applying the *n-ary* function to those $n$ arguments.

The Prolog definition of **factorial** is

```
factorial(0,1).
factorial(N,Nfac)  :- N>=1,
                      M is N-1,
                      factorial(M,Mfac),
                      Nfac is N*Mfac.
```

```
?- factorial(4,N).
```

```
yes. N=24
```

```
?- factorial(4,24).
```

```
yes.
```

```
?- factorial(N,24).
```

```
Error: variable not instantiated to a number in
        expression!
```

For a second example, consider the problem of relationally defining the function $x^n$ for all non-negative integers $n$. We will denote a 3-*ary* relation, **power(X,N,Xn)**, to be true whenever both $X$ and $N$ are initially instantiated to a number and non-negative integer, respectively, and **Xn** is $X^N$. The simplest solution would be to define **power** so that **Xn** is obtained by multiplying **x** by itself $N - 1$ times:

```
power(_,0,1).
power(X,N,Xn) :- N>0,
                 M is N-1,
                 power(X,M,Xm),
                 Xn is X*Xm.
```

```
?- power(2,3,P).
```

```
yes. P=8
```

```
?- power(3,2,9).
```

```
yes.
```

```
?- power(X,2,9).
```

```
yes.
Error: variable not instantiated to a number in
       expression!
```

Although this program certainly computes the denoted relation faithfully, it is not very efficient. Specifically, the time required by the program is proportional to the exponent **N**. By making a few straightforward algebraic observations, we can improve the situation considerably.

The general rule used herein can be decomposed into two cases: that where $N$ is *even* and $N$ is *odd*. When $N$ is odd, we will use the same principle of obtaining $X^N$ by computing $X^{N-1}$ and multiplying it by $X$. However, when $N$ is even, we observe that

$$X^N = (X^2)^{N/2}$$

This observation means that the required time can now be reduced to being roughly proportional to $\log_2 N$, a considerable improvement! The new definition of **power** is

```
power(_,0,1).
power(X,N,Xn) :- N>0,
                 odd(N),
                 M is N-1,
                 power(X,M,Xm),
                 Xn is X*Xm.
```

```
power(X,N,Xn) :- N>0,
                 even(N),
                 X2 is X*X,
                 M is N//2,
                 power(X2,M,Xn).

even(X) :- 0 is X mod 2.

odd(X) :- 1 is X mod 2.

?- power(5,4,X).

yes. X=625

?- power(5,4,625).

yes.

?- power(5,N,625).

Error: variable not instantiated to a number in
       expression!
```

For a third example, we will consider a problem that involves both the factorial and power functions. Suppose we want to define a relation to compute the function $e^x$ for all real numbers $x$. It has been known for some time that $e^x$ can be equated with an *infinite series* of terms, which we will call the *exponential series*:

$$e^x = 1 + x + \frac{x^2}{2!} + \frac{x^3}{3!} + \cdots$$

Using the relations we defined for computing the factorial and power functions, it is clear that we can compute each of these terms. There are, however, a multitude of related problems we must resolve. First, although we can compute any one of these terms, we certainly cannot compute an infinity of them! We can instead approximate $e^x$ by computing a finite number of the terms. Since the exponential series tends to converge to $e^x$ very rapidly, a small number of terms will typically suffice.

We will define a 3-*ary* relation, **exp1(X,N,ExpX)**, that unifies **ExpX** with the first **N** terms of the exponential series for $e^X$ whenever **X** is initially unified to a number and **N** is initially unified to a nonnegative integer. The method used to compute **ExpX** will be to compute and sum each of the terms successively:

```
expl(_,0,1).
expl(X,N,ExpX)  :- power(X,N,Xn),
                   factorial(N,Nfac),
                   Term is Xn/Nfac,
                   M is N-1,
                   expl(X,M,ExpM),
                   ExpX is Term+ExpM.

?- expl(1,10,P).

yes. P = 2.7182
```

This program, like the naive version of the relation **power**, computes the denoted relation but is unnecessarily inefficient. For one thing, consider the successive computation of the term numerators, $x^i$, $0 \le i \le n$. It should be clear that given $x^j$, we can determine $x^{j+1}$ with a single multiplication. However, the naive routine recalculates the numerators without exploiting this fact.

To rectify this problem, we note that when we are computing only the first $n+1$ terms of the exponential series, the series becomes a *polynomial*,

$$c_n x^n + c_{n-1} x^{n-1} + \cdots + c_1 x + c_0 \tag{1}$$

where $c_i = \frac{1}{i!}$, $0 \le i \le n$.

The most efficient method of evaluating a polynomial is *Horner's rule*. To understand the validity of Horner's rule, consider first the form equation **(1)** takes if we factor an $x$ from the $n$ terms involving $x$:

$$(c_n x^{n-1} + c_{n-1} x^{n-2} + \cdots + c_1)x + c_0 \tag{2}$$

If we repeat the factoring process on equation **(2)** $n-1$ more times, we get Horner's rule:

$$(\cdots (c_n x + c_{n-1})x + \cdots + c_1)x + c_0 \tag{3}$$

The significance of Horner's rule is that an $n$th-order polynomial [i.e., one fitting the form of equation (1)] can be evaluated for any value of $x$ using $n$ multiplications and $n$ additions, which is optimal! If we substitute the coefficients for the polynomial approximation of the exponential series into equation (3), the result is

$$(\cdots (\frac{x}{n!} + \frac{1}{n-1!})x + \cdots + 1)x + 1 \tag{4}$$

We have made the power computations efficient, but the coefficient computations require on the order of $n^2$ multiplications. Again, this is grossly inefficient. If we make the same clever use of factoring on the coefficients, we obtain a very efficient form for evaluating the polynomial approximation of the exponential series:

$$(\cdots((\frac{x}{n} + 1)\frac{x}{n-1} + 1)\frac{x}{n-2} + \cdots + 1)x + 1 \tag{5}$$

We will define a 3-*ary* relation, **exp2 (X, N, ExpX)**, that relates its components in the same way as **exp1**, but using the form of the polynomial given by equation (5). This relation will relegate most of the work to a 4-*ary* relation **horner (X, N, I, S)**, where **X**, **N**, and **I** must be initially instantiated to numbers (**N** to a nonnegative integer) and which is true if **S** unifies with the product of **I** and the polynomial given in equation (5) for the given values of **X** and **N**:

```
exp1(X,N,ExpX) :- horner(X,N,1,ExpX).

horner(_,0,S,S).
horner(X,N,I,S) :- T is I*X/N+1,
                   M is N-1,
                   horner(X,M,T,S).

?- exp2(2,12,P).

yes.  P = 7.389053
```

## ■ SUMMARY

1. One can express both integers and real numbers in Prolog, and do both integer and real computations. Real numbers can be represented in both fixed-point and floating-point form.

2. The syntax for queries and rule conditions is different from the prefix form used for conventional relations. Specifically, *V* **is** *Expr* is true whenever *V* is a variable or a number, *Expr* evaluates to a number, and *V* unifies with *Expr*. This syntax is more similar to that used in popular programming languages and is more convenient for this reason.

3. Arithmetic expressions are represented in infix form, as in popular programming languages, again, for convenience. There are a modest number of arithmetic operators, exponential, logarithmic, and sinusoidal functions, bit manipulation functions, and relational operators.

## ■ BIBLIOGRAPHY NOTES

Each implementation of Prolog has a particular set of numerical relations. The arithmetic functions and numerical relations given in this chapter are those in EdCAAD C-Prolog. Additional material on them can be found in Clocksin and Mellish. Examples of numeric problems in symbolic computing abound in most books on recursive programming, recursive programming languages, and symbolic computing.

W. F. Clocksin and C. S. Mellish (1981) Programming in Prolog. Springer-Verlag, New York.

## ■ EXERCISES

1. The relation **exp1**, as we defined it, works when the powers are positive. Simply generalizing it to work for negative powers would produce very inaccurate results. The terms in the sum alternate in sign, and the subtractions drop digits. Rewrite the relation making use of the fact that $x^{-n} = 1/x^n$.

2. Consider the following definition of the well known Ackermann's function defined on integer arguments:

$$
\begin{aligned}
a(i, 0) &= 1 & (i \geq 1) \\
a(i, 1) &= 2 & (i \geq 1) \\
a(0, j) &= 2j & (j \geq 0) \\
a(i, j) &= a(i - 1, a(i, j - 1)) & (i \geq 1, j \geq 1)
\end{aligned}
$$

Define a 3-ary Prolog relation **ackermann(I,J,A)** that is true whenever **I** and **J** are initially instantiated to nonnegative integers and **A** is $a(I, J)$.

3. There are several problems with computing Ackermann's function; one is the time required to obtain a solution (it grows exponentially with the size of $I$) and the other is with the size of the result and intermediate values used to obtain the result (they also grow exponentially with the size of $I$). Takeuchi's function, shown below, also runs very slowly, but its argument values and result never grow large.

$$
\begin{aligned}
tak(i, j, k) &= k & (i \leq j) \\
tak(i, j, k) &= tak(tak(i - 1, j, k), tak(j - 1, k, i), tak(k - 1, i, j)) & \\
& & \text{(otherwise)}
\end{aligned}
$$

Define a 4-ary Prolog relation **tak(I,J,K,Tak)** that is true whenever **I**, **J**, and **K** are initially instantiated to integers and **Tak** is $tak(I, J, K)$.

4. Let $\alpha = (a_1, a_2, \ldots, a_n)$ and $\beta = (b_1, b_2, \ldots, b_n)$ be two vectors, and define the *dot product* of $\alpha$ and $\beta$ to be

$$\alpha \cdot \beta = a_1 b_1 + a_2 b_2 + \cdots + a_n b_n = \sum_{k=1}^{n} a_k b_k$$

Define a 3-ary Prolog relation **dot(Alpha,Beta,Dot_Product)** that is true whenever **Alpha** and **Beta** are initially instantiated to lists of integers of length $n$, $n \geq 1$, corresponding to two vectors, and **Dot_Product** is the dot product of those two vectors.

5. The simplest method of computing the real zeros of a continuous function $f(x)$ in an interval $a \leq x \leq b$ is the *bisection method*. The bisection method relies on the assumption that an interval $x_1 \leq x \leq x_2$ is known to contain a zero of $f$. Mathematically, this means that the values of the function in the interval must change sign, that is, $f(x_1)f(x_2) < 0$.

Like the binary search, bisection is a divide-and-conquer method that iteratively decreases the size of the interval by one-half until a solution is found. The idea is to examine the value of $f$ at the midpoint of the interval, $f((x_1 + x_2)/2)$; if the value is zero, then $(x_1 + x_2)/2$ is a zero of $f$; if not, then there must be a sign change in at least one of the intervals $(x_1, (x_1 + x_2)/2)$ and $((x_1 + x_2)/2, x_2)$. Select one such interval and repeat the process. Define a 3-ary Prolog relation **bisection(X1,X2,Zero)** that is true whenever a relation **f(X,Y)** is defined for evaluating some function $f$ that is continuous in the interval $(X1, X2)$ on values $X$ to obtain $Y = f(X)$, a zero of $f$ exists on the interval $(X1, X2)$, where **X1** and **X2** are initially instantiated to real values, and **Zero** is a zero of $f$. You may assume $f$ to have a zero at $X$ if $|f(X)| < 0.01$.

## ANSWERS

1. **exp3(_,0,1).**
   ```
   exp3(X,N,ExpX)  :- X>0,
                      exp1(X,N,ExpX).
   exp3(X,N,ExpX)  :- X<0,
                      PosX is -X,
                      exp1(PosX,N,ExpTemp),
                      ExpX is 1/ExpTemp.
   ```

*Note:* The fact **exp1(_,0,1).** in the definition of **exp1** is no longer needed with this definition of **exp3**.

2. 
```
ackermann(_,0,0).
ackermann(I,1,2) :- I>=0.
ackermann(0,J,K)  :- J>=0,
                     K is J*2.
ackermann(I,J,K)  :- I>=1,
                     J>=1,
                     I1 is I-1,
                     J1 is J-1,
                     ackermann(I,J1,K1),
                     ackermann(I1,K1,K).
```

3. 
```
tak(I,J,K,K)  :- I=<J.
tak(I,J,K,P)  :- I1 is I-1,
                 J1 is J-1,
                 K1 is K-1,
                 tak(I1,J,K,P1),
                 tak(J1,K,I,P2),
                 tak(K1,I,J,P3),
                 tak(P1,P2,P3,P).
```

4. 
```
dot([A1],[B1],C)  :- C is A1*B1.
dot([A1|AL],[B1|BL],C)  :- C1 is A1*B1,
                           dot(AL,BL,C2),
                           C is C1+C2.
```

5. 
```
bisection(X1,X2,Zero)  :- Midpoint is (X1+X2)/2,
                          f(Midpoint,Y),
                          bisect(X1,X2,Midpoint,
                                 Y,Zero).

bisect(_,_,Midpoint,Y,Midpoint)  :- abs(Y,A),
                                    A<0.01.
bisect(X1,X2,Midpoint,Y,Zero)  :- f(X1,Y1),
                                  Y*Y1<0,
                                  bisection(X1,
                                            Midpoint,
                                            Zero).
bisect(X1,X2,Midpoint,Y,Zero)  :- f(X2,Y2),
                                  Y*Y2<0,
                                  bisection(Midpoint,
                                            X2,Zero).

abs(X,X)  :- X>=0.
abs(X,Y)  :- X<0,
             Y is 0-X.
```

# CHAPTER 32

# INPUT AND OUTPUT

In this chapter we discuss the Prolog relations for reading information into a program and writing information from a program. There are Prolog relations for the input and output of both *character data* and *terms*, and for selecting the input file and output file under program control.

We will begin with the default environment, where information is read from standard input and written to standard output. Standard input typically comes from a terminal keyboard, and standard output is typically the terminal screen.

## ■ CHARACTER OUTPUT

The EdCAAD C-Prolog relation for writing characters is called **put**. It has a single argument, which is assumed to be instantiated to a valid ASCII code[1].

---

[1] ASCII is an acronym for *American Standard Code for Information Interchange*.

Given a valid argument, **put** will always succeed and cannot be re-satisfied (i.e., backtracking on **put** will always fail). To illustrate **put**, suppose we wish to write the word "**prolog**" to output.

The ASCII codes for "**p**", "**r**", "**o**", "**l**", and "**g**" are 112, 114, 111, 108, and 103, respectively. Therefore, the query

```
?- put(112), put(114), put(111), put(108), put(111),
   put(103).
```

would succeed and, as a side effect, write the string **prolog** to output.

Several other built-in relations are useful for writing to output. The first is **nl**, a 0-*ary* relation that always succeeds, can never be resatisfied, and writes a *newline* control character sequence to output as a side effect.

Thus, if we instead wanted to write the string **pro** on a line, and **log** on the next line, that is,

```
pro
log
```

we could execute the query

```
?- put(112), put(114), put(111), nl, put(108),
   put(111), put(103).
```

Another useful relation is **tab**, which takes a single argument that is instantiated to an integer. Given a valid argument $X$, **tab**($X$) always succeeds, can never be resatisfied, and writes $X$ blanks to output as a side effect. Note that when $X \leq 0$ there is no side effect.

To write the string **pro log** on a line, we could execute the query

```
?- put(112), put(114), put(111), tab(1), put(108),
   put(111), put(103).
```

Note that the definition of **tab** in EdCAAD C-Prolog can be simply stated relationally in terms of **put** as follows:

```
tab(X) :- X=<0, !.
tab(X) :- put(32),
          X1 is X-1,
          tab(X1).
```

where 32 is the ASCII code for the blank.

You may be distressed by the ostensible need to manually encode characters to be written to output. If so, you will be pleased to know about the built-in relation **name**, which relates any atomic name to its ASCII string representation.

The relation **name** takes two arguments, the first being an atom or a number and the second a list of the ASCII codes corresponding to the characters of the first argument[2]

Thus, the query

```
?- name(prolog, [112,114,111,108,111,103]).
```

would succeed, as would the query

```
?- name(A, [108,97,115,101,114,95,100,105,115,107]).
```

for **A=laser_disk**, the query

```
?- name(otis,S).
```

for **S=[111,116,105,115]**, the query

```
?- name(1984,N).
```
\vbig

\noindent
for {\pt N}={\pt [49,57,56,52]}, and the query

\vbig
\begin{verbatim}
```
  ?- name(nakamichi,"nakamichi").
```

With the relation **name** at our disposal, it becomes useful to have a relation for writing strings. We can generalize **put** from single characters to strings by defining a relation **put_string** that takes a single argument instantiated to a string.

```
put_string([]).
put_string([C|L]) :- put(C),
                     put_string(L).
```

---

[2]Recall that a Prolog *string* is a sequence of symbols X delimited by quotes, that is, "X", and is represented by the list of ASCII character codes corresponding to the symbols of X.

### BUILT-IN RELATIONS FOR CHARACTER OUTPUT

| | |
|---|---|
| **put** (*Ascii*) | succeeds whenever *Ascii* is instantiated to a valid ASCII code and as a side effect writes the character with ASCII code *Ascii* to the current output file. |
| **name** (*Atomic*, *List*) | succeeds whenever *List* is the list of ASCII character codes for the characters in Prolog atom or number *Atomic*. |
| *Note:* | At least one of the two arguments must be instantiated, or else an error message is produced. |

## ■ CHARACTER INPUT

Reading characters from input can be done using either **get0** or **get**. The relation **get0** has a single argument and will always succeed if the argument is uninstantiated. Its function is to read the next input character and to advance the "input file pointer."[3]

If **C** is uninstantiated, then it instantiates to the ASCII code of the input character that is read. If **C** is instantiated, then it must have the same value as the input character that is read, or else the query fails.

In any case, **get0** can never be resatisfied. That is, once a character is read it can never be reread. This can be troublesome in lexical scanning applications and is usually managed by reading ahead before processing input data.

The second relation is called **get**. The relation **get** is identical in function to **get0**, with the exception that it will read *the next printing character* from the input stream. That is, it skips over nonprinting characters until it finds a printing character to read.

The printing characters are those that display on your screen. More specifically, printing characters have ASCII codes greater than 32. We often make use of **get** to automatically scan around delimiting characters when reading text.

There is one additional input relation, called **skip**. The relation **skip** has a single argument, which must be instantiated to an integer. It scans characters from the input stream until it finds one with an ASCII code matching the value of its argument. After **skip** completes successfully, further input requests are processed beginning with the next character in the input stream.

---

[3]The *input file pointer* is an internal system variable used to keep track of the next available character for input in the input file. It is automatically updated by the system so that the Prolog programmer need not manage this detail.

---

### BUILT-IN RELATIONS FOR CHARACTER INPUT

**get0** (*Ascii*)    succeeds whenever *Ascii* unifies with the ASCII code of the next character read from the current input file. It also causes the input file pointer to be advanced to the next available character in the input file.

**get** (*Ascii*)    succeeds whenever *Ascii* unifies with the ASCII code of the next *printing* character read from the current input file. It also causes the input file pointer to be advanced to the next available character in the input file.

**skip** (*Ascii*)    succeeds whenever *Ascii* unifies with the ASCII code of a character readable from the current input file, and, as a side effect, moves the input file pointer to the position following that character (effectively skipping over all input preceding that character).

---

## ■ TERM OUTPUT

The more common need in the output of program data is to write out the instantiated values of variables. This can be accomplished using the relation **write**, which takes a term as its single argument.

The query **write(T)** will always succeed and can never be resatisfied. It causes, as a side effect, the value of the term **T** to be written to output. For simple cases, such as writing out the current value of a variable, we simply give that variable as the argument to **write**. For example, the query

```
?- T is 3*5, write(T).
```

would write **15** to output.

We can also use **write** to print literal strings. The query

```
?- T is 3*5, write('The value of T is: '), write(T).
```

would write **The value of T is: 15** to output.

When an uninstantiated variable is a component of a term that is the argument to **write**, we get a seemingly cryptic value like **_239** written to output. The **_239** represents the memory element allocated to this uninstantiated variable by the interpreter.

The **write** relation can also be used with output lists; for example, the evaluation of the query

---

### BUILT-IN RELATIONS FOR TERM OUTPUT

**write**(*Term*)   always succeeds and as a side effect writes the term *Term* to the current output file.

---

```
?- write([a|[x,y|[z]]]).
```

would produce **[a,x,y,z]** as output.

Finally, **write** can display output structures. For example, if **X** was instantiated to **t2(3,5)** and **Y** to **nil**, then the evaluation of the query

```
?- write(t2(X,Y)).
```

would display the structure **t2(t2(3,5),nil)**.

Suppose you wished to write out the elements of a list, each element on a separate line. The relation **write_nl** defined next takes a list as its argument and does just that.

```
write_nl([]) :- !.
write_nl([T|L]) :- write(T),
                   nl,
                   write_nl(L).
```

## ■ TERM INPUT

To input terms in EdCAAD C-Prolog, we use the built-in relation **read**. The relation **read** takes a term as its single argument. The term must be followed by a period and some nonprinting character, such as the carriage return.

The query **read(T)** will always succeed when **T** is uninstantiated and can never be resatisfied. If **T** is instantiated, it must match up with the term that is read from the input stream.

Thus, the query

```
?- read(T), write(T).
```

with **T** initially uninstantiated, and the input "**i_am_a_term.**" followed by a carriage return, would succeed and produce as output "**i_am_a_term.**"

To illustrate term I/O in action, let us consider the problem of designing a user interface for a set manipulation program. A set will be represented as a list, and the program can perform the functions *insert*, *delete*, and *min*, where:

*insert* places an element into the set if it is not already present.

*delete* removes an element of the set if that element is currently a member of the set.

*min* returns the minimal element currently residing in the set.

The program is set in motion by the query **set(S)**, with **S** instantiated to the initial value of the set. Once initialized, the program will prompt the user with the message:

**please enter a set operation:**

The user will then respond in one of the following ways:

1. Enter the term **insert**, to insert an element into the set. The program will then respond with the request:

   **specify the element to be inserted:**

   The user will respond by supplying the element as a term.

2. Enter the term **delete**, to delete an element from the set. The program will then respond with the request:

   **specify the element to be deleted:**

   The user will respond by supplying the element as a term.

3. Enter the term **min**, to find out the minimal-valued element currently in the set. The program will respond with that element.

4. Enter the term **current**, to find out the current elements in the set. The program will respond with the set.

5. Enter the term **enough**, to terminate the session. The program will terminate successfully.

6. If a term other than these is read in, the program will respond with *unknown command....*

After each command (other than **enough**), the program will again prompt the user with the request:

**please enter a set operation:**

The process then repeats itself.

We will design our program through two relations. The first will have a single argument that is the current set and will prompt the user, read the response, and then send the current set and the response on to the other relation for processing.

The second relation will have a rule for handling each distinct command, and one for handling the "unknown command" case. We will assume that the set manipulation relations for doing insertion, deletion, and min-element are called **set_insert**, **set_delete**, and **set_min**, respectively, and the relation for printing out the current set is called **write_set**. For our purposes, we will simply treat these relations as "black boxes."

The program is defined as:

```
set(Set) :- nl,
            write('please enter a set operation:  '),
            read(Command),
            execute_command(Set,Command).

execute_command(Set,insert) :- nl,
            write('specify element to be inserted: '),
            read(Element),
            set_insert(Element,Set,New_Set),
            set(New_Set), !.

execute_command(Set,min) :- set_min(Set,Min_element),
  nl,
  write('smallest element currently in the set is: '),
  write(Min_element),
  set(Set), !.

execute_command(Set,delete) :- nl,
            write('specify the element to be deleted: '),
            read(Element),
            set_delete(Element,Set,New_Set),
            set(New_Set), !.

execute_command(Set,current) :- nl,
                                write_set(Set),
                                set(Set), !.

execute_command(_,enough) :- nl,
            write('That's all folks...'),
            nl,
            !.

execute_command(Set,_) :- nl,
                          write('Unknown command...'),
                          nl,
                          !.
```

---

### BUILT-IN RELATIONS FOR TERM INPUT

**read(***Term***)**   succeeds whenever *Term* unifies with the next term read from the current input file.

---

An example of a session with the set manipulation program is given here:

```
?- set([]).
please enter a set operation:   insert.
specify the element to be inserted:   cat.
please enter a set operation:   insert.
specify the element to be inserted:   bat.
please enter a set operation:   insert.
specify the element to be inserted:   dog.
please enter a set operation:   min.
smallest element currently in the set is bat
please enter a set operation:   delete.
specify the element to be deleted:   bat.
please enter a set operation:   min.
smallest element currently in the set is cat
please enter a set operation:   current.
the current set is {cat,dog}
please enter a set operation:   enough.
that's all folks...
```

## ▪ FILE HANDLING

In more sophisticated applications, it is often necessary not only to read and write from files other than standard input and output, but to read and write to multiple files in the single execution of a Prolog program. There are built-in EdCAAD C-Prolog relations that effect such file manipulation. We consider those for input and output separately.

### INPUT FILE MANIPULATION

There are three commands for manipulating input files: **see**, **seen**, and **seeing**. The query **see(F)** will succeed whenever **F** is instantiated to an existing file name. It causes that file to be opened and the current input stream to initiate at the beginning of the file.

## BUILT-IN RELATIONS FOR INPUT FILE MANIPULATION

| | |
|---|---|
| **see** (*Filename*) | succeeds whenever *Filename* is instantiated to a valid system file name and as a side effect causes that file to be opened as the current input file. |
| **seeing** (*Filename*) | succeeds whenever *Filename* unifies with the name of the current input file. |
| **seen** | always succeeds and as a side effect closes the current input file and then makes standard input the current input file. |

The query **see(F)** can never be resatisfied. Furthermore, should we backtrack over it, *the current input file set by its successful execution will not be reset to what it previously was.*

Once the **see(F)** has succeeded, all character and term input commands are processed from that file until either another file is specified as current input via **see**, or it is closed. To close the current input file, we use the command **seen**. It closes the current input file and redefines the current input file to be standard input, that is, the keyboard.

Should you wish to find out the name of the current input file at any point, simply execute **seeing(C)**, which succeeds if **C** unifies with the name of that file.

You may have up to 15 input and output files open at any time.

## OUTPUT FILE MANIPULATION

Similar to input file handling, there are three built-in relations for handling output files: **tell**, **told**, and **telling**. The query **tell(F)** will succeed whenever **F** is instantiated to an existing file name. It causes that file to be opened and the current output stream to initiate at the beginning of the file. Like **see**, **tell(F)** can never be resatisfied, and, should we backtrack over it, *the current output file set by its successful execution will not be reset to the previous output file.*

Once the **tell(F)** has succeeded, all character and term output queries are processed from that file until another output file is established as current via **tell**, or it is closed. To close the current output file, we use the command **told**. It closes the current output file and redefines the current output file to be standard output, that is, the screen.

Should you wish to find out the name of the current output file at any point, simply execute **telling(C)**, which succeeds if **C** unifies with the name of that file.

---

BUILT-IN RELATIONS FOR OUTPUT FILE MANIPULATION

| | |
|---|---|
| **tell()** | succeeds whenever is instantiated to a valid system file name and as a side effect causes that file to be opened as the current output file. |
| **telling()** | succeeds whenever unifies with the name of the current output file. |
| **told** | always succeeds and as a side effect closes the current output file and then makes standard output the current output file. |

---

## ■ SUMMARY

1. The built-in relation for writing characters is called **put**. The relation **put** takes a single argument, which is assumed to be instantiated to a valid ASCII code. Given a valid argument, **put** will always succeed and cannot be resatisfied.

2. Several other built-in relations are useful for writing to output. One such relation is **nl**, which always succeeds, can never be resatisfied, and writes a *newline* control character sequence to output as a side effect.

   Another useful relation is **tab**, which takes a single argument that is instantiated to an integer. Given a valid argument $X$, **tab(X)** always succeeds, can never be resatisfied, and writes $X$ blanks to output as a side effect. When $X<=0$, there is no side effect.

3. The built-in relation **name** relates any atomic name to its ASCII string representation. It takes two arguments, the first an atom or a number and the second a list of the ASCII codes corresponding to the characters of the first argument.

4. Reading characters from input can be done using either **get0** or **get**. The relation **get0** has a single argument and will always succeed if the argument is uninstantiated. Its function is to read the next input character.

   The relation **get** is identical in function to **get0**, with the exception that it will read the next printing character from the input stream. That is, it skips over nonprinting characters until it finds a printing character to read.

   A third input command is called **skip**. The relation **skip** has a single argument, which must be instantiated to an integer. It scans characters from the input stream until it finds one with an ASCII code matching the value of its argument. After **skip** completes successfully, further input requests are processed, beginning with the next character in the input stream.

5. The relation **write** is used for term output. The query **write(T)** will always succeed and can never be resatisfied. It causes as a side effect the value of the term **T** to be written to output.

6. To input terms in Prolog, we use the relation **read**. The relation **read** takes a term as its single argument. The term to be read must be followed by a period (.) and some nonprinting character, such as the carriage return.

   The query **read(T)** will always succeed when **T** is uninstantiated and can never be resatisfied. If **T** is instantiated, it must match up with the term that is read from the input stream.

7. There are three commands for manipulating input files: **see**, **seen**, and **seeing**. The query **see(F)** will succeed whenever **F** is instantiated to an existing file name. It causes that file to be opened and the current input stream to initiate at the beginning of the file.

   The query **see(F)** can never be resatisfied and, should we backtrack over it, the current input file set by its successful execution will not be reset to what it previously was.

   To close the current input file, we query the relation **seen**. It closes the current input file and redefines the current input file to be standard input, that is, the terminal keyboard.

   The relation **seeing** is used to determine the name of the current input file.

8. Similar to input file handling, there are three commands for handling output files: **tell**, **told**, and **telling**. The query **tell(F)** will succeed whenever **F** is instantiated to an existing file name. It causes that file to be opened and the current output stream to initiate at the beginning of the file. Like **see**, **tell(F)** can never be resatisfied and, should we backtrack over it, the current output file set by its successful execution will not be reset to the previous output file.

   To close the current output file, we query the relation **told**. It closes the current output file and redefines the current output file to be standard input, that is, the screen.

   The relation **telling** is used to determine the name of the current output file.

9. You may have up to 15 input and output files open at any time.

# ■ EXERCISES

1. Define a 1-*ary* Prolog relation **scan_echo(Terminator)** that scans characters from the input stream and echos them to the output stream until the character **Terminator** is read. It is assumed that **Terminator** is initially instantiated to a single character. Do not echo **Terminator** after it is scanned.

2. Define a 1-*ary* Prolog relation **scan_integer(Integer)** that scans decimal digits from the input stream until a nondecimal digit character is read and then unifies **Integer** with the numeric value of the decimal integer scanned. Should the first character read not be a decimal digit, **Integer** is unified with zero. Note that the ASCII codes for the decimal digits $0, 1, ..., 9$ are $48, 49, ..., 57$, respectively.

## ANSWERS

```
1. scan_echo(Terminator) :- name(Terminator,[Ascii]),
                            sc_ec(Ascii).
   sc_ec(Ascii) :- get0(Char),
                   ( Char=Ascii ;
                   /* or */
                   put(Char),
                   sc_ec(Ascii)).

2. scan_integer(Integer) :- scan_read(0,Integer).

   scan_read(Sum,Integer) :- get0(Char),
                             scan_int(Char,Sum,Integer).

   scan_int(Char,I,I) :- Char<48 ; Char>57.
   scan_int(Char,Sum,Integer) :- Char>=48,
                                 Char=<57,
                                 J is Char-48,
                                 New_Sum is Sum*10+J,
                                 scan_read(New_Sum,
                                           Integer).
```

# DECLARATIVE AND PROCEDURAL SEMANTICS OF LOGIC PROGRAMS

We have occasionally alluded to Prolog as a *logic programming* language. In this chapter, we will pursue the relationship between the *procedural* and *declarative* interpretation of logic programs. Our tutorial on Prolog emphasized the denotational style of programming. As such, we tended to portray more of a *declarative* explanation of Prolog programs than an operational one. Logic programs also have an operational interpretation that is reflected through their *procedural semantics*.

We will see that there is a nice *duality* between the procedural and declarative semantics of logic programs that allows us to view them in distinct but closely related ways. This duality makes such difficult problems as *formal program specification, program validation/verification,* and methodical *derivation of logic programs from specifications* more tractable.

In discussions of logic, it is always useful to separate syntax from semantics. We will present a *syntactic specification* of logic programs, and then give a declarative and procedural semantics for valid syntactic

---

## SYNTAX OF LOGIC PROGRAMS

| | | |
|---|---|---|
| *logic program* | is | a conjunction (logical *and*) of a finite set of *Horn clauses*, |

$$H_1 \wedge H_2 \wedge \cdots \wedge H_k$$

The conjunction symbol is "$\wedge$"

| | | |
|---|---|---|
| *clause* | is | a disjunction (logical *or*) of a finite set of *literals*, |

$$L_1 \vee L_2 \vee \cdots \vee L_m$$

each of which is either a *positive* or a *negative* literal. The disjunction symbol is "$\vee$"

| | | |
|---|---|---|
| *positive literal* | is | an *atomic formula*, |

$$at f(t_1, \ldots, t_n)$$

| | | |
|---|---|---|
| *negative literal* | is | a negation (logical *not*) of an *atomic formula*, |

$$\neg\, at f(t_1, \ldots, t_n)$$

where $t_1, \ldots, t_n$ are *terms*. The negation symbol is "$\neg$"

---

forms. We will then compare logic programs to Prolog programs, which can be viewed as a special case of logic programs.

The syntax of logic programs will be presented as a *top-down* specification. That is, we will start with a logic program as a unit, define it in terms of slightly simpler units, and continue in this way until the primitive, self-evident elements have all been defined.

Finally, each of the variables in a clause is *universally quantified*. That is, if $C$ is a clause containing variables $v_1, v_2, \ldots, v_m$, then the complete clause is interpreted as

$$\forall v_1 \forall v_2 \cdots \forall v_m\ C(v_1, v_2, \ldots, v_m)$$

where $C(v_1, v_2, \ldots, v_m)$ is any clause containing the variables $v_1, v_2, \ldots, v_m$ and "$\forall$" is the universal quantifier. The interpretation of the clause is read:

## SYNTAX OF HORN CLAUSES

*Horn clause*  is  a clause that contains either no positive literals,

$$\neg B_1 \ \lor \neg B_2 \ \lor \quad \cdots \quad \lor \neg B_m \quad (m \geq 0)$$

or a single positive literal and zero or more negative literals,

$$A \ \lor \ \neg B_1 \ \lor \neg B_2 \ \lor \quad \cdots \quad \lor \neg B_n \quad (n \geq 0)$$

*Note:*  The name *Horn clause* comes from the logician Alfred Horn, who first pointed out the significance of such clauses in 1951.

## SYNTAX OF TERMS

*term*        is  either a *constant*, a *variable*, or an *expression*.

*variable*    is  a name that can assume a term as its value.

*expression*  is  a structure. Recall that Prolog structures have the form $f(t_1, \ldots, t_j)$, where $f$ is the functor and $t_1, \ldots, t_j$ are terms. Lists are also examples of structures.

*constant*    is  a special case of expression, that is, the 0-*ary* expression.

For all values of the variables $v_1, v_2, \ldots, v_m$, the clause $C(v_1, v_2, \ldots, v_m)$ is true-valued.

Let us now address the declarative and procedural semantics of Horn clauses. From the interpretation standpoint, we can divide Horn clauses into three groups.

1. The Horn clause containing no literals is called the *empty clause*. Declaratively, the empty clause denotes the value *false*. As we will subsequently see, the logical imperative of the *resolution method* (on which logic programming is founded) is to *refute* (or *contradict*) the logic program comprised of the Horn clauses. Thus, in this sense, *false* connotes success.

In the procedural sense, the empty clause is a *halt statement*. Again, this can be interpreted as success; it represents the successful resolution of a goal query.

2. The Horn clause containing one or more negative literals and no positive literals,

$$\neg G_1 \lor \neg G_2 \lor \cdots \lor \neg G_n$$

is procedurally interpreted as a *goal statement*. In particular, each $\neg G_i$ is a *goal literal* or *procedure call* $(1 \le i \le n)$.

3. The Horn clause containing one positive literal and zero or more negative literals,

$$H \lor \neg G_1 \lor \neg G_2 \lor \cdots \lor \neg G_n$$

is procedurally interpreted as a *procedure definition*. In particular, $H$ is the *head* of the procedure, and $\neg G_1 \lor \neg G_2 \lor \cdots \lor \neg G_n$ is the *body* of the procedure. Again, each $\neg G_i$ is a goal literal or procedure call.

We can reformulate the logical representation of a procedure definition by using the logical equivalence

$$(X \supset Y) \equiv (\neg X \lor Y)$$

for any logical sentences $X$ and $Y$, where "$\supset$" is *logical implication*.

Substituting $\neg G_1 \lor \neg G_2 \lor \cdots \lor \neg G_n$ for $\neg X$, and $H$ for $Y$, we obtain the equivalent logical statement

$$(G_1 \land G_2 \land \cdots \land G_n) \supset H$$

Note that by negating the body of the statement, we replace the negative literals by their positive counterparts and replace each $\land$ with a $\lor$. This results from applying one of DeMorgan's laws, for example

$$(\neg X \lor \neg Y) \equiv \neg(X \land Y)$$

In addition, the occurrences of variables in the goal statement that were universally quantified in the original form of the clause are now *existentially quantified*.

This is a consequence of the logical equivalence

$$\neg(\forall x_1 \forall x_2 \cdots \forall x_n \, C(x_1, x_2, \ldots, x_n)) \equiv (\exists x_1 \exists x_2 \cdots \exists x_n) \neg C(x_1, x_2, \ldots, x_n)$$

## EQUIVALENCE OF TWO REPRESENTATIONS OF HORN CLAUSE PROCEDURES

Let $x_1, \ldots, x_j$ be the variables that occur in the literal $H$.
Let $y_1, \ldots, y_k$ be the variables other than $x_1, \ldots, x_j$ that occur in the Horn clause

$$(H \vee \neg G_1 \vee \neg G_2 \vee \cdots \vee \neg G_n)$$

$$\forall x_1 \cdots \forall x_j \, \forall y_1 \cdots \forall y_k \, (H \vee \neg G_1 \vee \neg G_2 \vee \cdots \vee \neg G_n) \equiv$$

$$\forall x_1 \cdots \forall x_j \, \forall y_1 \cdots \forall y_k \, (\neg G_1 \vee \neg G_2 \vee \cdots \vee \neg G_n \vee H) \equiv$$

$$\forall x_1 \cdots \forall x_j ((\forall y_1 \cdots \forall y_k \, (\neg G_1 \vee \neg G_2 \vee \cdots \vee \neg G_n)) \vee H)$$

Let $\neg X$ be $(\neg G_1 \vee \neg G_2 \vee \cdots \vee \neg G_n)$, and $Y$ be $H$. Then,
$X$ is $(G_1 \wedge G_2 \wedge \cdots \wedge G_n)$,
and

$$\forall x_1 \cdots \forall x_j ((\forall y_1 \cdots \forall y_k \, (\neg G_1 \vee \neg G_2 \vee \cdots \vee \neg G_n)) \vee H) \equiv$$

$$\forall x_1 \cdots \forall x_j (\neg (\forall y_1 \cdots \forall y_k \, (\neg G_1 \vee \neg G_2 \vee \cdots \vee \neg G_n)) \supset H) \equiv$$

$$\forall x_1 \cdots \forall x_j ((\exists y_1 \cdots \exists y_k \, \neg (\neg G_1 \vee \neg G_2 \vee \cdots \vee \neg G_n)) \supset H) \equiv$$

$$\forall x_1 \cdots \forall x_j ((\exists y_1 \cdots \exists y_k \, (G_1 \wedge G_2 \wedge \cdots \wedge G_n)) \supset H)$$

The interpretation of the clause

$$(\exists x_1 \exists x_2 \cdots \exists x_n) \, \neg \, C(x_1, x_2, \ldots, x_n)$$

is there exist values for variables $x_1, x_2, \ldots, x_n$ such that $C(x_1, x_2, \ldots, x_n)$ is false valued.

Thus, if $v_1, \ldots, v_m$ are the variables occurring in the head literal of the clause, and $w_1, \ldots, w_n$ are the variables occurring in the goal statement of the clause, then we read the clause

For all values of $v_1, \ldots, v_m$ there exist values of $w_1, \ldots, w_n$ such that $(G_1 \wedge G_2 \wedge \cdots \wedge G_n) \supset H$ is true.

The representation of the clause in this way, and the associated interpretation, show why a clause (or *rule* of Prolog) is often referred to as an *implication*. You can use whichever form you feel most comfortable with.

In the special case where there are no negative literals, the clause is called an *unqualified assertion of fact*, or simply a *fact*. In the procedural sense, a *logic program* is simply a set of procedure definitions.

We now consider the declarative and procedural semantics of Horn clause computations. Given a logic program, we supply a goal statement to initiate a *computation*. Let

$$\neg G_1 \vee \neg G_2 \vee \cdots \vee \neg G_{i-1} \vee \neg G_i \vee \neg G_{i+1} \vee \cdots \vee \neg G_n \qquad (1)$$

be an arbitrary goal statement with the variables of the statement assumed to be universally quantified. Further, assume that the logic program contains a procedure definition

$$G \vee \neg B_1 \vee \neg B_2 \vee \cdots \vee \neg B_m \tag{2}$$

such that goal literal $\neg G_i$ unifies with head literal $G$. Then *resolution* may occur in which the old goal statement is replaced by

$$\neg G_1 \vee \neg G_2 \vee \cdots \vee \neg G_{i-1} \vee \neg B_1 \vee \neg B_2 \vee \cdots \vee \neg B_m \vee \neg G_{i+1} \vee \cdots \vee \neg G_n \tag{3}$$

This is the basic computational step in a logic program execution. To see why this is justified, recall that the goal of a computation is the derivation of the empty clause, or *false*. Thus, to refute the goal statement (1), each goal $\neg G_j, 1 \le j \le n$, must be refuted.

Consider the goal $\neg G_i$ in (1). Clearly $\neg G_i$ is either *true* or *false*. If $\neg G_i$ is *false*, then (1) is *true* if and only if

$$\neg G_1 \vee \neg G_2 \vee \cdots \vee \neg G_{i-1} \vee \neg G_{i+1} \vee \cdots \vee \neg G_n$$

is *true*.

Suppose $\neg G_i$ is *true*. Given the assumed truth of procedure (2), $G_i$ is *false* only if

$$\neg B_1 \vee \neg B_2 \vee \cdots \vee \neg B_m$$

is *true*.

In summary, (1) is *true* only if

$$\neg G_1 \vee \neg G_2 \vee \cdots \vee \neg G_{i-1} \vee \neg G_{i+1} \vee \cdots \vee \neg G_n$$

is *true, or*

$$\neg B_1 \vee \neg B_2 \vee \cdots \vee \neg B_m$$

is *true*. Replacing the word *or* by the logical connective $\vee$ produces (3).

To illustrate the declarative interpretation of logic programs, consider a simple procedure for determining whether a term is an element of a list. In Prolog, we could give the following procedure:

```
member(X, [X|Y]).
member(X, [Q|Y]) :- member(X, Y).
```

The declarative representation of this logic program would be

```
member(X,[X|Y]).
member(X,[Q|Y]) ∨ ¬member(X,Y).
```

We will initiate a computation with the following goal statement:

`{¬member(y,[w,x,y]).`

The computation will then proceed as follows:

1. Resolve `¬member(y,[w,x,y])` with `member(X,[Q|Y]) ∨ ¬member(X,Y)` to obtain the new goal `¬member(y,[x,y])`.

2. Resolve `¬member(y,[x,y])` with `member(X,[Q|Y]) ∨ ¬member(X,Y)` to obtain the new goal `¬member(y,[y])`.

3. Resolve `¬member(y,[y])` with `member(X,[X|Y])` to obtain the empty statement.

4. The empty statement signifies *halt* and the computation terminates successfully.

In overviewing the declarative interpretation of logic programs, it is interesting to note the *nondeterminism* generally present in computations. That is, for any particular goal statement, we freely choose the goal literal we wish to resolve with a procedure definition. Although this offers considerable flexibility in the computation process, it is not characteristic of common programming languages.[1] This is where we can see a deviation of Prolog from logic programs.

Although the syntax of Prolog is essentially that of logic programs, we can observe that, although the order of literals in the goal statements and procedure definition bodies of logic programs are not significant (since the ∨ operation is both commutative and associative), we have strict evaluation order in Prolog.

First, there is the left-to-right evaluation of goal literals in a procedure body, and second, there is the top-to-bottom search of the logic program data base to find the first successful head literal to unify with the goal. These *deterministic* computation rules make programming in logic simpler and more familiar. However, they are generally unacceptable in the broader area of *theorem proving*, as they cause the proof system to be *incomplete*, that is, to be unable to prove certain logical truths.

The role of nondeterministic logic programming may become more important, though, as highly parallel computers are used to evaluate logic programs. In the so-called fifth-generation computer systems, the added evaluation flexibility afforded by nondeterminism may pave the way to more efficient execution of logic programs.

---

[1]We find it interesting that Fortran is one of the few programming languages in widespread use that permits nondeterministic evaluation of expressions.

# ■ SUMMARY

1. Prolog, as a special case of a logic programming language, uses a strict *deterministic* procedure for guiding its computations. Logic programming languages are generally more liberal with their computation rules, which are *nondeterministic*.

2. Logic programs have both a *declarative* and a *procedural* semantics. The declarative semantics provide a formal logical interpretation of a program, whereas the procedural semantics interpret a program in terms of its computations.

   The duality of these semantics makes logic programs more conducive to formal analysis and synthesis and tends to promote reliability.

# ■ BIBLIOGRAPHY NOTES

Logic programming grew out of developments in automated theorem-proving for first-order statements represented in clausal form. The success of the *resolution method* benefited from the work of Skolem, Herbrand, Prawitz, Gilmore, Davis and Putnam, and culminated with the classic paper of J. A. Robinson.

Resolution was a positive step toward a computational theory of theorem-proving. The early work of Horn and the subsequent work of Colmerauer and Kowalski established a procedural interpretation of logic. That is, the process of proving certain forms of first-order logic statements can be viewed computationally in terms of procedure calls, parameter passing, and the computation of values.

The definitive paper on the procedural and declarative semantics of logic programs is that of Van Emden and Kowalski.

A. Colmerauer (1973) Les systemes-Q ou un formalisme pour analyser et synthetiser des phrases sur ordinateur. *Publication Interne No. 43*, Dept. d'Informatique, University of Montreal, Canada.

M. Davis and H. Putnam (1960) A computing procedure for quantification theory. *J. ACM* **7**(3), 201–215.

P. Gilmore (1960) A proof method for quantification theory. *IBM J. Res. Dev.* **4**, 28–35.

J. Herbrand (1930) Investigations in proof theory. In J. van Heijenoort (ed.), *From Frege to Gödel*, Harvard University Press, Cambridge, Mass., 525–581.

A. Horn (1951) On sentences which are true of direct unions of algebras. *J. Symbolic Logic*, **16**, 14–21.

R. A. Kowalski (1974) Predicate logic as a programming language. *Proceedings of IFIP 74*, North-Holland Publishing, Amsterdam, 569–574.

R. A. Kowalski (1979) Algorithms=logic+control. *Comm. ACM* **22**(7), 424–436.

D. Prawitz (1960) An improved proof procedure. *Theoria* **26** 102–139.

J. A. Robinson (1965) A machine-oriented logic based on the resolution principle. *J. ACM* **12**(1), 23–41.

T. Skolem (1920) Logico-combinatorial investigation in the satisfiability or provability of mathematical propositions. In J. van Heijenoort (ed.), *From Frege to Gödel*, Harvard University Press, Cambridge, Mass., 1967.

M. H. Van Emden and R. A. Kowalski (1976) The semantics of predicate logic as a programming language: A machine-oriented logic based on the resolution principle. *J. ACM* **23**(4), 733–742.

## ▪ EXERCISES

1. Convert the Prolog relation definition shown here to the equivalent disjunctive logical form.

```
fact(X,1)  :- le(X,1).
fact(X,F)  :- gt(X,1),
              subt1(X,X1),
              fact(X1,F1),
              mult(X,F1,F).
```

2. Convert the disjunctive logical form representation of the Prolog relation definition given in Exercise 1 into the equivalent logical implication form.

3. Given the following set of Horn clauses that define the relations *reverse* and *append*, prove the truth of the predicate *reverse([a, b], [b, a])*.

   *append([],L,L)*
   *append([A—X],Y,[A—Z]) ∨ ¬ append(X,Y,Z)*
   *reverse([],[])*
   *reverse([A—L],R) ∨ ¬ reverse(L,L1) ∨ ¬ append(L1,[A],R)*

## ANSWERS

1. $fact(X,1) \vee \neg\, le(X,1)$

   $fact(X,F) \vee \neg\, gt(X,1) \vee \neg\, subt1(X,X1) \vee \neg\, fact(X1,F1) \vee \neg\, mult(X,F1,F)$

2. $le(X,1) \supset fact(X,1)$

   $fact(X,F) \vee 7gt(X,1) \vee \neg\, subt1(X,X1) \vee \neg\, fact(X1,F1) \vee \neg\, mult(X,F1,F)$
   $\supset fact(X,F)$

3. $\neg\, reverse([a,b],[b,a]) \wedge reverse([A—L],R) \vee \quad \neg\, reverse(L,L11) \vee$
   $\neg\, append(L11,[A],R) \supset \neg\, reverse([b],L11) \vee \neg\, append(L11,[a],[b,a])$

   $\neg\, reverse([b],L11) \vee \quad \neg\, append(L11,[a],[b,a]) \wedge reverse([A—L],R)$
   $\vee \;\neg\, reverse(L,L12) \vee \;\neg\, append(L12,[A],R) \supset \neg\, reverse([\,],L12) \vee$
   $\neg\, append(L12,[b],L11) \vee \neg\, append(L11,[a],[b,a])$

   $\neg\, reverse([\,],L12) \vee \neg\, append(L12,[b],L11) \vee \neg\, append(L11,[a],[b,a])$
   $\wedge reverse([\,],[\,]) \supset \neg\, append([\,],[b],L11) \vee \neg\, append(L11,[a],[b,a])$

   $\neg\, append([\,],[b],L11) \vee \quad \neg\, append(L11,[a],[b,a]) \wedge append([\,],L,L) \supset$
   $\neg\, append([b],[a],[b,a])$

   $\neg\, append([b],[a],[b,a]) \wedge append([A—X],Y,[A—Z]) \vee \neg\, append(X,Y,Z)$
   $\supset append([\,],[a],[a])$

   $append([\,],[a],[a]) \wedge append([\,],L,L) \supset empty\_statement$

# SECTION III

# LISP VS. PROLOG

# LISP VS. PROLOG: HOW DO THEY RELATE?

Functions, in mathematics, are defined as subsets of Cartesian products of domain sets and range sets.[1] Such a subset determines a function if and only if it contains at most one ordered pair for each element of the domain set. The domain set determines potential arguments for the function, and the range set determines potential values of the function. When $(x, y)$ is an ordered pair in a function set, $y$ denotes the value of the function corresponding to the argument $x$.

For example, if the domain set contains the elements $d$ and $e$ and the range set contains the elements $r$, $s$, and $t$, then the set $\{(d, r), (e, s)\}$ is a function. So are the sets $\{(d, r), (e, r)\}$ and $\{(d, t), (e, t)\}$ (the last two sets are constant functions; they deliver the same value for each argument).

On the other hand, the set $\{(d, r), (d, s), (e, r)\}$ is not a function because it contains two different ordered pairs with the same domain component, $(d, r)$ and $(d, s)$. It is, however, a "relation."

---

[1] The Cartesian product of a domain set and a range set is the set of all ordered pairs in which the first component comes from the domain set and second from the range set. $D \times R = \{(d, r) : d \in D \text{ and } r \in R\}$

Relations, in mathematics, are defined simply as subsets of Cartesian products, placing no restrictions on first components with respect to second components. The domain/range dichotomy, important in distinguishing arguments from values in "function" subsets of Cartesian products, plays no special role in "relation" subsets because of the unrestricted nature of the relationship between the components in ordered pairs forming mathematical relations.

Similarly, functional programs carefully discriminate between computational inputs (arguments of functions, corresponding to elements of the domain of the function in the mathematical formulation) and outputs (values of functions, elements of the range). Relational programs, on the other hand, do not designate particular components as input components and others as output components. Any of the components can play either role, depending on the nature of the invocation.

The function **reverse**, which reverses the order of the elements of lists, will serve as an example. As a function in the mathematical sense, **reverse** has the set of finite sequences as its domain and the same set as its range. This makes it a subset of the Cartesian product of the set of finite sequences with itself. This same subset also forms a relation in the mathematical sense. (Any mathematical function is also a relation because functions are subsets of Cartesian products with certain constraints on the relationship between domain and range components, whereas mathematical relations are unrestricted subsets of Cartesian products.)

As a function in the computational sense, expressed in Lisp, for example, **reverse** delivers a new sequence as a value only if an invocation supplies it with a sequence as an argument.

| Lisp Function Definition | Invocations | Results |
|---|---|---|

```
(defun rev (x)
  (if (null x)
      x
      (append (rev (cdr x)
              (list (car x))))))
```

| Invocations | Results |
|---|---|
| (rev '(a b c)) | (c b a) |
| (rev '(c b a)) | (a b c) |

On the other hand, as a computational relation expressed in Prolog, an invocation of **reverse** (that is, a query using **reverse**) can supply an input value in either component, and the result of the computation will deliver a value for the other component satisfying the **reverse** relation. Or an invocation may supply input values in both components, in which case the result will indicate whether the indicated ordered pair satisfies the **reverse** relation. In this way Prolog honors the mathematical notion of a relation by not distinguishing between input components and output components of ordered pairs.

| **Prolog Relation Definition** | **Invocations** | **Results** |
|---|---|---|
| `rev([],[]).` | `rev([a,b,c], Y).` | Yes. |
| | | Y=[c,b,a] |
| `rev([W|X],Y) :- rev(X,Z),` | `rev(X, [c,b,a]).` | Yes. |
| | | X=[a,b,c] |
| `append(Z,[W],Y).` | `rev([a,b,c], [c,b,a])` | Yes. |

The treatment of input/output mode in components points out a fundamental difference between Lisp and Prolog programs. Prolog's flexibility in this area comes from the potential for extra computation in the process of unification, which provides the basis for interpreting Prolog programs, compared to that of the substitution process that forms the basis of computation in Lisp systems. Prolog programs that take advantage of this capability are likely to be more succinct than their Lisp counterparts.[2]

Most of the Prolog programs in this text fail to take advantage of the interchangeability of input and output components in invocations. The notion first arose in connection with the **append** relation, which can operate in either direction to recognize prefixes or suffixes of lists as well as "pasted-together" lists. The most extensive use of the idea in this text is in the Prolog implementation of the Wang theorem prover, which makes the Prolog program shorter than the equivalent Lisp program (compare the definition of the function **prove** in Lisp to the definition of the relation **prove** in Prolog in Chapter 31).

Automatic pattern matching between invocations and definitions provides Prolog with another notational advantage over Lisp. The definition of a relation in Prolog takes the form of a collection of facts and rules, each of which involves a different pattern of component values. To interpret a query, the Prolog system uses the fact or rule with a component pattern that matches that of the query. For example, to interpret the query **rev([], [])**, Prolog would use the first fact in the definition of the reverse relation because the components in the query match those in the fact. On the other hand, Prolog could not use that fact to answer the query **rev([a,b,c], [c,b,a])** because the components in the query, being nonempty lists, cannot match those of the fact. They do, however, match the components of the rule following it, and Prolog uses that rule to answer the query.

Modern functional languages, such as Turner's Miranda, incorporate similar pattern-matching capabilities. This makes it possible to define functions in terms of case lists involving certain argument values without embedding tests for the cases in the body of the function.

---

[2]Prolog and Lisp are both "Turing equivalent" systems; that is, any computable relationship can be expressed in either language. If one notation were "more powerful" than the other, it probably would be on the basis of economy of expression, not generality of scope.

```
Definition of the Reverse Function in a modern
functional notation
```

```
Pattern matching form            If-test form (archaic)

      rev [] = []            rev x  = x              if x=[]
rev [x|seq] = append                = append(rev (cdr x))
              (rev seq)                       [car x]
              [x]                               otherwise
```

Because pattern matching is compatible with functional programming, we view it as a notational convenience of Prolog, but not as a fundamental difference between relational and functional programming. However, the input/output symmetry of Prolog versus Lisp's use of arguments as input-mode only is a difference that syntactic transformations cannot account for.

On the other hand, Lisp and functional notations in general have some advantages over Prolog. One has to do with the ability to combine functions to make more complex expressions, and another is that availability of higher-order functions.

For example, a merge-sort computation involves a combination of splitting and merging functions. A Lisp program expresses this via function composition, but Prolog lacks this concept and must designate intermediate variables to communicate partial results between stages. The Prolog program that follows uses the intermediate variables $A$, $B$, $SA$, and $SB$. The Lisp program uses an intermediate variable, *pair*, corresponding to $A$ and $B$ in the Prolog program [also corresponding to the pair $(a, b)$ in the modern functional version], to avoid rewriting the expression that splits the input sequence into two parts, but the Lisp program combines the merge and sort functions into one expression, avoiding the need for the intermediate variables $SA$ and $SB$ to carry sorted subsequences to the merge step.

**Lisp function**                    **Prolog relation**

```
defun sort (seq)           sort([], []).
  (if (null seq)           sort(Seq,Srt) :- split(Seq,A,B),
     '()                                     sort(A,SA),
     (let ((pair (split seq)))               sort(B,SB),
       (merge (sort (car pair))              merge(SA,SB,Srt
              (sort (cadr pair)))
   )))
```

### Functional form, modern notation

```
sort [] = []
sort seq = merge (sort a) (sort b)
            where (a,b) = split seq
```

Higher-order functions provide Lisp with another advantage over Prolog.[3] Functional programmers have found that nonrecursive equations communicate to other people the meaning of a program more effectively than do recursive equations. Recursion cannot be avoided in a general sense, but higher-order functions can express common patterns of recursion. Programs can then suppress their recursive portions by invoking these functions.

For example, Lisp's **mapcar** function applies a given function to each element of a list and delivers a list of the results. The common pattern of recursion here is that of constructing a result list with its first element the value of the given function applied to the first element of the given list and the rest of whose elements are those derived from the same formula applied to the rest of the components of the given list.

```
(defun mapcar (f seq)
  (if (null seq)
      '()
      (cons (funcall f (car seq)) (mapcar f (cdr seq)))
))
```

A user of **mapcar** understands that it constructs a list of function results without having to think about the recursion that defines **mapcar**.

```
(mapcar #'f (list x1 x2 ... xn)) = (list (f x1) (f x2)
                                     ... (f xn))
```

A good functional programmer will decide what common patterns of recursion a computation requires, encode those as higher-order functions, and use the higher-order functions instead of repeating the recursive equations. This way of expressing computations makes it possible for people who want to understand the program to invest the time required to understand a particular recursion pattern only once (to come to an understanding of the higher-order function), then make use of that investment at many places in the program. This is the same type of economy gained by defining ordinary functions (the economy of not having to repeat the definition for each pattern of data). In this sense it is familiar to all programmers.

---

[3]Prolog supports a limited capability to express higher-order relations, but Lisp has a more generally useful facility in this area.

We have pointed out two advantages of Prolog over Lisp (pattern matching and symmetric treatment of input/output mode) and two advantages of Lisp over Prolog (function composition and higher-order functions). Pattern matching and function composition provide primarily syntactic conveniences, but symmetric input/output mode and higher-order functions fundamentally improve expressive power.

Because Prolog uses unification rather than substitution as a basis for computation, Prolog programmers give up some of the control that Lisp programmers have over the process of program interpretation. That is, Lisp programs tend to be more computationally specific, whereas Prolog programs leave more options open to the interpreter. A clever interpreter might be able to take advantage of these options, producing a more economical computation than one derived from a more closely specified presentation. In other cases the interpreter will be overwhelmed by the possibilities, and the resulting computation will be less efficient than one directed in more detail by the program.

Higher-order functions in Lisp also provide an opportunity for suppressing computational details. Programmers can expect intrinsic higher-order functions, such as **mapcar**, to perform in a nearly optimal fashion with respect to the underlying computer system. Higher-order functions defined in a program might be singled out for special attention with regard to optimization. For example, a compiler might be directed to expend extra resources to find a good mapping of such functions onto the hardware, or system programmers might develop special implementations of the functions to take best advantage of the computing system.

No one yet knows which system, functional programming or relational programming, presents greater advantages. History favors less computationally specific languages as eventual winners in computational speed as well as in expressive power.[4] Because Lisp and Prolog both have advantages of this kind that the other language lacks, it seems reasonable to guess that some combination of the ideas of both languages will find their way into the denotational programming languages of the future.

## ■ BIBLIOGRAPHY NOTES

The relationship between functional and relational languages has provided fertile ground for programming language research. Most of the literature on the subject uses the term "logic programming" in the sense that we have used "relational programming." Much of the early work in the area appears in an excellent collection of papers edited by DeGroot and Lindstrom, but new results appear frequently. Many researchers

---

[4]For example, the numeric formula $a*b+c*d$ leaves more options open to the computing system than a sequence of loads, stores, multiplies, and adds, and higher-level languages universally prefer such formulas to sequences of simpler operations.

(Kieburtz provides an excellent example; others appear in the DeGroot/ Lindstrom book) have attempted to combine the advantages of relational and functional programming systems. Although none of these efforts have yet resulted in a commercial programming system, it seems reasonable to expect one eventually. The notion of pattern matching on arguments to select alternative computational formulas, a basic feature of Prolog but not Lisp, has been adopted by many programming languages, both functional (e.g., Turner's Miranda) and relational.

Doug DeGroot and Gary Lindstrom (1986) *Logic Programming: Functions, Relations, and Equations.* Prentice–Hall, Englewood Cliffs, N. J.

Richard B. Kieburtz (1987) *Functions + Logic in Theory and Practice.* Oregon Graduate Center, Beaverton, Oregon.

David Turner (1987) *Miranda System Manual.* Software Research Limited, Canterbury, England.

# ■ EXERCISES

1. Consider using the sort relation with both components in input mode to test a sequence for the "sorted" property. Will a Prolog program along the lines of the one in this chapter serve this purpose? How would it compare for this purpose with the following relation?

```
sorted([],[]).
sorted([A],[A]).
sorted([A,B|Seq],[A,B|Seq]) :- order(A,B),
                                sorted([B|Seq],[B|Seq]).
```

2. What would be the meaning of an invocation of the foregoing "sorted" relation with its first component in input mode and its second in output mode? What would it mean to use either the sort or the sorted relation with the first component in output mode?

3. Write a higher-order function, **maptree**, that constructs a tree of function values from a tree of data nodes. Assume that a tree is represented by a list with components that either are leaves (lists with a special first component identifying the list as a leaf) or are, themselves, trees represented in the same way.

```
(maptree #'f  tr)  is    a tree with the same shape
                         as tr, but with leaves
                         containing values delivered
                         by f:
```

> x is a leaf of tr if and
> only if (f x) is the
> corresponding leaf of
> (maptree #'f tr)

## ANSWERS

1. The sort relation defined in the chapter can be used to test a sequence for the "sorted" property, but will require $n*\log(n)$ time to do so. The simpler relation defined in the exercise will make the test in linear time.

2. The sorted relation, when used in a query with a sorted list as the first component (input mode) and a variable as the second component (output mode), will deliver a copy of the first component. If the first component is not sorted, the query will be answered "no". It works the same way if the second component is input and the first output mode.

   It will be a real learning experience for you to try the sort relation with a variable as the first component and a sorted list as the second. You may want to use the following definitions for the split and merge relations:

```
split ([],[],[]).
split ([X], [] [X]).
split ([X,Y|Seq], [X|A], [Y|B]) :- split(Seq,
                                               A, B).
merge([], [], []).
merge([X], [], [X]).
merge([X|SA], [Y|SB], [X,Y|Srt]) := order(X,Y),
                                     merge(SA,SB,Srt).
merge([X|SA], [Y|SB], [Y,X|Srt]) := order(Y,X),
                                     merge(SA,SB,Srt).
```

3. 
```
tree is (node... )
node is tree
      or leaf

(defun maptree (f tr)
  (mapcar  #'(lamda (node)
                (if (leaf node)
                    (funcall f node)
                    (maptree f node) ))
          tr))
```

# SECTION IV

# APPLICATIONS

# C HAPTER 35

■

# TWO-OPPONENT GAMES

Games with two opponents who alternate in taking actions fall into a general pattern that could be called minimax tree games. At each stage in such a game, one player or the other is obliged to take an action. The rules of the game specify a set of allowable actions for each stage, and each action presents a new stage of the game to the other player, who is then obliged to select one of the actions permitted by the rules. The opponents have opposite goals: what is good for one player is bad for the other, and vice versa.

These goals may be viewed as numeric scores. With this view, one player will seek to conclude the game with the highest possible score, and the other will seek to end it on the lowest score.

We stipulate in our model that player 1 (the player obliged to make the first move in the game) seeks a high score and player 2 a low score, but this stipulation could be reversed without changing the ideas of algorithmic game-playing discussed in this chapter.

At the beginning of the game, player 1 selects an action that appears to lead to the highest possible score. This choice will eliminate some scores that were attainable before the move. Player 2 then looks at the options and selects an action that appears to lead to the lowest possible score. In selecting their moves, competent players consider the actions their opponents may take. For example, suppose player 1 had a choice of two moves, one leaving player 2 with a choice between a score of 1 and 10 and another leaving player 2 with a choice between a score of 5 and 6. The second move would be the more conservative choice for player 1 because it guarantees a score of at least 5; the first move leaves open the possibility of a higher score (10), but also permits a more likely score of 1. Our game-playing algorithms will always make the conservative choice on the assumption that both players are equally competent.

However, the algorithms could be modified easily to gamble on an opponent missing an opportunity. One way to do this would be to weight potential scores resulting from a move with the likelihood that the opponent will foresee the consequences of that move. The algorithms could then use the weighted scores rather than the actual scores as a basis for making decisions. This trick could also adapt the tree-game approach to games in which the players do not have access to complete (perfect) information. Tic-tac-toe and double-dummy bridge, the games we use for examples in this chapter, are "perfect-information" games, as are games such as checkers and chess. To handle partial-information games such as contract bridge, backgammon, or Monopoly, the tree would be expanded to include collections of possible game situations. Each collection would be weighted with an estimate of its relative likelihood of being the actual game situation. Scaling resulting scores by the weights associated with game situations, as in the "imperfect players" strategy, would then lead to the selection of optimal moves.

Similarly, the assumption that the players alternate in making moves does not restrict the applicability of the algorithms: In situations where one player makes several moves in a row, the rules of the game could be modified to insert no-action moves for the other player at appropriate points without changing the nature of the game. In this sense, the algorithms discussed in this chapter accommodate a greater variety of two-opponent games than might be apparent from the basic assumptions.

We use the term *tree* to describe the structure of the game. At each stage a player has a set of allowable actions, and each action leads to a different set of allowable actions for the other player. This structure conforms to the graph theoretic notion of a tree consisting of a nonempty set of nodes, each of which is either itself a tree (i.e., a set of nodes) or a leaf. A game, in our sense, is a tree in which the leaf nodes are numbers designating scores and the subtree nodes are sets of possible actions for one player or the other. Player 1 selects one of the nodes in the tree representing the full game. If that node is a leaf, the game is over and the score is the number that the leaf designates. On the other hand, if player 1 selects a node that is a tree, then player 2 selects one of its nodes, which may be a leaf (terminating the game) or a tree from which player 1 must select a node, and so on.

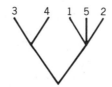

FIGURE **35.1** A minimax tree-game requiring exactly two moves

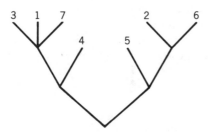

FIGURE **35.2** A minimax tree-game requiring either 2 or 3 moves.

Figures 35.1 and 35.2 display some game trees represented in a traditional way: Leaf nodes are depicted as numbers and subtree nodes are depicted as branch points with lines emanating upward to the nodes comprising the subtree. The term *minimax* describes the alternation between seeking a maximum score and a minimum score that occurs at alternating levels in the game tree.

Consider the game of Figure 35.1. Player 1, the first to move, has a choice of two actions (the game tree in Figure 35.1 is a set of two subtrees, represented by the two lines emanating upward from the bottom branch point). Suppose player 1 selects the node on the left. Then player 2, seeking to minimize the score, will choose the leaf indicating a score of 3. On the other hand, if player 1 selects the node on the right, player 2 will select a score of 1. Therefore, a careful player 1 will select the node on the left.

The game in Figure 35.2 requires more analysis because it potentially involves more moves. If player 1 selects the node on the left in Figure 35.2, player 2 will have to consider which of two moves to select. One of these moves produces a score of 4 immediately, and the other presents player 1 with a choice of three scores: 3, 1, and 7. Since player 1 would select the score 7, player 2 will choose the leaf containing 4 rather than the tree of moves for player 1. A similar analysis of the starting move on the right shows that the game would end with a score of 5 if player 1 started the game by selecting that move. Player 1, having made this analysis, chooses the move on the right to start the game, player 2 chooses the leaf containing 5, and the game is over in two moves.

The essential aspect of the analysis is that player 1 seeks to maximize the score, and player 2 to minimize, by looking ahead to the end of the game and choosing a move that puts the game on course to the optimal score from the point of view of the player selecting the move. If A designates the scoring function of player 1 and B that of player 2, then A and B form a pair of mutually dependent functions. When either scoring function encounters a leaf, hence no further choice, its value is the number at that leaf. On the other hand, when scoring function A faces a set of nodes to choose from, it selects the largest value it can find after the scoring function B has been applied to each node in the set. Vice versa for scoring function B.

In Lisp, we may represent a game tree as a nonempty list of subtrees and/or leaves, and the scoring functions A and B operate on these lists.

# ■ LISP PROGRAM SEGMENT A

```
            gtree  is  number
                   or  ( gtree gtree... )


(defun A(g)
   (if (leaf g)
       g
       (maxl (mapcar   B  g))
   ))

(defun B(g)
   (if (leaf g)
       g
       (minl (mapcar   A  g))
   ))

(defun leaf(g) (numberp g))
(defun score(g) g)

(defun maxl(glst)    (accumulate   #'maxs (cdr glst)
                                          (car glst)))
(defun minl(glst)    (accumulate   #'mins (cdr glst)
                                          (car glst)))

(defun accumulate( associativebinaryoperation
                   operands
                   initialvalue)
```

```
    (if (null operands)
        initialvalue
        (accumulate  associativebinaryoperation
                     (cdr operands)
                     (funcall associativebinaryoperation
                              initialvalue (car operands)))
    ))

  (defun maxs(g1 g2)
    (if (>= (score g1) (score g2))
        g1
        g2
     ))

  (defun mins(g1 g2)
    (if (<= (score g1) (score g2))
        g1
        g2
     ))

    (A  '( ((3 1 7)  4) (5  (2 5)) ) )
;is  (maxl (list (B '((3 1 7) 4)))
;                (B '(5 (2 6)))  ))
;is  (maxl (list (minl (list (A '(3 1 7))
;                            4           ))
;                (minl (list 5
;                            (A '(2 6))  )) ))
;is  (maxl (list (minl (list (maxl (list (B 3) (B 1) (B 7)))
;                            4           ))
;                (minl (list 5
;                            (maxl (list (B 2) (B 6))) ))
))
;is  (maxl (list (minl (list (maxl (list 3 1 7))
;                            4           ))
;                (minl (list 5
;                            (maxl (list 2 6)) )) ))
;is  (maxl (list (minl (list 7
;                            4           ))
;                (minl (list 5
;                            6           )) ))
;is  (maxl (list 4
;                5))
;is  5
;
```

End Lisp Program Segment A

# ■ PROLOG PROGRAM SEGMENT A

```
              gtree   is   number
                      or   [ gtree [ , gtree]... ]

a(G,G) :- leaf(G).

a(G,S) :- not(leaf(G)),
          mapcar(b,G,Mins),
          max(Mins,S).

b(G,G) :- leaf(G).

b(G,S) :- not(leaf(G)),
          mapcar(a,G,Maxs),
          min(Maxs,S).

mapcar(_,[],[]).
mapcar(R,[X|Y],[RX|RY]) :- apply(R,X,RX),
                           mapcar(R,Y,RY).

apply(R,X,RX) :- F =..[R,X,RX],
                 call(F).

leaf(G) :- number(G).

score(G,G).

max([X],X).
max([X,Y|Z],M) :- better_score(X,Y),
                  max([X|Z],M).
max([X,Y|Z],M) :- better_score(Y,X),
                  max([Y|Z],M).

min([X],X).
min([X,Y|Z],M) :- better_score(X,Y),
                  min([Y|Z],M).
min([X,Y|Z],M) :- better_score(Y,X),
                  min([X|Z],M).

better_score(S1,S2) :- S1 >= S2.

?- a([ [[3,1,7],4], [5,[2,5]] ],Score).
yes. Score=5
```

End Prolog Program Segment A

In tree games requiring long sequences of moves, human analysts sometimes make mistakes leading to suboptimal moves. Our program represents an algorithm known as *minimax search* that always finds an optimal move when carried out completely. However, it calls for much more computation than another algorithm that produces the same result. This algorithm, known as *alpha-beta search*, uses a combination of pumping (Chapter 11, Chapter 21) and lookahead to decrease the number of moves that need be considered during the computation. The trick has to do with knowing a bound on a maximum or minimum value being sought and abandoning a route when it becomes apparent that the route can do no better than the known bound. For example, the A function selects a maximum among a list of numbers that are delivered by the B function. Once one of the B values is known, it becomes a lower bound on the maximum being sought. If other B evaluations are notified of this bound, they can abort if they find that the bound cannot be exceeded among the possibilities they are considering.

We will derive a program for alpha-beta search by gradually transforming the minimax search program. Basically, we will be trying to pass along information about the status of the search to other stages of the search so that they can shut down when it becomes obvious that they will be fruitless.[1]

The transformation begins by expanding the functions to eliminate the use of the higher order function **mapcar**. We pump the maximum value onto one of the arguments in this transformation. For example, the job of A1 is to select a maximum from a list of B values; the argument **alpha** represents a running maximum, the largest value so far encountered in the search.

## ■ LISP PROGRAM SEGMENT B

```
(defun A(g)
   (if (leaf g)
       g
       (A1 (B (car g))  (cdr g))
   ))

(defun A1(alpha          ; running maximum of B values
           glstB)        ; game-tree list whose
                         ; max B val is sought
   (if (null glstB)
```

[1]This departs from the traditional approach that explains $\alpha$-$\beta$ in terms of the search process it generates. The "program transformation" approach used here seems more in keeping with our emphasis on programs as denotational specifications rather than as process generators.

```
        alpha
        (A1 (maxs alpha
                  (B (car glstB)))
             (cdr glstB))
    ))

  (defun B(g)
     (if (leaf g)
         g
         (B1 (A (car g))  (cdr g))
     ))

  (defun B1(beta          ; running minimum of A values
             glstA)       ; game-tree list whose
                          ; min A val is sought
     (if (null glstA)
         beta
         (B1 (mins beta
                   (A (car glstA)))
              (cdr glstA))
     ))
```

END LISP PROGRAM SEGMENT B

# ■ PROLOG PROGRAM SEGMENT B

```
a(Ga,Ga).
a([Gb|Ha],Sa) :- b(Gb,Sb),
                 a1(Sb,Ha,Sa).

a1(Alpha,[],Alpha). /* a1 accumulates max b-value   */
a1(Alpha,            /* running maximum of b-values  */
   [Gb|Ha],          /* game-tree list whose         */
                     /* max b-value is sought        */
    Sa) :-           /* score for player a           */
        b(Gb,Sb),
         ((better_score(Alpha,Sb),
           a1(Alpha,Ha,Sa))          ;
    /* or */
           (better_score(Sb,Alpha),
            a1(Sb,Ha,Sa))).

b(Gb,Gb) :- number(Gb).
b([Ga|Hb],Sb) :- a(Ga,Sa),
                 b1(Sa,Hb,Sb).
```

```
b1(Beta,[],Beta).      /* b1 accumulates min a-value    */
b1(Beta,               /* running minimum of a-values   */
   [Ga|Hb],            /* game-tree list whose          */
                       /* min a-value is sought         */
   Sb) :-              /* score for player b            */
         a(Ga,Sa),
         ((better_score(Sa,Beta),
           b1(Beta,Hb,Sb))              ;
     /* or */
           (better_score(Beta,Sa),
           b1(Sa,Hb,Sb))).
```

END PROLOG PROGRAM SEGMENT B

Then we further expand the functions, substituting the defining expression for B in place of its invocation in the definition of A1, and similarly replacing the invocation of A in the definition of B1. This expansion for A1 is illustrated here; the expansion of B1 is analogous.

# ■ LISP PROGRAM SEGMENT C

```
(defun A1(alpha        ; running maximum of B values
          glstB)       ; game-tree list whose
                       ; max B val is sought
   (if (null glstB)
       alpha
       (A1 (maxs alpha
                 (if (leaf (car glstB)) ;(B (car glstB))
                     (car glstB)
                     (B1 (A (car (car glstB)))
                         (cdr (car glstB))))))
           (cdr glstB))
   ))
```

END LISP PROGRAM SEGMENT C

# ■ PROLOG PROGRAM SEGMENT C

```
a1(Alpha,[],Alpha). /* a1 accumulates max b-value    */
a1(Alpha,           /* running maximum of b-values   */
   [Gb|Ha],         /* game-tree list whose          */
```

```
                          /* max b-value is sought       */
  Sa) :-                  /* score for player a          */
        leaf(Gb),
        ((better_score(Alpha,Gb),
          a1(Alpha,Ha,Sa))              ;
   /* or */
          (better_score(Gb,Alpha),
           a1(Gb,Ha,Sa))).
a1(Alpha,              /* running maximum of b-values   */
   [[Ga|Hb]|Ha],       /* game-tree list whose          */
                       /* max b-value is sought         */
  Sa) :-               /* score for player a            */
        a(Ga,Beta),
        b(Hb,Beta),
        ((better_score(Alpha,Beta),
          a1(Alpha,Ha,Sa))             ;
   /* or */
          (better_score(Beta,Alpha),
           a1(Beta,Ha,Sa))).
```

END PROLOG PROGRAM SEGMENT C

From this we see that where **maxs** is invoked in the definition of A1, its arguments will take one of two forms depending on whether or not the first element of the game-tree list is a leaf. We distribute this decision outside the invocation of A1, as follows.

# ■ LISP PROGRAM SEGMENT D

```
(defun A1(alpha         ; running maximum of B values
          glstB)        ; game-tree list whose
                        ; max B val is sought
   (if (null glstB)
       alpha
       (if (leaf (car glstB))
           (A1 (maxs alpha
                     (car glstB)
               (cdr glstB)))
           (A1 (maxs alpha
                     (B1 (A (car (car glstB)))
                         (cdr (car glstB))))
               (cdr glstB))
   )))
```

END LISP PROGRAM SEGMENT D

# ■ THERE IS NO PROLOG PROGRAM SEGMENT D

Now we observe that we can pass along the required information and delay the complete evaluation of B1, leaving open the possibility of reducing the overall amount of computation by deeper analysis of the code. We delay the evaluation of B1 by replacing the second invocation of A1 in its definition by the invocation of a new function A2. The arguments of A2 will include the four pieces of basic information needed to carry out the computation: (1) alpha, the running maximum in the computation of A1, (2) the result of applying the function A to the first subtree of the first game tree of the game tree list, (3) the other subtrees in the first game tree of the game tree list, and (4) all the game trees in the game tree list, except the first one (the B values of the game trees are needed in A1's search for a maximum).

# ■ LISP PROGRAM SEGMENT E

```
(defun A1(alpha        ; running maximum of B values
          glstB)       ; game tree list whose
                       ; max B val is sought
   (if (null glstB)
       alpha
       (if (leaf (car glstB))
           (A1 (maxs alpha
                     (car glstB))
               (cdr glstB))
           (A2 alpha
               (A (car (car glstB)))
               (cdr (car glstB))
               (cdr glstB))
       )))
```

END LISP PROGRAM SEGMENT E

# ■ PROLOG PROGRAM SEGMENT E

```
a1(Alpha,[],Alpha).  /* a1 accumulates max b-value    */
a1(Alpha,             /* running maximum of b-values   */
   [Gb|Ha],           /* game tree list whose          */
                      /* max b-value is sought         */
   Sa)  :-            /* score for player a            */
        leaf(Gb),
```

```
    ((better_score(Alpha,Gb),
      al(Alpha,Ha,Sa))              ;
 /* or */
      (better_score(Gb,Alpha),
       al(Gb,Ha,Sa))).
```

END PROLOG PROGRAM SEGMENT E

The second and third arguments of A2 provide the information needed to make the B1 computation that we excised from the definition of A1. The second argument is one of several A values that B1 must examine to find a minimum; thus, it becomes a running minimum in B1's search process. The third argument provides the other game trees among whose A values B1 might find the minimum it seeks. The trick comes in recognizing that the B value that could be computed from these arguments will be needed for the overall computation only if it could exceed **alpha**. If it cannot exceed **alpha**, A2 will select either **alpha** or one of the B values computed on the remainder of the game trees in the game tree list; A2 would not select the B value that could be computed from its second and third arguments if that B value could not exceed the other B values available.

This B value (i.e., the one that could be computed from the second and third arguments of A2) is a minimum of a collection of A values, one of which is the second argument of A2. This means that this B value cannot exceed the second argument of A2. Therefore, if the second argument of A2 is smaller than its first argument, the B value in question is irrelevant to the overall computation and can be dropped. This is the rationale behind the following definition of A2.

## ▪ LISP PROGRAM SEGMENT F

```
(defun A2 (alpha          ; running maximum of B values
           beta           ; running minimum of A values
           glstA          ; game tree list whose
                          ; min A val is sought
           glstB)         ; game tree list whose
                          ; max B val is sought
  (if (>= (score alpha) (score beta))
      (A1 alpha glstB)
      (if (null glstA) ; and beta > alpha
          (A1 beta glstB)
          (A2 alpha
              (mins beta (A (car glstA)))
              (cdr glstA)
```

```
                    glstB)
        )))

(defun B1(beta          ; running minimum of A values
          glstA)        ; game tree list whose
                        ; min A val is sought
    (if (null glstA)
        beta
        (if (leaf (car glstA))
            (B1 (mins beta
                      (car glstA))
                (cdr glstA))
            (B2 beta
                (B (car (car glstA)))
                (cdr (car glstA))
                (cdr glstA))
        )))

(defun B2(beta          ; running minimum of A values
          alpha         ; running maximum of B values
          glstB         ; game tree list whose
                        ; max B val is sought
          glstA)        ; game tree list whose
                        ; min A val is sought
    (if (<= (score beta) (score alpha))
        (B1 beta glstA)
        (if (null glstB) ; and alpha < beta
            (B1 alpha glstA)
            (B2 beta
                (maxs alpha (B (car glstB)))
                (cdr glstB)
                glstA)
        )))
```

END LISP PROGRAM SEGMENT F

## ■ PROLOG PROGRAM SEGMENT F

```
a1(Alpha,          /* running maximum of b-values   */
   [[Ga|Hb]|Ha],   /* game tree list whose          */
                   /* max b-value is sought         */
   Sa) :-          /* score for player a            */
        a(Ga,Beta),
        a2(Alpha,Beta,Hb,Ha,Sa).
```

```
a2(Alpha,Beta,_,_,Alpha) :- better_score(Alpha,Beta).
a2(Alpha,              /* running maximum of b-values   */
   Beta,               /* running maximum of a-values   */
   [],                 /* game tree list whose          */
                       /* min a-value is sought         */
   Ha,                 /* game tree list whose          */
                       /* max b-value is sought         */
   Ra) :-              /* result for player a           */
        better_score(Beta,Alpha),
        a1(Beta,Ha,Ra).
a2(Alpha,              /* running maximum of b-values   */
   Beta,               /* running maximum of a-values   */
   [Ga|Hb],            /* game tree list whose          */
                       /* min a-value is sought         */
   Ha,                 /* game tree list whose          */
                       /* max b-value is sought         */
   Ra) :-              /* result for player a           */
        a(Ga,RGa),
        ((better_score(RGa,Beta),
          a2(Alpha,Beta,Hb,Ha,Ra)) ;   /* or */
         (better_score(Beta,RGa),
          a2(Alpha,RGa,Hb,Ha,Ra))).
```

END PROLOG PROGRAM SEGMENT F

The alpha-beta search never expends more effort than the minimax search. It may expend much less effort, depending on how the game tree is represented (in particular, depending on the ordering of the nodes in the representation of the tree). On optimally arranged trees, the fraction of computation required by alpha-beta compared to minimax decreases rapidly toward zero as the size of the game tree increases. For the game tree shown in Figure 35.3, alpha-beta search takes roughly half as long as minimax when the subtrees appear in the list representation in the same left-to-right order in which they appear in the diagram. This ratio would tend to decrease for larger game trees. In the tic-tac-toe games that we study in this chapter, the alpha-beta algorithm is about 10 times faster than the simple minimax algorithm. In games of greater complexity, such as the card games we study at the end of this chapter, the alpha-beta algorithm is so much faster than the simple minimax that we did not have the patience to time it.[2]

---

[2] The number of nodes to choose from at a node in a game tree is known as the *branching factor* at that node. The total number, $n$, of nodes over all depth levels in a game tree that has a constant branching factor (i.e., presents the same number of alternative moves at each stage of the game) is the branching factor, $b$, multiplied by itself $d$ times, where $d$ is the depth of the tree. That is, $n = b^d$.

The minimax algorithm examines all these nodes, but the alpha-beta algorithm examines

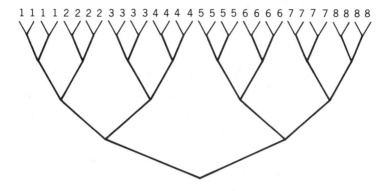

**FIGURE 35.3** A six-move tree game.

As pointed out early in this chapter, the tree-game approach with minimax (or alpha-beta) search can form the basis for game-playing algorithms for almost any two-opponent game. However, the huge size of the tree for any interesting game makes complete elaboration of the tree as a data structure at best impractical (actually, inconceivable might be a better description; in many cases the number of nodes in the tree would exceed the number of atoms in the known universe). For such games, the algorithm must be able to generate portions of the game tree on demand.[3]

Furthermore, the desired result of a game-playing algorithm is not the optimal score, but the sequence of moves that lead to that score. Generation of the game tree will involve

1. Producing a set of possible moves, given a particular game situation.

2. Creating a new situation, given an existing one and a move.

3. Creating a result, including a score, from a situation that ends the game.

Algorithms to handle these aspects of game-tree generation will be

---

only some of them. In an optimal case, the alpha-beta algorithm examines $b^{\lfloor (d+1)/2 \rfloor} + b^{\lceil (d-1)/2 \rceil} - 1$ nodes. Therefore, it is reasonable to hope that the amount of effort consumed by an alpha-beta search will amount to a small multiple of the square root of the amount of effort consumed by the naive minimax search.

[3]The explicit specification of the tree as data, as we have done so far, is known as an *extensive representation* of the tree; on the other hand, a representation of the tree as an algorithm that can produce portions of the tree on demand is known as an *intensive representation*. This extensive versus intensive dichotomy is sometimes used to delineate between different mechanisms for computing functions: a table of argument-value pairs (which supports computation of the function by table lookup) is an extensive representation, whereas a representation by a "formula" would be an intensive representation. The distinction gets blurred when we try to define formula. For example, the two functions in Figure 35.4 deliver the same values on arguments in the set of whole numbers between -2 and +2. Both are formulas, in a sense, but one has a definite extensive flavor and the other intensive.

$$fext(-2) \;=\; 2$$
$$fext(-1) \;=\; 1$$
$$fext(0) \;=\; 0$$
$$fext(1) \;=\; 1$$
$$fext(2) \;=\; 2$$

$$fint(x) \;=\; x \quad if \; x \geq 0$$
$$fint(x) \;=\; -x \quad if \; x < 0$$

FIGURE 35.4

available to our search algorithm. To produce the sequence of moves that lead to the optimal score, we will pump individual moves onto a sequence as the search proceeds. Retaining the sequence of moves during the search serves a dual purpose: It permits delivering the sequence as part of the final result, and it makes the game situation available for further tree generation.

In addition to having access to tree generators, the search algorithm will need to be able to test for leaves and to compare score values from the game tree leaves. Because these operations will depend on the representation of the tree, they will vary from game to game and will need to be written anew for each game and supplied to the search program.

Using these ideas, we rewrite our search algorithm as shown here.

# ■ LISP PROGRAM SEGMENT G

```
; situation -- a game state, including the sequence
;               of moves that produced the state and
;               enough information to compute the
;               final result (including score)
;               if the game state is terminal
;               (i.e., ends the game).

; moves      -- a function that generates a list of
;               possible moves, given situation

; move       -- a function that generates a new
;               situation, given a move to be made
;               and a situation

; score      -- a function that extracts the numeric
;               score from a game result
```

```
;  leaf        -- a predicate that is true iff its
;                 argument is a terminal game
;                 situation

;  result      -- a function that constructs a game
;                 result from a terminal game situation

(defun A(situation)
   (if (leaf situation)
       (result situation)
       (let ((Amoves (moves situation)))
            (A1 (B (move (car Amoves) situation))
                (cdr Amoves)
                situation)
       )))


(defun A1(alpha Amoves Asituation)
   (if (null Amoves)
       alpha
       (let ((Bsituation (move (car Amoves) Asituation)))
            (if (leaf Bsituation)
                (A1 (maxr alpha (result Bsituation))
                    (cdr Amoves)
                    Asituation)
                (let ((Bmoves (moves Bsituation)))
                     (A2 alpha
                         (A (move (car Bmoves)
                                  Bsituation))
                         (cdr Bmoves)
                         Bsituation
                         (cdr Amoves)
                         Asituation)
                )))))


(defun A2(alpha beta Bmoves Bsituation Amoves Asituation)
   (if (>= (score alpha) (score beta))
       (A1 alpha Amoves Asituation)
       (if (null Bmoves)
           (A1 beta Amoves Asituation)
           (A2 alpha
               (minr beta (A (move (car Bmoves)
                                   Bsituation)))
               (cdr Bmoves)
               Bsituation
               Amoves
               Asituation)
```

```
        )))

(defun B(situation)
   (if (leaf situation)
       (result situation)
       (let ((Bmoves (moves situation)))
            (B1 (A (move (car Bmoves) situation))
                (cdr Bmoves)
                situation)
       )))

(defun B1(beta Bmoves Bsituation)
   (if (null Bmoves)
       beta
       (let ((Asituation (move (car Bmoves) Bsituation)))
            (if (leaf Asituation)
                (B1 (minr beta (result Asituation))
                    (cdr Bmoves)
                    Bsituation)
                (let ((Amoves (moves Asituation)))
                     (B2 beta
                         (B (move (car Amoves)
                                  Asituation))
                         (cdr Amoves)
                         Asituation
                         (cdr Bmoves)
                         Bsituation)
                )))))

(defun B2(beta alpha Amoves Asituation Bmoves Bsituation)
   (if (<= (score beta) (score alpha))
       (B1 beta Bmoves Bsituation)
       (if (null Amoves)
           (B1 alpha Bmoves Bsituation)
           (B2 beta
               (maxr alpha (B (move (car Amoves)
                                    Asituation)))
               (cdr Amoves)
               Asituation
               Bmoves
               Bsituation)
       )))

(defun maxr(result1 result2)
   (if (>= (score result1) (score result2))
       result1
```

```
            result2
    ))

(defun minr(result1 result2)
    (if (<= (score result1) (score result2))
        result1
        result2
    ))
```

END LISP PROGRAM SEGMENT G

## ■ PROLOG PROGRAM SEGMENT G

```
/*
situation        -- a game state, including the sequence
                    of moves that produced the state and
                    enough information to compute the
                    final result (including score) if the
                    game state is terminal.

moves(S,Mlist)   -- Mlist is the list of possible moves
                    from situation S.

move(M,S,NewS)   -- the situation NewS arises after move M
                    from situation S.

score(R,Sc)      -- Sc is the numeric score reflected in
                    game result R.

leaf(S)          -- the situation S completes the game.

result(S,R)      -- the game result R follows from the
                    terminal situation S.
*/

a(Sa,Ra) :- leaf(Sa),
            result(Sa,Ra).
a(Sa,Ra) :- moves(Sa,[Ma|Amoves]),
            move(Ma,Sa,Sb),
            b(Sb,Rb),
            a1(Rb,Amoves,Sa,Ra).

a1(Alpha,              /* best result for player A using
                          moves not in 2nd argument     */
   [],                 /* some moves player A can make  */
```

```
        _,                      /* situation with player A to
                                   move       */
     Alpha).                    /* best result for player A       */

 a1(Alpha,                      /* best result for player A using
                                   moves not in 2nd argument       */
     [Amove|Amoves],            /* some moves player A can make   */
     Asituation,                /* situation with player A to
                                   move       */
     Aresult) :-                /* best result for player A        */
             move(Amove,Asituation,Bsituation),
               ((leaf(Bsituation),
                 result(Bsituation,Bresult),
                 maxr(Alpha,Bresult,NewAlpha),
                 a1(NewAlpha,Amoves,Asituation,Aresult))
                                /* or */
                 (not(leaf(Bsituation)),
                  moves(Bsituation,[Bmove|Bmoves]),
                  move(Bmove,Bsituation,NewAsituation),
                  a(NewAsituation,NewAresult),
                  a2(Alpha,
                     NewAresult,
                     Bmoves,
                     Bsituation,
                     Amoves,
                     Asituation,
                     Aresult))).

 a2(Alpha,                      /* best result for player A not
                                   using moves in Amoves         */
     Beta,                      /* best result for player B using
                                   moves in Bmoves               */
     Bmoves,                    /* some moves player B can make from
                                   Bsituation                    */
     Bsituation,                /* situation for move by player B after
                                   a move from Asituation        */
     Amoves,                    /* some moves player A can make from
                                   Asituation                    */
     Asituation,                /* situation with player A to move
 */
     Aresult) :-                /* best result for player A from
                                   Asituation                    */
                   ((score(Alpha,SAlpha),
                     score(Beta,SBeta),
                     SAlpha>=SBeta,
```

```
                        a1(Alpha,Amoves,Asituation,Aresult))   ;
        /* or */
                    a2h(Alpha,
                        Beta,
                        Bmoves,
                        Bsituation,
                        Amoves,
                        Asituation,
                        Aresult)).

a2h(_,
    Beta,
    [],
    _,
    Amoves,
    Asituation,
    Aresult) :-
                a1(Beta,Amoves,Asituation,Aresult).
a2h(Alpha,
    Beta,
    [Bmove|Bmoves],
    Bsituation,
    Amoves,
    Asituation,
    Aresult) :-  move(Bmove,Bsituation,NewAsituation),
                 a(NewAsituation,NewAresult),
                 minr(Beta,NewAresult,NewBeta),
                 a2(Alpha,
                    NewBeta,
                    Bmoves,
                    Bsituation,
                    Amoves,
                    Asituation,
                    Aresult).

b(Sb,Rb)  :- leaf(Sb),
             result(Sb,Rb).
b(Sb,Rb)  :- moves(Sb,[Mb|Bmoves]),
             move(Mb,Sb,Sa),
             a(Sa,Ra),
             b1(Ra,Bmoves,Sb,Rb).

b1(Beta,                 /* best result for player B using
                            moves not in 2nd argument      */
    [],                  /* some moves player B can make   */
    _,                   /* situation with player B to
```

```
                              move                          */
   Beta).                 /* best result for player B       */

b1(Beta,                  /* best result for player B using
                             moves not in 2nd argument      */
   [Bmove|Bmoves],        /* some moves player B can make   */
   Bsituation,            /* situation with player B to
                             move                           */
   Bresult) :-            /* best result for player B        */
            move(Bmove,Bsituation,Asituation),
            ((leaf(Asituation),
              result(Asituation,Aresult),
              minr(Beta,Aresult,NewBeta),
              b1(NewBeta,Bmoves,Bsituation,Bresult)) ;
       /* or */
              (not(leaf(Asituation)),
              moves(Asituation,[Amove|Amoves]),
              move(Amove,Asituation,NewBsituation),
              b(NewBsituation,NewBresult),
              b2(Beta,
                 NewBresult,
                 Amoves,
                 Asituation,
                 Bmoves,
                 Bsituation,
                 Bresult))).

b2(Beta,                  /* best result for player B not
                             using moves in Bmoves          */
   Alpha,                 /* best result for player A using
                             moves in Amoves                */
   Amoves,                /* some moves player A can make
                             from Asituation                */
   Asituation,            /* situation for move by player A
                             after a move from Bsituation   */
   Bmoves,                /* some moves player B can make
                             from Bsituation                */
   Bsituation,            /* situation with player B to
                             move                           */
   Bresult) :-            /* best result for player B from
                             Bsituation                     */
            ((score(Beta,SBeta),
              score(Alpha,SAlpha),
              SBeta=<SAlpha,
              b1(Beta,Bmoves,Bsituation,Bresult))  ;
       /* or */
```

```
                        b2h(Beta,
                            Alpha,
                            Amoves,
                            Asituation,
                            Bmoves,
                            Bsituation,
                            Bresult)).

b2h(_,
    Alpha,
    [],
    _,
    Bmoves,
    Bsituation,
    Bresult) :-
                b1(Alpha,Bmoves,Bsituation,Bresult).
b2h(Beta,
    Alpha,
    [Amove|Amoves],
    Asituation,
    Bmoves,
    Bsituation,
    Bresult) :-  move(Amove,Asituation,NewBsituation),
                 b(NewBsituation,NewBresult),
                 maxr(Alpha,NewBresult,NewAlpha),
                 b2(Beta,
                    NewAlpha,
                    Amoves,
                    Asituation,
                    Bmoves,
                    Bsituation,
                    Bresult).

maxr(R1,R2,MaxR) :- score(R1,Sc1),
                    score(R2,Sc2),
                    ((Sc1 >= Sc2, MaxR=R1)    ;
              /* or */
                     (Sc2 >= Sc1, MaxR=R2)).

minr(R1,R2,MaxR) :- score(R1,Sc1),
                    score(R2,Sc2),
                    ((Sc1 =< Sc2, MaxR=R1)    ;
              /* or */
                     (Sc2 =< Sc1, MaxR=R2)).
```

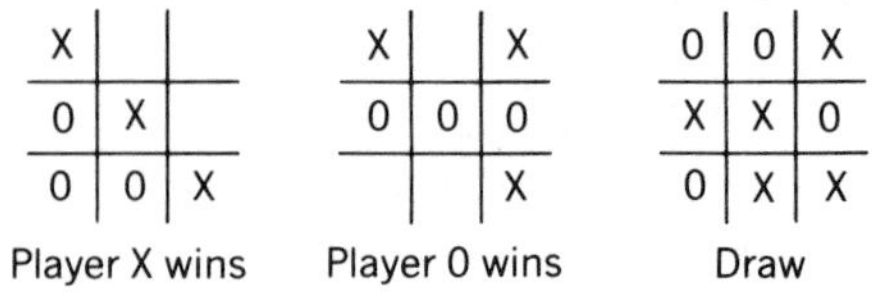

Player X wins    Player 0 wins    Draw

Figure **35.5** Tic-tac-toe

## END PROLOG PROGRAM SEGMENT G

To use the version of the search algorithm that generates the game tree on the fly, we must design data structures to represent game situations, moves, and game results and develop procedures to generate and operate on these structures. Naturally, these data structures and procedures are specialized to the game being played.

We will illustrate the use of the search algorithms with two games: tic-tac-toe, a simple game to illustrate the ideas, and double-dummy endgames in bridge, an interesting game that will require creative use of the algorithms.

Tic-tac-toe is a game played on a 3-by-3 rectangular grid. Players alternately mark empty squares on the grid, seeking to claim three squares in a straight line, vertically, horizontally, or diagonally. If neither player succeeds in forming a line before all nine squares are marked, the game is a draw; otherwise, the player forming the line wins.

Our first step calls for designing data structures to represent game situations and results. Because we want to be able to reconstruct the entire move sequence, we will mark squares with a digit (0, 1, 2, ..., 9) to indicate when a player marked a square. An odd digit (1, 3, 5, or 9) indicates that player 1 occupies the square; a nonzero even digit (2, 4, 6, or 8), player 2. A zero digit signifies an empty square. We represent the squares as a sequence of nine digits, the first three for the top row, left to right, the next three for the second row, and so on. A move will be represented by an integer between 1 and 9, indicating which grid position is to be marked (grid positions being numbered left to right, top to bottom).

## ■ LISP PROGRAM SEGMENT H

```
;    grid    is    (move-number    move-number    move-number
;                   move-number    move-number    move-number
;                   move-number    move-number    move-number)

;    situation    is    (num-moves    grid)    --    num-moves is
```

```
;                                        the number of
;                                        marked squares
;                                        in grid
;    result        is   (score  grid)

;    score         is   -2        -- player 2 wins
;                       0         -- draw
;                       1         -- player 1 wins

;    move-number   is   digit     -- zero indicates
;                                     empty square
;                                     odd number:  X- move,
;                                                  in sequence
;                                     even:        O-move,
;                                                  in sequence
;    num-moves     is   digit

;    digit         is   0
;                  or   1
;                  or   2
;                       .
;                       .
;                       .
;                  or   9
```

END LISP PROGRAM SEGMENT H

## ▪ PROLOG PROGRAM SEGMENT H

```
/*
Grid         is   grid(Move-number,Move-number,Move-number
                       Move-number,Move-number,Move-number
                       Move-number,Move-number,Move-number)

Situation    is   sit(Num-moves,Grid)

Result       is   res(Score,Grid)

score        is   -2        -- player 2 wins
                  0         -- draw
                  1         -- player 1 wins

Move-number  is   Digit     -- zero indicates empty square
                               odd number:  X-move,
                                            in sequence
```

```
                              even:        O-move,
                                           in sequence
Num-moves     is  Digit

Digit         is  0
              or  1
              or  2
                  .
                  .
                  .
              or  9
*/
```

END PROLOG PROGRAM SEGMENT H

To represent game situations, we will use this grid along with a number (0, 1, ..., 9) to indicate how many squares are marked. The initial game situation is (0 (0 0 0   0 0 0   0 0 0)). A move will be represented by a number designating a grid position to be marked with a move number. A game result will be a score along with a grid indicating all the moves of the game. Our search algorithms assume that high scores are more desirable for player 1 and that low scores favor player 2. In line with this assumption, we use 0 to represent a win by player 2 (the least desirable result for player 1), we use 1 for a draw (the next most desirable result for player 1), and we use 2 for a win by player 1 [e.g., (5 (5 0 0   4 1 0   2 0 3)) could represent the result depicted in Figure 35.5 in which player X wins].

Now all we need for a program to play tic-tac-toe are the procedures for operating on these data structures.

## ■ LISP PROGRAM SEGMENT I

```lisp
(defun moves(situation)              ; construct list of
                                     ; legal moves
   (zerospots (cadr situation) 1))

(defun move(m situation)             ; make move m to get
   (list (+ 1 (car situation))       ; new situation
         (newgrid (+ 1 (car situation))
              m
              (cadr situation)))))

(defun score(result) ; extract score from result
   (car result))               ; 1: player 1 wins;
```

```
                                 ; -2: player 2 wins; 0: draw

(defun leaf(situation)          ; non-NIL iff situation
   (or (equal (car situation) 9)   ; is terminal
       (win  situation)
   ))

(defun result(terminalsituation)  ; construct result
   (let ((score (win  terminalsituation)))        ; from
        (if (equal NIL score)     ; terminalsituation
            (list 0    (cadr terminalsituation))
            (list score (cadr terminalsituation))
        )))

(defun newgrid(movenumber k grid) ; insert movenumber
                                  ; at grid pos'n  k
   (let ((ht (split '() grid (- k 1))))
        (revappend (first ht)
                   (cons movenumber (cdr (second ht)))))
   ))

(defun split(base lst n) ; (list (append (reverse
                         ; first-n-elems-of-lst)
   (if (= n 0)           ;                   base)
       (list base lst)   ; lst-without-first-n-elements
       (split (cons (car lst) base) (cdr lst) (- n 1))
    ))

(defun zerospots(gridtail position)  ; construct list
                                     ; of positions
   (if (null gridtail)               ; of empty squares
                                     ; in gridtail
      '()                            ; numbering
                                     ; gridtail
                                     ; positions
      (if (equal 0 (car gridtail))   ; left to right
          (cons position             ; from position
                (zerospots (cdr gridtail) (+ 1 position)))
          (zerospots (cdr gridtail) (+ 1 position))
       )))

(defun win( situation)                     ; 1 if player
                                           ; 1 wins
   (and (>= (car situation) 3)             ; -2 if player
                                           ; 2 wins
        (let ((grid (cadr situation)))     ; NIL
```

```
                                              ; otherwise
              (let ((tl (mark (first   grid)))  ; top
                                              ; left
                                              ; square
                    (tc (mark (second  grid)))  ; top
                                              ; center
                    (tr (mark (third   grid)))  ; top
                                              ; right
                    (ml (mark (fourth  grid)))  ; middle
                                              ; left
                    (c  (mark (fifth   grid)))  ; center
                                              ; square
                    (mr (mark (sixth   grid)))  ; middle
                                              ; right
                    (bl (mark (seventh grid)))  ; bottom
                                              ; left
                    (bc (mark (eighth  grid)))  ; bottom
                                              ; center
                    (br (mark (ninth   grid)))) ; bottom
                                              ; right
                (or (markedalike tl  c br)  ; diagonal
                                              ; down
                    (markedalike bl  c tr)  ; diagonal
                                              ; up
                    (markedalike tl tc tr)  ; top row
                    (markedalike ml c  mr)  ; middle
                                              ; row
                    (markedalike bl bc br)  ; bottom
                                              ; row
                    (markedalike tl ml bl)  ; left
                                              ; column
                    (markedalike tc c  bc)  ; middle
                                              ; column
                    (markedalike tr mr br)  ; right
                                              ; column
              )))))

(defun mark(movenumber)          ;  0 if square empty
   (if (= movenumber 0)          ;  1 if square marked
                                 ;  by player 1
       0                         ; -2 if square marked
                                 ;  by player 2
       (if (oddp movenumber)
           1
           -2)
   ))
```

```
(defun markedalike(mark1 mark2 mark3)   ; 2 if all marks
                                        ; are player 1
    (and (/= 0 mark1)                   ; 1 if all marks
                                        ; are player 2
         (= mark1 mark2)                ; otherwise, NIL
         (= mark2 mark3)
         mark1
    ))
```

END LISP PROGRAM SEGMENT I

# ■ PROLOG PROGRAM SEGMENT I

```
moves(sit(_,Grid),Mlist) :- empty_spots(Grid,Mlist).

move(Position,                   /* pos'n of empty spot    */
                                 /*   in Grid              */
     sit(MovNum,Grid),           /* situation before move  */
     sit(NxtMov,NxtGrid)) :- /* situation after move       */
                             NxtMov is MovNum+1,
                             Grid=..[grid|Spots],
                             mark_spot(NxtMov,
                                       Position,
                                       Spots,
                                       [],
                                       NewSpots),
                             NxtGrid=..[grid|NewSpots].

score(res(Score,_),Score).

leaf(sit(9,_)).
leaf(sit(MovNum,Grid)) :- MovNum<9,
                          win(Grid,_).

result(sit(_,Grid),
       res(Score,Grid)) :- ((win(Grid,Sc), Score=Sc) ;
                            /* or */
                            Score=0).

empty_spots(Grid,Mlist) :- Grid=..[grid|Spots],
                           zero_spots(Spots,1,Mlist).

zero_spots([],_,[]).
zero_spots([0|Spots],
```

```
                Position,
                [Position|Moves]) :- NewPos is Position+1,
                                zero_spots(Spots,
                                        NewPos,Moves).


zero_spots([Mark|Spots],
            Position,
            Moves) :- Mark>0,
                    NewPos is Position+1,
                    zero_spots(Spots,NewPos,Moves).


mark_spot(MovNum,
            1,
            [_|Spots],
            PreSpots,
            NewSpots) :-
                        rev_append(PreSpots,
                                [MovNum|Spots],NewSpots).
mark_spot(MovNum,
            Position,
            [Spot|Spots],
            PreSpots,
            NewSpots) :- NewPos is Position-1,
                    mark_spot(MovNum,
                                NewPos,
                                Spots,
                                [Spot|PreSpots],
                                NewSpots).
rev_append([],L,L).
rev_append([A|X],Y,L) :- rev_append(X,[A|Y],L).


win(Grid,Score) :- xo_grid(Grid,XO_Grid),
                    win_grid(XO_Grid,Score).


xo_grid(grid(TL,TC,TR,
            ML,C,  MR,
            BL,BC,BR),
        grid(XO_TL,XO_TC,XO_TR,
            XO_ML,XO_C,  XO_MR,
            XO_BL,XO_BC,XO_BR)) :-
                                xo_spot(TL,XO_TL),
                                xo_spot(TC,XO_TC),
                                xo_spot(TR,XO_TR),
                                xo_spot(ML,XO_ML),
                                xo_spot(C,XO_C),
                                xo_spot(MR,XO_MR),
```

```
                                       xo_spot(BL,XO_BL),
                                       xo_spot(BC,XO_BC),
                                       xo_spot(BR,XO_BR).

xo_spot(0,empty).
xo_spot(MovNum,x)  :- 1 is MovNum mod 2.    /* odd moves  */
                                            /* are player */
                                            /* x          */
xo_spot(MovNum,o)  :- MovNum>0,
                      0 is MovNum mod 2.    /* even moves */
                                            /* are player */
                                            /* o          */

win_grid(grid(x,x,x,

               _,_,_,
               _,_,_),1).
win_grid(grid(_,_,_,
               x,x,x,
               _,_,_),1).
win_grid(grid(_,_,_,

               _,_,_,
               x,x,x),1).
win_grid(grid(x,_,_,
               x,_,_,
               x,_,_),1).
win_grid(grid(_,_,x,
               _,_,x,
               _,_,x),1).
win_grid(grid(_,x,_,
               _,x,_,
               _,x,_),1).
win_grid(grid(x,_,_,
               _,x,_,
               _,_,x),1).
win_grid(grid(_,_,x,
               _,x,_,
               x,_,_),1).

win_grid(grid(o,o,o,

               _,_,_,
               _,_,_),-2).
win_grid(grid(_,_,_,
               o,o,o,
               _,_,_),-2).
win_grid(grid(_,_,_,

               _,_,_,
```

```
              o,o,o),-2).
win_grid(grid(o,_,_,
              o,_,_,
              o,_,_),-2).
win_grid(grid(_,_,o,
              _,_,o,
              _,_,o),-2).
win_grid(grid(_,o,_,
              _,o,_,
              _,o,_),-2).
win_grid(grid(o,_,_,
              _,o,_,
              _,_,o),-2).
win_grid(grid(_,_,o,
              _,o,_,
              o,_,_),-2).
```

END PROLOG PROGRAM SEGMENT I

Using these procedures, we can start a game from the empty grid, or we can analyze an endgame by setting up a situation describing a partially completed game and feeding this situation as input to the search procedures.

Since the program plays perfectly and because tic-tac-toe always leads to a draw if neither player makes a mistake, games beginning from the empty grid always end in a draw. However, game situations in which one player has gained an advantage end in a win for that player. The invocations and results that follow illustrate the performance of the tic-tac-toe program.

■ LISP PROGRAM SEGMENT J

```
Example Game 1:  full game, draw
   (A        '(0 (0 0 0           ; full game,       . . .
                   0 0 0           ; empty grid        . . .
                   0 0 0)))        ;                    . . .
   result:  (0 (1 3 4              ;    X X O
               6 2 7              ;    O O X
               5 8 9))            ;    X O X  - draw


Example Game 2:  endgame, advantage X
   (A        '(2 (1 0 0            ; advantage X:    X . .
                   0 0 0           ;                  . . .
```

```
              2 0 0)))              ;                      O . .
result:   (1 (1 3 4                ;     X X O
              6 5 7                ;     O X X
              2 8 9))              ;     O O X  - win for X
```

Note:   The traditional winning move for X from this
        position is to mark the upper right hand corner.
        However, our algorithm marks the middle square
        on the top row, an equally effective move even
        though it falls outside conventional tic-tac-toe
        tactics.  Both moves (upper right corner and top
        row middle square) force a win for X, regardless
        of O's next move.

        Endgames 2a and 2b below continue game 2 in two
        ways:
        (a) The unconventional X-move to the top row
            middle square, as selected by our algorithm;
        (b) The traditional X-move, the upper right
            corner.

Example Game 2a:   Unconventional winning move for X
                   from the opening in Game 2.

```
(B         '(3 (1 3 0               ; advantage X:   X X .
               0 0 0                ;                . . .
               2 0 0)))             ;                O . .
Result:   (1 (1 3 4                 ;    X X O
              6 5 7                 ;    O X X
              2 8 9)))              ;    O O X  - win for X
```

Example Game 2b:   Traditional winning move for X
                   from the opening in Game 2.

```
(B         '(3 (1 0 3               ; advantage X:   X . X
               0 0 0                ;                . . .
               2 0 0)))             ;                O . .
Result:   (1 (1 4 3                 ;    X O X
              6 7 0                 ;    O X .
              2 0 5)))              ;    O . X  - win for X
```

Note:   After one player makes a move that forces a win,
        regardless of the other player's actions (e.g.,
        move 3 in games 2, 2a, and 2b), all moves for the
        losing player are equivalent (all are completely
        ineffective).  Our algorithm may select any of
        these equivalent moves, even those that appear

to be throwing the game (e.g., the sixth move in games 2a and 2b).

Example Game 3:  Endgame, advantage O

```
(B       '(3   (1 3 0         ; advantage O:   X X .
               0 0 0          ;                . . .
               0 0 2)))       ;                . . O
Result:    (-2 (1 3 4         ;      X X O
                5 0 6         ;      X . O
                0 0 2))       ;      . . O
```

Note:  Again, X seems to be throwing the game at move 5, but any other move would be equally ineffective.

END LISP PROGRAM SEGMENT J

# ■ PROLOG PROGRAM SEGMENT J

Example Game 1:  Full game, draw

```
?- a(sit(3,grid(0,0,0,        /* full game  . . .  */
             0,0,0,           /* empty grid . . .  */
             0,0,0)),Result). /*            . . .  */

yes. Result=[0,grid(1 3 4     /*  X X O          */
             6 2 7            /*  O O X          */
             5 8 9)]          /*  X O X  - draw */
```

Example Game 2:  Endgame, advantage X
```
?- a(sit(2,grid(1,0,0,        /* adv. X:  X . .  */
             0,0,0,           /*          . . .  */
             2,0,0)),Result). /*          O . .  */

yes. Result=[1,grid(1 3 4     /*  X X O            */
             6 5 7            /*  O X X            */
             2 8 9)]          /*  O O X - win for X */
```

Note:  The traditional winning move for X from this position is to mark the upper right hand corner. However, our algorithm marks the middle square on the top row, an equally effective move even

though it falls outside conventional tic-tac-toe
tactics.  Both moves (upper right corner and top
row middle square) force a win for X, regardless
of O's next move.

Endgames 2a and 2b below continue game 2 in two
ways:
  (a) The unconventional X-move to the top row
      middle square, as selected by our algorithm;
  (b) The traditional X-move, the upper right
      corner.

Example Game 2a:  Unconventional winning move for X
                  from the opening in Game 2.
```
?- b(sit(3,grid(1,3,0,           /* adv. X:  X X .  */
              0,0,0,             /*          . . .  */
              2,0,0)),Result).  /*          O . .  */

yes. Result=[1,grid(1 3 4        /*  X X O           */
               6 5 7             /*  O X X           */
               2 8 9)]           /*  O O X - win for X */
```

Example Game 2b:  Traditional winning move for X
                  from the opening in Game 2.

```
?- b(sit(3,grid(1,0,3,           /* adv. X:  X . X  */
              0,0,0,             /*          . . .  */
              2,0,0)),Result).  /*          O . .  */

yes. Result=[1,grid(1 4 3        /*  X O X           */
               6 7 0             /*  O X .           */
               2 0 5)]           /*  O . X - win for X */
```

  Note:  After one player makes a move that forces a win,
         regardless of the other player's actions (e.g.,
         move 3 in games 2, 2a, and 2b), all moves for the
         losing player are equivalent (all are completely
         ineffective).  Our algorithm may select any of
         these equivalent moves, even those that appear
         to be throwing the game (e.g., the sixth move
         in games 2a and 2b).

Example Game 3:  Endgame, advantage O

```
?- b(sit(3,grid(1,3,0,           /* adv. O:  X X .  */
```

```
                 0,0,0,                /*              . . .    */
                 0,0,2)),Result). /*                  . . O    */

yes. Result=[-2,grid(1 3 4         /*   X X O                  */
                       5 0 6         /*   X . O                  */
                       0 0 2)]       /*   . . O - win for O */
```

```
Note:   Again, X seems to be throwing the game at move
        5, but any other move would be equally
        ineffective.
```

## END PROLOG PROGRAM SEGMENT J

Now let's look at a more interesting game. Bridge is a card game in which the object is to win tricks by playing the highest of four cards played in each round. There are two opposing teams, two members on each team. The goal of each team is to win as many tricks as possible.[4] The two team members sit across from each other at the table, and play proceeds clockwise from the lead, which resides with the player who won the most recent trick. After the player with the lead plays a lead card, the member sitting in the next clockwise position (who will be from the other team) plays a card, and so on around the table until both teams have played two cards. The player who plays the highest card wins the trick and acquires the lead. Play continues in this manner one trick at a time. Each player begins with the same number of cards, and this number is, of course, the total number of tricks in the game. In a full game there are 13 tricks, but we will be dealing with endgames in which there will be, in general, a lessor number of tricks.

The cards are divided into four groups, "suits," and rank ordered with each suit. The suits are labeled clubs, diamonds, hearts, and spades. In each trick, players must follow suit (i.e., play a card from the same suit as that of the lead card in the trick), except that player who holds no card in the lead suit is not required to follow suit.

The winning card of the trick is the highest card played in the lead suit.[5] A game is complete when all of the cards have been played.

To apply our search algorithms to the game of bridge, we will represent each player's holding by a sequence of four lists, one list for each suit. Each suit-list contains numbers representing the cards held in that suit: 1 indicates the deuce of clubs, 2 the three of clubs, ..., 13 the ace of clubs, ..., 52 the ace of spades.

A game situation contains six components:

---

[4]In contract bridge, the most popular form of bridge, the goal is a little more complex, but we will be dealing with as simplified game known as double-dummy bridge, where the goal is simply to win as many tricks as possible for the team.

[5]This is known as no-trump play. Some of the exercises in this chapter deal with trump play, in which one suit has some privileges over the others.

1. A sequence of four hands (listed in clockwise order around the table and referred to as hands 1, 2, 3, and 4 in the order that they appear in the list).

2. A sequence of tricks, as played to arrive at the represented situation.

3. A number indicating how many moves have been made.

4. A number, 1, 2, 3, or 4, indicating the lead hand in the trick being played.

5. A number, 0, 1, 2, or 3, indicating how many cards have been played on the trick in progress.

6. A number indicating how many tricks have been won by the team holding hands 1 and 3.

A game result has two components: components (6) and (2) of a terminal situation. Thus, a game result indicates the number of tricks won by the team holding hands 1 and 3 and includes a sequence of tricks leading to that score.

## ■ LISP PROGRAM SEGMENT K

```
situation              is   ( hands
                            tricks
                            number-of-moves
                            leader
                            number-of-plays-in-trick
                            tricks-won-by-1&3)
hands                  is   (hand hand hand hand)
hand                   is   (clubs diamonds
                            hearts spades)
clubs                  is   (club-card...  )
diamonds               is   (diamond-card...)
hearts                 is   (heart-card...  )
spades                 is   (spade-card...  )
club-card              is   number -- 1 - 13:
                            1 denotes deuce, 13 ace
```

| diamond-card | is | number -- 14 - 26:<br>14 denotes deuce, 26 ace |
| heart-card | is | number -- 27 - 39:<br>27 denotes deuce, 39 ace |
| spade-card | is | number -- 40 - 52:<br>40 denotes deuce, 52 ace |
| tricks | is | (trick...) |
| trick | is | (card...  ) |
| card | is | club-card |
| | or | diamond-card |
| | or | heart-card |
| | or | spade-card |
| number-of-moves | is | number –<br>indicates number of moves<br>made to arrive at situation<br>(includes no-play moves) |
| leader | is | player number |
| number-of-plays-in-trick | is | number -- 0 to 4 |
| player-number | is | 1 – player 1 |
| | is | 2 – player 2 |
| | is | 3 – player 3 |
| | is | 4 – player 4 |
| tricks-won-by-1&3 | is | number --<br>indicates number of tricks won<br>by the team of players 1 and 3 |
| move | is | card |
| | or | none -- indicates no play |
| result | is | (tricks tricks-won-by-1&3) |

END LISP PROGRAM SEGMENT K

## ■ PROLOG PROGRAM SEGMENT K

| situation | is | sit( hands,<br>tricks,<br>number-of-moves,<br>leader,<br>number-of-plays-in-trick<br>tricks-won-by-1&3) |
| hands | is | hands(hand,hand,hand,hand) |
| hand | is | (clubs,diamonds,hearts,spades) |
| clubs | is | (club-card...  ) |
| diamonds | is | (diamond-card...) |
| hearts | is | (heart-card...  ) |
| spades | is | (spade-card...  ) |

| | | |
|---|---|---|
| club-card | is | number -- 1 - 13: |
| | | 1 denotes deuce, 13 ace |
| diamond-card | is | number -- 14 - 26: |
| | | 14 denotes deuce, 26 ace |
| club-card | is | number -- 27 - 39: |
| | | 27 denotes deuce, 39 ace |
| club-card | is | number -- 40 - 52: |
| | | 40 denotes deuce, 52 ace |
| tricks | is | (trick...) |
| trick | is | (card... ) |
| card | is | club-card |
| | or | diamond-card |
| | or | heart-card |
| | or | spade-card |
| number-of-moves | is | number -- |
| | | indicates number of moves made to arrive at situation (includes no-play moves) |
| leader | is | player number |
| number-of-plays-in-trick | is | number -- 0 to 4 |
| player-number | is | 1 — player 1 |
| | is | 2 — player 2 |
| | is | 3 — player 3 |
| | is | 4 — player 4 |
| tricks-won-by-1&3 | is | number -- |
| | | indicates number of tricks won by the team of players 1 and 3 |
| move | is | card |
| | or | none -- indicates no play |
| result | is | (tricks tricks-won-by-1&3) |

## END PROLOG PROGRAM SEGMENT K

Double-dummy bridge is a two-opponent game: each team is one of the opponents. However, the opponents do not always alternate in making moves. For example, if player 1 leads at the first trick and player 4 wins it, the sequence of moves is Team A (player 1 leads), Team B (player 2 follows), Team A (player 3 follows), Team B (player 4 wins), Team B again (player 4 leads), and so on. Whenever the lead switches, on consecutive tricks, from one team to the other, it causes this type of glitch in the alternation of moves. Because our search algorithms assume a strict alternation of moves between opponents, we must retain this property (or adapt our search algorithms to a specialized form for bridge, which is harder than retaining the alternating-moves property).

To retain alternation between opponents, we design the move generator to deliver a no-play move as the only option when the parity of the number of moves matches the parity of the player (i.e., if both the number-of-moves and hand-to-play are even, or are odd, no-play becomes the only move available). This will keep the levels of the game tree synchronized with the alternation between searching for the maximal and minimal results in the search algorithm.

The other procedures needed to make the search algorithms play bridge apply the rules in a straightforward way to the data structures we have designed to represent bridge-game situations, moves, and results.

# ■ LISP PROGRAM SEGMENT L

```
(defun moves(situation)   ; construct list of cards next
                          ; player may play
  (let ((hand (extracthand (handtoplay situation)
                           (hands situation)))))
      (if (firstplayintrick situation)
          (if (synchronized situation)
              (allcardsofhand hand)
              (list (noplay)))
          (let ((cardsinsuit (extractsuit
                                (leadsuit
                                  (currenttrick
                                   (tricks situation)))
                              hand)))
            (if (some cardsinsuit)
                cardsinsuit
                (allcardsofhand hand)
            )))))

(defun move(card situation)            ; play card, build
                                       ; new situation
  (if (equal card (noplay))
      (buildsituation (hands situation)    ; synchronize
                      (tricks situation)   ; gametree when
                                           ; card=noplay
                      (+ 1 (numberofmoves situation))
                      (leader situation)
                      (playsintrick situation)
                      (trickswon situation))
      (let ((hap (playcardfromhand card    ; hap: hands
                                   ;          after play
                    (hands situation)
```

```
                                    (handtoplay situation)))
           (tap (if (firstplayintrick situation)
                                        ; tap: tricks
                  (startnewtrick  card ;       after play
                             (tricks situation))
                  (addcardtotrick card
                             (tricks situation)))))
           (nap (+ 1 (numberofmoves situation)))))
                                        ; nap: num moves
                                        ;       after play
           (if (not (lastplayintrick situation))
               (buildsituation hap      ; record play,
                          tap           ; incomplete trick
                          nap
                          (leader situation)
                          (+ 1 (playsintrick situation))
                          (trickswon situation))
           (let ((wot (winneroftrick   ; wot: winner
of
                          (leader situation)   ; trick
                          (currenttrick tap))))
                  (buildsituation hap     ; record play,
                             tap      ; completed trick
                             nap
                             wot
                             0
                             (incrementtrickswon
                                wot
                                (trickswon situation))
           )))))

(defun score(result)   (first result))

(defun leaf(situation)
  (let ((hns (hands situation)))
      (and (emptyhand (extracthand (player1) hns))
           (emptyhand (extracthand (player2) hns))
           (emptyhand (extracthand (player3) hns))
           (emptyhand (extracthand (player4) hns))
      )))

(defun result(terminalsituation)
  (list (trickswon terminalsituation)
        (tricks    terminalsituation)))

(defun emptyhand(hand)
```

```
  (and (null (extractsuit (clubs)    hand))
       (null (extractsuit (diamonds) hand))
       (null (extractsuit (hearts)   hand))
       (null (extractsuit (spades)   hand))
  ))

(defun buildsituation(hands
                      tricks
                      numberofmoves
                      leader
                      playsintrick
                      trickswon)
  (list hands tricks numberofmoves leader playsintrick
                                           trickswon))

(defun hands(situation)            (first situation))

(defun tricks(situation)           (second situation))

(defun numberofmoves(situation)    (third situation))

(defun leader(situation)           (fourth situation))

(defun playsintrick(situation)     (fifth situation))

(defun trickswon(situation)        (sixth situation))

(defun handtoplay(situation)
  (incrementplayer (leader situation)
                   (playsintrick situation)))

(defun extractsuit(suit hand)  (nth suit hand))

(defun suit(card)  (floor (- card 1) 13))
(defun clubs)(0)
(defun diamonds)(1)
(defun hearts)(2)
(defun spades)(3)

(defun bettercard(card cardtobeat)           ; true iff
  (and (equal (suit card) (suit cardtobeat)) ; card beats
       (> card cardtobeat)                   ; cardtobeat
  ))

(defun extracthand(playernumber hands)
  (nth (- playernumber 1) hands))
```

```
(defun allcardsofhand(hand) (append
                                (extractsuit (clubs) hand)
                                (extractsuit (diamonds) hand)
                                (extractsuit (hearts) hand)
                                (extractsuit (spades) hand)))

(defun some(cardlist) (not (null cardlist)))

(defun playcardfromhand(card somehands handtoplay)
  (if (= handtoplay 1)
      (cons (removecardfromhand card (car somehands)
                                        (suit card))
            (cdr somehands))
      (cons (car somehands)
            (playcardfromhand card (cdr somehands)
                                        (- handtoplay 1)))
  ))

(defun removecardfromhand( card partialhand position)
  (if (= position 0)
      (cons (remove card (car partialhand))
            (cdr partialhand))
      (cons (car partialhand)
            (removecardfromhand card (cdr partialhand)
                                        (- position 1)))
  ))

(defun noplay() 'none)

(defun synchronized(situation)
  (/= (mod (handtoplay situation) 2)
      (mod (numberofmoves situation) 2)
  ))

(defun player1) (1)
(defun player2) (2)
(defun player3) (3)
(defun player4) (4)

(defun nextplayer(player) (incrementplayer player 1))

(defun incrementplayer(player incr)
  (+ 1 (mod (+ incr (- player 1)) 4)))

(defun startnewtrick(card tricks)    ; delivers new tricks
```

```
    (cons (list card)                     ; structure with
          tricks))                        ; most recent trick
                                          ; containing only
                                          ; the given card


(defun addcardtotrick(card tricks)   ;  adds given card to
  (cons (cons card (currenttrick tricks))   ; the current
        (coveredtricks tricks)))            ; trick

(defun currenttrick(tricks)   ; delivers most recent trick
  (car tricks))

(defun coveredtricks(tricks)   ; delivers all tricks except
  (cdr tricks))                          ; the most recent one

(defun firstcardintrick(trick)      ; delivers lead card
  (car (last trick)))                    ; in given trick

(defun leadsuit(trick)              ; delivers suit of lead
  (suit (firstcardintrick trick)))   ; card in given trick

(defun firstplayintrick(situation)
  (equal  0  (playsintrick situation)))

(defun lastplayintrick(situation)
  (equal 3  (playsintrick situation)))

(defun winneroftrick(leader trick)
   (incrementplayer leader (- (winningplay trick) 1)))

(defun winningplay(trick) ; winning play-number (1, 2, 3,
                          ; or 4)
  (seekwinningplay 4 1 (firstcardintrick trick) trick))

(defun seekwinningplay(playnumber       ; pumping helper
                       bossplay       ; for winning play
                       bosscard
                       unconsideredcards)
  (if (= playnumber 1)
      bossplay
      (let ((card (car unconsideredcards)))
           (if (bettercard card bosscard)
               (seekwinningplay (- playnumber 1)
                                playnumber
                                card
                                (cdr unconsideredcards))
```

```
       (seekwinningplay (- playnumber 1)
                        bossplay
                        bosscard
                        (cdr unconsideredcards))
    ))))

(defun incrementtrickswon(winneroftrick
                          trickswonbyplayers1and3)
   (+ (mod winneroftrick 2)  trickswonbyplayers1and3))
```

END LISP PROGRAM SEGMENT L


# ■ PROLOG PROGRAM SEGMENT L

```
moves(Situation,Plays)  :- hand_to_play(Situation,Htp),
                           extract_hand(Htp,Situation,Hnd),
                           numplays(Situation,NumPlays),
                           ((newtrick(NumPlays),
                             ((synchronized(Situation),
                               all_cards_of_hand(Hnd,
                                                 Plays)) ;
                             /* or */
                             (not(synchronized
                                          (Situation)),
                               Plays=[none])))         ;
                           /* or */
                            (not(newtrick(NumPlays)),
                             leadsuit(Situation,Leadsuit),
                             extract_suit(Leadsuit,Hnd,
                                          Cards_in_Suit),
                             (some(Cards_in_Suit,Plays)  ;
                             /* or */
                             all_cards_of_hand(Hnd,
                                               Plays)))).

move(none,
     sit(Hands,Tricks,NumMov,Leader,NumPlay,TrksWon),
     sit(Hands,Tricks,Nap   ,Leader,NumPlay,TrksWon)) :-
         Nap is NumMov+1.
move(Card,
     sit(Hands,Tricks,NumMov,Leader,NumPlay,TrksWon),
     sit(Hap  ,Tap   ,Nap   ,Leader,Npap   ,TrksWon)) :-
         Card\==none,
         not(last_play_in_trick(NumPlay)),
         hand_to_play(sit(Hands,Tricks,NumMov,Leader,
```

```
                                   NumPlay,TrksWon),Htp),
          play_card(Card,Hands,Htp,Hap),
          update_tricks(Card,NumPlay,Tricks,Tap),
          Nap is NumMov+1,
          Npap is NumPlay+1.
move(Card,
     sit(Hands,Tricks,NumMov,Leader,NumPlay,TrksWon),
     sit(Hap  ,Tap  ,Nap  ,Wot  ,0     ,Twap  )) :-
          Card\==none,
          last_play_in_trick(NumPlay),
          hand_to_play(sit(Hands,Tricks,NumMov,Leader,
                           NumPlay,TrksWon),Htp),
          play_card(Card,Hands,Htp,Hap),
          update_tricks(Card,NumPlay,Tricks,Tap),
          Nap is NumMov+1,
          winner_of_trick(Leader,Tap,Wot),
          update_tricks_won(Wot,TrksWon,Twap).

score(res(TrksWon,_),TrksWon).

leaf(sit(hands(hand([],[],[],[]),
               hand([],[],[],[]),
               hand([],[],[],[]),
               hand([],[],[],[])),_,_,_,_,_)).

result(sit(_,Tricks,_,_,_,TrksWon),res(TrksWon,Tricks)).

hand_to_play(sit(_,_,_,Leader,NumPlays,_),
             Htp) :-
                     increment_player(Leader,NumPlays,
                                         Htp).

extract_hand(Player,
             sit(Hands,_,_,_,_,_),
             Hnd) :-
                     arg(Player,Hands,Hnd).

numplays(sit(_,_,_,_,NumPlays,_),NumPlays).

newtrick(0).

synchronized(Situation) :- hand_to_play(Situation,Htp),
                           arg(3,Situation,NumMov),
                           Htp mod 2 =\= NumMov mod 2.

all_cards_of_hand(hand(C,D,H,S),CDHS) :- append(H,S,HS),
```

```
                                        append(D,HS,
                                               DHS),
                                        append(C,DHS,
                                               CDHS).


leadsuit(sit(_,[Trk|_],_,_,_,_),
         Leadsuit) :-
                      first_card_in_trick(Trk,Card),
                      suit(Card,Leadsuit).

suit(Card,Suit) :- Suit is (Card-1)//13 +1.

extract_suit(Suit,Hand,Cards) :- arg(Suit,Hand,Cards).

first_card_in_trick(Trick,Card) :- append(_,[Card],Trick).

some([X|L],[X|L]).

play_card(Card,hands(Hand1,      Hand2,Hand3,Hand4),
              1,hands(New_Hand,  Hand2,Hand3,Hand4)) :-
          suit(Card,Suit),
          remove_card(Card,Suit,Hand1,New_Hand).
play_card(Card,hands(Hand1,Hand2,      Hand3,Hand4),
              2,hands(Hand1,New_Hand,  Hand3,Hand4)) :-
          suit(Card,Suit),
          remove_card(Card,Suit,Hand2,New_Hand).
play_card(Card,hands(Hand1,Hand2,Hand3,      Hand4),
              3,hands(Hand1,Hand2,New_Hand,  Hand4)) :-
          suit(Card,Suit),
          remove_card(Card,Suit,Hand3,New_Hand).
play_card(Card,hands(Hand1,Hand2,Hand3,Hand4),
              4,hands(Hand1,Hand2,Hand3,New_Hand)) :-
          suit(Card,Suit),
          remove_card(Card,Suit,Hand4,New_Hand).

remove_card(Card,1,hand(Clubs,Diamonds,Hearts,Spades),
                    hand(New_Clubs,Diamonds,Hearts,Spades))
:-
          delete_element(Card,Clubs,New_Clubs).
remove_card(Card,2,hand(Clubs,Diamonds,Hearts,Spades),
                    hand(Clubs,New_Diamonds,Hearts,Spades))
:-
          delete_element(Card,Diamonds,New_Diamonds).
remove_card(Card,3,hand(Clubs,Diamonds,Hearts,Spades),
                    hand(Clubs,Diamonds,New_Hearts,Spades))
:-
```

```
                delete_element(Card,Hearts,New_Hearts).
remove_card(Card,4,hand(Clubs,Diamonds,Hearts,Spades),
                hand(Clubs,Diamonds,Hearts,New_Spades))
:-
                delete_element(Card,Spades,New_Spades).

delete_element(X,L,NewL) :- append(P,[X|S],L),
                              append(P,S,NewL).

update_tricks(Card,0         ,Tricks          ,[ [Card]
                                                 |Tricks]).
update_tricks(Card,NumPlay,[Trick|Tricks],[ [Card|Trick]
                                              |Tricks]) :-
                NumPlay>0.

last_play_in_trick(3).

update_tricks_won(1,TricksWon,Twap) :- Twap is TricksWon+1.
update_tricks_won(3,TricksWon,Twap) :- Twap is TricksWon+1.
update_tricks_won(2,TricksWon,TricksWon).
update_tricks_won(4,TricksWon,TricksWon).

increment_player(P,Incr,NewP) :- NewP is ((P-1+Incr)
                                           mod 4) +1.

winner_of_trick(Leader,[Trick|_],Wot) :- winning_play
                                           (Trick,Wp),
                                           increment_player
                                           (Leader,Wp,Wot).

winning_play([C4,C3,C2,C1],Wp) :- suit(C1,Suit),
                                    winner([C2,C3,C4],C1,
                                      0,Suit,0,Wp).

winner([],_,BossPlayNum,_,_,BossPlayNum).
winner([Card|Cards],
      BossCard,
      BossPlayNum,
      Suit,
      PlayNum,
      Wp) :-
              NewPlayNum is PlayNum+1,
            ((suit(Card,Suit),
               Card>BossCard,
             winner(Cards,Card, NewPlayNum,
                   Suit,NewPlayNum,Wp))  ;
```

```
/* or */
    winner(Cards,BossCard,BossPlayNum,
           Suit,NewPlayNum,Wp)).
```

## END PROLOG PROGRAM SEGMENT L

The following invocations illustrate the use of the double-dummy bridge-playing algorithm on some interesting hands, and the results are summarized in the accompanying diagrams. For fun, you might want to work out some of the hands in advance to prove to yourself that the program is solving nontrivial problems.

The example hands are bridge endgames of five tricks or fewer. A five trick endgame requires 20 plays in all. The last four plays (i.e., the last trick) present no choices because each hand contains only one card at that point. Therefore, the game tree can be viewed as a tree of depth 16. Before that last trick, the game tree's branching factor ranges from one to five, depending on the situation. The average branching factor is between two and three. At a depth of 16, this generates a tree containing between a few million and a few tens of millions of nodes. Even if the alpha-beta algorithm gets lucky and follows the "square-root rule" of effort discussed in footnote 2, this means that we can expect our program to search at least between a few thousand and a few tens of thousands of nodes. If the computer is able to examine only a few nodes per second, then we should not expect it to complete an endgame analysis in less than a few minutes; and it could take several days, or even several weeks, even if the game tree happens to be well suited to alpha-beta search. Our computer labored several hours per game to compute the results displayed in the examples.

# ∎ PROLOG PROGRAM SEGMENT M

```
/* example, Love's book on squeezes (p.218)
             --
             A 10 8
             9
             6
8 7                    --
K 6                    Q J
Q                      J
--                     J 10
             J 10
             4
             --      South to lead
```

```
                              Q 9                          */

?- a(sit(hands(hand([11,8],[]   ,[29]        ,[49,48]),
                                            /* South */
              hand([]    ,[24],[38,31]  ,[46,45]),
                                            /* West  */
              hand([5]   ,[21],[39,35,33],[]      ),
                                            /* North */
              hand([10,9],[23],[37,36]   ,[]      )),
                                            /* East  */
          [],                /* tricks played        */
          0 ,                /* number of moves       */
          1 ,                /* leader                */
          0 ,                /* number of plays in    */
                             /* current trick         */
          0),                /* tricks won by 1&3     */
       Result).

yes. Result= res(5,[   [36 39 31 29]
                       /* trick 5: h4   h6  hA   hJ */
                    [37 33 45 48]
                       /* trick 4: s10 s8  h8   hQ  */
                    [23 35 38  8]
                       /* trick 3: c9  hK  h10 dJ  */
                    [ 9 21 24 11]
                       /* trick 2: cQ  dQ  d9  c10 */
                    [10  5 46 49]])
                       /* trick 1: sJ  s8 c6  cJ  */


          /* example, Love's book on squeezes (p.226)

                       K 9 3
                       --        North to lead
                       7
          --                       J
          10 7 5 2                 Q J
          --                       J 10
          10                       --
                       --
                       A 6
                       A 8
                       5                          */

?- a(sit(hands(hand([4],[26,20],[39,31        ],[  ]),
```

```
                                                    /* South  */
                hand([9],[        ],[35,32,30,27],[   ]),
                                                    /* West   */
                hand([6],[        ],[38,34,28   ],[46]),
                                                    /* North  */
                hand([]  ,[23,22],[37,36        ],[49])),
                                                    /* East   */
        [],                     /* tricks played           */
        0 ,                     /* number of moves          */
        3 ,                     /* leader                    */
        0 ,                     /* number of plays in        */
                                /* current trick             */
        0),                     /* tricks won by 1&3         */
    Result).
```

```
yes. Result= res(4,[   [49 46 27 20]
                            /* trick 5:  d8   h2  s8  sJ   */
                       [22 28 30 26]
                            /* trick 4:  dA   h5  h3  d10  */
                       [32 39 36 34]
                            /* trick 3:  h9   hJ  hA  h7   */
                       [31 37 38 35]
                            /* trick 2:  d10  dK  dQ  d6   */
                       [ 9  4 23  6]])
                            /* trick 1:  c7   dJ  c5  c10  */
```

## END PROLOG PROGRAM SEGMENT M

Tic-tac-toe and double-dummy bridge are games of perfect information: No part of the game situation is hidden from either player, and all possible future situations are predictable from a given situation. Contract bridge, the type of bridge that is most popular, is not a game of complete information. As in double-dummy bridge, each team hold two hands. However, one team, known as the *declarer*, has one player making moves from two hands, the declaring hand and the dummy. The other team, known as the *defenders*, has one player for each of its hands. After the initial lead from the defender to the right of the dummy, the dummy appears face up, and the declarer calls for a card from that hand. All the hands except the dummy are closed from view. Thus, each player can see two hands, his own and the dummy, which amounts to half the unplayed cards. To make an intelligent play, a player must consider the possible contents of the closed hands, weigh these possibilities with their statistical likelihoods, and make a play based on the most positive outcome given the odds. In our model, this would amount to a whole collection of possible game trees at each node. The algorithm, to play optimally, would have to perform a search on all these trees, compute their final scores, and weight each score with the probability associated with the configuration of hands leading to the score. The algorithm would then choose the move to optimize the score in a statistical sense.

This means that the amount of computation needed to play contract bridge is vastly greater than that needed for the double-dummy game. To write a practical program to play contract bridge, some of the possibilities would have to be ignored or their outcomes estimated with minimal computation. With this type of change, the search functions described in this chapter would be useful even in this very complex situation. In fact, most game-playing programs use some version of alpha-beta search as a basis for evaluating potential moves. Typically the search is terminated after a certain number of moves have been considered, even though a leaf has not been reached. At that point, a heuristic formula estimates the value of the situation from one player's point of view, and the program uses this estimate in place of a score for the situation.[6] The accuracy of the estimate determines the skill of the game playing program, and most of the effort in developing good game playing programs centers around the design of heuristic formulas. These formulas are highly specialized. Developing them requires expert understanding of the game and a tremendous amount of experimentation.

## ▪ PROGRAM NOTES

A few of the Prolog relations in this chapter take advantage of pattern matching to avoid explicit tests and special functions to do the testing. For example, the Prolog relations describing double-dummy bridge test for empty hands via pattern matching. The Lisp functions, on the other hand, include a special function, **emptyhand**, to test for this condition.

Several of the Lisp functions take advantage of functional composition to avoid intermediate variables. For example, the relation **a** in the Prolog implementation of alpha-beta search uses four intermediate variables, $Sa$, $Sb$, $Ra$, and $Rb$, to carry values between terms. The corresponding Lisp function **A** needs no intermediate variables comparable to these. Similarly, the Prolog relation **maxr** uses intermediate variables $Sc1$ and $Sc2$ that are unnecessary in the corresponding Lisp function.

Function composition is used in a slightly different way in the Lisp alpha-beta search function **A2** to avoid the need for the helping relation **a2h** that appears in the definition of the Prolog relation **a2**. (Actually,

---

[6]Game-playing programs for any interesting game require some type of heuristic estimation because complete analyses by alpha-beta search can never be feasible. Samuel (1963) estimates that a complete analysis of a single move in a game of checkers would take a billion trillion centuries on a machine that could examine a billion game tree nodes per second.

**a2h** is not strictly necessary, but without it the program would be substantially longer.)

The differences between the Lisp and Prolog presentations of the computations in this chapter differ primarily in syntactic details (uses of pattern matching and function composition), not in really fundamental ways (uses of varying input/output modes or higher-order functions). All the Prolog relations express functional relationships (i.e., one component in each relation serves as the output component and only one output value is valid for each specific combination of input values). None of them take advantage of the generalization that mathematical relations provide over mathematical functions, nor of Prolog's tolerance of differing input/output modes for components of relations. The Lisp functions, for their part, take no significant advantage of higher order functions (but the projects suggest a way in which they could). Thus, the Lisp functions and Prolog relations of this chapter present the desired input/output relationship in basically the same form.

# ■ BIBLIOGRAPHY NOTES

Wand developed an automatic program transformation technique that could derive the alpha-beta search algorithm from the minimax algorithm The derivation in this chapter follows the procedure described in his work.

A hand of contract bridge begins with a sequence of "bids" in which the players both describe their hands (incompletely) and estimate the number of tricks they can take, given a trump suit or no-trump. The team making the highest bid wins the contract and becomes the declaring team. The bidding sequence is a game the object of which is to arrive at an optimal contract for the team. Wasserman developed a bridge-bidding algorithm with considerable skill when compared to experienced human players The bridge hands in this chapter were taken from Love's book on squeeze plays.

One of the first programs to play a competent game of substantial complexity was Samuel's checkers player, developed in the early 1960s. It employed alpha-beta search and heuristic formulas (and a great many assembly-language programming tricks) to get acceptable performance on the IBM 704 computer.

Clyde E. Love (1959). *Bridge Squeezes Complete or Winning End Play Strategy*, Dover, New York.

A. L. Samuel (1963). Some studies in machine learning using the game of checkers. In E. A. Feigenbaum and J. Feldman, (eds.), *Computers and Thought*, McGraw–Hill, New York, pp. 71-105.

Mitchell Wand (1980). Continuation-based program transformation strategies. *J. ACM* **27**(1), 164–180.

A. I. Wasserman (1970). Realization of a skillful bridge bidding program. *Fall Joint Computer Conference* **37**, 433–444.

## ■ PROJECTS[7]

1. The programs of this chapter analyze a game tree and deliver an optimal score for a perfectly played game, along with a sequence of moves leading to that score. However, there are usually a great many play sequences leading to the optimal score, and the one chosen by our programs may leave the impression that one player or the other is throwing the game away. (Annotations in the example tic-tac-toe and double-dummy bridge games of this chapter point out plays of this kind.) This occurs because after one side makes a crucial play that inevitably leads to the optimal score, regardless of the actions of the opponent, the opponent may as well make bad moves as good ones. One way to make the delivered results reflect more interesting game sequences is to make **maxr** and **minr**, the functions that compare results, more selective. As specified in this chapter, **maxr** and **minr** do not exhibit a preference when asked about two results with the same score. The results are equivalent, and the functions simply choose one of them.

   The alternate specifications of **maxr** and **minr** that follow invoke another function, **moreinteresting**, that chooses one of two equivalent results based on some criterion of interest with respect to the game sequences.

   ```
   (defun maxr(result1 result2)
      (if (= (score result1) (score result2))
          (moreinteresting result1 result2)
          (if (> (score result1) (score result2))
              result1
              result2
   )))
   ```

   ```
   (defun minr(result1 result2)
      (if (= (score result1) (score result2))
          (moreinteresting result1 result2)
   ```

---

[7]We use the term *Projects* because the following are larger than the exercises of earlier chapters.

```
(if (< (score result1) (score result2))
    result1
    result2
)))
```

Write a selection function, **moreinteresting**, for the tic-tac-toe game. A criterion of interest that you might consider is to choose the game with the latest nonblocking move. For example, if the third move in one result fails to block a two-in-a-row line of the opponent's marks, and the other result has no such play until the fifth move, then the latter result is "more interesting," by this criterion. A similar criterion has to do with making winning moves as early as possible. A result that passes up a winning move early in the game might be considered less interesting than one that makes the winning move at that point. Or maybe such a game would be considered more interesting; either way, you could incorporate this consideration in your selection function.

Write a selection function for double-dummy bridge. Games that play low cards early, retaining high cards for later play, might be favored, for example.

2. When a double-dummy bridge hand contains an adjacent sequence of cards, any card from the sequence leads to the same score. (A sequence of cards is adjacent if all are from the same suit and no other hand contains a card of that suit that beats the lowest card in the sequence and loses to the highest card in the sequence.) A move generator could save effort in the game tree search if it generated only one move for the sequence instead of all the moves that could be made from the sequence. Alter the moves function of our bridge program to save effort in this way.

3. The bridge games that our program handles are no-trump games. Naming a trump suit changes the rules for winning a trick: The highest card in the trump suit played on the trick wins the trick. If no cards in the trump suit were played on the trick, the highest card in the suit lead wins the trick, as in no-trump games. Thus, a player holding no cards in the suit lead may play a card in the trump suit in an attempt to win the trick.

Revise the situation data structure and the move algorithm in our bridge playing program to handle play in a trump suit as well as no-trump.

4. *Go-Moku* is a game similar to tic-tac-toe, but on a larger grid (19 by 19) and with a requirement of five marks in a row to win (horizontal, vertical, or diagonal). Provide the necessary move generators and analysis routines to enable our search algorithms to play modified Go-Moku on an *n*-by-*n* grid (write the routines so that you can

vary *n* easily). Run the programs on grids of various sizes and with various initial conditions to study different endgames. (A 19-by-19 grid will be too large for your computer system to handle; start with 5-by-5 and go up slowly from there.)

5. Modify the analysis routines in your Go-Moku program from Project 2 so that they estimate the score after searching to a certain depth. Provide different estimation formulas for the different players and study the resulting skill levels.

6. **Heuristics:** No computer will ever be powerful enough to use alpha-beta search and full-game analysis to play a perfect game of bridge (or chess, or any other game complex enough to interest people). At some point in the analysis, game-playing programs using alpha-beta search will have to choose moves based on estimates of the final score from a given position. For example, a move analyzer for bridge might estimate that a finesse would produce an extra half trick and choose that play without doing a complete analysis of all the alternatives. Serious game-playing programs have thousands of such "heuristic" estimates, which attempt to suggest a good move without rigorous justification, usually following some traditional, "common sense" procedure.

Modify the analysis functions in the Go-Moku program from the foregoing project so that they choose a move and estimate a score based on some heuristics after searching to a certain depth. Provide different heuristics for different players, and study the resulting skill levels.

7. **Higher-order Functions:** The functions **A**, **A1**, and **A2** in the Lisp implementation of alpha-beta search are the same as **B**, **B1**, and **B2**, except for their uses of **maxr** and **minr**. Rewrite these functions as **G**, **G1**, and **G2**, adding two additional arguments to each function. One new argument will be a function that selects the better of two results for one player. The other argument, a function selecting the better result for the other player.

The **G**, **G1**, and **G2** will take the place of **A**, **A1**, **A2**, **B**, **B1**, and **B2**, halving the amount of code. The invocations

```
(G situation maxr minr)
```

and

```
(A situation)
```

will be equivalent.

Similarly,

**(G situation minr maxr)**

and

**(B situation)**

will be equivalent.

*Note:* A similar trick in the Prolog implementation would be difficult to pull off because the support for higher-order relations is so clumsy.

## CHAPTER 36

# LANGUAGE PARSING

A basic problem in computing is the translation of symbolic programming languages into a machine-interpretable form. This is most often accomplished by *lexical analysis, syntactic analysis, semantic analysis,* and finally, *code generation.* We will look at the problem of *syntax-directed translation,* which involves both syntax analysis (*parsing*) and the generation of a translated form of the program.

The chapter begins with the fundamentals of symbolic languages, their specification with *context-free grammars,* and canonical representations of the generation of sentences from context-free grammars (*parse trees*). We then discuss a popular method of parsing called *recursive-descent parsing* and develop a Lisp implementation of a recursive-descent parser.

A more difficult problem is the translation of (subsets of) *natural languages,* such as English. Although the capabilities of contemporary natural language processers are limited, progress continues to be made. We first consider the use of *Definite Clause Grammars* and the use of Prolog for parsing sentences of the language they generate. Then we generalize the definite clause grammar formalism to allow for the explicit associa-

**370**

tion of *semantics* with grammatical rules. A discussion of the resulting *Definite Clause Translation Grammars* and the Prolog parsers for the languages they generate completes the tutorial on language parsing.

Keep in mind that our coverage of lexical and syntactic analysis and natural language processing serves only to introduce you to these problems and some solution strategies. The bibliographic notes point to deeper sources of information.

# ■ FUNDAMENTALS OF PARSING

Let us consider the problem of determining whether a program of a certain language is syntactically correct, and if so, producing an alternate but semantically equivalent form to be compiled. This is generally called *parsing*.

A parser typically receives tokens from a scanner, as input, and produces information to guide the remainder of the translation, as output. The specification of the programming language being translated will be discussed first. Next, a few methods of parsing are discussed, as well as a classic form for representing the output of a parser: a *parse tree*. We then explore *recursive descent parsing* with Lisp and *definite clause grammar* parsing with Prolog.

## LANGUAGES AND GRAMMARS

To specify a language to be recognized by a parser, we will employ *context-free grammars* (hereafter simply called *grammars*). The use of grammars for specifying languages to be parsed offers several advantages. Specifically, they serve as a formal representation suitable for both machine and human interpretation.

A grammar has four components:

A set of *terminal symbols* $(\sum)$

A set of *non-terminal symbols* $(V)$

A special *start symbol* $(S)$, $S \in V$

A set of *rewriting rules* (or *productions*) $(P)$

The terminal symbols are simply the atomic elements of strings in the language specified by the grammar. As such, they form the input elements to the parser. The nonterminal symbols are grammatical variables that denote sequences of terminal symbols. The start symbol is a special nonterminal symbol that denotes the set of all terminal symbol strings that are "generated" by the grammar; that is, *the language generated by the grammar.*

The productions are the rules that describe how strings can be generated by the grammar. A popular form for expressing the productions of a grammar is BNF (*Backus-Naur Form*). A description of BNF sufficient for describing the syntax of Lisp and Prolog was given in Chapter 2. We now elaborate on that description to allow for simple, succinct, and precise grammatical descriptions of language syntax.

Each BNF *production* is of the form

$$N \rightarrow R$$

where $N$ is any nonterminal symbol and $R$ is any (possibly empty) string of terminal and nonterminal symbols. It can be read as: "$N$ can be rewritten as $R$", or "$N$ generates the set of strings denoted by $R$."

When $N$ can be rewritten by more than one such $R$, we use a production of the form

$$N \rightarrow R_1 \mid \cdots \mid R_m$$

To illustrate the specification of languages with grammars, we will specify a language with familiar constructs.[1] To improve readability, we will italicize the nonterminals and type the terminals in boldface. The major statements of the language are

*identifier* := *expression*
**if** *relational_expression* **then** *statement* **else** *statement*
**while** *relational_expression* **do** *statement*
**read** *identifier*
**write** *expression*

There are several things to note about the statements of our language. First, the language is inherently recursive; that is, statements can be formed using statements. Next, we need to know how statements are "glued" together to form complete programs. Finally, other components of statements, for example, *identifiers and expressions*, must also be specified.

All these properties of the language can be captured with a grammar. We will bite the bullet and exhibit the grammar, and then pick it apart to convey how it generates the language of interest. The grammar is shown in Figure 36.1. The terminal symbol set is

---

[1]The use of the "$\rightarrow$" symbol in rewriting rules $N \rightarrow R$ serves the same purpose as our use of *is* in describing the syntax of $N$ as "$N$ is R." Similarly, the use of the symbol $\mid$ serves the same purpose as our use of *or* in describing the syntax of $N$ as "$N$ is $R_1$ or $R_2$." To express repetition of a syntactic construct, the ellipsis "..." is often used. In particular, "[ ] ..." is used to indicate that the item delimited by the square brackets may occur zero or more times at the corresponding point in the construct being defined.

1. *program*       →    *statement* [ ; *statement* ] ...
2. *statement*      →    **identifier** := *expression* |
                                    **if** *relational_expr* **then** *statement*
                                                               **else** *statement* |
                                    **while** *relational_expr* **do** *statement* |
                                    **read identifier** |
                                    **write identifier** |
                                    { *program* }
3. *relational_expr* →    *expression relational_opr expression*
4. *expression*      →    *term opr1 expression* |
                                    *term*
5. *term*           →    *factor opr2 term* |
                                    *factor*
6. *factor*        →    **identifier** |
                                    **integer** |
                                    ( *expression* )
7. *relational_opr* →    = | < | > | ≤ | ≥ | ≠
8. *opr1*          →    + | −
9. *opr2*          →    * | /

**Figure 36.1** Simple context-free grammar represented in BNF.

{**if**,**then**,**else**,**while**,**do**,**read**,**write**, ;,:=,=,<,>,≤,≥,≠, *,/,+,-,{,},(,) }

whereas the nonterminal set is

{ *program, statement, expression, relational_expr, factor, term, opr1, opr2* }

The special start symbol is *program*; thus, to examine the language generated by the grammar, we begin with production 1. Production 1 states that a *program* is a sequence of one or more *statements*, with each adjacent pair of *statements* delimited by ";".

Production 2 gives the assortment of valid *statements*. There is an assignment statement, an if-then-else statement, a while statement, a read statement, and a write statement, in addition to any *program* (i.e., any sequence of one or more statements) delimited by set braces, { and }.

Productions 3 and 7 define a *relational_expr* to be any two expressions connected by one of the *relational_oprs*, which are {=,<,>,≤,≥,≠}.

Productions 4, 5, 6, 8, and 9 define an *expression* to be a conventional arithmetic expression, with the operands being either **identifier**'s or **integer**'s and the (binary) operators being {*,/,+,-}, and with the option for using parentheses to explicitly impose evaluation order.

Note that we decomposed the definition of an *expression* into something hierarchical. This is done to impose, through the grammar and parsing algorithm, a form of *implicit* evaluation order. In particular, an *opr2* (i.e., * or /) will have precedence over an *opr1* (i.e., + or -).

To elucidate on this further, we need to investigate the parsing process. This is the topic of the next section.

## PARSING AND PARSE TREES

Given a program, we attempt to see if it is syntactically valid by checking whether the program could be derived from the grammar specifying the programming language. If there does exist a derivation of the program from the grammar, we produce as output a *tree representation of the derivation*. The latter is called a *parse tree*. The nodes of the parse tree can also be labeled with semantic directives to facilitate code generation.

Consider the following program segment:

```
if x=y then z:=0 else write (x+y)/2
```

where **x**, **y**, and **z** are **identifiers**, and **0** and **2** are **integers**.

If the program is in the language specified by the grammar, there must exist a derivation of the program from the grammar. We will demonstrate such a derivation, beginning with the start symbol *program*. Each step of the derivation shows the application of a single rewriting rule of the grammar to one of the nonterminal symbols in the string derived from *program*. The derivation of the program from the grammar might proceed as follows:

> *program*
>   *(start symbol of the grammar)*
> *statement*
>   *(production 1)*
> **if** *relational_expr* **then** *statement* **else** *statement*
>   *(production 2)*
> **if** *expression relational_opr expression* **then** *statement* **else** *statement*
>   *(production 3)*
> **if** *term relational_opr expression* **then** *statement* **else** *statement*
>   *(production 4)*
> **if** *factor relational_opr expression* **then** *statement* **else** *statement*
>   *(production 5)*
> **if identifier** *relational_opr expression* **then** *statement* **else** *statement*
>   *(production 6)*
> **if** x *relational_opr expression* **then** *statement* **else** *statement*
>   *(x is an identifier)*
> **if** x = *expression* **then** *statement* **else** *statement*
>   *(production 7)*
> **if** x = *term* **then** *statement* **else** *statement*

*(production 4)*
**if** x = *factor* **then** *statement* **else** *statement*
*(production 5)*
**if** x = **identifier then** *statement* **else** *statement*
*(production 6)*
**if** x = y **then** *statement* **else** *statement*
*(y is an identifier)*
**if** x = y **then** identifier := *expression* **else** *statement*
*(production 2)*
**if** x = y **then** z := *expression* **else** *statement*
*(z is an identifier)*
**if** x = y **then** z := *term* **else** *statement*
*(production 4)*
**if** x = y **then** z := *factor* **else** *statement*
*(production 5)*
**if** x = y **then** z := **integer else** *statement*
*(production 6)*
**if** x = y **then** z := *0* **else** *statement*
*(0 is an integer)*
**if** x = y **then** z := *0* **else write** *expression*
*(production 2)*
**if** x = y **then** z := *0* **else write** *term*
*(production 4)*
**if** x = y **then** z := *0* **else write** *factor opr2 term*
*(production 5)*
**if** x = y **then** z := *0* **else write** ( *expression* ) *opr2 term*
*(production 6)*
**if** x = y **then** z := *0* **else write** ( *term opr1 expression* ) *opr2 term*
*(production 4)*
**if** x = y **then** z := *0* **else write** ( *factor opr1 expression* ) *opr2 term*
*(production 5)*
**if** x = y **then** z := *0* **else write** ( **identifier** *opr1 expression* ) *opr2 term*
*(production 6)*
**if** x = y **then** z := *0* **else write** ( x *opr1 expression* ) *opr2 term*
*(x is an identifier)*
**if** x = y **then** z := *0* **else write** ( x + *expression* ) *opr2 term*
*(production 8)*
**if** x = y **then** z := *0* **else write** ( x + *term* ) *opr2 term*
*(production 4)*
**if** x = y **then** z := *0* **else write** ( x + *factor* ) *opr2 term*
*(production 5)*
**if** x = y **then** z := *0* **else write** ( x + **identifier** ) *opr2 term*
*(production 6)*
**if** x = y **then** z := *0* **else write** ( x + y ) *opr2 term*
*(y is an identifier)*
**if** x = y **then** z := *0* **else write** ( x + y ) / *term*

*(production 9)*
**if x = y then z :=** *0* **else write ( x + y )** / *factor*
*(production 5)*
**if x = y then z :=** *0* **else write ( x + y )** / **integer**
*(production 6)*
**if x = y then z :=** *0* **else write ( x + y )** / 2
*(2 is an integer)*

Our illustration of the derivation process was sufficient to show the general idea, but there is a much better way of representing a derivation for both the translator and the human reader: the *parse tree*. A parse tree is a tree with the interior nodes labeled by nonterminal symbols and leaf nodes labeled by either terminal or nonterminal symbols. Further, if *N* is a nonterminal symbol labeling an interior node with immediate subtree structure,

then the grammar must contain a rewriting rule $N \rightarrow ABC$. Consider, for example, the derivation of the string

    x - y / 2

from the nonterminal symbol *expression* in the example grammar. The parse tree representation of the derivation is shown in Figure 36.2.

The string obtained by concatenating the labels of a parse tree in left to right order (at any point in its construction) yields the *frontier* of the tree. For example, the frontier of the simple parse tree above with root node *N* and leaf nodes *A*, *B*, and *C*, is *ABC*. For parse trees representing complete derivations of strings from a grammar, the frontier of such trees is exactly the string derived from the grammar. Thus, for the parse tree representation of the string "**x - y / 2**" from the nonterminal symbol *expression* shown in Figure 36.2, the frontier of that tree is simply "**x - y / 2**".

It can be seen that the parse tree representation captures the hierarchical structure of the sentence syntax. Thus, for example, the order of evaluation of the operators becomes clear. In the foregoing derivation, we are subtracting from **x** the string derived from *term*, which is **y/z**.

Now, let us focus in on some significant properties of grammars and derivations and try to clear up some of the questions you may have in mind.

You most likely noticed that this derivation was not unique. At any stage of the derivation in which the derived string contained two or more

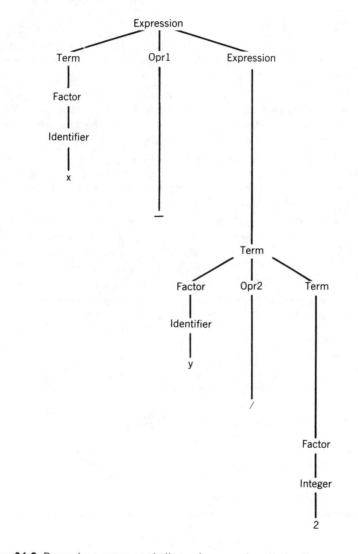

**Figure 36.2** Parse tree representation of expression derivation

nonterminal symbols, we had the option of expanding any one of them in the next step. A property of context-free grammars/languages assures us that if there is a derivation of the input string from the derived string, then any of the nonterminals can be expanded in the next step of the derivation, and there will be a derivation of the input string from the resulting string.

We happened to always expand the *leftmost* nonterminal string in each step of the derivation. This results in what is appropriately called a *leftmost derivation*. A consequence of the property of context-free grammars stated is that *if there exists a derivation of an input string from a (context-free) grammar, then there exists a leftmost derivation.*

The parsing algorithm we will introduce in the next section actually simulates a leftmost derivation. If you did not catch the leftmost expansions in the example derivation, go back through it again: It is important. Before we move onto the parsing algorithm section, there are a few other points to note.

Although we can always count on a leftmost derivation to lead to success if the input string is syntactically valid, there is one other element of uncertainty in derivations. In general, for a given nonterminal symbol we wish to rewrite, there are several ways to rewrite it. However, some choices may lead to a successful derivation, whereas other will lead to a dead end.

For example, consider the derivation of the string **x+y*z** from the nonterminal symbol *expression* in the example grammar. It might seem reasonable to proceed as follows:

| | |
|---|---|
| *expression* | (initially) |
| *term* | (production 4) |
| *factor opr2 term* | (production 5) |
| **identifier** *opr2 term* | (production 6) |
| x *opr2 term* | (**x** is an identifier) |

At this point, it becomes clear that we cannot derive the input string, for which there does exist a derivation. The error was in the initial expansion of *expression*, not the selection of *expression* for expansion.

It is desirable to build grammars and parsers for those grammars where it is always possible to select the proper rewriting rule at each step of a derivation. When this is not possible, some form of *backtracking* must be employed. Although backtracking can help to guarantee that a derivation will be found, it can cause other problems. This is beyond the scope of the chapter; consult a text on compilers for details. We will restrict our attention to those grammars for which there exist such "nonbacktracking" parsers.

# ■ RECURSIVE DESCENT PARSING IN LISP

In previous sections we saw that grammars were recursive structures for specifying languages. It should not be surprising that functional languages such as Lisp are highly conducive to the syntax-driven translation of context-free languages. In our discussion of parsing in Lisp, we will make several simplifying assumptions. First, it is assumed that the input to the parser is a list of tokens produced and organized by some scanner. Second, we will assume that every token sequence is syntactically correct (i.e., is a string generated by the grammar). Writing a scanner and building in effective syntax-error processing are excellent topics of further work for the ambitious.

Recursive descent parsing is a form of *top-down parsing*. Top-down parsing is, in turn, a form of syntax analysis in which a parse tree for the input sentence is built starting with a root node labeled with the grammar start symbol and thereafter growing as determined by a *leftmost derivation* until the *frontier* of the parse tree is exactly the input sentence.

For example, the parse tree given in Figure 36.2 which represents the derivation of the sentence

```
x - y / 2
```

from the nonterminal symbol *expression* in the grammar given in Figure 36.1 was constructed by a top-down parse if the order in which the internal nodes is expanded were exactly top-to-bottom in the depiction of the tree.

In the recursive descent method of top-down parsing, a primary function is defined for each nonterminal symbol of the grammar. Each such function for a nonterminal symbol $A$ is a mapping from a sequence of tokens, *token-list-in*, to a pair of lists, *translated-out* and *token-list-out*. The input sequence *token-list-in* has a prefix that is a sentence generated by $A$ [i.e., there exist strings $P$ and $S$ such that **append**($P$, $S$, *token-list-in*) and $P$ are generated by $A$ in the grammar]. The list *translated-out* is a translated form of $P$ (as determined by supplemental translation rules), and list *token-list-out* is the remainder of *token-list-in* following the token sequence that is generated by nonterminal $A$ (i.e., $S$, as earlier). Hereafter, a list containing the pair *translated-out* and *token-list-out* will be referred to as a *parse pair*.

For example, if we were performing a recursive descent parse of the segment

```
z:=0 else write (x+y)/2
```

of the complete sentence that was generated by *program* in Figure 36.1,

```
if x=y then z:=0 else write (x+y)/2
```

we would encounter the need to parse the construct **z:=0** from the non-terminal symbol *statement* in the grammar.

A primary function **statement** for nonterminal symbol *statement* would map the list[2]

```
(z ":=" 0 else write ( x "+" y ) "/" 2
```

into a parse pair

```
( ( (assign (var z) (const 0)) )
  (else write ( x "+" y ) "/" 2)
)
```

where the list

```
( (assign (var z) (const 0)) )
```

represents a translated form of the token list "**z** "**:=**" **0**", and

```
(else write ( x "+" y ) "/" 2)
```

is the token list that follows the prefix of *token-list-in* that was translated.

In the Lisp programs we will present, the argument name **token_list** is typically used for *token-list-in*, and **parse_pair** identifies a list containing *translated-out* and *token-list-out*. In constructing a recursive descent parser for the grammar in Figure 36.1, we'll begin with the starting symbol *program*. Consider the following single production for *program*:

*program* → *statement_sequence*

We define a primary function, **program**, and a supporting function, **statement_sequence**, as follows:

```
(defun program (token_list)
       (statement_sequence (statement token_list))
)

(defun statement_sequence (parse_pair)
       (if (equal ";" (caadr parse_pair))
           (let ( (program_parse_pair
                     (program (cdadr parse_pair))) )
```

---

[2]Special symbols used as atomic elements in the list are represented as strings.

```
                (and
                        (list (cons (car parse_pair)
                                    (car program_parse_pair))
                              (cadr program_parse_pair)
                        )
                )
        )
                (list (list (car parse_pair))
                      (cadr parse_pair))
        )
)
```

The function **program** parses a token sequence, hereafter called a *statement sequence*, of the form

*statement [; statement]...*

The value of the function is a parse pair, the first component of which is a list of lists, each of which represents a translated *statement*. The *token-list-out* component will be **nil** if *token-list-in* was a complete program, and a token list beginning with the symbol "}" if *token-list-in* was prefixed with a statement block of the form "{ *statement [ ; statement] ... }*".

```
-> (program ' (x ":=" y ";" if x ">" 0
                              then x ":=" x "+" 1
                              else read x))

( ( (assign (var x) (var y))
    (if (">" (var x) (const 0))
            (assign (var x) ("+" (var x) (const 1)))
            (read (var x))
    )
  )
  nil
)


-> (program ' (if x ">" 0 then x ":=" y
              else "{" read x ";" write x "+" 1 "}"))

( ( (if (">" (var x) (const 0)) (assign (var x) (var y))
                              ( (read (var x))
                                (write ("+" (var x)
                                            (const 1))))
    )
```

```
  )
  nil
)
```

The function **statement_sequence** takes a parse pair ( *translated-out token-list-out* ) as its argument, where *translated-out* is the result of translating the leading *statement* in a statement sequence, and *token-list-out* is a token list of the form [ *; statement* ] ... . If the leading symbol in the token list is "*;*", then the remainder of the statement sequence is parsed, and the result of translating the leading statement is placed at the front of the translated form of the remaining statement sequence. If the leading symbol in the token list is *not* "*;*", then an entire *program* has been parsed. That is, either the token list is empty or the token list begins with a }, thus signifying the end of the program component of a statement block.

```
-> (statement_sequence '((assign (var x) (var y))
                         (if x ">" 0
                         then x ":=" x "+" 1
                         else read x)
                         )
   )

( ( (assign (var x) (var y))
    (if (">" (var x) (const 0))
            (assign (var x) ("+" (var x) (const 1)))
            (read (var x))
    )
  )
  nil
)


-> (statement_sequence '((read (var x))
                         (write x "+" 1 "}")))

( ( (read (var x)) (write ("+" (var x) (const 1))) )
  ("}")
)
```

Let us now turn our attention to the parsing of individual statements via the function **statement**. There are many forms of *statement*s, as revealed by the collection of productions that define it:

*statement* → **identifier :=** *expression*
*statement* → **if** *relational_expr* **then** *statement* **else** *statement*
*statement* → **while** *relational_expr* **do** *statement*

*statement* → **read** *identifier*
*statement* → **write** *expression*
*statement* → { *program* }

The existence of several forms of *statements* suggests the use of an **or** function in the definition of **statement**, as shown next:

```
(defun statement (token_list)

                ; assignment statement
        (or (and (identifier (car token_list))
                (equal ":=" (cadr token_list))
                (let ( (expr_parse_pair
                        (expr (cddr token_list))) )
                    (list (list 'assign
                                (list 'var
                                    (car token_list))
                                (car expr_parse_pair))
                        (cadr expr_parse_pair)
                    )
        )
            )

                ; if-then-else statement
            (and (equal 'if (car token_list))
                (let ( (relop_parse_pair (relop_expr
                            (cdr token_list))))
                    (equal 'then
                            (caadr relop_parse_pair))
                    (let ( (then_parse_pair
        (statement
    )
                            (cdadr relop_parse_pair)))
                        (equal 'else
                            (caadr then_parse_pair))
                        (let ( (else_parse_pair
    (statement
        )
                            (cdadr then_parse_pair)))
                            (list (list 'if
                                (car relop_parse_pair)
                                (car then_parse_pair)
                                (car else_parse_pair)
                                )
                                (cadr else_parse_pair)
                    )
```

```
)
  )
            )
        )

              ; while-do statement
      (and (equal 'while (car token_list))
           (let ( (relop_parse_pair (relop_expr
                                    (cdr token_list))))
                (equal 'do (caadr relop_parse_pair))
                (let ( (do_parse_pair
  (statement
                          (cdadr relop_parse_pair)))
)
                    (list (list 'while
                           (car relop_parse_pair)
                           (car do_parse_pair)
                          )
                           (cadr do_parse_pair)
                    )
    )
)
        )

              ; read statement
      (and (equal 'read (car token_list))
           (identifier (cadr token_list))
           (list (list 'read (list 'var
                           (cadr token_list)))
                  (cddr token_list)
           )
      )

              ; write statement
      (and (equal 'write (car token_list))
           (let ( (expr_parse_pair
                  (expr (cdr token_list))) )
                (list (list 'write
                          (car expr_parse_pair)
                      )
                       (cadr expr_parse_pair)
                )
)
        )

        (and (equal "{" (car token_list))
```

```
                    (statement_block (program
                                        (cdr token_list)))
            )
        )
    )
```

For each different form of a *statement*, the constituent parts are parsed from left to right. In the case of the assignment statement, a sequence of **identifier**, **:=**, and *expression* are sought. If the entire sequence is found, the results of parsing the individual parts are combined to form a *translated-out* list of the form " **(assign (var *id*) *expr*)** ", where ***id*** is the **identifier** of the statement and ***expr*** is the translated form of the *expression* of the statement.

```
-> (statement '(x ":=" y ";" if x ">" 0 then x ":=" x "+"
1 else read x))

( (assign (var x) (var y))
  (";" if x ">" 0 then x ":=" x "+" 1 else read x)
)
```

The other forms of *statement*s are handled similarly. In the case of the if-then-else statement, a sequence of **if**, *relational_expression*, **then**, *statement*, **else**, and *statement* are sought. Such sequences are mapped into a *translated-out* list of the form " **(if *rel_expr* then_stmt else_stmt)** ", where ***rel_expr*** is the translated form of the *relational_ expression*, **then_stmt** is the translated form of the then-part *statement*, and ***else_stmt*** is the translated form of the else-part *statement* of the if-then-else statement.

```
-> (statement '(if x ">" 0
                  then x ":=" x "+" 1
                  else read x ";" x ":=" y))

( (if (">" (var x) (const 0))
      (assign (var x) ("+" (var x) (const 1)))
      (read (var x))
  )
  (";" x ":=" y)
)
```

In the case of the while-do statement, a sequence of **while**, *rela-tional_expression*, **do**, and *statement* are sought. Such sequences are mapped into a *translated-out* list of the form " **(while *rel_expr* do_stmt)** ", where ***rel_expr*** is the translated form of the *relational_expression*, ***do_stmt*** is the translated form of the do *statement*.

```
-> (statement '(while x ">" 0 do x ":=" x "-" 1))

( (while (">" (var x) (const 0))
              (assign (var x) ("-" (var x) (const 1))))
  nil
)
```

The read and write statements are analogous. Statement blocks delimited by "{" and "}" are simply translated into the translated form of the *program* contained in the block.

```
(defun statement_block (parse_pair)
      (if (equal (car (cadr parse_pair)) "}")
          (list (car parse_pair)
                (cdr (cadr parse_pair))
          )
          'nil
      )
)

-> (statement '("{" read q ";"
                    write q "*" 2 "}" ";" x ":=" y "-"
                z))

( ((read (var q)) (write ("*" (var q) (const 2))))
  (x ":=" y "-" z)
)
```

Relational expressions are simply formed by an *expression* followed by a relational operator (*relational_opr*), followed by an *expression*, as shown here:

*relational_expr* → *expression relational_opr expression*
*relational_opr* → = — < — > — ≤ — ≥ — ≠

Relational expressions occur after the keyword **if** in *if-then-else* constructs, or the keyword **while** in *while-do* constructs. They are represented in the token list in infix notation, with the operator being a *relational_opr* and the operands any two *expressions*. Their *translated-out* form is a prefix representation, with the operator followed by the translated forms of the left and right operands, respectively.[3]

```
(defun relop_expr (token_list)
      (let ( (expr1_parse_pair (expr token_list)) )
```

---

[3]The single symbol representations of the inequalities are given as two symbols in the Prolog parser. This is simply due to the lack of single symbol inequality symbols on most keyboards.

```
              (rel_opr (caadr exprl_parse_pair))
              (let ( (exprr_parse_pair
                      (expr (cdadr exprl_parse_pair))) )
                    (list (list (caadr exprl_parse_pair)
                                (car exprl_parse_pair)
                                (car exprr_parse_pair)
                          )
                          (cadr exprr_parse_pair)
                    )
         )
)

(defun rel_opr (token)
       (or (equal token "=")
           (equal token "<=")
           (equal token ">=")
           (equal token ">")
           (equal token "<")
           (equal token "!=")
       )
)
-> (relop_expr '(x ">" y "+" 1 then x ":=" x "+" 1
                                 else write x "*" z))

( (">" (var x) ("+" (var y) (const 1)))
  (then x ":=" x "+" 1 else write x "*" z)
)
```

The parsing of arithmetic expressions is similar in the general methodology used, but there is an additional dimension: *operator precedence*. Our hierarchical specification of *expression* in the grammar produces the following precedence hierarchy:

**integer**   **identifier**
( *expr* )
*     /
+    -

where terminal symbols on the same line have equal precedence, and the lines are given in decreasing order of precedence.

The precedence relation is naturally enforced in recursive descent parsing. For example, in parsing the expression "$x + y * z$", we note that an expression is interpreted in a top-down parse with respect to the grammar in Figure 36.1 as "*expression + term*", where *expression* derives **x** and *term* derives **y * z**.

To top-down parse an *expression*, specified in Figure 36.1 as

$$expression \quad \rightarrow \quad term \; opr1 \; expression \; |$$
$$term$$

we can parse the leading *term,* and then resolve whether it is followed
by an *opr1* operator and an *expression,* or if it is the complete *expression.* The parsing of a *term* is a facsimile of our method for handling an
*expression.*

```
(defun expr (token_list)
        (exprprime (term token_list))
)

(defun exprprime (parse_pair)
        (or (and (or (equal (caadr parse_pair) "+")
                     (equal (caadr parse_pair) "-")
                 )
                 (let ( (exprprime_parse_pair
                           (exprprime
                             (term (cdadr parse_pair))))
                       )
                       (list (list (caadr parse_pair)
                              (car parse_pair)
                              (car exprprime_parse_pair)
                              )
                              (cadr exprprime_parse_pair)
                       )
                 )
            )
            parse_pair
        )
)

(defun term (token_list)
        (termprime (factor token_list))
)

(defun termprime (parse_pair)
        (or (and (or (equal (caadr parse_pair) "*")
                     (equal (caadr parse_pair) "/")
                 )
                 (let ( (termprime_parse_pair
                           (termprime (factor
```

```
                                      (cdadr parse_pair))))
          )
                        (list (list
                                (caadr parse_pair)
                                (car parse_pair)
                                (car termprime_parse_pair)
                              )
                              (cadr termprime_parse_pair)
                        )
)
              )
          parse_pair
        )
)


(defun factor (token_list)
      (or (and (equal (car token_list) "(")
              (let ( (expr_parse_pair
                        (expr (cdr token_list)))
                     (equal (caadr expr_parse_pair)
                            ")")
       )
                      (list (car expr_parse_pair)
                            (cdadr expr_parse_pair))
)
          )
          (and (identifier (car token_list))
              (list (list 'var (car token_list))
                           (cdr token_list))
          )
          (and (numberp (car token_list))
              (list (list 'const (car token_list))
                           (cdr token_list))
          )
        )
)

(defun identifier (token)
      (and (litatom token) (not (stringp token)))
)

-> (expr '(x "+" y "*" z))

( ("+" (var x) ("*" (var y) (var z)))
   ()
```

```
)

-> (expr '(w "+" "(" a "-" b ")" "*" x "+" y "*" z))

( ("+" (var w) ("+" ("*" ("-" (var a) (var b)) (var x))
                ("*"  (var y)  (var z))))
   ()
)
```

The complete Lisp implementation of a recursive descent parser for
the grammar in Figure 36.1 is given here.

```
(defun program (token_list)
       (statement_sequence (statement token_list))
)

(defun statement_sequence (parse_pair)
       (if (equal ";" (caadr parse_pair))
           (and (let ( (program_parse_pair
                         (program (cdadr parse_pair))))
                     (list (cons (car parse_pair)
                           (car program_parse_pair))
                           (cadr program_parse_pair)
                     )
)
           )
           (list (list (car parse_pair))
                 (cadr parse_pair))
       )
)

(defun statement (token_list)

               ; assignment statement
       (or (and (identifier (car token_list))
                (equal ":=" (cadr token_list))
                (let ( (expr_parse_pair
                         (expr (cddr token_list))) )
                     (list (list 'assign
                             (list 'var (car token_list))
                             (car expr_parse_pair))
                           (cadr expr_parse_pair)
                     )
)
           )
               )
```

```
                        ; if-then-else statement
               (and (equal 'if (car token_list))
                    (let ( (relop_parse_pair (relop_expr
                               (cdr token_list))))
                       (equal 'then
                               (caadr relop_parse_pair))
                       (let ( (then_parse_pair
      (statement

                                  (cdadr relop_parse_pair)))
    )
                            (equal 'else
                              (caadr then_parse_pair))
                          (let ( (else_parse_pair
  (statement

                                (cdadr then_parse_pair)))
         )
                            (list (list 'if
                              (car relop_parse_pair)
                              (car then_parse_pair)
                              (car else_parse_pair)
                                 )
                              (cadr else_parse_pair)
                              )
    )
      )
  )
           )


                    ; while-do statement
               (and (equal 'while (car token_list))
                    (let ( (relop_parse_pair (relop_expr
                                 (cdr token_list))))
                       (equal 'do
                               (caadr relop_parse_pair))
                       (let ( (do_parse_pair
      (statement

                                  (cdadr relop_parse_pair)))
    )
                            (list (list 'while
                                (car relop_parse_pair)
                                (car do_parse_pair)
                                )
                             (cadr do_parse_pair)
                              )
    )
      )
  )
```

```
            )
                ; read statement
            (and (equal 'read (car token_list))
                 (identifier (cadr token_list))
                 (list (list 'read (list 'var
                                (cadr token_list)))
                      (cddr token_list)
                 )
            )

                ; write statement
            (and (equal 'write (car token_list))
                 (let ( (expr_parse_pair
                     (expr (cdr token_list))) )
                     (list (list 'write
                                  (car expr_parse_pair)
                            )
                           (cadr expr_parse_pair)
                     )
            )
            )

            (and (equal "{" (car token_list))
                 (statement_block (program
                                    (cdr token_list)))
            )
        )
)

(defun statement_block (parse_pair)
        (if (equal (car (cadr parse_pair)) "}")
                        (list (car parse_pair)
                              (cdr (cadr parse_pair))
                        )
                                        'nil
        )
)

(defun relop_expr (token_list)
        (let ( (exprl_parse_pair (expr token_list)) )
            (rel_opr (caadr exprl_parse_pair))
            (let ( (exprr_parse_pair
                (expr (cdadr exprl_parse_pair))))
                (list (list (caadr exprl_parse_pair)
                            (car exprl_parse_pair)
```

```
                                        (car exprr_parse_pair)
                        )
                            (cadr exprr_parse_pair)
                    )
        )
            )
)


(defun rel_opr (token)
        (or (equal token "=")
            (equal token "<=")
            (equal token ">=")
            (equal token ">")
            (equal token "<")
            (equal token "!=")
        )
)


(defun expr (token_list)
        (exprprime (term token_list))
)


(defun exprprime (parse_pair)
        (or (and (or (equal (caadr parse_pair) "+")
                     (equal (caadr parse_pair) "-")
                 )
                 (let ( (exprprime_parse_pair
                        (exprprime (term
                                (cdadr parse_pair))))
        )
                        (list (list (caadr parse_pair)
                            (car parse_pair)
                            (car exprprime_parse_pair)
                            )
                            (cadr exprprime_parse_pair)
                    )
)
            )
            parse_pair
        )
)


(defun term (token_list)
        (termprime (factor token_list))
)
```

```
(defun termprime (parse_pair)
       (or (and (or (equal (caadr parse_pair) "*")
                    (equal (caadr parse_pair) "/")
                )
                (let ( (termprime_parse_pair
                        (termprime
                           (factor (cdadr parse_pair)))))
    )
                    (list (list (caadr parse_pair)
                       (car parse_pair)
                       (car termprime_parse_pair)
                       )
                       (cadr termprime_parse_pair)
                    )
)
           )
           parse_pair
       )
)


(defun factor (token_list)
       (or (and (equal (car token_list) "(")
                (let ( (expr_parse_pair
                        (expr (cdr token_list))) )
                   (equal (caadr expr_parse_pair) ")")
                   (list (car expr_parse_pair)
                        (cdadr expr_parse_pair))
)
           )
           (and (identifier (car token_list))
                (list (list 'var (car token_list))
                   (cdr token_list))
           )
           (and (numberp (car token_list))
                (list (list 'const (car token_list))
                   (cdr token_list))
           )
       )
)

(defun identifier (token)
       (and (litatom token) (not (stringp token)))
)
```

1. *sentence* → *noun_phrase verb_phrase*

2. *noun_phrase* → *determiner noun rel_clause* | *name*

3. *verb_phrase* → *transitive_phrase* | *intransitive_phrase*

4. *transitive_phrase* → *verb noun_phrase*

5. *intransitive_phrase* → *verb*

6. *rel_clause* → **who** *verb_phrase* | Λ

7. *determiner* → **a** | **every**

8. *noun* → **man** | **woman**

9. *name* → **chris** | **katie**

10. *verb* → **lives** | **loves**

FIGURE **36.3** Grammar 2.1

## ▪ DEFINITE CLAUSE GRAMMAR PARSING IN PROLOG

A related problem to that of translating programming languages is the translation of natural languages, such as English or German. The major difficulty with translating natural languages is the lack of unambiguous grammatical models for such languages. As such, this remains an active area of research.

If we consider subsets of natural languages that can be described by context-free grammars, things become more tractable. In fact, the parsing problem becomes somewhat similar to the problem of computer language parsing we tackled in the previous section. We will pursue several approachs based on the notions of *definite clause grammars* (DCG's), as described in Pereira, and *definite clause translation grammars* (DCTG's), as described in Abramson. (See Bibliography Notes.)

Definite clause grammars are formalisms introduced by Colmerauer in which rules are specified as clauses of the first-order predicate calculus. To illustrate DCG's, we begin with an example. The grammar in Figure 36.3 is a BNF representation of a simple subset of English that is based on an example given in Abramson. Note that the symbol "Λ" represents the *empty string* (i.e., the string containing zero symbols).

This grammar captures some simple and common English sentence structures. Specifically,

|  |  |  |
|---|---|---|
| *sentence* | is | a *noun_phrase* followed by a *verb_phrase*. |
| *noun_phrase* | is | either a *determiner* followed by a *noun* followed by a *rel_clause* (relative clause), or a *name*. |
| *verb_phrase* | is | either a *transitive_phrase* or an *intransitive_phrase*. |
| *transitive_phrase* | is | a *verb* followed by the direct object *noun_phrase*. |
| *intransitive_phrase* | is | a *verb*. |
| *rel_clause* | is | the relative pronoun **who** followed by a *verb_phrase*. |

The *determiners* are **a** and **every**, the *nouns* are **man** and **woman**, the *names* are **chris** and **katie**, and the *verbs* are **lives** and **loves**.

For sentences generated by the grammar, we can exhibit parse trees that expose the hierarchical structure of the sentence. The sentence

```
a woman who loves chris loves a man who loves katie
```

has the parse tree shown in Figure 36.4.

The construction of parsers from grammars is a natural application of Prolog. In effect, we will map the productions of the grammar into Prolog statements and use the Prolog interpreter as the parser. As the mapping of productions into statements is typically straightforward, Prolog is a natural implementation language for parsing. We will assume, for simplicity, that the input to the parser is a list of tokens produced and organized by some scanner, and that the token list is syntactically correct (i.e., the token list is a sentence generated by the grammar).

Each collection of *n* productions for a nonterminal symbol *A* are mapped into *n* statements of a Prolog definition of relation *A*, in addition to some supporting relation definitions. In the simplest case, the relation *A* is of the form

*non_terminal(Token_list,Remaining_list,Phrase)*

where *non_terminal* is the nonterminal symbol, *Token_list* is a list of tokens to be parsed, *Remaining_list* is a "suffix" of *Token_list* [i.e., *Token_list* is denoted by **append**(*L*, *Remaining_list* , *Token_list* ) for some list *L*], and *Phrase* is the grammatical phrase determined by parsing token list *L*.

For example, consider the example grammar with starting symbol *sentence*. The single production for *sentence* is

*sentence* → *noun_phrase verb_phrase*

This production can be mapped into the Prolog rule

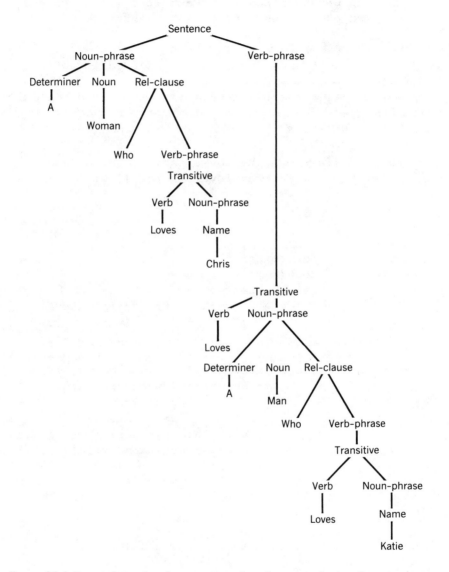

**Figure 36.4** Parse tree for "**a woman who loves chris loves a man who loves katie**"

```
sentence(Token_list,Rest_list,sentence(Noun_phrase,
                                        Verb_phrase)) :-

    noun_phrase(Token_list,Rest_list_1,Noun_phrase),
    verb_phrase(Rest_list_1,Rest_list,Verb_phrase).
```

which is read "**Token_list** is a string consisting of a sentence with translated noun phrase **Noun_phrase** and translated verb phrase **Verb_phrase**, followed by the string **Rest_list**".

To parse a complete sentence generated by the grammar, relate the **Token_list** containing the elements of the sentence with an empty **Rest_list** and a variable representing the parsed sentence.

```
?- sentence([a,woman,who,loves,chris,loves,a,man,
                    who,loves,katie],[],P).


yes.
P=
sentence(
  noun_phrase(determiner(a),
              noun(woman),
              rel_clause(who,
                          verb_phrase(transitive
                                        (verb(loves),
                                        noun_phrase
                                          (name(chris))))))),
  verb_phrase(transitive(verb(loves),
                  noun_phrase(determiner(a),
                              noun(man),
                              rel_clause(who,
                          verb_phrase(transitive(verb(loves),
                          noun_phrase(name(katie)))))))))
```

The clauses for the nonterminal symbols *noun_phrase*, *verb_phrase*, *transitive_phrase*, *intransitive_phrase*, and *rel_clause* are analogous.

For example, the production for *noun_phrase*,

*noun_phrase* → *determiner noun rel_clause* | *name*

is mapped into the following relation definition:

```
noun_phrase([Name|Rest_list],Rest_list,
            noun_phrase(name(Name))) :- name(Name).
noun_phrase([Determiner,Noun|Token_list],
            Rest_list,
            noun_phrase(determiner(Determiner),
```

```
                        noun(Noun),R_clause)) :-
    determiner(Determiner),
    noun(Noun),
    rel_clause(Token_list,Rest_list,R_clause).
```

The fact simply verifies that the leading token is a *name,* and, if so, relates the *Token_list* to a *Rest_list* that is the remainder of *Token_list* after token *Name,* and the structure **name**(*Name*).

```
?- noun_phrase([chris,loves,a,woman],R,P).
```

```
yes.  R=[loves,a,woman]  P=name(chris)
```

The rule verifies that the leading tokens are a *determiner* followed by a *noun* followed by a *rel_clause.* If so, it relates the *Token_list* to a *Rest_list* that is the remainder of *Token_list* after the noun phrase, and the structure **noun_phrase**(**determiner**(*Determiner*)**,noun**(*Noun*)**,***R_clause*), where *Determiner* and *Noun* are the leading tokens of *Token_list,* and *R_clause* is the translated form of the following *rel_clause.*

```
?- noun_phrase([a,woman,who,loves,chris,loves,a,man,
                    who,loves,katie],R,P).
```

```
yes.  R=[loves,a,man,who,loves,katie]
      P= noun_phrase(determiner(a),
                     noun(woman),
                     rel_clause(who,
             verb_phrase(transitive(verb(loves),
                                    noun_phrase(name(chris)))))))
```

The relations for *determiner, noun, name,* and *verb* are unary relations that relate the valid tokens associated with each of these nonterminals as specified by the grammar.

The complete parsing program is shown here.

```
sentence(Token_list,Rest_list,sentence(Noun_phrase,
                                        Verb_phrase)) :-

    noun_phrase(Token_list,Rest_list_1,Noun_phrase),
    verb_phrase(Rest_list_1,Rest_list,Verb_phrase).

noun_phrase([Name|Rest_list],Rest_list,
            noun_phrase(name(Name))) :- name(Name).
noun_phrase([Determiner,Noun|Token_list],
            Rest_list,
            noun_phrase(determiner(Determiner),
                        noun(Noun),R_clause)) :-
```

```
            determiner(Determiner),
            noun(Noun),
            rel_clause(Token_list,Rest_list,R_clause).

  verb_phrase(Token_list,Rest_list,verb_phrase(VP))  :-
            transitive(Token_list,Rest_list,VP)      ;
            intransitive(Token_list,Rest_list,VP).

  transitive([Verb|Token_list],Rest_list,
            transitive(verb(Verb),NP))  :-
            verb(Verb),
            noun_phrase(Token_list,Rest_list,NP).

  intransitive([Verb|Rest_list],Rest_list,
            intransitive(verb(Verb)))  :- verb(Verb).

  rel_clause([who|Token_list],Rest_list,
            rel_clause(who,VP))  :-
            verb_phrase(Token_list,Rest_list,VP).

  determiner(a).
  determiner(every).

  noun(man).
  noun(woman).

  name(chris).
  name(katie).

  verb(lives).
  verb(loves).
```

One problem with the grammar in Figure 36.3 is its inability to guarantee coordinated subject and verb *plurality*. A *singular sentence* is a sentence with a *singular noun phrase* and a *singular verb phrase*, whereas a *plural sentence* is a sentence with a *plural noun phrase* and a *plural verb phrase*.

There are several ways to extend the grammar to handle plurality. The first is to simply add clauses to cover the enumeration of possible sentence structures. Thus, a segment of the grammar extended in this way might include the following productions:

*sentence → singular_sentence | plural_sentence*
*singular_sentence → singular_noun_phrase singular_verb_phrase*
*singular_noun_phrase → singular_determiner singular_noun*
    *singular_rel_clause | singular_name*

1. *sentence → sentence(P)*

2. *sentence(P) → noun_phrase(P) verb_phrase(P)*

3. *noun_phrase(P) → determiner(P) noun(P) rel_clause(P)* | *name(P)*

4. *verb_phrase(P) → transitive_phrase(P)* | *intransitive_phrase(P)*

5. *transitive_phrase(P) → verb(P) noun_phrase(P)*

6. *intransitive_phrase(P) → verb(P)*

7. *rel_clause(P) →* **who** *verb_phrase(P)* | Λ

8. *determiner(singular) →* **a**

9. *determiner(plural) →* **many**

10. *noun(singular) →* **man** | **woman**

11. *noun(plural) →* **men** | **women**

12. *name(singular) →* **chris** | **katie**

13. *verb(singular) →* **dreams** | **loves**

14. *verb(plural) →* **dream** | **love**

**FIGURE 36.5** Grammar 2.3

Although this can be made to work, it is generally undesirable to enumerate large numbers of cases. Enumeration by cases can often be eliminated by parameterization, which is our second option. That is, we index each sentential substructure that has variable plurality with an index for either singular or plural. Indexing the grammar in Figure 36.3 in this way yields the "extended" BNF grammar given in Figure 36.5.

The generalized grammar is mapped to Prolog clauses that closely resemble those used to parse sentences of the grammar in Figure 36.3 with the exception that an additional argument is added in those cases where plurality need be resolved. A Prolog parser for the grammar in Figure 36.5 is given next.

```
sentence(Token_list,Rest_list,S) :-
     sentence(Token_list,Rest_list,singular,S) ;
     sentence(Token_list,Rest_list,plural,S) .

sentence(Token_list,Rest_list,Plurality,
       sentence(Noun_phrase,Verb_phrase)) :-
     noun_phrase(Token_list,Rest_list_1,Plurality,
```

```
                        Noun_phrase),
        verb_phrase(Rest_list_1,Rest_list,Plurality,
                        Verb_phrase).

noun_phrase([Name|Rest_list],Rest_list,Plurality,
            noun_phrase(name(Name)))) :-
            sname(Plurality,Name).
noun_phrase([Determiner,Noun|Token_list],
            Rest_list,
            Plurality,
            noun_phrase(determiner(Determiner),
                        noun(Noun),R_clause)) :-
    determiner(Plurality,Determiner),
    noun(Plurality,Noun),
    rel_clause(Token_list,Rest_list,Plurality,
                R_clause).

verb_phrase(Token_list,Rest_list,Plurality,
            verb_phrase(VP)) :-
            transitive(Token_list,Rest_list,
            Plurality,VP)        ;
            intransitive(Token_list,Rest_list,
            Plurality,VP).

transitive([Verb|Token_list],Rest_list,Plurality,
            transitive(verb(Verb),NP)) :-
            verb(Plurality,Verb),
            noun_phrase(Token_list,Rest_list,
                        Plurality,NP).

intransitive([Verb|Rest_list],Rest_list,Plurality,
              intransitive(verb(Verb))) :-
            verb(Plurality,Verb).

rel_clause([who|Token_list],Rest_list,Plurality,
            rel_clause(who,VP)) :-
            verb_phrase(Token_list,Rest_list,
            Plurality,VP).

determiner(singular,a).
determiner(plural,many).

noun(singular,man).
noun(singular,woman).
noun(plural,men).
noun(plural,women).
```

```
sname(singular,chris).
sname(singular,katie).

verb(singular,dreams).
verb(singular,loves).
verb(plural,dream).
verb(plural,love).


?- sentence([many,women,who,dream,love,a,man,
                    who,dreams],[],P).

yes.
P= sentence(
     noun_phrase(determiner(many),
             noun(women),
             rel_clause(who,
         verb_phrase(intransitive(verb(dream)))))),
     verb_phrase(transitive(verb(love),
                 noun_phrase(determiner(a),
                         noun(man),
                         rel_clause(who,
         verb_phrase(intransitive(verb(dreams)))))))))
```

# ■ DEFINITE CLAUSE TRANSLATION GRAMMARS

A third approach to generalizing the grammar to handle more complex parsing problems is to attach semantic rules to the productions of the grammar. The semantic rules allow the parser to invoke procedures that perform tasks such as plurality checking or dictionary lookup in cases where the interpretation of words or phrases is ambiguous (e.g., the word loves can be used as a transitive verb, as in *"jack loves jill*, as an intransitive verb, as in *"one who loves"*, or as a plural noun, as in *"her many loves"*).

An example of such a grammar is the *definite clause translation grammar* (DCTG) described in Abramson. A production of a DCTG has the form

*Left_part* : := *Right_part* <:> *Semantics*

The *Left_part* : := *Right_part* component captures the syntactic properties of the strings generated by the production and allows "hooks" to be embedded for computations of the semantic component. For example, any nonterminal symbol in *Right_part* may have a variable associated with it. Each time that nonterminal symbol is mapped to a parse tree during the parse of a sentence, the variable assumes that parse tree as its value. This allows for the analysis of the parse tree rooted by the nonterminal symbol constructed during a parse.

Given a nonterminal symbol *nt* and Prolog variable *X*, let

$$nt\verb|^^|X$$

relate *X* to a parse tree rooted by *nt*.

Another option is the use of embedded Prolog queries in the *Right_part*. For example, if we were writing a DCTG production for a *sentence*, as previously defined, we might attach the variable *N* to the *noun_phrase* and the variable *V* to the *verb_phrase* of the sentence. The production could then finish with a query relation *agreement(N,V)*, which verifies that the *noun_phrase* and *verb_phrase* agree in plurality. In DCTG productions, Prolog queries in the *Right_part* are delimited by curly brackets, "{" and "}".

The semantic component of a DCTG production, *Semantics*, associates relation definitions—with a parse tree rooted by a node labeled with the nonterminal symbol *Left_part*—that specify the properties of that parse tree. In general, *Semantics* consists of either a single statement or a list of statements $C_1, \ldots, C_m$ represented as a parenthesized list:

$$(C_1, \ldots, C_m)$$

Each statement is either an unconditional attribute (i.e., an asserted fact) or a conditional attribute of the form

*Attribute* : : - *Semantic_conditions.*

where *Attribute* is a relation representing a property of the production and *Semantic_conditions* are relations representing sufficient conditions for *Attribute*.

Attributes are generally used for consistency checking and conversion of a string to an alternate form (e.g., a prefix representation of the sentence). Using an example given in Abramson, we construct a DCTG grammar for the language specified in the grammar in Figure 36.3, and provide for its translation into a prefix representation. For simplicity, we will describe the DCTG productions in a bottom-up fashion, starting with the simpler rules and working up to the more complex.

The simplest elements in our grammar are *names*. As *names* refer to fixed objects, they can be mapped to constant terms. The relation *logic(chris)* simply asserts *chris* as a constant term. Thus, we have the productions

*name* : := *chris*
**<:>**
*logic(chris).*

*name* : := *katie*
**<:>**
*logic(katie).*

The nouns are interpreted as relations. The use of the noun **man** is interpreted as *"an object X such that X is a man"*. Further, as nouns have plurality, we must attach a plurality attribute to each specific noun. The productions for the nouns are then

*noun* : := *man*
**<:>**
*(plurality(singular)),*
*(logic(X,man(X)))*

*noun* : := *woman*
**<:>**
*(plurality(singular)),*
*(logic(X,woman(X)))*

Handling verbs is similar, but the additional transitivity attribute must also be accounted for. Note that as some verbs may be used as both transitives and intransitives, choices need be specified in the semantic attribute component for the verb. The productions for our two verbs are then

*verb* : := *lives*
**<:>**
*(plurality(singular)),*
*(logic(intransitive,X,lives(X))).*

*verb* : := *loves*
**<:>**
*(plurality(singular)),*
*(logic(transitive,X,Y,loves(X,Y))).*
*(logic(intransitive,X,loves(X))).*

In the case of intransitive verbs (e.g., **lives**), *"logic(intransitive,X,lives(X))"* asserts that *"X lives"*, where $X$ is the subject of the verb **lives**. Similarly for transitives such as **loves**, *"logic(transitive,X,Y,loves(X,Y))"* asserts that *"X loves Y"*, where $X$ is the subject and $Y$ is the direct object of the verb *loves*.

Constructing productions for determiners becomes more complex, in that explicit quantification is needed. Consider first the determiner **every**, which is used in sentences of the form

For every noun $X$, if $X$ possesses the property specified by the relative clause (say *P1*), then either the *verb* is true with respect to $X$ (should the verb be intransitive) or the *verb* is true with respect to $X$ and the direct object.

Letting *P2* represent the verb applied to the noun (or the verb applied to the noun and direct object), we get the following production for the determiner **every**:

> *determiner* : := *every*
> <:>
> *(plurality(singular)),*
> *(logic(X,P1,P2,for_all(X,implies(P1,P2)))).*

For example, the sentence

```
every man who loves loves katie
```

has noun phrase "**every man who loves**" and verb phrase "**loves katie**". The determiner of the noun phrase is "**every**", the noun is "**man**", and the relative clause is "**who loves**". The verb phrase consists of the transitive verb "**loves**" and the direct object "**katie**", which is in turn a noun phrase comprised of the name "**katie**". The translated representation of the sentence is then

```
for_all(X,implies(and(man(X),loves(X)),loves(X,katie)))
```

Rephrased prosaically, this representation is read

*for all* **X**, **X** *is a* **man** *and* **X loves** *implies that* **X loves katie**

The case for determiner **a** is analogous, with the exception that the *for_all* quantifier is replaced with a *there_exists* quantifier, and logical implication is replaced with logical conjunction. The result is the production

> *determiner* : := *a*
> <:>
> *(plurality(singular)),*
> *(logic(X,P1,P2,there_exists(X,and(P1,P2)))).*

Thus, the sentence

```
a woman that loves loves Chris
```

has noun phrase "**a woman who loves**" and verb phrase "**loves Chris**". The determiner of the noun phrase is "**a**", the noun is "**woman**", and the relative clause is "**who loves**". The verb phrase consists of the transitive verb "**loves**" and the direct object "**Chris**", which is in turn a noun phrase comprised of the name "**Chris**". The translated representation of the sentence is then

```
there_exists(X,and(and(woman(X),loves(X)),
loves(X,Chris)))
```

Rephrased prosaically, this representation is read

*there exists X such that X is a woman and X loves, and X loves Chris*

The *relative clauses* (for relative pronoun **who**) are next. First, note that the plurality of a relative clause is determined by the plurality of its constituent *verb_phrase*. Its prefix translation relates an object X specified by the noun addressed by the relative clause, and the verb phrase that specifies a property it possesses.

If *P1* is the predicate that relates the noun to X and *P2* the predicate determined by the *verb_phrase* of the clause, we obtain the production

```
rel_clause ::= who , verb_phrase^^V.
<:>
(plurality(PL) ::- V^^plurality(PL)),
(logic(X,P1,and(P1,P2)) ::- V^^logic(X,P2)).
```

Note that *P2* is determined by the logical properties of the parse tree for the verb phrase of the clause. In the examples for the determiners above, it is shown how relative clauses were handled for the case of intransitive verb phrases. To illustrate the case where the verb phrase is transitive, consider the sentence

**Katie loves a woman who loves Chris**

with noun phrase "**Katie**", consisting of the name "**Katie**", and with the transitive verb phrase "**loves a woman who loves Chris**". The direct object of the verb phrase "**a woman who loves Chris**" is then represented as

**there exists(X,and(woman(X),loves(X,Chris)))**

Two forms of noun phrases are permitted under the grammar in Figure 36.3 The first is a *name*; the second is a *determiner* followed by a *noun* followed by a *rel_clause* (i.e., relative clause). Plurality for names is always singular, whereas the plurality of the more general form of the noun phrase is jointly determined by the plurality of the determiner, noun, and relative clause, which must all be the same.

The translated form of a noun phrase comprised of a name is *logic(X,P, P)*, where *X* is the subject of the noun phrase and *P* is a predicate that either relates the verb of the following verb phrase to the subject of the noun phrase (for intransitive verb phrases) or the verb of the following verb phrase to the subject and direct object (for transitive verb phrases). The DCTG production is given next:

> *noun_phrase* : := *name^^N.*
> *<:>*
> *(plurality(singular)),*
> *(logic(X,P,P)* : :- *N^^logic(X)).*

For the more general form of noun phrases, the representation *logic(X, P1,P)* is used, where *X* is defined as before, *P1* is defined as *P* is before, and *P* is a quantified formula that integrates the determiner, noun, relative clause, and the verb phrase that follows the noun phrase.

> *noun_phrase* : := *determiner^^D , noun^^N, rel_clause^^R.*
> *<:>*
> *(plurality(PL)* : :- *D^^plurality(PL), N^^plurality(PL),*
>     *R^^plurality(PL)),*
> *(logic(X,P1,P)* : :- *D^^logic(X,P2,P1,P), N^^logic(X,P3),*
>     *R^^logic(X,P3,P2)).*

There are two forms of verb phrases, one for transitive verbs and the other for intransitive verbs. Consider first the intransitive verb phrases.

The plurality of an intransitive verb phrase is determined by the plurality of the intransitive verb. Logically, given the subject of the verb *X* and the verb *vi*, we form a predicate that relates the verb to its subject, that is, *vi(X)*. For transitive verb phrases, there is the transitive verb *vt* and the representation of its direct object *N*, and the translation gives the binary relation *vt(X,N)*. The DCTG productions for verb phrases are then

> *verb_phrase* : := *verb^^V, intransitive(V).*
> *<:>*
> *(plurality(PL)* : :- *V^^plurality(PL)),*
> *(logic(X,P)* : :- *V^^logic(intransitive,X,P)).*
> *verb_phrase* : := *verb^^V, transitive(V), noun_phrase^^N.*
> *<:>*
> *(plurality(PL)* : :- *V^^plurality(PL), N^^plurality(PL1)),*
> *(logic(X,P)* : :- *V^^logic(transitive,X,Y,P1),*
>         *N^^noun_phrase(Y,P1,P)).*

Finally, sentences simply consist of the verb that relates a translated representation of the noun phrase.

*sentence* : := *noun_phrase^^N, verb_phrase^^V, {agreement(N,V)}.*
*<:>*
*(logic(P) : :- N^^logic(X,P1,P), V^^logic(X,P)).*

The last item of business is to supply the relation definitions for the conditions that were embedded in the right side of DCTG productions. The definitions for *agreement, transitive,* and *intransitive* are given next:

*agreement(N,V) : := N^^plurality(PL), V^^plurality(PL).*
*transitive(V) : := V^^logic(transitive,_,_,_).*
*intransitive(V) : := V^^logic(intransitive,_,_,_).*

The complete DCTG grammar is shown in Figure 36.6, and the derivation and result of the translation of the sentence

**Every man who loves loves a woman who loves a who that loves**

that appears in Abramson is given below. For those interested, an algorithm for translating a DCTG grammar into a Prolog parser for the language generated by the grammar is given in Abramson.

**Figure 36.6**

*sentence* : := *noun_phrase^^N, verb_phrase^^V, {agreement(N,V)}.*
*<:>*
*(logic(P) : :- N^^logic(X,P1,P), V^^logic(X,P1)).*
*verb_phrase* : := *verb^^V, {intransitive(V)}.*
*<:>*
*(plurality(PL) : :- V^^plurality(PL)),*
*(logic(X,P) : :- V^^logic(intransitive,X,P)).*
*verb_phrase* : := *verb^^V, {transitive(V)}, noun_phrase^^N.*
*<:>*
*(plurality(PL) : :- V^^plurality(PL), N^^plurality(PL1)),*
*(logic(X,P) : :- V^^logic(transitive,X,Y,P1), N^^noun_phrase(Y,P1,P)).*
*noun_phrase* : := *name^^N.*
*<:>*
*(plurality(singular)),*
*(logic(X,P,P) : :- N^^logic(X)).*
*noun_phrase* : := *determiner^^D , noun^^N, rel_clause^^R.*
*<:>*
*(plurality(PL) : :- D^^plurality(PL), N^^plurality(PL), R^^plurality(PL)),*
*(logic(X,P1,P) : :- D^^logic(X,P2,P1,P), N^^logic(X,P3), R^^logic(X,P3,P2)).*

*rel_clause* : := **who** , *verb_phrase*^^*V*.
*<:>*
*(plurality(PL)* : :- *V*^^*plurality(PL)),*
*(logic(X,P1,and(P1,P2))* : :- *V*^^*logic(X,P2)).*

*determiner* : := **every**
*<:>*
*(plurality(singular)),*
*(logic(X,P1,P2,for_all(X,implies(P1,P2)))).*

*determiner* : := **a**
*<:>*
*(plurality(singular)),*
*(logic(X,P1,P2,there_exists(X,and(P1,P2)))).*

*verb* : := **lives**
*<:>*
*(plurality(singular)),*
*(logic(intransitive,X,lives(X))).*

*verb* : := **loves**
*<:>*
*(plurality(singular)),*
*(logic(transitive,X,Y,loves(X,Y))).*
*(logic(intransitive,X,loves(X))).*

*noun* : := **man**
*<:>*
*(plurality(singular)),*
*(logic(X,man(X))).*

*noun* : := **woman**
*<:>*
*(plurality(singular)),*
*(logic(X,woman(X))).*

*name* : := **chris**
*<:>*
*logic(chris).*

*name* : := **katie**
*<:>*
*logic(katie).*

■ BIBLIOGRAPHY NOTES

There are many good books on parsing and compiling techniques, including Barrett and Couch, Waite and Goos, and Aho, Sethi, and Ullman. Warren discusses logic programming in compiler writing. Winograd is an excellent text on natural language parsing. The October 1983 special

```
sentence(
   noun_phrase(
      determiner(every),
      noun(man),
      rel_clause(
         who,
         verb_phrase(
            intransitive(
               verb(loves))))),
      verb_phrase(
         transitive(
            verb(loves),
            noun_phrase(
               determiner(a),
               noun(woman),
               rel_clause(
                  who,
                  verb_phrase(
                     transitive(
                        verb(loves),
                        noun_phrase(
                           determiner(a),
                           noun(man),
                           rel_clause(
                              who,
                              verb_phrase(
```
```
intransitive(verb(loves)))))))))))))
```

**Translated Form of the Sentence** "Every man that loves loves a woman that loves a man that loves"

```
for_all(X1,
      implies(and(man(X1),loves(X1)),
               there_exists(X2,
                              and(and(woman(X2),
                                    there_exists(X3,
```
```
and(and(man(X3),loves(X3)),
```
```
loves(X2,X3)))),
```
```
                                    loves(X1,X2)))))
```

FIGURE **36.7** Prefix Form of the Parse Tree Constructed for the Sentence "Every man who loves loves a woman who loves a man who loves" issue of *IEEE Computer* on *"Knowledge Representation"* contains several tutorial articles on the subject. A nice comparative survey article on definite clause grammars for language analysis is given by Pereira and Warren. More recent results on logic grammars are given in Dahl and Abramson.

H. Abramson (1983) *Definite Clause Translation Grammars.* University of British Columbia, Department of Computer Science.

A. V. Aho, R. Sethi, and J. D. Ullman (1986) *Compilers: Principles, Techniques, and Tools.* Addison–Wesley, Reading, Mass.

W. A. Barrett and J. D. Couch (1979) *Compiler Construction: Theory and Practice.* Science Research Associates, Chicago.

V. Dahl (1983) *Current Trends in Logic Grammars.* Proceedings of the 1983 Logic Programming Workshop, Praia da Falesia, Algarve, Portugal, June 1983.

F. C. N. Pereira and D. H. D. Warren (1980) Definite clause grammars for language analysis—a survey of the formalism and a comparison with augmented transition networks. *Artificial Intelligence* **13**, 231–278.

W. M. Waite and G. Goos (1984) *Compiler Construction.* Springer-Verlag, New York.

D. H. D. Warren (1980) Logic programming and compiler writing. *Software Practice and Experience* **10**, 97–125.

T. Winograd (1983) *Language as a Cognitive Process*, Vol. 1; *Syntax.* Addison–Wesley, Reading, Mass.

# ▪ PROJECTS

1. Specify a BNF grammar for the set of decimal integers, fixed point reals, and floating-point reals. State your assumptions about the validity of leading zeros and the use of special symbols in representing floating-point reals.

2. Construct a recursive descent parser in Lisp for the grammar of Exercise 1.

3. Construct a definite clause parser in Prolog for the grammar of Exercise 1.

4. Attach semantic processing functions or relations to the parsers of Exercises 2 and 3 to enable them to produce the numerical value of the parsed strings.

# CHAPTER 37

# AUTOMATED THEOREM PROVING

*Automated theorem proving* is an area of artificial intelligence that has been successfully used in a variety of applications, including program analysis and verification, program synthesis, digital system design, expert reasoning, robotics, and mathematical discovery. Automated theorem provers have been used to provide proofs of complex open problems and simplified proofs of complex and controversial arguments.[1]

Some notable examples of successful theorem provers are that of Boyer and Moore (Table 37.1); Overbeek, Wos, Winker, Lusk, and Smith (Table 37.2); Andrews (Table 37.3); and Wen-tsün (Table 37.4). The tables 37, 37.2, 37.3, and 37.4 contain some of the important theorems proven automatically by these mechanical theorem provers. The goal of mechanizing the theorem-proving process dates back at least to Leibniz (1646–1716). In the early twentieth century, the mathematician David Hilbert

---

[1] There have been very few cases where automated theorem provers have discovered simpler proofs. One documented case is discussed by Wos and Winker in "Open Questions Solved with the Assistance of Aura", pages 73–88 in Bledsoe and Loveland (1984).

**TABLE 37.1**
BOYER AND MOORE THEOREM-PROVER

---

The existence and uniqueness of prime factorizations (Boyer and Moore, 1979)

Fermat's Theorem (Boyer and Moore, 1982):

$$M^{(p-1)} = 1 \ (mod \ p) \ if \ p \ is \ prime \ and \ does \ not \ divide \ M$$

Wilson's Theorem (Moore, 1983):

$$(p-1)! = -1 \ (mod \ p) \ if \ p \ is \ prime$$

Gauss' law of quadratic reciprocity

The existence of non-primitive recursive functions

The soundness and completeness of a propositional calculus decision procedure (Boyer and Moore, 1979)

The Turing completeness of the Pure LISP programming language (Bledsoe and Loveland, 84)

The recursive unsolvability of the halting problem [Boyer and Moore, 1984]

The termination of Takeuchi's Function (Moore, 1979)

---

**TABLE 37.2**
OVERBEEK, WOS, WINKER, LUSK, AND SMITH THEOREM PROVER

---

The existence of a finite semigroup admitting a nontrivial antiautomorphism but admitting no non-trivial involution (Winker, Wos, and Lusk, 1981)

Independence of several axioms of the ternary Boolean algebra (Winker and Wos, 1978)

Proofs for open questions in the equivalential calculus (Wos, 84a)

---

**TABLE 37.3**
ANDREW'S THEOREM PROVER

---

Cantor's theorem (Bledsoe and Loveland, 1984)

Proofs in higher-order logic (Bledsoe and Loveland, 1984)

---

conjectured the existence of an algorithm for determining the validity of any formula of the first-order predicate calculus applied to the domain of integers, and he challenged his colleagues to find such an algorithm. To

**TABLE 37.4**
WEN-TSUN'S THEOREM PROVER

Proofs for nontrivial theorems in elementary geometry (Bledsoe and Loveland, 1984)

Proofs for nontrivial theorems in elementary differential geometry (Bledsoe and Loveland, 1984)

the surprise of Hilbert and many others, Kurt Gödel demonstrated in his famous incompleteness theorem of 1931 that no such procedure could exist.

It should be noted that Gödel's incompleteness theorem does not reduce the goal of automating theorem proving to an exercise in futility. Rather, it conveys the fact that we cannot hope to construct an algorithm to settle *all* the questions that exist about domains of interest. The practical feasibility of deciding *many* of the important questions mechanically remains a possibility.

The work of Herbrand (1967), Gilmore (1960), Davis and Putnam (1960), and Robinson (1965) resulted in a mechanical method based on a single inference rule, called the *resolution rule*. The resolution rule is the basis of many of today's theorem provers. It provides the foundation for logic programming and Prolog. General theorem proving in the first-order predicate calculus is too complex to cover in a single chapter of a book of this sort. The bibliographic section at the end of the chapter points to additional sources on this topic.

A closely related and interesting problem is that of proving theorems of the *propositional calculus*.[2] Unlike the first-order predicate calculus, there exist systems for deciding the validity of all formulas of the propositional calculus. We will address a landmark propositional theorem-proving system that was developed by Wang (1960). Using an IBM 704 computer in 1959, Wang used his system to efficiently prove all the (approximately 220) theorems of Russell and Whitehead's *Principia Mathematica*, which are formulas of the propositional calculus.

First we present the syntax and semantics of propositional formulas. Then we cover the propositional theorem-proving system of Wang, followed by its Lisp and Prolog implementations. We finish the chapter with logic puzzles, their propositional representation, and their computer-aided solution.

---

[2]More than 30 years ago, J. Barkely Rosser cautioned mathematicians to avoid the term "proposition" in connection with formal statements in symbolic logic [Rosser53]. He felt that "proposition" carries a connotation of meaning, whereas formal statements in the notation of symbolic logic are devoid of meaning. Only their form is important. Keep this in mind as you read this chapter. Our program will manipulate forms, not meanings.

# ■ PROPOSITIONAL CALCULUS

The propositional calculus is a formal language for constructing declarative sentences that are always either *true* or *false*, exclusively. We call such declarative sentences *propositions*. Some examples of propositions are

A bluejay is a bird

and

All birds fly

Each simple proposition, like the foregoing examples, is assumed to have a *truth value*, that is, *true* or *false*. The proposition obtains a truth value as a result of a *truth assignment*. It is usually useful to associate symbols with both truth values and propositions. We will use **T** and **F** for the truth values *true* and *false*, respectively. **T** and **F** are called *propositional constants*. For propositions, letter symbols such as *P*, *Q*, and *R* will be used. *P*, *Q*, and *R* generally represent fixed but unknown propositions and are therefore called *propositional variables*.

A simple proposition is generally not very interesting in isolation. More complex propositions, called *compound propositions*, are formed using *logical connectives*. An example of a compound proposition is

**if** A bluejay is a bird **and** all birds fly **then** a bluejay flies

Each sentence of the propositional calculus is formed by connecting propositional constants and variables with logical connectives. The set of *well-formed formulas* (wff) of the propositional calculus is defined recursively.

**Definition 37.1.** The set of *well-formed formulas*, or *wffs* of the propositional calculus is defined as

Each of the propositional constants, **T** and **F**, are wffs.

A propositional variable is a wff.

If $A$ is a wff, then so is $\sim A$.

If $A$ and $C$ are wffs, then so are $(A \lor C)$, $(A \land C)$, $(A \supset C)$, and $(A \equiv C)$.

If $A$ is a wff, then so is $(A)$.

Nothing else is a wff.

A wff may have a truth value (*true* or *false*) associated with it. These truth values derive from the following rules, which are recursive.

**TABLE 37.5**

TRUTH TABLE FOR THE LOGICAL CONNECTIVES

| $P$ | $Q$ | $\sim P$ | $(P \wedge Q)$ | $(P \vee Q)$ | $(P \supset Q)$ | $(P \equiv Q)$ |
|---|---|---|---|---|---|---|
| T | T | F | T | T | T | T |
| T | F | F | F | T | F | F |
| F | T | T | F | T | T | F |
| F | F | T | F | F | T | T |

**T,F:** The truth values of the propositional constants **T** and **F** are *true* and *false*, respectively.

variables: A propositional variable has the same truth value either *true* or *false*, throughout a wff.

$\sim A$: The truth value of $\sim A$ is *true* if the truth value of $A$ is *false* and *false* if the truth value of $A$ is *true*.

$(A)$: The truth value of $(A)$ is the same as the truth value of $A$.

$(A \vee C)$: $(A \vee C)$ has the truth value *false* if both $A$ and $C$ have the truth value *false*; otherwise, $(A \vee C)$ has the truth value *true*.

$(A \wedge C)$: $(A \wedge C)$ has the truth value *true* if both $A$ and $C$ have the truth value *true*; otherwise, $(A \wedge C)$ has the truth value *false*.

$(A \supset C)$: $(A \supset C)$ has the truth value *false* if $A$ has the truth value *true* and $C$ has the truth value *false*; otherwise $(A \supset C)$ has the truth value *true*.

$(A \equiv C)$: $(A \equiv C)$ has the truth value *true* if $A$ and $C$ have the same truth value; otherwise, $(A \equiv C)$ has the truth value *false*.

**Shorthand:** Sometimes we write $A \vee B \vee C$ to denote the wff $(A \vee B) \vee C$. Similarly, we sometimes write $A \wedge B \wedge C$ for $(A \wedge B) \wedge C$.

The truth tables for each of the connectives are given in Table 37.5. The truth tables reveal some of the algebraic properties of the connectives (e.g., $\vee$ and $\wedge$ are commutative and associative, while $\supset$ is not commutative).

Consider the wff

$$(\sim P \supset (\sim Q)) \equiv (P \vee (Q \supset R))$$

To determine the truth value of the wff, we generally need to supply truth values to each of the propositional variables and evaluate the wff

**TABLE 37.6**
TRUTH TABLE FOR THE WFF $(\sim P \supset (\sim Q)) \equiv (P \vee (Q \supset R))$

| $P$ | $Q$ | $R$ | $\sim P$ | $\sim Q$ | $\sim P \supset (\sim Q)$ | $Q \supset R$ | $P \vee (Q \supset R)$ | $(\sim P \supset (\sim Q))$ $\equiv (P \vee (Q \supset R))$ |
|---|---|---|---|---|---|---|---|---|
| F | F | F | T | T | T | T | T | T |
| F | F | T | T | T | T | T | T | T |
| F | T | F | T | F | F | F | F | T |
| F | T | T | T | F | F | T | T | F |
| T | F | F | F | T | T | T | T | T |
| T | F | T | F | T | T | T | T | T |
| T | T | F | F | F | T | F | T | T |
| T | T | T | F | F | T | T | T | T |

**TABLE 37.7**
TRUTH TABLE FOR THE WFFS $(\sim Q \wedge (P \supset Q)) \supset (\sim P)$ AND $P \wedge (P \supset Q) \wedge (\sim Q)$

| $P$ | $Q$ | $\sim P$ | $\sim Q$ | $P \supset Q$ | $(\sim Q \wedge (P \supset Q)) \supset (\sim P)$ | $P \wedge (P \supset Q) \wedge (\sim Q)$ |
|---|---|---|---|---|---|---|
| F | F | T | T | T | T | F |
| F | T | T | F | T | T | F |
| T | F | F | T | F | T | F |
| T | T | F | F | T | T | F |

that results from substituting the corresponding truth variables for each variable, using the interpretations of the logical connectives. A truth table is useful for this purpose. Specifically, we construct a truth table for a wff $A$ by constructing truth tables for each wff contained in $A$. For the foregoing wff, we get the truth table given in Table 37.6. From the truth table it is easy to see that the wff is *true* under the truth assignment $\{P = F, Q = T, R = F\}$, and *false* under the truth assignment $\{P = F, Q = T, R = T\}$.

In theorem proving, there are two classes of wffs that have special significance: *tautologies* and *contradictions*. Consider the two wffs

$(\sim Q \wedge (P \supset Q)) \supset (\sim P)$

and

$P \wedge (P \supset Q) \wedge (\sim Q)$

and their respective truth tables given in Table 37.7.

The wff $(\sim Q \wedge (P \supset Q)) \supset (\sim P)$ has the interesting property that it is *true* under *all* variable truth assignments, while the wff $P \wedge (P \supset Q) \wedge (\sim Q)$

has the property that it is *false* under *all* variable truth assignments. Propositional wffs that are *true* under all variable truth assignments are called *tautologies*, whereas wffs that are *false* under all variable truth assignments are called *contradictions*.

The goal of a propositional theorem prover is either to demonstrate that a wff $A$ is a tautology or to demonstrate that $\sim (A)$ is a contradiction. Note that showing that $\sim (A)$ is a contradiction is tantamount to proving that $A$ is a tautology. We now consider Wang's mechanical system for deciding whether any wff of the propositional calculus is a tautology (a *valid* wff) or not a tautology (an *invalid* wff).

# ■ WANG'S PROPOSITIONAL THEOREM PROVER

In mechanizing theorem proving, it is useful to use a *normal form* to represent wffs. A normal form standardizes the presentation of equivalent wffs, which simplifies the task of mechanical processing. We will use a normal form known as the *logical consequence*, which has the following form.

$$A_1, A_2, \ldots, A_m \ \vdash \ C_1, C_2, \ldots, C_n \quad (m \geq 0, \ n \geq 0)$$

Each of $A_1, A_2, \ldots, A_m$ are wffs called *premises*, and each of $C_1, C_2, \ldots, C_n$ are wffs called *conclusions*. The syntactic mark "$\vdash$" serves as a delimiter that separates premises from conclusions.

The truth value of a logical consequence is determined using the following interpretation:

*At least one of the conclusions is true if all the premises are true*

Put more formally, a logical consequence $A_1, A_2, \ldots, A_m \ \vdash \ C_1, C_2, \ldots, C_n$ is *true* (i.e., a *valid* proposition) if and only if the propositional wff $A_1 \wedge A_2 \wedge \cdots \wedge A_m \ \supset \ C_1 \vee C_2 \vee \cdots \vee C_n$ is a tautology.

The *modus tollens* rule is an example of a valid proposition. It states that

*If $P \supset Q$ and $Q$ is false then $P$ is false*

or, in the form of a logical consequence,

$P \supset Q, \sim Q \ \vdash \sim P$

or, in the form of a wff,

$((P \supset Q) \wedge (\sim Q)) \ \supset \ (\sim P)$

The validity of *modus tollens* can be verified by constructing a truth table for the wff $((P \supset Q) \wedge (\sim Q)) \supset (\sim P)$. Alternatively, it can be verified by a sequence of simplifications that an automatic theorem prover could discover by matching syntactic patterns occurring in $P \supset Q, \sim Q \vdash \sim P$ with those occurring in a collection of transformational rules that we call *System W*.

System W, which forms the basis of Wang's propositional theorem proving system, is a collection of 11 rules, each of which provides a way to simplify a logical consequence. The theorem prover uses System W to verify or deny a given proposition by looking through the list of rules in System W to find one that has the same form as the given proposition. On finding such a rule, the theorem prover applies the simplification or conclusion suggested by the rule. Eventually, this leads to a simplification that confirms or rejects the proposition.

We will present each of the rules of System W and verify its validity. Then we will show how the rules can be used to verify a simple logical consequence.

Three of the rules (W.1, W.2a, and W.3) state conditions under which the validity of a logical consequence can be immediately determined. When an automatic theorem prover encounters one of these rules, its job is completed. The other rules (W.0, W.2b, W.4–W.9) spell out situations in which a given logical consequence can be simplified. These rules are used by automatic theorem provers to transform given logical consequences into new ones in such a way that steady progress toward a determination of validity is made.

In our presentation of the rules, $\lambda$ will denote a collection of "conjuncted" wffs, that is, $(A_1 \wedge A_2 \wedge \cdots \wedge A_m)$, and $\xi$ will denote a collection of "disjuncted" wffs, that is, $(C_1 \vee C_2 \vee \cdots \vee C_n)$, unless we specify an alternate form for $\lambda$ or $\xi$.

**Rule W.0:**   A wff $A$ is a tautology if and only if $\mathbf{T} \vdash A$ is valid.

*Proof:* By definition, $\mathbf{T} \vdash A$ is valid if and only if $\mathbf{T} \supset A$ is a tautology. From the interpretation of $\supset$, we note that for all wffs $A$, $\mathbf{T} \supset A$ is *false* if $A$ is false and $\mathbf{T} \supset A$ is *true* if $A$ is true. That is, $(\mathbf{T} \supset A) \equiv A$, which means that $\mathbf{T} \supset A$ is a tautology if and only if $A$ is a tautology.

**Rule W.1:**   The logical consequence $A_1, A_2, \ldots, A_m \vdash C_1, C_2, \ldots, C_n$ is valid if the same propositional variable occurs as both a premise, $A_i$, and a conclusion, $C_j$.

In other words, rule W.1 states that a proposition is valid whenever it has a premise and a conclusion that are identical and contain no logical connectives.

*Proof:* Consider the logical consequence $\lambda_1, P, \lambda_2 \vdash \xi_1, P, \xi_2$ for any propositional variable $P$, and the corresponding wff $(\lambda_1 \wedge P \wedge \lambda_2) \supset (\xi_1 \vee P \vee \xi_2)$. If $P$ is *false*, the wff simplifies to $\mathbf{F} \supset (\xi_1 \vee \xi_2)$, which is $\mathbf{T}$ for all

$\xi_1$ and $\xi_2$. If $P$ is *true*, the wff simplifies to $(\lambda_1 \wedge \lambda_2) \supset \mathbf{T}$, which is *true* for all $\lambda_1$ and $\lambda_2$. Thus, the wff $(\lambda_1 \wedge P \wedge \lambda_2) \supset (\xi_1 \vee P \vee \xi_2)$ is a tautology; that is to say, $\lambda_1, P, \lambda_2 \vdash \xi_1, P, \xi_2$ is valid.

**Rule W.2a:** If the truth value $\mathbf{F}$ is an element of the premise, or the truth value $\mathbf{T}$ is an element of the conclusion, then the logical consequence is valid.

In other words, rule W.2a states that $\mathbf{F}$ implies everything and that everything implies $\mathbf{T}$.

*Proof:* If $\mathbf{F}$ is an element of the premise, then the premise must have the form $\lambda_1, \mathbf{F}, \lambda_2$, which simplifies to $\mathbf{F}$, and $\mathbf{F} \supset \xi$ is *true* for all $\xi$. Similarly, if $\mathbf{T}$ is an element of the conclusion, then the conclusion must have the form $\xi_1, \mathbf{T}, \xi_2$, which simplifies to $\mathbf{T}$, and and $\lambda \supset \mathbf{T}$ is *true* for all $\lambda$. We conclude that the logical consequence is valid.

**Rule W.2b:** The logical consequence $\lambda_1, \mathbf{T}, \lambda_2 \vdash \xi$ is valid if and only if the logical consequence $\lambda_1, \lambda_2 \vdash \xi$ is valid. Similarly, the logical consequence $\lambda \vdash \xi_1, \mathbf{F}, \xi_2$ is valid if and only if the logical consequence $\lambda \vdash \xi_1, \xi_2$ is valid.

Rule W.2b simply extends rule W.2a with the observation that $\mathbf{T}$ is an identity operator with respect to $\wedge$, and that $\mathbf{F}$ is an identity operator with respect to $\vee$.

*Proof:* Simply observe that both $(\lambda_1 \wedge \mathbf{T} \wedge \lambda_2) \equiv (\lambda_1 \wedge \lambda_2)$ and $(\xi_1 \vee \mathbf{F} \vee \xi_2) \equiv (\xi_1 \vee \xi_2)$ are *true* for all wff sets $\lambda_1, \lambda_2, \xi_1,$ and $\xi_2$.

**Rule W.3:** If neither the premise nor conclusion contains wffs with logical connectives, and no propositional variable is common to the premise and conclusion, then the logical consequence is invalid.

That is, the presence of a common propositional variable in the premise and conclusion is a necessary condition for validity should the logical consequence contain no logical connectives. (It is also a sufficient condition for validity, as stated in rule W.1.)

*Proof:* Simply assign the value *true* to each propositional variable in the premise and the value *false* to each propositional variable in the conclusion, and the corresponding wff reduces to $\mathbf{T} \supset \mathbf{F}$, which is always false.

The remaining rules deal with the logical connectives. Each rule is designed to remove one connective from a wff in the premise or conclusion. Using these rules, the "size" of the logical consequence can be reduced until only propositional variables and constants remain. At this point, either Rule W.1 or Rule W.2a indicate success or Rule W.3 indicates failure.

**Rule W.4:**  The logical consequence $\lambda_1, \sim P, \lambda_2 \vdash \xi$ is valid if and only if the logical consequence $\lambda_1, \lambda_2 \vdash P, \xi$ is valid. Similarly, the logical consequence $\lambda \vdash \xi_1, \sim P, \xi_2$ is valid if and only if the logical consequence $P, \lambda \vdash \xi_1, \xi_2$ is valid.

*Proof:* Consider the logical consequence $\lambda_1, \sim P, \lambda_2 \vdash \xi$ and the corresponding wff $\lambda_1 \wedge (\sim P) \wedge \lambda_2 \supset \xi$. Applying the tautologies $(A \supset C) \equiv (\sim A \vee C)$ and DeMorgan's law [that is, $(\sim (P \wedge Q)) \equiv ((\sim P) \vee (\sim Q))$][3] to the wff produces the equivalent wff

$$((\sim \lambda_1) \vee (\sim (\sim P)) \vee (\sim \lambda_2)) \vee \xi$$

Since $\vee$ is commutative and associative, this is in turn equivalent to

$$((\sim \lambda_1) \vee (\sim \lambda_2)) \vee (\sim (\sim P)) \vee \xi$$

The *involution rule* states that for all propositions $P$, $P$ is equivalent to $(\sim (\sim P))$, and thus allows us to replace $(\sim (\sim P))$ with $P$, giving

$$((\sim \lambda_1) \vee (\sim \lambda_2)) \vee (P \vee \xi)$$

Finally, we use the same rule we used above to eliminate the $\supset$, to re-introduce it, i.e.

$$(\sim (\sim \lambda_1) \wedge (\sim (\sim \lambda_2)) \supset (P \vee \xi)$$

and eliminate the superfluous $\sim$ connectives to obtain

$$(\lambda_1 \wedge \lambda_2) \supset (P \vee \xi)$$

which is the wff corresponding to the logical connective $\lambda_1, \lambda_2 \vdash P, \xi$.

The argument for showing that $\lambda \vdash \xi_1, \sim P, \xi_2$ is valid if and only if $P, \lambda \vdash \xi_1, \xi_2$ is valid is a facsimile and is left as an exercise.

**Rule W.5:**  The logical consequence $\lambda_1, A \wedge C, \lambda_2 \vdash \xi$ is valid if and only if the logical consequence $\lambda_1, A, C, \lambda_2 \vdash \xi$ is valid. Similarly, the logical consequence $\lambda \vdash \xi_1, P \vee Q, \xi_2$ is valid if and only if the logical consequence $\lambda \vdash \xi_1, P, Q, \xi_2$ is valid.

*Proof:* Simply note that "," represents $\wedge$ in the premise and $\vee$ in the conclusion.

---

[3]Both the logical equivalence $(A \supset C) \equiv (\sim A \vee C)$ and DeMorgan's law can be verified as tautologies using truth tables. Try it as an exercise.

**Rule W.6:** The logical consequence $\lambda_1, A \equiv C, \lambda_2 \vdash \xi$ is valid if and only if the logical consequence $\lambda_1, (A \supset C), (C \supset A), \lambda_2 \vdash \xi$ is valid. Similarly, the logical consequence $\lambda \vdash \xi_1, A \equiv C, \xi_2$ is valid if and only if the logical consequence $\lambda \vdash \xi_1, (A \supset C) \wedge (C \supset A), \xi_2$ is valid.

*Proof:* The wff $A \equiv C$ is *true* if and only if both the wffs $A \supset C$ and $C \supset A$ are *true* (i.e. $(A \supset C) \wedge (C \supset A)$ is *true*).

**Rule W.7:** The logical consequence $\lambda_1, A \supset C, \lambda_2 \vdash \xi$ is valid if and only if the logical consequence $\lambda_1, ((\sim A) \vee C), \lambda_2 \vdash \xi$ is valid. Similarly, the logical consequence $\lambda \vdash \xi_1, A \supset C, \xi_2$ is valid if and only if the logical consequence $\lambda \vdash \xi_1, ((\sim A) \vee C), \xi_2$ is valid.

*Proof:* The wff $A \supset C$ is *true* if and only if the wff $((\sim A) \vee C)$ is *true*.

The next two rules are called *splitting rules*, since they split a logical consequence $X$ into two simpler logical consequences $X_1$ and $X_2$, where $X$ is valid if and only if both $X_1$ and $X_2$ are valid.

**Rule W.8:** The logical consequence $\lambda_1, A \vee C, \lambda_2 \vdash \xi$ is valid if and only if both the logical consequences $\lambda_1, A, \lambda_2 \vdash \xi$ and $\lambda_1, C, \lambda_2 \vdash \xi$ are valid.

*Proof:* A sequence of logical equivalences will be used to validate the claim.

$$
\begin{aligned}
(\lambda_1 \wedge (A \vee C) \wedge \lambda_2) \supset \xi &\equiv \\
((A \vee C) \wedge \lambda_1 \wedge \lambda_2) \supset \xi &\equiv && (\textit{commutativity of } \wedge) \\
\sim (A \vee C) \vee (\sim \lambda_1) \vee (\sim \lambda_2) \vee \xi &\equiv && ((X \supset Y) \equiv (\sim X \vee Y)) \\
((\sim A) \wedge (\sim C)) \vee ((\sim \lambda_1) \vee (\sim \lambda_2) \vee \xi) &\equiv && (\textit{De Morgan's Law}) \\
((\sim A) \vee (\sim \lambda_1) \vee (\sim \lambda_2) \vee \xi) \wedge & \\
\quad ((\sim C) \vee (\sim \lambda_1) \vee (\sim \lambda_2) \vee \xi) &\equiv && (\textit{distribute } \vee \textit{ over } \wedge) \\
(\sim (A \wedge \lambda_1 \wedge \lambda_2) \vee \xi) \wedge (\sim (C \wedge \lambda_1 \wedge \lambda_2) \vee \xi) &\equiv && (\textit{De Morgan's law}) \\
((A \wedge \lambda_1 \wedge \lambda_2) \supset \xi) \wedge ((C \wedge \lambda_1 \wedge \lambda_2) \supset \xi) && && ((X \supset Y) \equiv (\sim X \vee Y))
\end{aligned}
$$

**Rule W.9:** The logical consequence $\lambda \vdash \xi_1, A \wedge C, \xi_2$ is valid if and only if both the logical consequences $\lambda \vdash \xi_1, A, \xi_2$ and $\lambda \vdash \xi_1, C, \xi_2$ are valid.

*Proof:* Again, a sequence of logical equivalences will be used to validate the claim.

$$
\begin{aligned}
\lambda \supset (\xi_1 \vee (A \wedge C) \vee \xi_2) &\equiv \\
(\sim \lambda) \vee \xi_1 \vee (A \wedge C) \vee \xi_2 &\equiv && ((X \supset Y) \equiv (\sim X \vee Y)) \\
(A \wedge C) \vee (\sim \lambda) \vee \xi_1 \vee \xi_2 &\equiv && (\textit{commutativity and} \\
& && \textit{associativity of } \vee) \\
(A \vee (\sim \lambda) \vee \xi_1 \vee \xi_2) \wedge (C \vee (\sim \lambda) \vee \xi_1 \vee \xi_2) &\equiv && (\textit{distribute } \vee \textit{ over } \wedge) \\
((\sim \lambda) \vee A \vee \xi_1 \vee \xi_2) \wedge ((\sim \lambda) \vee C \vee \xi_1 \vee \xi_2) &\equiv && (\textit{commutativity of } \vee) \\
(\lambda \supset (A \vee \xi_1 \vee \xi_2)) \wedge (\lambda \supset (C \vee \xi_1 \vee \xi_2)) && && ((X \supset Y) \equiv (\sim X \vee Y))
\end{aligned}
$$

This completes the definition of system W. Let us apply it to several wffs. Consider the wff

$$Q \vee (\sim (P \supset Q)) \vee (\sim P)$$

This wff can be shown to be a tautology using system W as follows.

| | |
|---|---|
| $\vdash\ Q \vee (\sim (P \supset Q)) \vee (\sim P)$ | *by Rule W.0* |
| $\vdash\ Q, (\sim (P \supset Q)) \vee (\sim P)$ | *by Rule W.5* |
| $\vdash\ Q, \sim (P \supset Q), (\sim P)$ | *by Rule W.5* |
| $P \supset Q \vdash Q, \sim P$ | *by Rule W.4* |
| $\sim P \vee Q \vdash Q, \sim P$ | *by Rule W.7* |
| $P, \sim P \vee Q \vdash Q$ | *by Rule W.4* |
| $P, \sim P \vdash Q$ | *Left Branch of Split, Rule W.8* |
| $P \vdash Q, P$ | *by Rule W.4* |
| $**Tautology***$ | *by Rule W.1* |
| $P, Q \vdash Q$ | *Right Branch of Split, Rule W.8* |
| $**Tautology***$ | *by Rule W.1* |
| $**PROVEN***$ | |

The wff

$$(\sim Q \supset Q) \equiv (P \vee Q)$$

can be shown to be invalid.

| | |
|---|---|
| $\vdash\ (\sim Q \supset Q) \equiv P \vee Q$ | |
| $\vdash\ ((\sim Q \supset Q) \supset (P \vee Q))$ | |
| $\quad \wedge ((P \vee Q) \supset (\sim Q \supset Q))$ | *by Rule W.6* |
| $\vdash\ ((\sim Q \supset Q) \supset (P \vee Q))$ | *Left Branch of Split, Rule W.8* |
| $\vdash\ \sim ((\sim Q) \supset Q) \vee (P \vee Q)$ | *by Rule W.7* |
| $\vdash\ \sim ((\sim Q) \supset Q), P \vee Q$ | *by Rule W.5* |
| $(\sim Q) \supset Q \vdash P \vee Q$ | *by Rule W.4* |
| $\sim (\sim Q) \vee Q \vdash P \vee Q$ | *by Rule W.7* |
| $\sim (\sim Q) \vee Q \vdash P, Q$ | *by Rule W.5* |
| $\sim (\sim Q) \vdash P, Q$ | *Left Branch of Split, Rule W.8* |
| $\vdash\ \sim Q, P, Q$ | *by Rule W.4* |
| $Q \vdash P, Q$ | *by Rule W.4* |
| $**Tautology***$ | *by Rule W.1* |
| $Q \vdash P, Q$ | *Right Branch of Split, Rule W.8* |
| $**Tautology***$ | *by Rule W.1* |

$$\vdash (P \lor Q) \supset (\sim (Q) \supset Q) \qquad \textit{Right Branch of Split, Rule W.8}$$
$$\vdash (\sim (P \lor Q)) \lor (\sim (Q) \supset Q) \qquad \textit{by Rule W.7}$$
$$\vdash \sim (P \lor Q), \sim (Q) \supset Q \qquad \textit{by Rule W.5}$$
$$P \lor Q \vdash \sim (Q) \supset Q \qquad \textit{by Rule W.4}$$
$$P \lor Q \vdash \sim (\sim (Q)) \lor Q \qquad \textit{by Rule W.7}$$
$$P \lor Q \vdash \sim (\sim (Q)), Q \qquad \textit{by Rule W.5}$$
$$\sim (Q), P \lor Q \vdash Q \qquad \textit{by Rule W.4}$$
$$P \lor Q \vdash Q \qquad \textit{by Rule W.4}$$
$$P \vdash Q \qquad \textit{Left Branch of Split, Rule W.8}$$
$$**INVALID*** \qquad \textit{by Rule W.3}$$

Before moving on to either the Lisp or Prolog implementation sections, we suggest you work through Exercises 1, 2, and 3 at the end of the chapter.

# ■ LISP IMPLEMENTATION OF WANG'S THEOREM PROVER

To implement system W in Lisp, a plan must be devised for applying the simplification and splitting rules, detecting tautologies, and detecting invalid wffs. The implementation we present is modeled after a Prolog program by Coelho, Cotta, and Pereira (1980). Basically, the program takes a wff as input and proves or disproves that the wff is a tautology using the rules of system W. Each step of the proof is annotated with the system W rule the step was based on.

The syntax of program input wffs can be defined recursively, as follows:

A literal $P$ is a wff

If $A$ is a wff, then (- $A$) is a wff

If $A$ and $B$ are wffs, then

$(A$ ++ $B)$ is a wff,

$(A$ & $B)$ is a wff,

$(A$ => $B)$ is a wff, and

$(A$ <=> $B)$ is a wff

Nothing else is a wff

The procedure **theorem** is the entry point in the program. It simply formats the wff as a logical consequence for the subsequent proof. In general, a logical consequence used by the program consists of four lists: **Prelit**, **Prewff**, **Conlit**, and **Conwff**, where **Prelit** is a list of propositional variables that occur as wffs in the premise, **Prewff** is a list of the

FORMATTING THE WFF FOR THE THEOREM PROVER

```
(defun theorem (Wff)
        (if (prove nil nil nil (list Wff))
            (print "***PROVEN:")
            (print "***INVALID:")
        )
        (print Wff)
)
```

remaining wffs of the premise, **Conlit** is a list of propositional variables that occur as wffs in the conclusion, and **Conwff** is a list of the remaining wffs of the conclusion. Note that while **Prelit** and **Conlit** contain only propositional variable wffs, there may be both propositional variable wffs and compound wffs in either of **Prewff** or **Conwff**.

There is no necessity to separate out the propositional variables that occur as wffs from the compound wffs. Rather, it serves as a convenience for applying either of rules W.1 or W.3. Given this format and a wff **Wff** input to the program, the initial logical consequence is formatted such that **Prelit**, **Prewff**, and **Conlit** are empty, and **Conwff** is a list containing **Wff**.

The procedure **prove** first attempts to apply a simplification procedure, **simplify**, to the logical consequence. There are simplification rules for doing such things as removing the propositional constant **T** (**F**) from the premise (conclusion) list (as described by rule W.2b), or rewriting a wff of the form $A \supset C$ by the equivalent wff $(\sim A) \vee C$. If simplification is successful, **prove** recurses on the simplified logical consequence. The simplification procedure will be described shortly.

If **simplify** is able to simply a wff in the logical consequence, the simplified consequence is returned as its value; otherwise, **NIL** is returned.

If the logical consequence has been simplified, then the proof recurses. Before doing so, it makes notes on the progress of the proof via the utility routine **outwff** on the simplified structure.

Should there be no opportunity for performing simplification, **prove** then attempts to apply one of the splitting rules (as described by rules W.8 and W.9). For example, given the logical consequence

$$P, \sim P \vee Q \vdash Q$$

Rule W.8 can be applied to decompose the goal of the proof to proving that both the logical consequences

## ATTEMPT TO SIMPLIFY THE PROOF

```
(defun prove (Prelit Prewff Conlit Conwff)
  (let (simplified_wff (simplify Prelit Prewff
                                 Conlit Conwff))
      (if (dtpr Simplified_Wff)
; if simplification was successful,
; continue proof on simplified wff.
          (prove_simpler_wff Simplified_Wff)
          (if (disjunct_in_wff Prewff)
;  otherwise, if there is a disjunction (++) in
; the premise wff, or a conjunction (&) in the
; conclusion wff, then apply a splitting rule.
              (split_premise Prelit Prewff Conlit
                             Conwff)
              (if (conjunct_in_wff Conwff)
                  (split_concl Prelit Prewff Conlit
                               Conwff)
                  (if (literal_in_wff Prewff)
;  otherwise, if there is a literal in either the
; premise or conclusion wff list, then move it to
; the corresponding literal list.
                      (move_prelit Prelit Prewff
                                   Conlit Conwff)
                      (if (literal_in_wff Conwff)
                          (move_conlit Prelit
                              Prewff Conlit Conwff)
                          (tautology Prelit Prewff
                                     Conlit Conwff)
; otherwise, perform a definitive valdity test.
      )))))
))
```

$$P, \sim P \vdash Q$$

and

$$P, Q \vdash Q$$

are valid.

## RECURSE ON SIMPLIFIED WFF

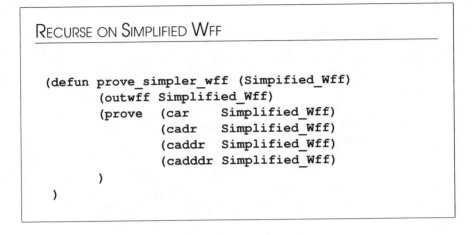

```
(defun prove_simpler_wff (Simpified_Wff)
        (outwff Simplified_Wff)
        (prove  (car     Simplified_Wff)
                (cadr    Simplified_Wff)
                (caddr   Simplified_Wff)
                (cadddr  Simplified_Wff)
        )
)
```

This requires the creation of two logical consequences from the given logical consequence, and invoking **prove** on each. The validity of the given logical consequence requires that both created logical consequences be proved valid.

The splitting-rule effectors simply print statements that show how the splitting in the proof is being carried out and call the **prove** procedure to attempt each of the two proofs.

Should there be a propositional variable (also called a *literal*) at the front of either the premise wff list or the conclusion wff list, it is moved into the corresponding literal list.

Finally, if none of these situations exist, the logical consequence can be determined to be either valid or invalid. This is done by checking for the presence of a literal in both the literal list of the premise and that of the conclusion, or the truth value **F** in the premise wff list, or the presence of the truth value **T** in the conclusion wff list. Should any of these conditions exist, the logical consequence is declared to be valid. Should none of these conditions hold, we can conclude that the logical consequence is invalid.

The simplification rules are a collection of *rewriting rules*, in which the form of a logical consequence $C_1$ is replaced by an alternate form $C_2$ with the property that $C_1$ is valid if and only if $C_2$ is valid. Each simplification is based on a rule of system W. When a simplification is applied during the execution of the program, the newly obtained logical consequence is listed along with the system W rule that justifies it.

## Split Premise/Conclusion Wff

```
(defun split_premise (Prelit Prewff Conlit Conwff)
      (and
            (leftbranch Prelit
                        (cons (extract_left_operand
                                        Prewff)
                        (cdr Prewff))
                        Conlit
                        Conwff
            )
            (rightbranch Prelit
                        (cons (extract_right_operand
                                        Prewff)
                        (cdr Prewff))
                        Conlit
                        Conwff
            )
      )
)

(defun split_concl (Prelit Prewff Conlit Conwff)
      (and
            (leftbranch Prelit
                        Prewff
                        Conlit
                        (cons (extract_left_operand
                                        Conwff)
                        (cdr Conwff))
            )
            (rightbranch Prelit
                        Prewff
                        Conlit
                        (cons (extract_right_operand
                                        Conwff)
                        (cdr Conwff))
            )
      )
)
```

## Splitting Rule Effectors

```
(defun leftbranch (Prelit Prewff Conlit Conwff)
       (print " Left Branch")
       (if (subproof Prelit Prewff Conlit Conwff)
           (print_left Prelit Prewff Conlit Conwff)
           nil
       )
)

(defun print_left (Prelit Prewff Conlit Conwff)
       (print "*** Left Branch Proven: ")
       (pwff Prelit Prewff Conlit Conwff)
)

(defun rightbranch (Prelit Prewff Conlit Conwff)
       (print " Right Branch")
       (if (subproof Prelit Prewff Conlit Conwff)
           (print_right Prelit Prewff Conlit Conwff)
           nil
       )
)

(defun print_right (Prelit Prewff Conlit Conwff)
       (print "*** Right Branch Proven: ")
       (pwff Prelit Prewff Conlit Conwff)
)

(defun subproof (Prelit Prewff Conlit Conwff)
       (print " SUBFORMULA: ")
       (pwff Prelit Prewff Conlit Conwff)
       (prove Prelit Prewff Conlit Conwff)
)
```

## MOVE LITERAL FROM WFF LIST TO LIST

```
(defun move_prelit (Prelit Prewff Conlit Conwff)
       (prove (union (list (car Prewff)) Prelit)
              (cdr Prewff)
              Conlit
              Conwff
       )
)

(defun move_conlit (Prelit Prewff Conlit Conwff)
       (prove Prelit
              Prewff
              (union (list (car Conwff)) Conlit)
              (cdr Conwff)
       )
)
```

## VALIDITY CHECKING RULES

```
(defun tautology (Prelit Prewff Conlit Conwff)
       (or (false_in_wff Prewff)
           (true_in_wff  Conwff)
           (intersectp Prelit Conlit)
       )
)
```

## SIMPLIFICATION RULES

```
(defun simplify (Prelit Prewff Conlit Conwff)
(if (true_in_wff Prewff) ;  true found in Premise
(list Prelit (cdr Prewff) Conlit Conwff "Rule W.2b")
(if (false_in_wff Conwff) ; false found in
                               ; Conclusion
(list Prelit Prewff Conlit (cdr Conwff) "Rule W.2b")
(if (implication_in_wff Prewff) ; Implication (=>)
                               ; found in Premise
                               ; Wff
(expand_imply_premise Prelit Prewff Conlit Conwff)
(if (equivalence_in_wff Prewff) ; Equivalence (<=>)
                               ; found in Premise
                               ; Wff.
(expand_equiv_premise Prelit Prewff Conlit Conwff)
(if (equivalence_in_wff Conwff) ; Equivalence (<=>)
                               ; found in
                               ; Conclusion Wff
(expand_equiv_conclusion Prelit Prewff
                         Conlit Conwff)
(if (negation_in_wff Prewff) ; Negation (-) found in
                             ; Premise Wff
(move_negate_premise Prelit Prewff Conlit Conwff)
(if (negation_in_wff Conwff) ; Negation (-) found in
                             ; Conclusion Wff
(move_negate_conclusion Prelit Prewff Conlit Conwff)
(if (conjunct_in_wff Prewff) ; Conjunction found in
                             ; Premise Wff
(simplify_conjunct Prelit Prewff Conlit Conwff)
(if (disjunct_in_wff Conwff) ; Disjunction found in
                             ; Conclusion Wff
(simplify_disjunct Prelit Prewff Conlit Conwff)
)))))))))
)
```

## EXPAND IMPLICATION IN PREMISE/CONCLUSION WFF

```
(defun expand_imply_premise (Prelit Prewff Conlit
                                 Conwff)
        (list Prelit (expand_imply Prewff) Conlit
            Conwff "Rule W.7")
)

(defun expand_imply_conclusion (Prelit Prewff Conlit
                                 Conwff)
        (list Prelit Prewff Conlit (expand_imply
            Conwff) "Rule W.7")
)

(defun expand_imply (Wff)
        (cons (list (list "-" (extract_left_operand
                                Wff))
                "++"
                (extract_right_operand Wff)
            )
            (cdr Wff)
        )
)
```

Set manipulation utility routines are provided for performing nonnull set intersection tests and set union on lists that represent sets. Note how the helping functions **interhelp** and **unionhelp** are used to avoid having to test the variable **L2** on each recursive step.

The operator/operand extraction routines are used as a mnemonic convenience for retrieving both operators and operands from the first wff contained in a nonempty wff list. For binary operators, their infix representation implies that the left operand is the first element of the wff, the operator is the second element, and the right operand is the third element. For unary operators, their prefix representation implies that the operator is the first element and the operand is the second element.

Finally, some print utilities for annotating proofs. The first, **outwff**, takes a list **Consequence** of five arguments, the premise literal list and wff list, the conclusion literal list and wff list, and a rule number string. In the second, **pwff**, the premise literal list and wff list, and the conclusion literal list and wff list, are passed in as the four arguments. In both cases, the function will return the value **T**.

## EXPAND EQUIVALENCE IN PREMISE/CONCLUSION WFF

```
(defun expand_equiv_premise (Prelit Prewff Conlit
                                    Conwff)
        (list Prelit (expand_equiv Prewff) Conlit
            Conwff "Rule W.6")
)

(defun expand_equiv_conclusion (Prelit Prewff Conlit
                                      Conwff)
        (list Prelit Prewff Conlit (expand_equiv
            Conwff) "Rule W.6")
)

(defun expand_equiv (Wff)
        (cons (list (list (extract_left_operand
                          Prewff)
                        "=>"
                        (extract_right_operand
                          Prewff)
                    )
                    "&"
                    (list (extract_right_operand
                          Prewff)
                        "=>"
                        (extract_left_operand
                          Prewff)
                    )
              )
            (cdr Prewff)
        )
)
```

## MOVE COMPLEMENT OF NEGATED WFF TO THE OTHER SIDE OF THE LOGICAL CONSEQUENCE

```
(defun move_negate_premise (Prelit Prewff Conlit
                                    Conwff)
      (list Prelit
            (cdr Prewff)
            Conlit
            (cons (extract_unary_operand Prewff)
                  Conwff)
            "Rule W.4"
      )
)

(defun move_negate_conclusion (Prelit Prewff Conlit
                                       Conwff)
      (list Prelit
            (cons (extract_unary_operand Conwff)
                  Prewff)
            Conlit
            (cdr Conwff)
            "Rule W.4"
      )
)
```

## SIMPLIFY CONJUNCTION (DISJUNCTION) IN PREMISE (CONCLUSION)

```
(defun simplify_conjunct (Prelit Prewff Conlit
                          Conwff)
       (list Prelit
             (eliminate_connective Prewff)
             (cons (extract_left_operand Prewff)
                   (cons (extract_right_operand
                          Prewff)
                         (cdr Prewff))
             )
             Conlit
             Conwff
             "Rule W.5"
       )
)

(defun simplify_disjunct (Prelit Prewff Conlit
                          Conwff)
       (list Prelit
             Prewff
             Conlit
             (eliminate_connective Conwff)
             "Rule W.5"
       )
)

(defun eliminate_connective (Wff)
       (cons (extract_left_operand Wff)
             (cons (extract_right_operand Wff)
                   (cdr Wff))
       )
)
```

## SET MANIPULATION UTILITY ROUTINES

```
(defun intersectp (L1 L2)
       (and (dtpr L2) (interhelp L1 L2))
)

(defun interhelp (L1 L2)
       (and (dtpr L1)
            (or (member (car L1) L2)
                (interhelp (cdr L1) L2))
       )
)

(defun union (L1 L2)
       (if (null L2) L1 (unionhelp L1 L2))
)

(defun unionhelp (L1 L2)
       (if (null L1)
           L2
           (if (member (car L1) L2)
               (unionhelp (cdr L1) L2)
               (cons (car L1)
                     (unionhelp (cdr L1) L2))
           )))
```

## WFF LIST OPERATOR/OPERAND EXTRACTION ROUTINES

```
(defun true_in_wff (WffList)
   (constcheck 'true WffList))
(defun false_in_wff (WffList)
    (constcheck 'false WffList))
(defun literal_in_wff (WffList)
   (and (dtpr WffList)
        (atom (car WffList))
        (not (or (true_in_wff WffList)
                 (false_in_wff WffList))) ))
(defun negation_in_wff (WffList)
   (uopcheck '- WffList))
(defun conjunct_in_wff (WffList)
   (bopcheck '& WffList))
(defun disjunct_in_wff (WffList)
   (bopcheck '++ WffList))
(defun implication_in_wff (WffList)
   (bopcheck '=> WffList))
(defun equivalence_in_wff (WffList)
   (bopcheck '<=> WffList))
(defun constcheck (const WffList)
   (and (dtpr WffList)
        (equal const (car WffList))))
(defun uopcheck (op WffList)
   (and (dtpr WffList)
        (listp (car WffList))
        (equal op (caar WffList))))
(defun bopcheck (op WffList)
   (and (dtpr WffList)
        (listp (car WffList))
        (equal op (cadar WffList))))
(defun extract_left_operand (WffList)
   (caar WffList))
(defun extract_right_operand (WffList)
   (caddar WffList))
(defun extract_unary_operand (WffList)
   (cadar WffList))
```

## Output Formatting Utility Routines

```
(defun outwff (Consequence)
   (print (list "premise(" (car Consequence) ","))
   (print (cadr Consequence))
   (print (list ") => conclusion("
                (caddr Consequence)))
   (print (list "," (cadddr Consequence)))
   (print (list ")      by "
                (caddddr Consequence)))
)

(defun pwff (Prelit Prewff Conlit Conwff)
   (print (list "premise(" Prelit))
   (print (list "," Prewff))
   (print (list ") => conclusion(" Conlit))
   (print (list "," Conwff))
   (print ")")
)
```

Tables 37.8 and 37.9 show the output of the theorem prover on a valid and invalid wff,

$(theorem\ (((p \lor q) \supset r) \lor (p \land q)) \supset (p \supset r))$
$(theorem\ (((p \lor q) \supset r) \lor (p \supset q)) \supset (p \supset r))$

respectively. Extraneous parentheses have been removed to reduce the width of the table entries.

# ■ Prolog Implementation of Wang's Theorem Prover

To implement system W in Prolog, a plan must be devised for applying the simplification rules and the splitting rules and for detecting tautologies and invalid wffs. The implementation we present is a modified version of a Prolog program that appeared in Coelho, Cotta, and Pereire (1980). Basically, the program takes a wff as input and proves or disproves that the wff is a tautology using the rules of system W. Each step of the proof is annotated with the system W rule the step was based on.

Using a top-down presentation then, the program, called **systemWP**, begins with some operator definitions.

The "operator" declarations allow the user of the Prolog implementation of system W to denote functors in a syntax similar to that of the propositional calculus. The infix functor "<=>" is used for the equivalence connective ($\equiv$), the infix functor "=>" for the implication connective ($\supset$), the infix functor "++" for the disjunction connective ($\lor$), the infix functor "&" for the conjunction connective ($\land$), and the prefix functor "-" for the negation connective ($\sim$).

The C-Prolog language allows operators to denote functors with varying properties. One property, *position*, allows the operator to be defined as prefix, infix, or postfix. The second property, *precedence*, helps the parser resolve ambiguities in interpreting the expression when multiple

## Operator Definitions

```
:- op(700,yfx,<=>).   /* equivalence */
:- op(650,yfx,=>).    /* implication */
:- op(600,yfx,++).    /* disjunction */
:- op(550,yfx,&).     /* conjunction */
:- op(500,fy,-).      /* negation    */
```

**TABLE 37.8**

AUTOMATIC TAUTOLOGY PROOF FOR $(((P \wedge Q) \supset R) \wedge (P \supset Q)) \supset (P \supset R)$

$FORMULA : (p\&q => r)\&(p => q) => (p => r)$

$premise([], []) => conclusion([], [-((p\&q => r)\&(p => q)) + +(p => r)]) by$ Rule 7
$premise([], []) => conclusion([], [-((p\&q => r)\&(p => q)), p => r]) by$ Rule 5
$premise([], [(p\&q => r)\&(p => q)]) => conclusion([], [p => r]) by$ Rule 4
$premise([], [(p\&q => r)\&(p => q)]) => conclusion([], [-p + +r]) by$ Rule 7
$premise([], [p\&q => r, p => q]) => conclusion([], [-p + +r]) by$ Rule 5
$premise([], [-(p\&q) + +r, p => q]) => conclusion([], [-p + +r]) by$ Rule 7
$premise([], [-(p\&q) + +r, p => q]) => conclusion([], [-p, r]) by$ Rule 5
$premise([], [p, -(p\&q) + +r, p => q]) => conclusion([], [r]) by$ Rule 4
$Left\ Branch\ SUBFORMULA : premise([p], [-(p\&q), p => q]) =>$
     $conclusion, [], [r])$
$premise([p], [p => q]) => conclusion([], [p\&q, r]) by$ Rule 4
$premise([p], [-p + +q]) => conclusion([], [p\&q, r]) by$ Rule 7
$Left\ Branch\ SUBFORMULA : premise([p], [-p]) => conclusion([], [p\&q, r])$
$premise([p], []) => conclusion([], [p, p\&q, r]) by$ Rule 4
$Left\ Branch\ SUBFORMULA : premise([p], []) => conclusion([p], [p, r])$
$* * Tautology$
$* * Left\ Branch\ PROVEN : premise([p], []) => conclusion([p], [p, r])$
$Right\ Branch\ SUBFORMULA : premise([p], []) => conclusion([p], [q, r])$
$* * Tautology$
$* * Right\ Branch\ PROVEN : premise([p], []) => conclusion([p], [q, r])$
$* * Left\ Branch\ PROVEN : premise([p], [-p]) => conclusion([], [p\&q, r])$
$Right\ Branch\ SUBFORMULA : premise([p], [q]) => conclusion([], [p\&q, r])$
$Left\ Branch\ SUBFORMULA : premise([p], [q]) => conclusion([], [p, r])$
$* * Tautology$
$* * Left\ Branch\ PROVEN : premise([p], [q]) => conclusion([], [p, r])$
$Right\ Branch\ SUBFORMULA : premise([p], [q]) => conclusion([], [q, r])$
$* * Tautology$
$* * Right\ Branch\ PROVEN : premise([p], [q]) => conclusion([], [q, r])$
$* * Right\ Branch\ PROVEN : premise([p], [q]) => conclusion([], [p\&q, r])$
$* * Left\ Branch\ PROVEN : premise([p], [-(p\&q), p => q]) =>$
     $conclusion([], [r])$
$Right\ Branch\ SUBFORMULA : premise([p], [r, p => q]) => conclusion([], [r])$
$premise([r, p], [-p + +q]) => conclusion([], [r]) by$ Rule 1
$Left\ Branch\ SUBFORMULA : premise([r, p], [-p]) => conclusion([], [r])$
$premise([r, p], []) => conclusion([], [p, r]) by$ Rule 5
$* * Tautology$
$* * Left\ Branch\ PROVEN : premise([r, p], [-p]) => conclusion([], [r])$
$Right\ Branch\ SUBFORMULA : premise([r, p], [q]) => conclusion([], [r])$
$* * Tautology$
$* * Right\ Branch\ PROVEN : premise([r, p], [q]) => conclusion([], [r])$
$* * Right\ Branch\ PROVEN : premise([p], [r, p => q]) => conclusion([], [r])$
$* * PROVEN : (p\&q => r)\&(p => q) => (p => r)$

**TABLE 37.9**

Automatic Invalidity Proof for $(((P \lor Q) \supset R) \lor (P \supset Q)) \supset (P \supset R)$

$FORMULA : (p + +q => r) + +p\&q => (p => r)$

$premise([], []) => conclusion([], [-((p + +q => r) + +p\&q) + +(p => r)])by\ Rule\ 7$

$pemise([], []) => conclusion([], [-((p + +q => r) + +p\&q), p => r])by\ Rule\ 5$

$premise([], [(p + +q => r) + +p\&q]) => conclusion([], [p => r])by\ Rule\ 4$

$premise([], [(p + +q => r) + +p\&q]) => conclusion([], [-p + +r])by\ Rule\ 7$

$premise([], [(p + +q => r) + +p\&q]) => conclusion([], [-p, r])by\ Rule\ 5$

$premise([], [p, (p + +q => r) + +p\&q]) => conclusion([], [r])by\ Rule\ 4$

$Left\ Branch\ SUBFORMULA : premise([p], [p + +q => r]) => conclusion([], [r])$

$premise([p], [-(p + +q) + +r]) => conclusion([], [r])by\ Rule\ 7$

$Left\ Branch\ SUBFORMULA : premise([p], [-(p + +q)]) => conclusion([], [r])$

$premise([p], []) => conclusion([], [p + +q, r])by\ Rule\ 4$

$premise([p], []) => conclusion([], [p, q, r])by\ Rule\ 5$

$**Tautology$

$**Left\ Branch\ PROVEN : premise([p], [-(p + +q)]) => conclusion([], [r])$

$Right\ Branch\ SUBFORMULA : premise([p], [r]) => conclusion([], [r])$

$**Tautology$

$**Right\ Branch\ PROVEN : premise([p], [r]) => conclusion([], [r])$

$**Left\ Branch\ PROVEN : premise([p], [p + +q => r]) => conclusion([], [r])$

$Right\ Branch\ SUBFORMULA : premise([p], [p\&q]) => conclusion([], [r])$

$premise([p], [p, q]) => conclusion([], [r])by\ Rule\ 7$

$**INVALID : (p + +q => r) + +p\&q => (p => r)$

interpretations are possible in the absence of parentheses. An integer with the functor in its operator declaration designates its precedence, an "associativity" resolves ambiguities when the parser encounters two operators with the same precedence.

A detailed discussion of this feature of Prolog is beyond the scope of this chapter, and is not needed in clarifying the example. Other texts on Prolog cover this aspect in greater depth. It should suffice to point out that

```
:- op(700,yfx,<=>). /* equivalence */
```

means that the functor "`<=>`" is infix and left-associative (i.e., evaluated left-to-right when faced with expressions such as "`p <=> q <=> r`"), that

```
:- op(500,fy,-).    /* negation   */
```

means that the functor "`-`" is prefix, and for the group of defined operators, the relative precedence of the functors in strictly increasing order is conveyed by the list (<=>,=>,++,&,-).

The procedure **theorem** is the entry point into the program. It simply formats the input wff as a logical consequence for the subsequent proof. In general, the form of a logical consequence used by the program is

```
premise(PreLit,PreWff) => conclusion(ConLit,ConWff)
```

where **PreLit** is a list of propositional variables that occur as wffs in the premise, **PreWff** is a list of the remaining wffs of the premise, **ConLit** is a list of propositional variables that occur as wffs in the conclusion, and **ConWff** is a list of the remaining wffs of the conclusion. Note that whereas **PreLit** and **ConLit** contain only propositional variable wffs, there may be both propositional variable wffs and compound wffs in either of **PreWff** or **ConWff**.

Given this format and a wff **Wff** input to the program, the initial logical consequence is formatted as

```
premise([],[]) => conclusion([],Wff)
```

The procedure **prove** first attempts to apply a simplification procedure to the logical consequence. There are simplification rules for doing such things as removing the propositional constant **T** (**F**) from the premise (conclusion) list (as described by Rule W.2b), or rewriting a wff of the form $A \supset C$ by the equivalent wff $(\sim A) \vee C$. If simplification is successful, **prove** recurses on the simplified logical consequence. The simplification procedure will be described shortly.

Should there be no opportunity for performing simplification, the program then attempts to apply one of the splitting rules (as described by Rules W.8 and W.9). For example, given the logical consequence

## FORMATTING THE WFF FOR THE THEOREM PROVER

```
theorem(Wff) :- nl,
                (prove(premise([],[]) =>
                        conclusion([],[Wff])),
                 writeln('*** PROVEN: '), write(Wff)
                ) ;
                (writeln('*** INVALID: '),
                 write(Wff)).
```

## ATTEMPT TO SIMPLIFY USING ONE OF THE REWRITING RULES

```
prove(Wff) :- simplify(Wff,NewWff,Rule),
              writeln(NewWff),
              annotate(Rule),
              prove(NewWff).
```

$$P, \sim P \lor Q \vdash Q$$

rule W.8 can be applied to decompose the goal of the proof to proving that both the logical consequences

$$P, \sim P \vdash Q$$

and

$$P, Q \vdash Q$$

are valid.

This requires the creation of two logical consequences from the given logical consequence, and invoking **prove** on each. The validity of the given logical consequence requires that both created logical consequences be proved valid.

Should there be a propositional variable (also called a *literal*) at the front of either the premise wff list or the conclusion wff list, it is moved into the corresponding literal list.

Finally, if none of these situations exist, the logical consequence can be determined to be either valid or invalid. This is done by checking for

## ATTEMPT TO APPLY A SPLITTING RULE

```
/*   ***** disjunction (++) in premise wff *****  */
 prove(premise(P_literals,[T1 ++ T2|Term]) =>
      Conclusion) :-
      left_branch(premise(P_literals,[T1|Term]) =>
                Conclusion),
      right_branch(premise(P_literals,[T2|Term]) =>
                Conclusion).

/*   **** conjunction (&) in conclusion wff ****  */
 prove(Premise => conclusion(C_literals,[T1 &
                               T2|Term])) :-
      left_branch(Premise =>
                conclusion(C_literals,[T1|Term])),
      right_branch(Premise =>
                conclusion(C_literals,[T2|Term])).
```

## MOVE LITERAL FROM WFF LIST TO LITERAL LIST

```
prove(premise(P_literals,[Literal|Term]) =>
      Conclusion) :-
      prove(premise([Literal|P_literals],Term) =>
          Conclusion).

prove(Premise =>
      conclusion(C_literals,[Literal|Term])) :-
      prove(Premise =>
          conclusion([Literal|C_literals],Term)).
```

---

Decide Whether the Logical Consequence is Valid

---

```
prove(Wff)  :- tautology(Wff),
               writeln('*** Tautology'),
               nl.
```

---

the presence of a literal in both the literal list of the premise and that of the conclusion, or the truth value **F** in the premise wff list, or the presence of the truth value **T** in the conclusion wff list. Should any of these conditions exist, the logical consequence is declared to be valid. Should none of these conditions hold, we can conclude that the logical consequence is invalid.

The simplification rules are a collection of *rewriting rules*, in which the form of a logical consequence $C_1$ is replaced by an alternate form $C_2$ with the property that $C_1$ is valid if and only if $C_2$ is valid. Each simplification is based on a rule of system **W**. When a simplification is applied during the execution of the program, the newly obtained logical consequence is listed along with the system **W** rule that justifies it.

The procedure for determining validity is fairly simple, as by the time the procedure is called the premise and conclusion of the logical consequence have been reduced to a list of propositional variables or key truth values. Validity is therefore determined by checking for the presence of any of the following: a literal in both the literal list of the premise and that of the conclusion, the truth value **F** in the premise wff list, or the presence of the truth value **T** in the conclusion wff list. Should any of these conditions exist, the logical consequence is declared to be valid. Should none of these conditions hold, we can conclude that the logical consequence is invalid.

The splitting rule effectors simply print statements that show how the splitting in the proof is being carried out and call the **prove** procedure to attempt each of the two proofs.

The final component of the procedure is the collection of set manipulation and utility routines.

Note that as the program was designed to produce output similar to that of the Lisp theorem prover in the previous section, tables 37.8 and 37.9 serve to show the output of the theorem prover on a valid and invalid wff,

$theorem(((((p \wedge q) \supset r) \wedge (p \supset q)) \supset (p \supset r))$
$theorem(((((p \vee q) \supset r) \vee (p \wedge q)) \supset (p \supset r))$

## Simplification Rules

```
/* ***  T (F) found in Premise (Conclusion)  *** */
simplify(premise(P_literals,[true|Term]) => Conclusion,
    premise(P_literals,Term) => Conclusion, 'Rule W.2b').
simplify(Premise => conclusion(C_literals,[false|Term])
                => Conclusion,
    Premise => conclusion(C_literals,Term), 'Rule W.2b').

/* ***  Implication (=>) found in either Premise
        or Conclusion Wff *** */
simplify(premise(P_literals,[T1 => T2|Term]) => Conclusion,
    premise(P_literals,[- T1 ++ T2|Term])
        => Conclusion, 'Rule W.7').
simplify(Premise => conclusion(C_literals,[T1 => T2|Term]),
    Premise => conclusion(C_literals,[- T1 ++ T2|Term]),
                        'Rule W.7').

/* ***  Equivalence (<=>) found in either Premise
        or Conclusion Wff *** */
simplify(premise(P_literals,[T1 <=> T2|Term]) => Conclusion,
    premise(P_literals,[T1 => T2,T2 => T1|Term])
        => Conclusion, 'Rule W.6').
simplify(Premise => conclusion(C_literals,[T1 <=> T2|Term]),
    Premise => conclusion(C_literals,
                        [(T1 => T2)&(T2 => T1)|Term]),
                        'Rule W.6').

/* ***  Negation (-) found in either Premise
        or Conclusion Wff *** */
simplify(premise(P_literals,[- T1|Term])
            => conclusion(C_literals,C_wff),
    premise(P_literals,Term)
        => conclusion(C_literals,[T1|C_wff]), 'Rule W.4').
simplify(premise(P_literals,P_wff)
            => conclusion(C_literals,[- T1|Term]),
    premise(P_literals,[T1|P_wff])
        => conclusion(C_literals,Term), 'Rule W.4').

/* ***  Conjunction (&) found in either Premise Wff *** */
simplify(premise(P_literals,[T1 & T2|Term]) => Conclusion,
    premise(P_literals,[T1,T2|Term]) => Conclusion, 'Rule W.5').

/* ***  Disjunction (++) found in either Conclusion Wff *** */
simplify(Premise => conclusion(C_literals,[T1 ++ T2|Term]),
    Premise => conclusion(C_literals,[T1,T2|Term]), 'Rule W.5').
```

## VALIDITY CHECKING RULES

```
tautology(premise(_,[false|_]) => _ ).
tautology(_ => conclusion(_,[true|_])).
tautology(premise(P_literals,_) =>
        conclusion(C_literals,_)) :-
        member(Literal,P_literals),
        member(Literal,C_literals).
```

## SPLITTING RULE EFFECTORS

```
left_branch(Wff) :- writeln(' Left Branch'),
            subproof(Wff),
            writeln('*** Left Branch PROVEN: '),
            write(Wff),
            nl.

right_branch(Wff) :- writeln(' Right Branch'),
            subproof(Wff),
            writeln('*** Right Branch PROVEN: '),
            write(Wff),
            nl.

    subproof(Wff) :- write(' SUBFORMULA: '),
                write(Wff),
                nl,
                prove(Wff).
```

### Set Manipulation and Utility Routines

```
member(X, [X|_]).
member(X, [_|L]) :- member(X, L).

writeln(T) :- nl,
              write(T).

annotate(Rule) :- write('     by '),
                  write(Rule),
                  nl.
```

respectively. Extraneous parentheses have been removed to reduce the width of the table entries.

## ■ Theorem Proving for Fun and Profit

Now that we have gone through the trials and tribulations of learning the propositional calculus and a formal system for proving tautologies of the propositional calculus and developing a program to express those ideas, it is time to put it all to work.

### A SIMPLE PROPOSITIONAL EXAMPLE

To begin with, consider the following propositional wff:

$$(P \supset Q) \land (Q \supset R)$$

This wff is clearly sufficient to guarantee the truth of the wff $P \supset R$. It simply asserts the transitive property of logical implication. It might also seem that the wff

$$(P \supset Q) \land (R \supset S) \land \neg(Q \supset R)$$

is sufficient to guarantee that $P$ does not imply $S$. It is somewhat difficult to determine this by eyeballing the wff, but we can construct a logical consequence from the wff,

$$((P \supset Q) \land (R \supset S) \land \neg(Q \supset R)) \supset \neg(P \supset S)$$

and apply system W. The result is shown next.

$\vdash ((P \supset Q) \wedge (R \supset S) \wedge (\sim (Q \supset R))) \supset (\sim (P \supset S))$

$\vdash \sim ((P \supset Q) \wedge (R \supset S) \wedge (\sim (Q \supset R))) \vee (\sim (P \supset S))$      *by Rule W.7*

$\vdash \sim ((P \supset Q) \wedge (R \supset S) \wedge (\sim (Q \supset R))), (\sim (P \supset S))$      *by Rule W.5*

$(P \supset Q) \wedge (R \supset S) \wedge (\sim (Q \supset R)) \vdash (\sim (P \supset S))$      *by Rule W.4*

$(P \supset S), (P \supset Q) \wedge (R \supset S) \wedge (\sim (Q \supset R)) \vdash$      *by Rule W.4*

$(\sim P \vee S), (P \supset Q) \wedge (R \supset S) \wedge (\sim (Q \supset R)) \vdash$      *by Rule W.7*

$\sim P, (P \supset Q) \wedge (R \supset S) \wedge (\sim (Q \supset R)) \vdash$      *Left Branch of Split, Rule W.8*

$(P \supset Q) \wedge (R \supset S) \wedge (\sim (Q \supset R)) \vdash P$      *by Rule W.4*

$(P \supset Q), (R \supset S) \wedge (\sim (Q \supset R)) \vdash P$      *by Rule W.5*

$(\sim P \vee Q), (R \supset S) \wedge (\sim (Q \supset R)) \vdash P$      *by Rule W.7*

$\sim P, (R \supset S) \wedge (\sim (Q \supset R)) \vdash P$      *Left Branch of Split, Rule W.8*

$(R \supset S), \sim (Q \supset R) \vdash P, P$      *by Rule W.5*

$(\sim R \vee S), \sim (Q \supset R) \vdash P, P$      *by Rule W.7*

$\sim R, \sim (Q \supset R) \vdash P, P$      *Left Branch of Split, Rule W.8*

$\sim (Q \supset R) \vdash R, P, P$      *by Rule W.4*

$\vdash Q \supset R, R, P, P$      *by Rule W.4*

$\vdash \sim Q, R, R, P, P$      *by Rule W.7*

$Q \vdash R, R, P, P$      *by Rule W.4*

$**INVALID***$      *by Rule W.3*

Close inspection of the proof reveals that the assignment of the truth value **F** to $P$ and $Q$ and the truth value **T** to $Q$ yield a wff value of **F**. We might consider how to "strengthen" the premise to ensure that the conclusion was false only when the premise was false. Can you see how this might be done?

The simplest solution is to add the conjuction $W \wedge \sim Z$ to the premise. Try constructing such a logical consequence and running it through system W. Another remedy you might try is to "weaken" the conclusion. This is left as an exercise.

A more challenging task is to use the system W program to help solve or verify logic puzzles. We will consider three puzzles to illustrate the possibilities.

## PUZZLE 1

The first puzzle places you deep in a bayou, in search of a small isolated eatery called the *House of Crawfish Gumbo*. You have reached a fork in the road, you and know that one branch leads to the *House of Crawfish Gumbo* whereas the other leads deep into alligator infested waters. However, there are no signs to provide directions. Your choice will determine whether you get to eat a dinner of succulent crawfish or become dinner for a hungry alligator. Now, the only hope appears to lie with the crusty geezer rocking in his chair and chewing tobacco on the porch of a log cabin. The problem is the fact that all people who chew tobacco either always tell the truth or always lie, and crusty geezers are only willing to answer one yes/no question for a stranger. What yes/no question should you ask the geezer to find the way to the *House of Crawfish Gumbo*?

Let $P$ stand for *the geezer always tells the truth*, and let $Q$ stand for *the left branch leads to the House of Crawfish Gumbo*. We want to construct a wff $W_1$ involving $P$ and $Q$ with the property that the crusty geezer's answer to the question

Is $W_1$ *true*?

will be *yes* when and only when $Q$ is *true*.

We will attack this problem using truth tables. In particular, the possible combinations of truth values for $P$ and $Q$ can be enumerated together with the answer we would want for the question $Q$ (*is $W_1$ true?*) and its relation to $W_1$. Thus, the truth table in terms of $P$ and $Q$ is given here.

| $P$ (The geezer tells the truth) | $Q$ (Left to the *House of Crawfish Gumbo*) | Desired answer to *is $W_1$ true* |
|---|---|---|
| true | true | yes ($W_1$) |
| true | false | no ($W_1$) |
| false | true | yes ($\sim W_1$) |
| false | false | no ($\sim W_1$) |

Note that we associate $W_1$ with the cases where $P$=*true*, $Q$=*true* and $P$=*true*, $Q$=*false* since $P$=*true* indicates a truthful answer to $Q$, whereas we associate $\sim W_1$ with the case where $P$=*false*, $Q$=*true* and $P$=*false*, $Q$=*false* since $P$=*false* indicates a fallacious answer to $Q$. From the truth table, it is clear then that $W_1$ must be *true* when either $P$=*true* and $Q$=*true*, or $P$=*false* and $Q$=*false*, and $W_1$ must be *false* when either $P$=*true* and $Q$=*false*, or $P$=*true* and $Q$=*false*. The truth table for $W_1$ is shown next.

| $P$ (The geezer tells the truth | $Q$ (Left to the *House of Crawfish Gumbo*) | $W_1$ |
|---|---|---|
| true | true | true |
| true | false | false |
| false | true | false |
| false | false | true |

Clearly, $W_1$ has the semantics of the equivalence connective applied to $P$ and $Q$. Therefore, the question we ask is

> Mr. Geezer, either you always tell the truth and the left branch leads to the *House of Crawfish Gumbo*, or you always lie and the right branch leads to the *House of Crawfish Gumbo*. Right?

Verify this question using the theorem prover.

## PUZZLE 2

The second puzzle presents a Cold War dilemma. The Russian KGB Committee for State Security has many moles implanted in the British MI6 Foreign Intelligence Service. All moles are trained to respond to any message that begins with the phrase:

*the borscht is better in Gorky Park*

For added security, one group of moles (code name: Boris) will always respond truthfully, whereas another group of moles (code name: Igor) will always lie, and a third group can either lie or tell the truth (code name: Natasha). You are working in the British MI5 Counterintelligence Service and are tailing two suspected moles (*Mole A* and *Mole B*). The two moles are approached by a third suspected mole (*Mole C*) who whispers "*the borscht is better in Gorky Park. Identify yourselves*".

The response from *Mole A* is "*Mole B is a Boris*", and the response from *Mole B* is "*Mole A is an Igor*".

You claim that one of *Mole A* or *Mole B* must be code name Natasha and must now prove it. Define the following propositional variables:

*P1*: *Mole A* is code name Boris.

*P2*: *Mole A* is code name Igor.

*P3*: *Mole A* is code name Natasha.

Q1: *Mole B* is code name Boris.

Q2: *Mole B* is code name Igor.

Q3: *Mole B* is code name Natasha.

We begin by noting that both *Mole A* and *Mole B* are exactly one of code name Boris, Igor, or Natasha. This can be expressed logically as:

$$(P1 \lor P2 \lor P3) \land (Q1 \lor Q2 \lor Q3) \land$$
$$(\sim (P1 \land P2)) \land (\sim (P1 \land P3)) \land (\sim (P2 \land P3)) \land$$
$$(\sim (Q1 \land Q2)) \land (\sim (Q1 \land Q3)) \land (\sim (Q2 \land Q3))$$

where

$$(P1 \lor P2 \lor P3) \land (Q1 \lor Q2 \lor Q3)$$

states that *Mole A* and *Mole B* must be *at least* one of code name Boris, Igor, or Natasha,

$$(\sim (P1 \land P2)) \land (\sim (P1 \land P3)) \land (\sim (P2 \land P3))$$

states that *Mole A* can be *at most* one of code name Boris, Igor, or Natasha, and

$$(\sim (Q1 \land Q2)) \land (\sim (Q1 \land Q3)) \land (\sim (Q2 \land Q3))$$

states that *Mole B* can be *at most* one of code name Boris, Igor, or Natasha.

Consider next *Mole B*, who is either lying or telling the truth. If *Mole B* is telling the truth then

$$P2 \land (Q1 \lor Q3) \land (Q2 \lor Q3)$$

is *true*, since *Mole A* must be code name Igor (*Mole B*'s statement), *Mole B* must be either code name Boris or Natasha (*Mole B* tells the truth), and since *Mole A* is a liar, *Mole B* must either be code name Igor or Natasha (*Mole A*'s statement). Similarly, if *Mole B* is lying then

$$(P1 \lor P3) \land (Q2 \lor Q3) \land (P2 \lor P3)$$

is *true*, *Mole A* cannot be code name Igor (*Mole B*'s statement), *Mole B* must be either code name Igor or Natasha (*Mole B* lies), and since *Mole B* is assumed to be lying, *Mole B* cannot be code name Boris and *Mole A* is lying (i.e. *Mole A* must either be code name Igor or Natasha).

We want to show that by assuming the foregoing, it always follows that either of *Mole A* or *Mole B* is code name Natasha (i.e., $P3 \lor Q3$ is *true*). Putting it all together yields the following wff:

$((P1 \lor P2 \lor P3) \land (Q1 \lor Q2 \lor Q3) \land$
$(\sim (P1 \land P2)) \land (\sim (P1 \land P3)) \land (\sim (P2 \land P3)) \land (\sim (Q1 \land Q2)) \land (\sim (Q1 \land Q3)) \land (\sim (Q2 \land Q3)) \land$
$((P2 \land (Q1 \lor Q3) \land (Q2 \lor Q3)) \lor ((P1 \lor P3) \land (Q2 \lor Q3) \land (P2 \lor P3)))) \supset$
$(P3 \lor Q3)$

Now, this is a pretty complex wff. The theorem prover takes about 22 minutes to validate it on a reasonable computing workstation. It was also able to demonstrate a much shorter (but still quite lengthy) proof for the wff:

$(\sim (P1 \land P2)) \land (\sim (P1 \land P3)) \land (\sim (P2 \land P3)) \land (\sim (Q1 \land Q2)) \land (\sim (Q1 \land Q3)) \land (\sim (Q2 \land Q3)) \land$
$((P2 \land (Q1 \lor Q3) \land (Q2 \lor Q3)) \lor ((P1 \lor P3) \land (Q2 \lor Q3) \land (P2 \lor P3)))) \supset$
$(P3 \lor Q3)$

The proof of the shorter wff effectively proves the larger wff, since the larger wff is of the form

$$(X \land Y) \supset Z$$

and the shorter proof is of the form

$$Y \supset Z$$

where $X$ is defined to be

$$((P1 \lor P2 \lor P3) \land (Q1 \lor Q2 \lor Q3)$$

$Y$ is defined to be

$(\sim (P1 \land P2)) \land (\sim (P1 \land P3)) \land (\sim (P2 \land P3)) \land (\sim (Q1 \land Q2)) \land (\sim (Q1 \land Q3)) \land (\sim (Q2 \land Q3)) \land$
$\land((P2 \land (Q1 \lor Q3) \land (Q2 \lor Q3)) \lor ((P1 \lor P3) \land (Q2 \lor Q3))$

and $Z$ is defined to be

$(P3 \lor Q3)$.

You should be able to convince yourself that if $Y \supset Z$, then $(X \land Y) \supset Z$, for all wffs $X, Y$, and $Z$. If you have trouble convincing yourself, why not submit it to the theorem prover and examine the resulting proof?

## Applying System W to a Simple Logical Consequence

$\sim P \;\wedge\; \sim Q \;\vdash\; P \supset Q$
$\Downarrow$
$\sim P \,,\, \sim Q \;\vdash\; P \supset Q$      Rule W.5
$\Downarrow$
$\sim Q \;\vdash\; P \,,P \supset Q$      Rule W.4
$\Downarrow$
$\vdash\; Q \,,P \,,P \supset Q$      Rule W.4
$\Downarrow$
$\vdash\; Q \,,P \,,\sim P \vee Q$      Rule W.7
$\Downarrow$
$\vdash\; Q \,,P \,,\sim P \,,Q$      Rule W.5
$\Downarrow$
$P \;\vdash\; Q \,,P \,,Q$      Rule W.4
$\Downarrow$
Valid      Rule W.1

## PUZZLE 3

The final puzzle we present is somewhat more difficult. The scenario is as follows:

> When on MI5 counterintelligence missions, you frequently encounter three moles, *Mole X*, *Mole Y*, and *Mole Z* and know that one is code name Boris, one is code name Igor, and one is code name Natasha. Unfortunately, you do not know which Mole is of each code name group. The good news is that you've uncovered their secret communication code (*the borscht is better in Gorky Park*), so you can get them to answer questions. The bad news is that you cannot ask more than three questions, each of which can only be answered with a yes or a no, or they might become suspicious.

The problem is to find the right three questions to ask, and then prove that the solution is correct. Each proof has a considerable number of steps, so the line-by-line output of the proofs is not shown. Lisp and Prolog implementations of the solution will also be provided as an added brownie point for your pending promotion.

The major problem faced in identifying the three moles is being able to get predictable answers to the questions. That is, we wish to address questions to either the Boris or Igor moles. Therefore, the first question will be designed to isolate a mole that is *not* code name Natasha. This mole will be be asked to answer the remaining questions.

Let $P1$ stand for *Mole X is code name Boris,* and let $Q1$ stand for *Mole Y is code name Natasha.*

We want to construct a wff $V_1$ involving $P1$ and $Q1$ with the property that the *Mole X's* answer to the question:

Is $V_1$ *true?*

will yield a mole that is not code name Natasha.

The truth table in terms of $P1$ and $Q1$ is given below.

| $P1$ Mole X is code name Boris | $Q1$ Mole Y is code name Natasha | Desired answer to is $V_1$ *true?* |
|---|---|---|
| *true* | *true* | (*Mole Z* is not code name Natasha) |
| *true* | *false* | (*Mole Y* is not code name Natasha) |
| *false* | *true* | (*Mole Z* is not code name Natasha) |
| *false* | *false* | (*Mole Y* is not code name Natasha) |

Therefore, we can ask the question:

*Mole X,* either you are code name Boris and *Mole Y* is code name Natasha, or you are not code name Boris and *Mole Y* is not code name Natasha. Right?

Should the answer from *Mole X* be yes, then *Mole Z* is not code name Natasha, and should the answer be no, then *Mole Y* is not code name Natasha.

To prove the correctness of this first step, you could set up a suitable wff and subject it to the theorem prover. Let $A1$ designate the wff representing some important assumptions, that is,

$A1:$ $((( P1 \wedge Q1) \supset (\sim Z)) \wedge ((P1 \wedge (\sim Q1)) \supset (\sim Y)) \wedge$
$((( \sim P1) \wedge Q1) \supset (\sim Z)) \wedge (((\sim P1) \wedge (\sim Q1)) \supset (\sim Y)))$

Let $B1$ designate the wff representing the case where *Mole X's* answer to $V_1$ is *true.*

$B1:$ $(P1 \wedge (P1 \iff Q1)) \vee ((\sim P1) \wedge (\sim (P1 \iff Q1)))$

Let $C1$ designate the wff representing the case where *Mole X's* answer to $V_1$ is *false.*

$C1:$ $(P1 \wedge (P1 \iff Q1)) \vee ((\sim P1) \wedge (\sim (P1 \iff Q1)))$

Then the wff that must be proven is

$$((A1 \wedge B1) \supset (\sim Z)) \wedge ((A1 \wedge C1) \supset (\sim Y))$$

It is suggested that you use the theorem prover to verify the two sub-wffs $(A1 \wedge B1) \supset (\sim Z))$ and $(A1 \wedge C1) \supset (\sim Y))$ separately, to reduce the time involved.

Let us continue on with the solution now. Let **T** be the mole that is not code name Natasha (i.e. designate **T** to be *Mole Z* when the answer is yes and *Mole Y* when the answer is no), and let $U$ and $V$ be the remaining two moles.

The second question (which is addressed to **T**) will determine which mole is code name Natasha. Let $P2$ stand for **T** *is code name Boris*, and let $Q2$ stand for $U$ *is code name Natasha*.

A wff $V_2$ involving $P2$ and $Q2$ must then be constructed, with the property that **T**'s answer to the question:

Is $V_2$ *true?*

will yield the mole that is code name Natasha.

The truth table in terms of $P2$ and $Q2$ is given here.

| P2 T is code name Boris | Q2 U is code name Natasha | Desired answer to is $V_2$ *true?* |
|---|---|---|
| true | true | ($U$ is code name Natasha) |
| true | false | ($V$ is code name Natasha) |
| false | true | ($U$ is code name Natasha) |
| false | false | ($V$ is code name Natasha) |

Therefore, we ask **T** the question:

Either you are code name Boris and $U$ is code name Natasha, or you are not code name Boris and $U$ is not code name Natasha. Right?

Should the answer from **T** be yes, then $U$ is code name Natasha, and should the answer be no, then $V$ is code name Natasha.

To prove the correctness of the second step, let $A2$ designate the wff representing some important assumptions, that is,

$A2$ : $(((P \wedge Q) \supset U) \wedge ((P \wedge (\sim Q)) \supset V) \wedge (((\sim P) \wedge Q) \supset U) \wedge (((\sim P) \wedge (\sim Q)) \supset V))$

where $U$ designates that $U$ is code name Natasha and $V$ designates that $V$ is code name Natasha.

Let $B2$ designate the wff representing the case where **T**'s answer to $V_2$ is *true*.

$B2:\ (P2 \wedge (P2 <=> Q2)) \vee ((\sim P2) \wedge (\sim (P2 <=> Q2)))$

Let $C2$ designate the wff representing the case where **T**'s answer to $V_2$ is *false*.

$C2:\ (P2 \wedge (P2 <=> Q2)) \vee ((\sim P2) \wedge (\sim (P2 <=> Q2)))$

Then the wff that must be proven is

$((A2 \wedge B2) \supset U) \wedge ((A2 \wedge C2) \supset V)$

The final job is to determine which of the remaining moles is code name Boris and which is code name Igor. One of the remaining moles is **T**, and the other is either $U$ or $V$, whichever was not code name Natasha. Let $W$ designate which of $U$ and $V$ is not code name Natasha.

The third question (which is again addressed to **T**) will determine whether **T** is code name Boris and $W$ is code name Igor, or vice versa. Let $P3$ stand for **T** *is code name Boris*, and let $Q3$ stand for $W$ *is code name Igor*.

Wff $V_3$ involving $P3$ and $Q3$ is then constructed with the property that **T**'s answer to the question:

Is $V_3$ *true*?

will be *true* if **T** is code name Boris and $W$ is code name Igor, and will be *false* if $W$ is code name Boris and **T** is code name Igor.

The truth table in terms of $P3$ and $Q3$ is given here.

| $P3$<br>**T** is<br>code name Boris | $Q3$<br>$W$ is<br>code name Igor | Desired answer to<br>is $V_3$ *true*? |
|:---:|:---:|:---:|
| *true* | *true* | (**T** is code name Boris,<br>$W$ is code name Igor) |
| *false* | *false* | ($W$ is code name Igor,<br>**T** is code name Boris) |

Note that there are only two entries since if $P3$ is *true* (i.e., **T** is code name Boris) then $Q3$ must be *true* (i.e., $W$ is code name Igor), and if $P3$ is *false* (i.e., **T** is code name Igor) then $Q3$ must be *false* (i.e., $W$ is code name Boris). Therefore, we ask **T** the question:

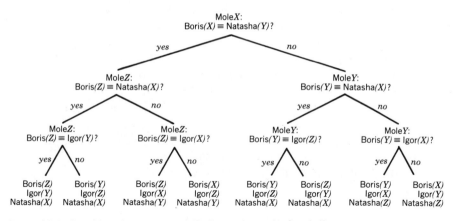

**FIGURE 37.1** Decision tree representation of puzzle 3 solution

Either you are code name Boris and $W$ is code name Igor, or you are not code name Boris and $W$ is not code name Igor. Right?

Should the answer from **T** be yes, then **T** is code name Boris and $W$ is code name Igor. Should the answer from **T** be no, then $W$ is code name Boris and **T** is code name Igor.

The construction of the proof of the third step is somewhat simpler and is left as an exercise at the end of this section.

A decision tree representation of the entire question/answer strategy used to crack the puzzle is shown in Figure 37.1.

The implementation of the identification system is simply a matter of mapping the logical questions into Lisp and Prolog procedures, and is left to you.

# ■ PROGRAM NOTES

The Lisp and Prolog programs in this chapter follow essentially the same pattern. Wang's theorem-proving algorithm requires no backtracking, so Prolog's backtracking resolution method fails, in this case, to provide any advantage over Lisp's "reduction-by-substitution" model of computation. We did have to face a problem in representing the input wffs to the Lisp and Prolog programs. As usual, we chose in both programs an input format compatible with the language's notation for data, but we also wanted to make the input format as close as possible to customary notation for symbolic logic.

In Lisp, this presented the dilemma of choosing between denoting logic operations (e.g., implication) with standard Lisp identifiers (e.g., implies) or with special symbols (e.g., =>). Leaning toward customary logic notation, we chose to use special symbols. This required the introduction of a new format for Lisp data; namely, enclosing atoms made from special symbols in quotation marks.

Prolog presented a slightly different dilemma. Our introduction to Prolog concentrated on functors denoted in prefix notation (with only a few exceptions, all of which were intrinsic functors such as " : -"). We could have represented wffs for the Prolog program in prefix-functor form [e.g., implies(P,Q)], but this seemed unduly clumsy. We chose instead to introduce the operator notation for functions, inserting just enough coverage of the idea to make the program understandable. Prolog provides much more in the way of operator notation than we detailed, and you may want to consult some of the references if the idea arouses your interest.

# ■ BIBLIOGRAPHY NOTES

There are many texts on mathematical logic. Examples of elementary-level texts are those of Hilbert and Ackermann and Rogers and the problem-solving text of Kowalski. Intermediate-level texts include those of Mendelson, Kleene, and the second chapter of Manna's text on the theory of computing.

The goal of mechanizing the theorem proving process dates back at least to Leibniz (1646–1716). Work on automating theorem proving was stimulated by Hilbert's goal of finding a complete and consistent system for proving all theorems of mathematics. In 1931, Gödel showed that the second-order predicate calculus was incomplete, and shortly thereafter, it was shown by Church and Turing that there was no algorithm for deciding the validity of wffs of the first-order predicate calculus.

Early theorem proving systems were of the *natural deduction* variety, particularly the system of Gentzen. Two of the first computer implementations of such systems are Newell, Shaw and Simon and Wang. Resolution theorem proving is founded on the work of Herbrand. Early, inefficient implementations were proposed by Davis and Putnam and Gilmore. These were improved by Prawitz and Davis, culminating in the resolution method of Robinson (1965).

Books containing substantial material on automated theorem proving include Chang and Lee, Nilsson, Loveland, Robinson (1979), Bundy, Bledsoe and Loveland, and Wos et al.

Some notable examples of successful theorem provers are that of Boyer and Moore (1979), Overbeek, Wos, Winker, Lusk, and Smith in Wos, Overbeek, Lusk, and Boyle (1984), Andrews in Miller, Cohen and Andrews (1962), and Wen-tsün.

Smullyan has compiled a nice collection of logic puzzles and included their solutions.

W. W. Bledsoe and D. W. Loveland, (eds.) (1984) *Automated Theorem Proving: After 25 Years*, Contemporary Mathematics, Vol. 29. American Mathematical Society, Providence, R.I.

R. S. Boyer and J. S. Moore, (1982) *A Computational Logic*. Academic Press, New York.

R. S. Boyer and J. S. Moore, (1982) *Proof Checking the RSA Public Key Encryption Algorithm*, Technical Report ICSCA-CMP-33, Institute for Computing Science and Computer Applications, University of Texas, Austin.

R. S. Boyer, and J. S. Moore, (1984) *A mechanical proof of the unsolvability of the Halting Problem. J. ACM*, **31**(3): 441–458.

A. Bundy, (1983) *The Computer Modelling of Mathematical Reasoning*, Academic Press, New York.

C. Chang and R. C. Lee, (1973) *Symbolic Logic and Mechanical Theorem Proving*, Academic Press, New York.

A. Church, (1936) *An unsolvable problem with elementary number theory. American J. Mathematics*, **58**. 345–363.

H. Coelho, J. C. Cotta, and L. M. Pereira, (1980) *How to Solve it With Prolog*, Ministério Da Habitação E Obras Públicas, Laboratório Nacional de Engenharia Civil, Lisbon, Portugal.

M. Davis, (1963) *Eliminating the irrelevant from mechanical proofs, Proceedings of the Symposium on Applied Mathematics* **18**: 15–30. (1963).

M. Davis, and H. Putnam, (1960) *A computing procedure for quantification theory, J. ACM* **7**(3): 201–215.

G. Gentzen, (1934) *Untersuchungen über das Logische Schliessen.* in M. E. Szabo (ed.) *The Collected Papers of Gerhard Gentzen*, North-Holland, Amsterdam, 68–132.

P. C. Gilmore, (1960) *A proof method for quantification theory, IBM J. Research and Development*, **4**: 28–35.

Gödel, (1931) *On formally undecidable propositions of principia mathematica and related systems I.* in J. Heijenoort (ed.) (1967) *From Frege to Gödel*, Harvard University Press, Cambridge, Mass., 592–617.

J. Herbrand, (1930) *Investigations in proof theory*, in J. Heijenoort (ed.) (1967) *From Frege to Gödel*, Harvard University Press, Cambridge, Mass., 525–581.

D. Hilbert, and W. Ackermann, (1950) *Principles of Mathematical Logic*, Chelsea Publishing, New York.

R. Kowalski, (1979) *Logic for Problem Solving*, North-Holland, New York.

S. C. Kleene, (1968) *Mathematical Logic*, Wiley, New York.

D. W. Loveland, (1978) *Automated Theorem Proving*, North-Holland, Amsterdam.

Z. Manna, (1974) *Mathematical Theory of Computation*, McGraw–Hill, New York.

E. Mendelson, (1964) *Introduction to Mathematical Logic*, Van Nostrand, Princeton, N.J.

D. A. Miller, E. L. Cohen, P. B. Andrews, (1982) *A look at TPS, Proceedings of the Sixth Conference on Automated Deduction.* In D. W. Loveland (ed.) (1982) *Lecture Notes in Computer Science* **138**.

J. S. Moore, (1979) *A mechanical proof of the termination of Takeuchi's function*, Information Processing Letters, **9**(4): 176–181.

A. Newell, J. C. Shaw, and H. A. Simon, (1957) *Empirical Explorations with the Logic Theory Machine:*, Proc. West. Joint Computer Conf., Vol. 15, pp. 218–238, 1957. Reprinted in E. Feigenbaum and J. Feldman (eds.), "Computers and Thought", pp. 109–133, McGraw–Hill, New York, 1963.

N. J. Nilsson, (1971) *Problem-Solving Methods in Artificial Intelligence*, McGraw–Hill, New York.

N. J. Nilsson, (1980) *Principles of Artificial Intelligence*, Tioga Publishing, Palo Alto, Calif.

D. Prawitz, (1960) *An improved proof procedure*. Theoria **26**: 102–139.

J. A. Robinson, (1965) *A machine-oriented logic based on the resolution principle*. J. ACM **12**(1): 23–41.

J. A. Robinson, (1979) *Logic: Form and Function. The Mechanization of Deductive Reasoning*, North-Holland, New York.

R. Rogers, (1971) *Mathematical Logic and Formalized Theories*, North-Holland, Amsterdam.

J. R. Rosser, (1953) *Logic for Mathematics*, McGraw–Hill, New York.

J. S. Moore, (1983) *A Mechanical Proof of Wilson's Theorem*, Department of Computer Sciences, University of Texas, Austin.

R. Smullyan, (1978) *What is the Name of this Book? The Riddle of Dracula and Other Logical Puzzles*, Prentice-Hall, Englewood Cliffs, N.J.

A. M. Turing, (1936) *On computable numbers, with an application to Entscheidungsproblem. Proceedings of the London Mathematical Society* **42**: 230–265.

H. Wang, (1960) *Toward mechanical mathematics. IBM J. Research and Development*, **4**: 2–22.

W. Wen-Tsŭn, (1982) *Mechanical theorem proving in elementary geometry and differential geometry, Proceedings of the 1980 Symposium on Differential Geometry and Differential Equations*, **2**. pp1073-1092.

S. Winker, L. Wos, (1978) *Automated generation of models and counter-examples and its application to open questions in ternary boolean algebra, Proceedings of the Eighth International Symposium on Multiple-Valued Logic*, Rosemont, Illinois, ACM/IEEE Publishers, 251–256.

S. Winker, L. Wos, and E. Lusk, (1981) *Semigroups, antiautomorphisms, and involutions: A computer solution to an open problem, I. Mathematics of Computation* **37**: 533–545.

L. Wos, R. Overbeek, E. Lusk, and J. Boyle, (1984) *Automated Reasoning: Introduction and Applications*, Prentice–Hall, Englewood Cliffs, N.J.

L. Wos, S. Winker, and E. Lusk, (1981) *An Automated Reasoning System, Proceedings of the National Computer Conference*, AFIPS Press.

L. Wos, S. Winker, B. Smith, R. Veroff, and L. Henschen, (1984) *A new use of an automated reasoning assistant: Open questions in equivalential calculus and the study of infinite domains. Artificial Intelligence* **22**: 303–356.

■ EXERCISES

1. Complete the proof of system W rule W.4.

2. Determine whether each of the propositional wffs given here is a tautology, a contradiction, or neither. Use either algebraic proofs or truth tables.

   (a) $(P \wedge Q) \wedge R \equiv P \wedge (Q \wedge R)$

   (b) $P \vee (Q \wedge R) \equiv (P \vee Q) \wedge (P \vee R)$

   (c) $P \wedge (Q \vee R) \supset (P \wedge Q) \vee R$

   (d) $(P \wedge Q) \vee R \supset P \wedge (Q \vee R)$

   (e) $(Q \supset R) \supset ((P \supset Q) \supset (P \supset R))$

3. Do the same analysis as in Exercise 2, but instead use system W.

4. There are several ways to combine the rules of system W so as to reduce the number of proof steps. Give some examples.

5. There is an interesting propositional operator "↑" called *Sheffer stroke*, which is defined as follows:

   $$T \uparrow T = F \quad T \uparrow F = T \quad F \uparrow T = T \quad F \uparrow F = T$$

   Show how to integrate the Sheffer stroke into system W.

6. Transform the following wff into a tautology by weakening the conclusion. Verify your wff using system W.

   $$((P \supset Q) \wedge (R \supset S) \wedge \neg(Q \supset R)) \supset \neg(P \supset S)$$

7. Suppose there are two moles, $X$ and $Y$, each of whom always tells the truth or always lies. If $X$ says: "At least one of us is a liar," use the propositional calculus to identify $X$ and $Y$ as truth-tellers or liars, and use the theorem prover to verify your conclusion.

8. Consider the following somewhat more difficult puzzle. The scenario is as follows:

   > When on MI5 counter-intelligence missions, you frequently encounter three moles, *Mole X*, *Mole Y*, and *Mole Z*, and know that one is code name Boris, one is code name Igor, and one is code name Natasha. Unfortunately, you do not know which Mole is of each code name group. The good news is that you have uncovered their secret communication code (*the borscht is better in Gorky Park*), so you can get them to answer questions. The bad news is that you can't ask more than three questions, each of which can only be answered with a yes or a no, or they might become suspicious.

The problem is to find the right three questions to ask and then prove that the solution is correct. The major problem faced in identifying the three moles is being able to get predictable answers to the questions. That is, we wish to address questions to either the Boris or Igor moles. Therefore, the first question will be designed to isolate a mole that is *not* code name Natasha. This mole will be be asked to answer the remaining questions. Good luck!

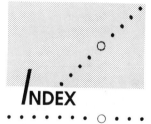

# INDEX

Abolish, Prolog, 244
Accumulation (pumping):
    Lisp, 86
    Prolog, 172, 173, 174, 177,
        179
Adaptive quadrature, 125
Addition: Lisp, 123
    Prolog, 268
ALFL, 4
Alligator, 450
Alpha–beta, 319, 364
Alpha–beta vs. minimax,
    326
Alphabetical order, 97, 184,
    192
Alpha reduction, 26
Alternative instantiation (;),
    151, 224
And: Lisp, 81
    Prolog, 139
And (wff), 417
And/or, Lisp, 79
And/or control flow, 196
Apostrophe, 21, 26
Append: Lisp, 40, 41
    Prolog, 165, 166
Applicative programming, 2
Arctangent: Lisp, 123
    Prolog, 165, 166
Area, quadrature, 125
Arg, test for, 246
Argument, function as, 31,
    115

Argument of function, 20,
    21
Argument matching, 156,
    306
Argument mode,
    input/output, 305
Arithmetic expression, 268
Arity, relation, 138, 146,
    158, 246
Assert, Prolog, 242, 243
Atom: Lisp, 14
    Lisp test, 50
    Prolog, 129, 130, 245
Atomic, Prolog, 245
Automata, 174
Automated theorem proving,
    413, 460
    Wang, 419

Backtrace: Lisp, 72
    Prolog, 257
Backtrack, in parsing, 378
Backtracking: Prolog, 207,
    218
    inhibit (!), 228, 229
Backup, Unix, 262
Backus, John, 4
Backus–Naur form, 14, 372
Bagof, 224
Bar: vertical (Prolog),132,
    133
    vertical (BNF), 372
BASIC, 2
Bells and whistles, 2

Beta reduction, 26
Bidding, bridge, 366
Bit manipulation, Prolog,
    269
BNF, 14, 372
Boolean: and, 81
    and/or, 79
    compare (numeric), 270
    compare (string), 93, 184,
        192
    not, 80
    or, 82
    Prolog, 245, 255
Boolean (true/false), 22
Bracket notation (Prolog
    list), 132, 133
Break levels, Prolog, 260
Bridge: bidding, 366
    card game, 348
    squeeze, 361
    trump, 367
Bug, avoid, 70
Building result (pumping), 86
Build list, Lisp, 34, 43
Burstall, 4

C, 2
C vs. Lisp/Prolog, 6
Cabin, log, 451
Calculus: lambda, 7, 117,
    174
    predicate, 7, 174
    propositional, 415
Call: function, 21

Call (*continued*)
function argument
(funcall), 115
Prolog, 233
Car, cadr, . . . , 32, 33
Cartesian product, 303
Cdr, cddr, . . . , 42
Chance, games of, 313, 363
Checkers, game of, 364
Church, Alonzo, 3
Circular definition, 59
Clause: Horn, 292, 293
Clause, Prolog, 242, 245, 292
Clause grammar, definite,
370, 395
Cobol, 2
Code generation, 370
Colmerauer, 3
Colon–hyphen (:-), Prolog,
139, 140
Coloring, graph, 216
Comma, Prolog, 139, 140,
200, 201
Common subexpression, 56
Compare: equal, 22, 23, 204,
269
numeric, 123, 269
string, 93, 184, 192
Compiler, parsing, 325
Complexity, computation,
178, 186, 189
Component: Lisp, 14
Lisp delete (cdr), 42
Lisp delete (remove), 65
Lisp extract (car), 32
Prolog, 133, 138, 146
Composition, function, 306
Computable, 1
Computation: essence of, 20
model, 1, 6, 7
rule, 51
speed, 178, 186, 189
state of, 330
trace, 76, 258
Computer program, 2
Concatenate lists, 41
Conclusion, Prolog, 139,
140, 146
Conclusion (wff), 421
Condition, Prolog, 139, 140,
146
Conditional, Lisp, 48
Conjuction, op (550, yfx, &),
440
Conjuction (wff), 417
Connective, logic, 416, 417
Conquer by dividing, 97,
182, 183
Cons, Lisp, 43
Consistent instantiation,
150, 208, 218

Construct list, Lisp, 34, 43
Consult, Prolog, 238
Context–free grammar, 372
Contract bridge, 348
Contradiction (wff), 418
Control flow, and/or, 196
Cosine: Lisp, 123
Prolog, 269
Crawfish gumbo, 450
Crusty geezer, 451
Current_atom, Prolog, 269
Current_functor, Prolog, 255
Current_predicate, Prolog,
255
Curry, 3
Cut (!), 228, 229, 257
Cut/fail, 233

Data: function, 20
function as, 31, 115
Lisp, 13, 14, 15, 16, 21
Prolog, 129, 130
pure, 21, 26
real world, 17
Davis, 3
DCTG (grammar), 403
Deadeye Dick, 15
Debug: Lisp, 70
Prolog, 251, 258
Declarative, Prolog, 291
Declarative programming, 2
Declarer, bridge, 365
Defender, bridge, 365
Definite clause grammar,
370, 395
Definition: Lisp function, 25
recursive (circular), 59
relation (Prolog), 140, 146
Defun, 25
as lambda expression, 117
Delayed evaluation, 48, 51,
63, 79
Delete element, Prolog, 183
Demand–driven, 48, 51, 63,
79
Denotational, 2, 15, 174, 232
Derivation, in parsing, 376,
379
Determiner, 401, 406
Determinism, 51
Diagram (parsing), 372
Disjunction, op (600, yfx,
++), 440
Disjunction (wff), 417
Divide and conquer, 97, 182,
183
Division, 123
Prolog, 268
Dog, mad, 23
Dot-dot-dot (. . .) ellipsis,
14, 374

Double dummy bridge, 348

Editor, Prolog, 261
Elba, 23
Element: Lisp, 15
Lisp delete (cdr), 42
Lisp delete (remove), 65
Lisp extract (car), 32
Ellipsis (. . .), 14, 372
Empty list, Lisp test (null),
51, 52
Equal: Lisp, 22, 23
Prolog, 203, 269
Equivalence, op (700, yfx,
<=>), 440
Equivalence (wff), 417
Eta reduction, 26
Evaluation: lazy, 48, 51, 63,
79
strategy, 51, 63
Exponential, 123
Expression, 373
Lisp, 21
numeric, 268
relational, 386
symbolic, 15
Extensive representation,
327
Extract component, Lisp car,
32

Fact, Prolog, 129, 130, 137,
138, 146
Fail, cut, 233
Failure, Prolog negation, 205
False always (contradiction),
418
False/true, 22, 416, 417
Federal tax code, 142
Fifth–generation, 4
File: backup, 262
current, 288
Lisp, 113
load, 113, 238, 241
open, 287
Prolog, 288
view from Prolog, 261
Finite state automata, 174
Fixed point number, Prolog,
267
Floating point number,
Prolog, 267
Format: function, 51
relation, 254
Formula, wff, 416, 417
Fortran, 2
FP, 4
Frege, 3
Friedman, Daniel, 51
Frontier, parse tree, 379
FSA, 174

Funcall, 115
Function, 19, 20
  application, 21
  as data, 31, 115
  definition, 25
  extensive vs. intensive, 327
  formatting, 51
  helping, 85
  higher order, 114, 307, 365, 368
  invocation history, 72
  lambda expression, 118
  lenient, 47, 48, 51, 63
  mathematical definition, 303
  numeric, 123
  strict, 48, 51, 63
Functional, 2
Function of function, 31, 115
Function of function value, 306
Function quote (#'), 31, 115
Functor: Prolog, 133, 255
  test for, 246

Game playing: bridge, 348
  checkers, 364
  Go–Moku, 367
  tic-tac-toe, 336
Game playing programs, 313
Games, perfect information, 313, 363
Games of chance, 315, 363
Gcd, 122
Geezer, crusty, 451
Get, Prolog, 282
Gilmore, 3
Goal, Prolog, 139
Goedel incompleteness, 413
Go-Moku, 367
Gorky Park, 452
Grammar: BNF
    specification, 374
  context–free, 370
  definite clause, 370, 395
  definite clause translation, 403
  natural language, 395, 400, 401
  programming language, 370
  rewrite rule, 371, 428, 446
  terminal/non–terminal, 371
Graph coloring, 216
Greater than, Prolog, 269
Greatest common divisor, 123
Grep, Unix, 262

Gumbo, 450

Hardcopy, Prolog, 256
Head, Prolog, 139
Helping function, 85
Henderson, 51
Herbrand, 3
Heuristic formula, 364, 368
Hierarchy (tree), 131
Higher order function, 114, 307, 365, 368
Hope, 4
Horn, 3
Horn clause, 292, 293
Hudak, Paul, 4

If, Lisp, 47, 48, 51, 63
If (:-), Prolog, 139,140
Implication: logical (:-), 140
  op (650, yfx,=>), 440
  wff, 417
Incompleteness, Goedel, 415
Inference, Prolog, 151
Infix compare, Prolog, 192
Inhibit backtracking (!), 228, 229
Input: function as, 31, 115
  Prolog, 281
Input/output: Lisp, 105
  Prolog, 278
Insertion sort, 99
Instantiation: alternative (;), 151, 224
  Prolog, 149, 150, 152, 208, 218
Integer, Prolog, 245, 267
Integral, quadrature, 125
Intensive representation, 327
Interpreter, parsing, 370
Intersection, set, 202, 205
Invalid (wff), 419
Invocation: function, 21
  function argument, 115
Is expression, Prolog, 268
Iteration (tail recursion), 90
Iterative, 2

Keller, Robert, 51
KGB, 452
Kowalski, 3
KRC, 4

Lambda calculus, 7, 117, 174
Lambda expression, 117, 118
Language: parsing, 325
  programming power, 305, 308
Language translation,
    natural, 395, 403
Latin, pig, 106
Layout, program, 51, 254

Lazy evaluation, 48, 51, 63, 79
Lazy T (⊢), 419
Leftmost derivation, 378, 379
Lenient function, 47, 48, 51, 63, 79
Less than, Prolog, 269
Let: as lambda expression, 117
  Lisp, 56, 57
Lexical analysis, 370
Lexical order, 97
Lisp, 2
  from car cdr cons, 43
  vs. conventional, 6
  vs. Prolog, 5, 303
List: empty (nil), 18
  extract component (car), 32
  Lisp, 13, 14, 15, 16
  Lisp build, 34, 43
  Lisp representation, 43
  Prolog, 132, 133
Listing, Prolog, 256
Literal: positive/negative, 293
  proposition, 444
Load file, Lisp, 113
  Prolog, 238, 241
Local value, 57
Logarithm, 123
Log cabin, 451
Logical connective, 416, 417
Logical implication (:-), 140
Logic function: Lisp and, 81
  Lisp and/or, 79
  Lisp not, 80
  Lisp or, 82
Logic program, 292
Looping (tail recursion), 90

Mad dog, 23
Mapcar, 30, 31
Matching, argument pattern, 156, 158, 306
Mathematical function, 303
Mathematical relation, 304
Max, Lisp, 123
Maximum, Prolog, 171, 172
McCarthy, 3
Member, Prolog, 163, 164, 203
Merge sort, 101
Milner, Robin, 4
Minimax, 366
  alpha–beta, 319
  function, 318
  tree games, 313
  vs. alpha–beta, 326

Minimum, Prolog, 171, 172, 183
Miranda, 4
Mod, 123
Mode, argument, 305
Model: computation, 1, 6, 7
  programming, 2, 3
Modus tollens, 420
Mole, 452
More, Unix, 261
Morris, 51
Multiplication: Lisp, 123
  Prolog, 268

Name: Prolog, 255, 281
  test for, 247
Name–value binding (let), 57
Natural language
  translation, 395, 403
Negation, op (500, fy, -), 440
Negation as failure, Prolog, 205
Nil, 18
Nil, Lisp test (null), 51, 52
Nondeterminism, 51
Nonprocedural, 2
Non–terminal symbol,
  grammar, 371
Nonvar, Prolog, 245
Not, Prolog, 203, 205, 233
Not (null), Lisp, 80
Not (wff), 417
No-trump, bridge, 348
Noun, 401, 405
Noun phrase, 401, 408
Null, Lisp, 51, 52
Number: compare, 123, 269
  Lisp, 121
  Prolog, 129, 245, 266, 267
Number-apostrophe (#'), 31, 115
Numeric expression, 268

Open file, 287
Operational, 2
Operator definition, op (700,
  yfx, =>), 440
Operator precedence, 270, 387
Or: embedded (;), 200, 201
  Lisp, 82
Or/and, Lisp, 79
Order, Prolog, 172, 183
Ordering (e.g., alphabetical),
  97, 183
Or (wff), 417
Output, Prolog term, 282
Output/input: Lisp, 105
  Prolog, 278

Palindrome, 3, 5, 23

Parameter, test for, 246
Parameter of function, 20
Parse pair, 379
Parse token, 379
Parse tree, 371, 374, 377
Parse tree frontier, 379
Parsing, 370
  top-down, 379
Partial result, let naming, 56
Partition, quicksort, 187, 188
Pascal, 2
Pattern matching, Prolog,
  156, 158, 306
Perfect information games,
  313, 363
Period, Prolog, 139, 140, 141
Period-period-period (. . .)
  ellipsis, 14, 372
Phrase, 401
Pig Latin, 106
Place mark variable (_), 150,
  159
Positive literal, Prolog, 292
Post, Emil, 3
Pound–apostrophe (#'), 31,
  115
Precedence: numeric
  operators, 270
  operator, 387
Predicate, Prolog, 245, 255
Predicate calculus, 7, 174
Prefix, Prolog, 167
Premise (wff), 419
Principle of substitution, 15
  26
Print, Lisp, 110
Print listing, Prolog, 256
Probablistic games, 313, 363
Procedural, 2, 174
  Prolog, 291
Procedure, Prolog, 140, 295
Product, Cartesian, 303
Production, BNF, 372
Program, 2
  layout, 51, 254
  listing, 257
  logic, 292
  parsing, 379
  transformation, 319
Programming language, 2, 4,
  parsing, 370
  power, 305, 308
  toy, 372
Programming model, 2, 3, 6,
  7,
Prolog, 2
  vs. conventional, 6
  vs. Lisp, 5, 303
Proof: theorem, 413, 460
  theorem (Wang), 419

theorem (Wang, Lisp), 425
Propagation, Prolog, 172,
  173, 174, 177, 179
Proposition: logic, 415, 416,
  417
  Prolog, 138, 146
Propositional calculus, 415
Propositional variable, 416,
  417
Pumping: Lisp, 86
Pumping, Prolog, 172, 173,
  174, 177, 179
Pure data, 21 26
Put, Prolog, 279, 281
Putnam, 3
Put_string, Prolog, 280

Quadrature, 125
Query, Prolog, 129, 130, 137,
  138, 141, 146, 151
Quicksort, 187
Quote: function, 31, 115
  Lisp, 21, 26

Read, Prolog, 281, 283, 286
Read file, Prolog, 261
Reconsult, Prolog, 241
Recursion: Prolog, 163
  tail, 90
Recursive definition, 59
Recursive–descent parser,
  370
Reduction: alpha, beta, eta,
  26
  pumping/accumulation,
  86
  substitution, 15
Relation: arity, 138, 146,
  158
  mathematical definition,
  304
  Prolog, 137, 138, 141, 148
Relational expression, 386
Relative clause, 401, 407
Remove, Lisp, 65
Remove element, Prolog,
  183
Resolution rule, 415
Rest of list, Lisp cdr, 42
Retract, Prolog, 244
Reverse, 5, 19
  Lisp, 22
  Prolog, 177, 178
Rewrite rule, grammar, 371,
  428, 446
Robinson, 3
Rosser, J. Barkley, 7
Rplaca, 4
Rule, Prolog, 137, 139, 146

SASL, 4

Search, Prolog, 150, 151, 152
Search for pattern, 262
See, Prolog, 287
Seeing, Prolog, 287
Selection, Prolog, 156, 158
Selection sort, 183, 184
Semantic analysis, 370
Semantic rules, grammar, 403
Semantics, declarative vs. procedural, 291
Semicolon, Prolog, 151, 200, 201
Sentence, 401, 409
    grammar, 395, 400, 401
Sentence diagram, parsing, 370
Set intersection, 203, 206
Setof, 227
Setq, 4
S-expression, 15
Shoenfinkel, 3
Sidewards, T (⊢), 421
Sine: Lisp, 123
    Prolog, 269
Single quote, 21, 26
Single stepping, 74
Skip, Prolog, 282
Skolem, 3
Solve, divide and conquer, 97, 182, 183
Sort: insertion, 99
    merge, 101
Sorting, quicksort, 187
Sorting (e.g., alphabetical), 97, 183
Speed, computation, 178, 186, 189
Spy, Prolog, 258, 260
Square root, Prolog, 269
Squeeze, bridge, 361
Standard-output, Lisp, 113
Start symbol, grammar, 371
State of computation, 328
Statement: parsing, 379, 380, 381
    Prolog, 146, 150, 207, 217
State transition diagram, 174
Statistical games, 313, 363
Step through program, 74
Stereo system, 20
Strategy games, 313
Strict function, 48, 51, 63
String-lessp, 93
Structure, Prolog, 129, 130, 133
Subexpression, common, 56
Subfunction (helper), 85
Sublist, Prolog, 198
Substitution, 15, 26

Prolog, 155, 156
Substitution (instantiation), 149, 208, 218
Subtraction, 123
    Prolog, 268
Symbolic atom: Lisp, 14
Symbolic atom, Prolog, 129, 130
Symbolic expression, 15
Syntactic analysis, 370
Syntax, BNF specification, 14, 372
Syntax–directed translation, 370
System W, 420

T, lazy (⊢), 421
Tab, Prolog, 279
Tail: Lisp list cdr, 42
Tail recursion, 90
Tangent: Lisp, 123
    Prolog, 269
Tautology (wff), 418
Tax code, 142
Tell, Prolog, 288
Telling, Prolog, 288
Term: Prolog, 129, 130, 137, 138, 146, 148, 293
    Prolog input, 286
    Prolog output, 282
    testing, 245
Terminal symbol, 371
Terminator (.), Prolog, 139, 140, 141
Test, Prolog term, 245
Theorem proving, 413, 460
    Wang, 419
    Wang (Lisp), 425
Tic-tac-toe, 336
Tilda (wff), 417
Time, computation, 178, 186, 189
Tobacco, chewing, 451
Token, parsing, 379
Told, Prolog, 288
Tollens, modus, 420
Top-down parsing, 379
Tournament, 187, 188, 189, 190, 191
Trace, Lisp, 76
Trace, Prolog, 258
Transformation, program, 319
Transitive phrase, 401, 405
Translation: natural language, 395, 403
    syntax-directed, 370
Translation grammar, 403
Transpose, 67
Tree, parse, 371, 376, 377

Tree frontier, parse, 379
Tree games, 313
Tree structure, 131, 135
Trig function: Lisp, 123
    Prolog, 270
True always (tautology), 418
True/false, 22, 416, 417
Trump, bridge, 367
Truth assignment, 416, 417
Truth or consequences, 451
Turing, Alan, 3
Turing equivalent, 305
Turner, David, 4
Two-opponent games, 313
Typing vs. thinking, 74

Underscore variable, 150, 159, 160, 233
Unequal, Prolog, 269
Unification, 155, 156, 158, 160, 305
Unifier, 156
Uninstantiated variable, 158
Unload, Prolog, 244
Untrace, Lisp, 76

Valid (wff), 419
Value, local, 57
Value–name binding (let), 57
Var, Prolog, 245
Variable: Prolog, 129, 131, 149, 150, 208, 218
    propositional, 416, 417
    uninstantiated, 158
    wild card (_), 150, 159, 160, 233
Verb, 401, 405
Vertical bar: BNF, 37
    Prolog, 132, 133
Vi editor, Prolog, 261
View file, Prolog, 261
Vitx, Prolog, 261
Vuillemin, 51

Wang System W, 420
Wang theorem prover, 419
    Lisp, 425
    Prolog, 425
Wff, well-formed formula, 416, 417
Wild card variable (_), 150, 159, 160
Wise, David, 51
Workspace, Prolog, 238, 241, 242, 244, 255
Write, Prolog, 279, 283

Yakity-Yak, 107
Yogurt, 59